VINEYARD INTERNATIONAL PUBLISHING
PO Box 53286
Kenilworth, 7745
Cape Town, South Africa

Reg. No.CK94/26543/23

The Scripture quotations in this publication are taken from The
New International Version. Copyright © 1985, Zondervan,
Grand Rapids, MI.

Published 1999, Vineyard International Publishing, Ladysmith

Cover by *Mercy Arts Studio*, Ladysmith
Photograph of John Wimber used by permission of
"Doin the Stuff", USA
Printed and bound by National Book Printers, Cape Town

ISBN 0 620 24319 8

# THE QUEST FOR THE RADICAL MIDDLE

## A HISTORY OF THE VINEYARD

BILL JACKSON

FOREWORD BY TODD HUNTER

APPENDIX ON LONNIE FRISBEE BY DAVID DI SABATINO

VINEYARD INTERNATIONAL PUBLISHING

*I dedicate this book, to my wonderful wife, Betsy. She is the love of my life. The last twenty years have gone by like the wind, and I couldn't have asked for a better friend, wife, mother and partner in ministry. Thanks, Honey, for taking care of the ranch while I pecked away up in the bedroom for all those months.*

# TABLE OF CONTENTS

# ACKNOWLEDGMENTS

T he original work for *The Quest for the Radical Middle: A History of the Vineyard* began in 1996 as I lectured on empowered evangelical church history in the Vineyard School of Pastoral Ministry at the Champaign Vineyard in Illinois. Many thanks to my students for letting me "practice" on them and for the many wonderful hours we spent together. I am deeply indebted to my former pastors and teammates, Happy Leman and Ben Hoerr, for their foresight to let me experiment with the school and to give me the luxury of doing the initial research on the history of the Vineyard. My four years in Champaign were good and fruitful years and I will always be thankful for them.

I would also like to thank especially Kenn Gulliksen, Todd Hunter and Steve Nicholson for their continual encouragement for the project, their reading of the various drafts and for their suggestions. Kenn was extremely helpful in working through the material, even though it was exhausting for him. He gave me great insight into Calvary Chapel and the genesis of the Vineyard. Now living in San Diego, I was able to get up to Anaheim to talk with Todd on numerous occasions and in every case he was kind enough to carve out time from his busy schedule to listen to my many questions. Steve Nicholson was my initial cheerleader in Illinois, as he was anxious to put a history into the hands of prospective Vineyard church planters.

There are many people who read various drafts and gave helpful critique. Thanks to John and Margie McClure for their thorough reading and helpful clarifications. Thanks also to Bill Dwyer and Jack Little for their help on the early days of the Vineyard. Bob Fulton was a great help on writing the missions chapter, as were my friends Fred Collum and Larry Larson. Marilyn Hanson and LeAnn Shulz from AVC are the greatest, always kind and helpful, even though all the calls from "Jax" probably got old after awhile.

Mike Bickle read at least two drafts and was kind enough to talk with me on the phone and give me his critique. I also talked to David Parker, Bert Waggoner, John Mumford and Sandy Miller to get their perspectives on the prophetic period. Thank you to Randy Clark, John Arnott and Fred Wright for their insights and perspectives on The Toronto Blessing. Thanks also to my team-mates here in San Diego, Don Williams, Gary Goodell, Bruce Henderson and Ron Ford for their willingness to read rough drafts and for their gracious comments. Thanks to Les Yoder for e-mailing me his Vineyard research.

I was delighted that scholars such as Peter Wagner and Jack Deere read the later drafts. They were not only helpful but very encouraging.

I am excited that David Di Sabatino, perhaps the leading expert on the Jesus Movement and the life of Lonnie Frisbee, has agreed to write on Lonnie's life and ministry to separate truth from myth. We share a similar passion for history that instantly bonded us. Thanks also to Lonnie's old room-mates, John Ruttkay and Marwan Bahu for some great times reminiscing about the Jesus People.

Thanks to my spiritual father, Dave Veerman, and my theological mentor, Gordon Fee, for helping me to understand something of the world of publishing.

I would like to thank my great friend, Jeff Stoner, for his role in getting me connected with The Toronto Blessing in its earliest phases and the healing that God brought to my life from that experience.

Many thanks to Derek Morphew and Stephan Vosloo from South Africa for their willingness to take a chance on a new writer and publish this under the VIP banner.

I couldn't have done this without my two friends and editors in the Northern Hemisphere, Robbie Hunt from Indianapolis and Ruth Wegman from Champaign. Blessings to you both! Not only were they invaluable team-mates in helping us to plant our first church in the 1980s, but they are both writing teachers. They spent a good portion of the snowy Midwest winter of 1998-99 pouring over every word of the manuscript and encouraging lively debate over the internet.

Thanks to our church, the Black Mountain Vineyard in North

County, San Diego, for allowing me to finish this while planting the church. Thanks especially to Dana Martinez, my friend, relative and computer guru who has worked tirelessly to keep my computer humming. Thanks also to Kathy Nutt for help on the bibliography. I am also deeply appreciative to my fellow elder, Tim Hoerr, for his friendship and encouragement.

Finally, thanks to my wonderful family, my dear wife Betsy, my sons Luke and John and my daughter Megan. May God bless you for being willing to give me away for all those weeks and months as I typed into the night, hit the road for another interview, and made one more phone call.

BILL JACKSON
*San Diego, California*
*April 1999*

# FOREWORD

I've been in the Vineyard since its inception. I know all the key players, and I don't know anyone who could perfectly recount our history. Even my closest friends and I sit around and disagree in friendly discussions about *what **really** happened*... but, I also don't know anyone who has worked harder than Bill Jackson to get it right.

The reader can be sure that *Jax* (as his friends call him) has no hidden motive and no ax to grind. His "rank 'n file" lens provides a valid starting point to piece together the complex pieces of the Vineyard story. Many of you went through this history with him and will share his perceptions and his questions. This book will no doubt open lively debate as to what we have learned.

From my vantage-point as one who was in John Wimber's inner circle, sometimes I see things from a different angle than Jax does, but I will say this, he has done his homework. I have read every draft of the book and can vouch for his integrity in tracing down the facts.

I commend this writing of Vineyard history as a good first step. I'm quite certain that other professional historians will come along and provide a more analytical history of the Vineyard, but I'm also convinced that they will pay tribute to *The Quest for the Radical Middle* as a contemporary account of a Vineyard pastor *who was there.*

I'm proud of the courage Jax demonstrates in diligently seeking an even-handed approach. It is not easy or fun to examine the mistakes of your own family. I encouraged him many times, however, to try to tell it like it was so that future generations will be able to learn from our trek to find the *radical middle.*

I've known Jax was bright, had an eye for the truly important and as a teacher could organize material. I didn't know, however, that he is also an engaging author. If you are interested in the Vineyard for any reason, you may not be able to put *The Quest for the Radical Middle* down once you've started. It is a fascinating, concise part of God's story in our little part of the Church called *Vineyard.*

TODD HUNTER
*National Director, Association of Vineyard Churches, USA*

# INTRODUCTION

I have a proud Christian heritage. My family first experienced Christ through the ministry of Young Life, and later was powerfully affected by Campus Life under the mentoring of men like Dave Veerman. We were nurtured at South Park Church in Park Ridge, Illinois which, during my freshman year at Wheaton College, gave birth to what is now Willow Creek Community Church in Barrington, Illinois, one of the largest evangelical churches in America. It was during my Wheaton days, however, that I had a personal encounter with the Holy Spirit that left me forever altered. I spoke in tongues when some classmates laid their hands on me, and I went through a tremendous renewal in my Christian life.

It was confusing to me that after such a wonderful event so few of my evangelical friends shared my enthusiasm. My room-mate and best friend, now a Presbyterian pastor, said to me, "You aren't one of those booga boogas now, are you?" He was joking, of course, but not really, and the incident describes perfectly the dilemma I now faced. Theologically I hadn't changed. I didn't think everybody had to speak in tongues, nor did I believe that one had to speak in tongues to have power or to be saved. Even though my experience was both biblical and life-changing, it was not embraced within my evangelicalism. I consequently experienced something of an identify crisis. I no longer knew who I was. I went about my evangelical business and spoke in tongues in private. There was no one I knew in my world that could either relate to or mentor me in the things of the Spirit into which I so longed to look.

I worked for Campus Life after graduating from Wheaton, but ran away with a friend to Southern California after my fiancée, Janet Moore, was killed in 1976. Divine circumstances led me to Calvary Chapel in San Diego where God opened my eyes to things in the Spirit that I had always wanted to see. I also met my wife, Betsy, and shortly after we were married, I led my Southern

California bride to Boston to attend Gordon-Conwell Theological Seminary. It wasn't the winters that drew us to Boston but the desire to study the Bible at an evangelical institution that had a Pentecostal scholar named Gordon Fee. I was hoping that the "Doc," as we affectionately called him, would be able to help us put together an evangelical theology of the Holy Spirit. I wasn't sure that there was such a thing, but if there was, I was hoping Dr. Fee would lead us to it.

Those were rich years. I was given exegetical tools that enabled me to study the Bible for myself. With these tools and the help of Dr. Fee and others, I was able to put a provisional theology of the Spirit together. The problem was that I still had no-one to mentor me in how it all really worked.

As Bets and I neared graduation, the obvious question was, "What do we do now?" We had an evangelical theology but a Pentecostal experience. In which direction should we go? I decided to try first to be ordained in the Assemblies of God, but they didn't want me because I didn't believe that tongues was the necessary sign of the fullness of the Spirit. We next tried to get into the Evangelical Free Church, but they didn't want me because I spoke in tongues! Because of my post-tribulational eschatology I knew that we couldn't fit the Calvary Chapel church network. What were we to do? Where did we fit?

Someone from our Calvary Chapel days saw me in the dining hall at the seminary and invited me to hear some guy named John Womber or Wumber or something like that who was part of a church called the Vineyard. I eventually got it right—it was Wimber. He was in town to teach on the subject of healing. It was the late spring of 1983; our first child was due in two weeks; we had nowhere to go except back to who-knows-what in San Diego. What did I have to lose?

That night I heard John Wimber deliver what was essentially a seminary lecture on the kingdom of God and I watched as God healed a lady of deafness in one ear. John's manner was laid back and natural, even funny, but not in an irreverent way. I had always dreamed as I read the gospels that Jesus' ministry would have been completely natural and not hyped, like some of the things I'd seen on TV. Oh, and did I mention that the music was great and nobody had to wear ties?

I went home to my pregnant wife and told her that I thought I had just found what we'd been looking for. I went back to the seminar the next day and asked John how to sign up. All he said was, "Come and hang out." These were not encouraging words for a young couple that had no money and was about to have a baby—but it was all we had.

After a soul-searching summer living at Betsy's sister's house in San Diego I was asked to direct the Year of the Bible Program at the U.S. Center for World Mission in Pasadena. This at least put us up near Wimber's church in Anaheim. While in Pasadena we helped plant the Arcadia Vineyard, attended Peter Wagner's 120 Fellowship at Lake Avenue Congregational Church, and drove down to Anaheim on Sunday nights to learn to pray for the sick. Before long we were sent out to plant the first Vineyard in Indianapolis.

I have shared some of my history with you to point out that I was the product of two worlds, the evangelical and the Pentecostal. I loved aspects of both but could embrace neither with my whole heart. I loved both Word and Spirit and didn't see why I had to divorce one from the other. I was somewhere in the middle. Years later Rich Nathan and Ken Wilson would write a book called *Empowered Evangelicals* which eloquently articulated this tension, for they and many others were experiencing it too. I like the term because it connotes a joining together of the best of both worlds. And that's what the Vineyard endeavors to be.

Many years later I found myself directing the Vineyard School of Pastoral Ministry (VSPM) at the Vineyard in Champaign, Illinois. One of the courses I taught was "An Empowered Evangelical View of Church History." It was a fabulous experience. Not only was I able to review and synthesize my evangelical roots, which I had already studied in seminary, but also to research for the first time the Pentecostal side of my heritage which had been filtered out of my evangelical education. I was mesmerized by reading the miracles of the Catholic mystics, the diary accounts of George Fox, the spiritual "affections" of Jonathan Edwards, the impact of the Cane Ridge revival, the nineteenth century faith-cure movement, the history of Azusa Street, and the healing ministries of men and women like Maria Woodworth-Etter, John G. Lake, Smith Wigglesworth and William Branham.

As I worked my way through church history up to the Vineyard, I found no coherent version of our story. Oh, the folk-lore is everywhere: one story on a Wimber tape with no context, one in a Peter Wagner book with no context, another in a John White book, and so on. Only someone who was a professional reader or who had been there from the beginning had any frame-work for understanding the stories. I knew a lot of it because I had been "hanging around" since 1983 and was an avid reader. But for the students I was teaching, whose sum total of Vineyard exposure was our local church, I realized that somebody out there ought to write the story down. After some thought and prayer I decided to give it a try myself.

What I am attempting is to write "my take" on the Vineyard as someone who has been sitting out with the rank and file at our pastors' conferences all these years. I have never been in the inner circle. Since John Wimber never had any interest in history projects, I have had to reconstruct the story from not only my memory and notes but from a myriad of sources such as books, magazines, personal conversations, e-mail messages, faxes and the like.

I have interspersed some of my own experiences in the story, not because I played any significant role, but to give readers a feel for what it was like as we were living it. At certain points I do give my perspective but have tried to differentiate between history and my interpretation of it, if the two can be separated. I have tried to be objective but it will be obvious to the reader that I am a "company man" and I know this affects my perception of events. If there is too much me in here, please chew the meat and spit out the bones.

It must be said up front that John Wimber has had an incredible impact on my Christian life. I sat at my desk and cried when I got the fax that he had died of a massive brain hemorrhage on November 16, 1997. While I did not agree with every decision that John made—the record will clearly show that he made mistakes—I believe in what Peter Wagner has called "followership" and have tried to honor him throughout.

I entrust this story to all those pastors in the conference chairs who tended the Father's vine with me over the years. You and your miraculous stories will not be told in these pages. The apostle John said of the Master that he "did many other things as well. If every one of them were written down, I suppose that even the whole world would not have room for the books that would be written." The same could be said for those out laboring faithfully in the fields. The pay's the same whether your story appears on these pages or not.

For those in International Vineyards, I am so sorry for how "American" this is. It is the only story I really know. I hope that it will someday be written better and more comprehensively than this first attempt.

May an understanding of the past give the present new meaning. Let us go forth for the glory of God, the advancement of the kingdom and the finishing of history (Matthew 24:14).

# CHAPTER ONE

# SETTING THE VINEYARD IN CONTEXT

# SETTING THE VINEYARD IN CONTEXT

## INTRODUCTION

In their excellent book charting the history of the American church from 1776-1990,[1] Roger Finke and Rodney Stark see the continued vitality of the church based on a continuum between what they call sects and churches. Sects represent those movements in high tension with the world system. Finke and Stark demonstrate through their research that as time goes on, those movements, under pressure to lower that tension, accommodate themselves to the culture to better fit in, thus becoming churches. In so doing, they begin to lose their ability to sustain the newfound life that had been the reason for their genesis. The religious sociologist Max Weber calls this process "the routinization of charisma,"[2] i.e., the natural process whereby new religious movements form structures and rituals to survive for the long haul. While an inevitable process for a religious organization to survive past its Charismatic founder, routinization must maintain a balance between organism and organization, between structure and life, lest it stagnate the movement. When the spontaneity that was initially so attractive is choked by the weight of the organization that was set in place to sustain it, the now-hardened bureaucracy snuffs the life out of the organism. What began as a reform movement now needs to be reformed—and so the cycle of church history is a history of routinization and renewal.

The process of continual reformation is based on a constellation of issues, the most basic being the sin nature within men and women. The law of spiritual entropy, sin within the flesh causing all things to become sick and break down, by its very nature calls for continual reformation. Spiritual entropy attacks *the radical middle*, the perfect balance between biblical truths in tension. There are a number of such tensions in the Bible. The following chart names just a few (in random order):

| Jesus is God | Jesus is Man |
|---|---|
| The kingdom of God as already here | The kingdom of God as not here yet |
| Being in the world | Being not of the world |
| Standing for unity | Standing for truth |
| Saved by faith, not by works | Faith without works is dead |
| Divine sovereignty | Human responsibility |
| Head, Word, reason | Heart, Spirit, experience |
| Organization, wineskin, kings (church leaders) | Organism, wine, prophets (charismatic itinerants) |
| Evangelism | Nurture |
| Will of God as a specific calling | Will of God as a general calling |
| Being natural | Being supernatural |
| Planning | Being Spirit-led |
| Everything (all gifts of the Spirit) | Decently and in order |

Biblical truth is found in the radical middle, holding propositions like these in tension. Satan's strategy has, from the very beginning, been to challenge these tensions. His first recorded words caused Eve to doubt God's motive in prohibiting Adam and Eve to eat from one of the trees in the garden when they could eat from all the rest. Satan tempted them to harmonize the apparent incongruity, and in so doing they lost the radical middle of affirming God's *yes* and God's *no* at the same time.

Of all the places of biblical tension, it is perhaps the Word/Spirit, head/heart, reason/experience, organization/organism continuum that provides the best lens through which to view the Vineyard. Throughout the history of the church, one can see the sect/church process outlined by Finke and Stark. A sect begins through the new experience of a forgotten biblical truth. In order to enhance the life of the organism, organization is built to sustain it. Eventually Weber's process of routinization ensues and religion of the heart soon becomes religion of the head as well as the heart. A biblical balance is achieved and the sect/church is on the cutting edge and able to survive. With the passage of time, however, the radical middle becomes hard to sustain, precisely because it is a place of tension. The law of spiritual entropy presses the movement to choose a pole and become one or the other, to harmonize the dissonance. The forces of evil push the new movement either away from biblical doctrine toward cultism or away from Spirit-led spontaneity toward dead orthodoxy and institutionalism. We might picture the continuum like this:

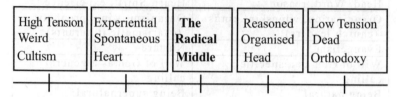

| High Tension Weird Cultism | Experiential Spontaneous Heart | **The Radical Middle** | Reasoned Organised Head | Low Tension Dead Orthodoxy |

We will use the rubric Word/Spirit to articulate this historical tension because it best exemplifies the core issues for our study. Gerald F. Hawthorne, in his book *The Presence & the Power: The Significance of the Holy Spirit in the Life and Ministry of Jesus,*[3] demonstrates that Jesus, the incarnate Word of God, ministered and performed miracles through the power of the Holy Spirit and not out of his deity (although he could have). In so doing, Jesus modeled for humanity that the Word and Spirit are in proper relationship to one another. The Word submits to the voice of the Spirit, and the Spirit blows in accordance with the parameters of the Word. Word and Spirit are in dynamic tension.

Satan's strategy, as we have hypothesized, is to pull a person, church or movement away from the *radical middle* toward one pole or the other. In this case he pits Word against Spirit, reason against experience, organization against organism. Church movements are fluid, starting on the Spirit side of the continuum as people crave experiential reality. Then they move toward the Word side as they seek to ground their experience in biblical objectivity. We will call the Word stream in church history *Evangelicalism* and the Spirit stream *Pentecostalism*. However inadequate these labels, the point is clear, and the words represent points of emphasis. By using these labels we are in no way saying that consensus orthodoxy has not or is not led by the Spirit; nor do we mean that experiential renewal movements have not or are not teaching the Word. What we are saying is that groups throughout history have tended toward one pole or the other. History shows that the Word without the Spirit quickly becomes dead orthodoxy, and the Spirit without the Word quickly becomes cultish.

The crucial issue for the Word/Spirit tension concerns how one is to know the will of God. The evangelical stream has always (and rightly) affirmed the Word as the true foundation; there is no new Truth because it has been once for all given to the saints (Jude 3). Evangelicals have also affirmed that there is only one meaning to a biblical text: the meaning of the original author. Spirit movements have "rediscovered" forgotten biblical truths, thus bringing new balance and life to what was dying through neglect. Unfortunately, renewal has often come at the price of doctrinal purity by offering interpretations based not on historical/ grammatical study, but on interpretations prompted by the "Spirit." Once off biblical/historical moorings, the slide toward cultism begins. The challenge is, as it has always been, to affirm both Word and Spirit and aim for the radical middle.

An in-depth discussion of these views is outside the scope of this work, but in order to set the Vineyard in its historical context, we will try to trace the broad outlines as the two perspectives work to balance each other. One might extrapolate a biblical text here and say that just as iron sharpens iron, so one perspective sharpens another (Proverbs 27:17). The quest for the radical middle in the Word/Spirit paradigm would culminate in a church growth explosion called Calvary Chapel in the 1960s and become the precursor to the Vineyard.

## Historic Evangelicalism[4]

From the time of the apostles, one could draw a time line charting those who gave their lives to preserve the intent of the apostolic writings. These writings, which became the New Testament, define what Christians believe and do until the return of Christ. Evangelicals are those who are committed to Christ's mission and Christ's doctrine as defined in the Bible. There is no new truth coming to the earth. Any revelation concerns application of truth already written. True interpretation means digging for the author's original intent in the Scripture, a discipline not only of prayer but also of language, grammar and ancient history.

The historic doctrines of the faith were hammered out in church councils by bishops in the early centuries, and were preserved by the Catholic and Eastern Orthodox churches until the Reformation. While the Middle Ages had seen a great demise in live orthodoxy, it was a young Catholic scholar named Martin Luther whom God used to call the church back to its apostolic moorings. In 1517 he nailed 95 items of debate on the door of Wittenburg Cathedral. The protest, or Protestant movement, had begun.

Out of the Reformation, a number of different reform movements arose in Germany, Switzerland and England. The so-called Reformed Tradition as articulated by John Calvin became the dominant, new, Protestant orthodoxy. It affirmed the absolute sovereignty of God. Jacob Arminius, a Dutch theologian, introduced a counter-system that affirmed human free will. Streams hereafter would prefer one system or the other. As centuries went on, the church was renewed again and again by such groups as the Puritans, the Pietists, the Moravians, the Anabaptists, and the Quakers, some more Reformed and others more Arminian.

There were two great periods of awakening that most affected British and American Christianity. The first Great Awakening began through the evangelistic fire of George Whitefield and John Wesley. Wesley was the first to build church silos (local churches) to hold the grain through the instigation of a "method," thus the name Methodists. Jonathan Edwards became the father of the Awakening in the colonies and one of the church's greatest theologians of the Reformed Tradition. We will speak more of him later. Out of this move of God came the rise of modern missions through the labors of a young shoemaker named William Carey.

A second Awakening occurred at the beginning of the nineteenth century. It began in the theological schools in New England and swept like a fire onto the southwestern frontier. Charles Finney, most remembered for his labors in the Northwest, was an Arminian who became the prototype for modern evangelistic crusades. He introduced new measures such as the use of protracted meetings and altar calls.

The post-Civil War era saw the rise of liberal theology, and live orthodoxy rose to oppose it. The defense encompassed both evangelicals in the mainline denominations led by the famous Princeton Reformed theologian B.B. Warfield, and a more independent voice called the Holiness Movement that developed into twentieth-century fundamentalism. Men like Jonathan Blanchard, who founded Wheaton College, and D.L. Moody, who became the great evangelist of the era, led the new independents, along with A.B Simpson, A.J. Gordon, and R.A. Torrey. When their doctrinal stance was written in a series of pamphlets called the *Fundamentals*, they became known as "fundamentalists." They were not the narrow group we know today but cutting-edge defenders of live orthodoxy.

A great divide occurred for the new crusaders during the Scopes Trial in 1925. The agnostic Clarence Darrow made a fool of the fundamentalist William Jennings Bryan in a court case over the issue of Darwinism. Even though Darrow lost the case, he made the fundamentalists look like backward hicks, and fundamentalism was forced into a narrow sub-culture during the 1930s, propagating itself through the formation of Bible schools.

What we now know as Evangelicalism emerged in the 1940s as a group of former fundamentalists brought live orthodoxy out into the public arena again. Billy Graham, an evangelist; Carl Henry, a theologian who started the magazine *Christianity Today*; and Harold John Ockenga, a pastor who founded both Gordon Divinity School (now Gordon-Conwell) and Fuller Theological Seminary, led the new movement in both evangelism (thus the name "Evangelical") and social action. A new wave of theologians also began to lead the Evangelicals back into the scholarly arena, and a whole host of evangelical publishing companies such as Wm. B. Eerdmans and Zondervan gave the movement the literature it needed.

God used Billy Graham most dramatically to bring the Evangelicals into the public arena. Billy's amazing career began with a crusade in Los Angeles that saw famous people converted to Christ. When they put Billy on the covers of the *LA Times* and *Newsweek*, the new Evangelicals were on the covers with him. A whole host of new evangelistic efforts were raised up to harvest souls such as Youth for Christ, Young Life, Campus Crusade for Christ and the Navigators. At mid-century the evangelical gospel was disseminating all over the world.

## HISTORIC PENTECOSTALISM[5]

Movements that have embraced the ministry of the Holy Spirit through spiritual gifts such as prophecy and healing have often been relegated to the fringes of orthodoxy because they neglected the Word. For example, in the second century a group called the Montanists (named for their leader, Montanus) sought to stir up the gifts of the Spirit. They were condemned by church leaders of the day as heretics due to their belief that extra-biblical prophecy was equal to the apostolic writings, but before they strayed from orthodoxy, they saw what appears to have been a true revival of the Spirit.[6]

One of the main reasons that the miraculous activity of the Holy Spirit was pushed toward the fringes of orthodoxy was the doctrine of cessationism first propounded by the church father Augustine.[7] In his book *On the True Religion*, Augustine laid the foundation not only for the doctrine of the Catholic Church but also for throttling the Spirit. Since he had never experienced the miraculous, he reasoned back to the Bible and concluded that the miraculous must have died out with the apostles. Miracles continued to occur but only among the saints and were considered acts one must be worthy to perform. Before Augustine died, however, he saw a healing and changed his position. In his most famous book, *The City of God*, he supports the miraculous, but it was too late. Consensus orthodoxy had the weapons it needed to keep the supernatural on the pages of the Bible and out of the churches.

Despite the wonderful changes in the church that occurred in the Protestant Reformation, both of the key reformers, Luther and Calvin, unfortunately accepted Augustine's cessationism. In so doing the culture was robbed of what William DeArtega has called "analogous experiences."[8] An analogous experience is a contemporary experience that parallels something that happened in the Bible. When people read that Jesus healed a fever, they are able to say, "Oh, I saw something like that once." DeArtega's contention is that if we say that we cannot experience the things of the Bible, then it is a short hop to rejecting the historicity of the Bible itself.

In the seventeenth century, George Fox, the founder of the Quakers, saw what was probably the greatest outbreak of spiritual gifts since the time of the apostles. His followers got their name because they often shook or "quaked" under the power of God. Fox's ideas became the forerunner of our modern theology of healing. While many believed that healing was available in the atonement of the cross (i.e., to anyone who believed), Fox proposed that it was based in the sovereignty of God (i.e., God's purposes dictated who was and wasn't healed). George Fox was a man before his time, and his more experiential center paved the way for a truly live orthodoxy and for future missionary zeal.

Jonathan Edwards, the father of the first Great Awakening in America, was, however, the first to develop a theological argument for renewal by the Spirit. When the Awakening broke out in his church in Northhampton, Massachusetts, it was accompanied by what Edwards called "supernatural affections." These affections were manifestations of the Spirit that affected people's bodies. People fell, cried out, groaned, and lay enraptured, his own wife for a period of days. When Edwards picked up his pen to defend experiential as well as reasoned faith, he was flying in the face of almost three hundred years of rejection of the validity of experience. Since the Reformers had placed the church on a purely empirical foundation, no one had stood to defend affections as reasonable. It should be noted that Edwards was a cessationist; while he embraced the idea that Christianity was to be experienced as well as reasoned, he did not see a place for spiritual gifts such as healing and prophecy in the church.

That began to change with the Cane Ridge revival during the second Great Awakening. Awesome power fell on camp meetings on the western frontiers of Kentucky and Tennessee drawing people from miles around. The historic controversy centered not on the number of people who were saved but on the strange phenomena that accompanied the Spirit's presence. People were said to fall, jerk, bark, laugh, and have periods of ecstatic singing and dancing. Consensus orthodoxy accepted the converts and the fruit but rejected the phenomena.

Meanwhile, across the Atlantic in London, a British pastor named Edward Irving began to propagate the view that the apostolic gifts would be returned to the church before the return of Christ. After investigating reports of healings, tongues, and prophecy in Scotland, Irving saw an outbreak of the same gifts in his church. He went on to teach some strange doctrines and was eventually condemned as a heretic, but modern Pentecostal scholars consider Irving the father of Pentecostalism.

The half-century after the Civil War saw a great buildup of Spirit activity that would explode in the twentieth century. The Holiness movement began to earnestly pray for the baptism of the Holy Ghost, which they equated with the power to live a holy life. Eventually, the cry for "the baptism" would be equated with power for service.

Rumors began to come over to America from Europe that God was beginning to heal the sick. European healers like Johann Blumhardt began to believe that sickness came from sin and healing was therefore guaranteed in the atonement if people would only believe. This put healing on an entirely different foundation than that of George Fox and laid the foundation for later Pentecostal theology. The American healing movement began with Ethan O. Allen but was taken into the public arena by Dr. Charles Cullis whose accomplishments were breathtaking. Noted evangelicals like A.J. Gordon and A.B. Simpson supported the healing movement, even though the followers of these men would reject that aspect of their ministries. Maria Woodworth-Etter and John Alexander Dowie were other healers during this period.

The turn of the century saw the Welsh Revival led by Evan Roberts. The key distinctive to Roberts' meetings was that he was committed to letting them be led by the Holy Spirit. Crying, falling, repentance, travailing prayer, conversions, and joyous singing characterized his meetings. While the revival physically broke Evan Roberts for lack of rest, the Holy Spirit jumped across the ocean and lit a fire that went all around the world.

Historic Pentecostalism was birthed in a dilapidated mission on Azusa Street in Los Angeles in 1906. It began as a revival that lasted day and night for three years, and in less than a century, it grew into the largest strata of Protestant Christianity in the world. The Azusa Street revival actually began in Kansas on January 1, 1901, when a young girl named Agnes Ozman spoke in tongues in a Bible school led by Charles Parham. Others began speaking in tongues, and Parham took his new Spirit baptism out on the road. God used William J. Seymour, a black holiness preacher and one of Parham's students, to father the revival. He was invited to speak in Los Angeles. When the power fell, the crowds became so great that they moved to the little mission, and from there revival spread all over the world.

A number of Pentecostal denominations formed out of the revival, the largest being the Assemblies of God. Aimee Semple McPherson was a noted evangelist of the period who went on to found the Four Square Gospel denomination. Other notable figures included Smith Wigglesworth and John G. Lake. These people and their denominations were largely rejected by the Holiness churches, the very people who had been praying for fifty years for "the baptism." When it came, it wasn't what they had anticipated. B.B. Warfield, the noted Princeton theologian, wrote *Counterfeit Miracles* restating Augustine's original cessationist thesis. Once again the movement of the Spirit was relegated to the fringes of orthodoxy.

Evangelicals were not the only ones who experienced a period of renewal at mid-century; second-generation Pentecostals had lived for years on the stories from the first generation. In one year, 1946, healing power was released on three sovereign vessels:

William Branham, Oral Roberts, and Kathryn Kuhlman. Another more localized revival broke out in Canada and became known as the Latter Rain movement. While historic Pentecostalism eventually rejected the Latter Rain for its doctrinal errors, it made important contributions that laid the groundwork for the Charismatic movement in the 1960s. Some of these contributions were the laying on of hands, the gifts of prophecy and healing, the "five-fold" ministry, and a new hymnody of Scripture-based choruses.

The Charismatic movement began when people from mainline denominations began to experience the baptism of the Spirit, the most notable being the Episcopal priest, Dennis Bennett. He was the first clergyman to speak in tongues and be allowed to stay in his denomination. The Charismatic movement also had a tremendous impact on the Catholic Church which had opened the door for renewal in Vatican II.

## THE JESUS MOVEMENT

During the late 1960s, when the Charismatic movement was at its height, the Holy Spirit moved in an incredible way on a new generation of young people. Many of the expressions of this move were Charismatic in their orientation; others were not. It didn't really matter by which net they were caught, thousands upon thousands of young people were saved from drugs, sex, and rock 'n roll between 1967 and the mid 1970s. The fish began biting everywhere; many of them were caught in tried-and-true organizations such as Youth for Christ and Campus Crusade for Christ, but many more were caught with brand new nets.

### THE SOCIAL MILIEU OF THE 1960S

A new generation had come to young adulthood. They were called the "baby-boomers," a generation named after the boom in births following the Second World War. They were "the pig in the python," a description of the population graph that showed a giant bulge in the number of babies born between 1946 and 1964—as if a python had just eaten a pig. They were the first generation to be raised on television, the generation that birthed rock 'n roll.

They were affluent, having been raised in the post-war surge in the economy when the American dream was more real than it had ever been, at least for middle-class white folks.

Francis Schaeffer, an American living with his family in Switzerland, was a major influence during this period. He and his wife, Edith, ministered to a whole parade of baby-boomers traveling through Europe to find truth, noted that this generation had been cheated.[9] Their parents had been raised in church by godly grandparents who got their values from a true relationship with Christ. Those parents, however, had gotten the values but not the relationship that gave the values meaning. They taught those values to their baby-boomer children but without any substance. When the boomers asked "Why?" their parents, without true relationship with Christ, could only say, "Because I said so." To a generation watching itself return from Southeast Asia in body bags, "because I said so" didn't cut it. From the kids' perspective, their parents' values were the reason the world was in such a mess.

A "generation gap" developed between the boomers and the "establishment." Occasionally, during social crisis, a generation is born that moves a quantum leap forward socially to an altogether different place. A gap develops. The cultural forms and values of the parents' generation are obsolete for the children who must carve out a new life, new values, new forms, new heroes, new gods, new art and new music. The two generations are like ships passing in the night, not hearing, not understanding, eventually becoming "people speaking without listening" (Simon and Garfunkel).

As the decade of the 1960s passed, one generation was living the American Dream while their children were living in a world that seemed out of control!

- The Cuban missile crisis left us frightened about a ubiquitous Communist takeover.
- China successfully field-tested their first nuclear bomb.
- John F. Kennedy, Martin Luther King Jr., and Bobby Kennedy were shot.
- Vietnam touched our lives nightly with Walter Cronkite's

body count.
- The six-day Arab-Israeli war seemed to some the beginning of Armageddon.
- The religion of the older generation was declared irrelevant. On April 8, 1966, the cover of *Time* magazine asked "Is God Dead?"
- Young people were confronted in secular terms with two alternatives, either escape the pain or work to overthrow the system. The youth culture escaped the pain through the big three: sex, drugs, and rock 'n roll. Men like Martin Luther King Jr. went after the system.
- The hippie movement had its genesis in the Haight Ashbury district in San Francisco. Beatniks and Bohemians of North Beach were pressured by the sex merchants to move to a low rent district called "Haight Ashbury." Word soon be gan to get out about experiences the new Haight residents were having with mind-altering drugs. In 1967-68, young people began to flock there from all over the world to crash the party and experiment with sex, drugs, and rock 'n roll.
- Other centers soon cropped up like Greenwich Village in New York, Old Town in Chicago, Griffith Park in Los Angeles, Mission Beach in San Diego, Yorkville in Toronto and many college campuses, especially U.C. at Berkeley in San Francisco. The steps and plaza of Sproul Hall became the Aereopagus of the modern age where anyone could speak openly on their views about anything.

## THE SEARCH FOR SPIRITUAL ANSWERS

When the Beatles' search for meaning led them via the emptiness of drugs to the Maharishi Mahesh Yogi, Eastern religion caught the world by storm. You could continue to "do your own thing" while trying to find inner peace. One could chant one's way to peace by saying a mantra to the Indian god Krishna. It was a lie, but many got hooked to their own destruction. Some young people intuitively knew that the way of love was the true path, but "flower power" didn't seem to lead them there. People were just as hateful "with flowers in their hair" (a song by Joni Mitchell).

Some sensed the apocalyptic dawning of the Age of Aquarius. Crosby, Stills, Nash & Young sang that it was "time to get back to the garden," but that didn't work either. They eventually broke up and David Crosby almost destroyed his life with drugs.

Some delved into the occult to find the answers. Astrologers claimed it was the Age of Aquarius. Youth experimented with Ouiji boards. Anton LaVey started the First Church of Satan for those enlightened Satanists who did not believe in the supernatural. Other Satanic cults, however, tapped into the real thing and performed weird sexual rites and formed covens for witches and warlocks to practice magic. People began to find the remains of bizarre sacrifices.

## THE JESUS MOVEMENT[10]

In 1966, John Lennon made an off-hand remark that the Beatles were more popular than Jesus Christ. He didn't realize that the youth culture was on the edge of a massive revival of love for Jesus Christ and that the Beatles were on the verge of disbanding. While the youth of the 60s were working out the emptiness of their genetic code of rebellion against authority, God was at work to counteract tragedy with glory.

## TED WISE

Ted Wise was a sail-maker from Saulsalito, California, and was one of the original hippies. He was a drug addict and into speed and LSD before they were popular. He sensed the emptiness of it all by 1966 and gave his life to Christ when he read the New Testament.

Wise was 33 when, helped by three Bay Area ministers (one of whom was Ed Plowman), he started one of the earliest storefront efforts to evangelize the youth culture in Haight Ashbury. Through the "Living Room," Wise was instrumental in the spiritual journeys of thousands of hippies who came to groove on the atmosphere in Haight.

Before long, Wise and his wife, Elizabeth, saw that those who were messed up on drugs needed to be removed from their environment, so they started a Christian commune in nearby Novato called the House of Acts.[11] Other such communes would follow in a chain reaction, thus starting the Christian commune movement, one of the major vehicles reaching the drug culture.

One of the residents of the House of Acts was a 19-year-old ex-drug addict named Lonnie Frisbee who had moved to Haight Asbury when he was sixteen, gotten saved, and begun a career of preaching to hippies. He eventually moved down to Costa Mesa near Los Angeles to help Chuck Smith, a pastor of a small church called Calvary Chapel. It was there that Lonnie became involved with another commune called the House of Miracles. The House of Miracles was one of the instrumental feeders for the explosion of conversions at Calvary Chapel. Within a few years, Smith's church would grow from 150 to several thousand as masses of young people came to Christ.

## HAL LINDSEY AND *THE LATE GREAT PLANET EARTH*

In 1970 Hal Lindsey published the book *The Late Great Planet Earth*.[12] In it he detailed what he believed to be the unfolding of events prior to the return of Christ. It was a classic restatement of pretribulational premillennialism in a package the youth culture could embrace.

The doctrine of the pretribulational rapture, therefore, became the eschatology of the Jesus Movement. Preachers such as the influential Chuck Smith and movies like *A Thief in the Night* gave the movement an apocalyptic edge. There was so much power to save souls that it seemed to many as if the end-time events were taking place before their eyes.

## GOSPEL ROCK 'N ROLL

Many of the young hippie converts were rock musicians. When Calvary Chapel exploded, a number of these musicians began to put together Christian bands. Chuck Girard and his band, *Love Song,* were converted and become one of the areas premier music groups. *The Second Chapter of Acts* was formed and the solo artist, Larry Norman, became the Christian equivalent to Bob Dylan writing such classics as "Why Does the Devil Get All the Good Music?"

With the creation of the music agency *Maranatha! Music*, Calvary Chapel was on the cutting edge of a whole new industry that would take the world by storm—gospel rock 'n roll. Now baby boomers not only had Jesus, but they also had a church to attend with music that was indigenous to them.

## BILL HYBELS AND THE RISE OF THE SEEKER-SENSITIVE CHURCHES

In 1972, two young men, Bill Hybels and Dave Holmbo began to lead the youth group at my home church, South Park Church in Park Ridge, Illinois. Out of their efforts God created the youth movement called "Son City" which impacted thousands of young people from the Chicago area. While there is probably not any direct tie to the Jesus Movement per se, God was in the air in those days. It was all one move of the Holy Spirit.

Eventually Hybels and Holmbo moved Son City out of the church and rented the Willow Creek Theater in nearby Palatine. This was the beginning of Willow Creek Community Church, one of the largest churches in America. Thousands of churches have patterned their Sunday morning services after Willow Creek's format that tries to win the seeker to Christianity through contemporary vehicles such as drama, media, and rock music. Gatherings for teaching the church take place on other nights.

## CALVARY CHAPEL[13]

The story of Calvary Chapel is significant for the history of the Vineyard because the Vineyard was birthed out of Calvary. It was, at the height of the Jesus Movement, a classic example of a quest for the radical middle between the Word/Spirit poles. The story begins with pastor Chuck Smith.

Chuck Smith grew up as a Christian in a Pentecostal denomination, and after going to Life Bible College, the Foursquare school in Los Angeles, he pastored churches for 17 years from that denomination. Because of pressure to grow, Smith tried every gimmick possible to grow his church. Week after week he prepared topical evangelistic sermons, but when he would get to church, he says there was never a "sinner in the bunch." He chastised his flock for not gathering the lost, but it never worked.

His third pastorate in Corona, California, started with 52 people. Before long they had grown to 17, five of whom were members of his own family! He was forced to get another job and began to work for an Alpha Beta supermarket. Here, however, he prospered and was strongly urged by his boss to quit the ministry and move into management. Smith took that decision to the Lord; either God would somehow bring in the money to cover his unpaid bills ($416), or he would quit the ministry and go into business. That same day someone called to say that God had laid it on their hearts to send Chuck $426.

God next moved the Smiths to pastor a church in Huntington Beach. Here Chuck began to admit that God had made him a pastor-teacher rather than an evangelist. He gave himself to teaching expositionally through books of the Bible and saw the church begin to prosper as people were fed the Word of God.

They eventually left Huntington Beach and moved to Los Seranos and then Costa Mesa where they began to experiment with home Bible studies. At this point God made it clear to Chuck that he was to break with his denomination. He was now working as a carpenter and continued with the home Bible studies. One of the studies in Corona began to take off and looked like it might be very fruitful.

The owner of the project he was building, however, was on the board of a little church in Costa Mesa called Calvary Chapel. They were on the verge of closing and needed a pastor. Chuck's wife Kay was not at all interested in leaving their new work in Corona, but God made it clear to her that He was speaking to Chuck about taking the small church. God provided a Spirit-filled pastor for the work in Corona, and the Smiths began to pastor Calvary Chapel in 1965.

Two years before this, God had sovereignly spoken to Chuck that he was going to become a shepherd over many flocks and that his ministry would grow so large that the building would not be able to hold the people. Unbeknown to Chuck, the Holy Spirit had also spoken to the little group at Calvary that He would bring Chuck to pastor them. They also knew from the Lord that when he got there he would be unhappy with the building and would want to remodel it. God would bless the church. It would go on the radio and would overflow with people. It would eventually move to a new facility on the bluffs overlooking the Bay and become world renown.

Chuck was surprised when, at lunch on his first Sunday, he was not rebuffed by his proposal to the elders to remodel the church. They went on the radio shortly thereafter but had to stop because so many people began showing up!

Much to Chuck's consternation, many of the new converts were hippies. Chuck couldn't stand hippies at first, but before long God gave him such a heart for them that he and Kay would often drive to Huntington Beach to watch and pray for them. About this time, the Smiths' daughter began to date a boy named John, an ex-hippie who had come to Christ. Through John, God began to open the doors to reaching hippies for Christ. One day John brought a hippie named Lonnie Frisbee whom he had picked up hitchhiking to Chuck's door - the first one he had ever met! Lonnie stayed with the Smiths for a couple of days, having just come from living in Ted Wise's "House of Acts" in San Francisco. Shortly thereafter, Lonnie helped a man named John Higgins start the Costa Mesa version of the same in a rented two bedroom house they called the "House of Miracles." It was May of 1968 and time for an explosion.

Within the first week, 21 hippies accepted Christ and moved into the house. By the end of the second week there were 35. Those who had been Christians a week or more were asked to leave to share Christ with others. That next week some of them went to Tahquitz Canyon to witness and found a young runaway sitting on a rock and holding drugs, books on oriental religion and a Bible. She was trying to find truth. The young Christians took her to the House of Miracles where she accepted Christ. The girl was returned to her parents but was back the next week with 10 of her friends. All ten were saved. The next week they brought 35 more from Riverside where they lived.

This led to a house ministry in Riverside, but it turned out to be an old hotel! A whole motorcycle gang was saved when they stopped to get rooms at the hotel, only to find that it was full of turned on hippie Christians. Other houses were started in Santa Ana, Garden Grove, Buena Park, Newport Beach, Costa Mesa, and Huntington Beach. They even started a ranch in Oregon.

Meanwhile, back at Calvary, the church was beginning to outgrow its facility. There was growing tension between the more traditional members and the hippies. The straw that broke the camel's back was when the church members hung a sign outside the entrance saying NO BARE FEET ALLOWED. Chuck was appalled and immediately took the sign down. There was a board meeting that night and Chuck challenged the men saying that the church was on trial and had to pass the test of love. They turned over their new carpet to Jesus and determined to learn to love the hippies as they were, just as God had loved them.

They quickly outgrew their facility and bought an 11-acre plot on the bluffs overlooking the Bay. They remodeled the existing building, but soon outgrew it and had to put up a huge circus tent until they could build something more permanent. While meeting in the tent, they began to grow exponentially. Calvary was made famous when magazines such as *Look*, *Time* and *Life* ran spreads showing their mass baptisms in a cove off Newport Beach. Brian Vachon records his observations in an article in *Look* in 1971:

*Each month, adult ministers from Calvary Chapel conduct massive baptisms in a gently rounded harbor area outside Newport Beach, California. At the baptism I attended, several thousand spectators came and circled the beach or sat up on the protective wall of rock. They sang and prayed, and fellowship was something I could almost grab in my hand. It was warm–happy.* [14]

Chuck writes,

*Scholars such as Peter Wagner (Fuller Theological Seminary) and Ron Enroth (Westmont College) have observed this phenomenon and noted that it is not likely anything of such colossal proportions has occurred in American history. One estimate put the total number of Calvary Chapel (Costa Mesa) baptisms performed over a two-year period during the mid-1970s at well over 8,000. Additionally, over 20,000 conversions to the Christian faith took place during that same period. According to church growth experts, Calvary Chapel's 10-year growth rate was almost 10,000 percent! Calvary Chapels have grown to nearly 400 affiliates [500 by 1995] in the United States and around the world. From humble beginnings, more than forty thousand people now call Calvary Chapel their home church. Calvary Chapel has become the third largest Protestant church in America and the largest in California.*[15]

My wife and I can both trace roots back to Calvary Chapel. My wife was a white-collar hippie on drugs and living in Ocean Beach in San Diego. She came to Christ when someone from the Navigators knocked on her door, and shortly thereafter she became one of the first members of Mike MacIntosh's Calvary Chapel in San Diego (now called Horizon, an affiliate of Calvary Chapel).

I, on the other hand, was a straight kid from a Christian church in the Chicago suburbs and had run away to Southern California after my fiancée had been killed. I was in a park on a Sunday morning just a few days after arriving and was reading my Bible and asking God where I was to go to church. A jogger ran by and seeing my Bible said, "How you doin', Brother?" He invited me to a church called Calvary Chapel. It met in a theater, and everyone was dressed like… well, Southern California. A girl came and sat on the stage with her guitar, closed her eyes, and went to be with Jesus. I had never seen anything like it before. A thousand people with their eyes closed, many with hands raised, singing and weeping to Jesus. No band, no flash, just broken people like me learning to love God and neighbor. I had found my home and, not realizing it then, my wife. I married the girl with the guitar a little over a year later. And like my lovely Betsy, I too was baptized in one of the mass baptisms in the ocean.

## The Philosophy of Calvary Chapel

In his section on "Philosophy" in *The History of Calvary Chapel*, Chuck Smith goes to great lengths to explain the key to his approach to the church. He believes that the job of the church, after its primary task of bringing glory to God, is not to evangelize but rather to build up the church for the work of ministry so they can reach maturity in Christ (Ephesians 4:12). Chuck sees his role as pastor-teacher to model the lifestyle of a servant and teach the Word of God. His radio, tape, and book ministry is called The Word for Today.

Calvary's main emphasis in church is to worship God and teach the Bible. Their worship involves songs produced by *Maranatha! Music* and Chuck's systematic teaching through the Bible. At the time of writing (1992) Chuck was going through the Bible with his congregation for the seventh time. Systematic teaching, he says, solves the basic problem of the minister struggling to find the text for the next week. It also keeps the preacher off pet subjects and forces him to teach the whole counsel of God.

Chuck believes that God showed him that if he would build up the church, Jesus would grow it. That indeed is what has happened. Calvary Chapel has been known for being one of the most successful evangelistic ministries in the history of America, producing some of the country's best evangelists in Raul Ruiz, Greg Laurie, and Mike MacIntosh. Interestingly, the evangelism did not begin until Chuck stopped trying to be an evangelist and settled down to be a pastor-teacher, systematically teaching his church the Bible.

Calvary reflects the laid back style of what Chuck considers to be 90% of the baby-boomers, especially those in Southern California.

People can come dressed however they please. Most of the services use contemporary music, but others include traditional hymns. The heart of the service is Chuck's Bible-based message which he concludes with an opportunity for people to respond to Christ.

Calvary Chapel reflects a theology that affirms the present-day ministry of the Holy Spirit, but Chuck minimizes the use of the more Charismatic gifts. Tongues and prophecy are not allowed to manifest in the main services; other venues are provided for their expression. He does not want the services to be a "circus." He wants the gifts to flow in a way that he feels brings balance to the tension between dead orthodoxy and out-of-control emotionalism, between Word and Spirit. He would see gifts such as prophecy and word of knowledge as inherent in the pastor's preaching and teaching.[16]

The church government in the Calvary churches allows the senior pastor to make the key decisions as he discerns the will of Jesus. He does so in conjunction with a board of elders that partners with him. He is not their hireling, but neither does he lord his authority over them.

Chuck is very strong on not doing anything out of vain ambition and emphasizes waiting for the Lord who promises to build his church. Calvary prays, waits, and moves out on the basis of what they think the Lord is saying. They are very laid-back and avoid anything resembling what one might view as mainstream philosophy or ideology (such as marketing) or church growth principles.

## SUMMARY

This brief overview of the Word and Spirit streams of church history sets the context for the emergence of the Vineyard movement. Like Calvary Chapel, the Vineyard is a search for the balance between Word and Spirit. As we will see, as Calvary began to routinize into a church planting movement, the Vineyard rose up to represent a more aggressive affirmation of the present-day ministry of the Holy Spirit. The Vineyard is an attempt to marry the life of the Spirit with solid exegesis and the fierce pragmatism that reflects John Wimber's years as a church growth consultant. As will be seen in the following pages, staying in the radical middle is plagued with land mines. The Vineyard, as is historically the case, is in a tremendous struggle to find the point of balance as the Evangelical and Pentecostal sides in the Vineyard endeavor to critique one another.

To begin our story we need to examine two streams: John Wimber and the Evangelicals, and Kenn Gulliksen and Calvary Chapel representing the "Pentecostals."[17]

CB

NOTES:

[1] *The Churching of America, 1776-1990: Winners and Losers in Our Religious Economy*, New Brunswick, NJ, Rutgers University Press, 1992

[2] *The Sociology of Religion*, Boston, MA, Beacon Press, 1993 (first published in Germany in 1922)

[3] Dallas, TX, Word Publishing, 1991

[4] While the volumes on evangelicalism are too numerous to list, two suggested studies are Christian Smith, *American Evangelicalism: Embattled and Thriving*, Chicago, IL, The University of Chicago Press, 1998; see also the excellent historical account by George Marsden, *Fundamentalism and American Culture: The Shaping of Twentieth Century Evangelicalism, 1870-1925*, New York, NY, Oxford University Press, 1980.

[5] As with evangelicalism, Pentecostal scholarship is voluminous. On renewal movements throughout the history of the church see Ronald Knox, *Enthusiasm*, South Bend, IN, University of Nortre Dame Press, 1995. On classic Pentecostalism from an outsiders perspective see Harvey Cox, *Fire from Heaven: The Rise of Pentecostal Spirituality and the Reshaping of Religion in the Twenty-First Century*, Reading, MA, Addison-Wesley Publishing Co., 1995. For an insiders view see either the thorough analysis by Walter Hollenweger, *The Pentecostals*, London, Eng., Student Christian Movement Press, 1972 or a quick overview by Vinson Synan, *In the Latter Days: The Outpouring of the Holy Spirit in the Twentieth Century*, Rev. Ed., Ann Arbor, MI, Servant Publications, 1991. For background of the healing revivals see "Healing Movements," by P. G. Chappell in Burgess, McGee and Alexander, eds., *Dictionary of Pentecostal and Charismatic Movements*, Grand Rapids

MI, Zondervan, 1988; see also D. E. Harrell's *All Things are Possible: The Healing and Charismatic Revivals in Modern America*, Bloomington IN, Indiana University Press, 1975.

[6] Some Charismatics in the 1960s saw the Montanists as proto Pentecostals.

[7] For a modern restatement of the cessationist thesis see John MacArthur, *Charismatic Chaos*, Grand Rapids, MI, Zondervan, 1992. For a refutation see Jack Deere, *Surprised by the Power of the Spirit*, Grand Rapids, MI, Zondervan, 1993.

[8] *Quenching the Spirit: Examining Centuries of Opposition to the Moving of the Holy Spirit*, Lake Mary, FL, Creation House, 1992, pp.84-87

[9] *How Should We Then Live?* Old Tappan, NJ, Fleming H. Revell, 1976, pp. 182ff

[10] See the unpublished MA thesis by David Di Sabatino, *The History of the Jesus Movement*. This thesis can be viewed and downloaded off the world wide web at www.ldolphin.org/jpindex.shtml. The thesis has also been published as *The Jesus People: An Annotated Bibliography and General Resource* (Westport, CT., Greenwood Press, 1999); see also Edward Plowman's *The Jesus Movement in America* (formerly *The Underground Church*), New York, Pyramid Books, 1971. Plowman was a pastor in San Francisco during this period and studied, researched and lived through what happened.

[11] *Time*, August 3, 1971

[12] Grand Rapids, MI, Zondervan

[13] Much of the following information about Calvary Chapel comes from a booklet written by Chuck Smith called *The History of Calvary Chapel* (Costa Mesa, CA, The Word for Today).

[14] "The Jesus Movement is Upon Us," February 9, 1971 (Vol. 35, No. 3, pp. 15-21

[15] Smith, p. 2

[16] Chuck's essential position was communicated to me in a fax from Kenn Gulliksen, August 6, 1998.

[17] I put "Pentecostals" in quotes because neither Gulliksen nor Chuck Smith would consider themselves Pentecostals. Indeed, Chuck Smith moved away from his Pentecostal, Foursquare heritage. I am using the term "Pentecostal" to mean that these men were representative of a stream that affirmed the present day ministry of the Spirit whereas Wimber was birthed in evangelical cessationism.

# CHAPTER TWO

# JOHN
# WIMBER

# JOHN WIMBER

After John Wimber died, Anglican Bishop David Pytches edited a memorial to him called *John Wimber*.[1]  In it, twenty-four writers pay tribute to him for his massive gifts to the body of Christ on behalf of Jesus.  Each one remembers him for different things, one as a family man, one as an evangelist, one as a musician and worshipper, yet another as "The Ecumenist." We now take a look at the formation of the man Peter Wagner called, "a moulder of an entire generation."[2]

## THE EARLY YEARS

### GROWING UP ALONE

John was born on February 25, 1934, in Kirksville, Missouri.[3] His father abandoned him on the day he was born and he was raised as an only child.[4]  He grew up learning nothing about God; the only thing he knew about "Jesus" was that it was a "cuss word."[5]  He would later describe himself as a fourth genera-tion pagan. He once said, "I didn't even know God had a book out!… I don't think I ever met a Christian—if I did he never blew his cover."[6]

John remembered that in 1952, his last year of high school, his grandfather was led to Christ during his final illness.[7]  Immediately before he died, he awoke from a coma, sat up, and declared to John's mother and grandmother, "I've been with Jesus. It's won-derful. It's beautiful. It's glory! It's glory!" He then lay down and fell asleep for the last time saying, "I'm coming, Jesus." John doesn't remember being at all impacted by this event.  He had a life to live.

As he grew up with no brothers or sisters, John spent long hours alone and learned to play over 20 different musical instru-ments, his favorite being the saxophone.  By age fifteen he had become an accomplished musician and after graduation from high school began a professional music career.  In 1953 he won first prize at the Lighthouse International Jazz Festival.  After graduating from junior college in 1954, he began to pursue music with a passion. In 1962 he bought an up-and-coming musical group called The Righteous Brothers and played sax for them. In 1964 they released their hit single, "You've Lost that Lovin' Feeling" and were booked to support the Beatles at the start of their American tour in San Francisco.[8] Things were looking up.

## GETTING IN TOUCH WITH THE SUPERNATURAL

John and Carol Wimber were married in 1955, and between 1950-1962 John made most of his living from music. By 1961 the Righteous Brothers had two albums in the top ten. John was twenty-seven years old that year and on top of the world, at least until he and his wife Carol began to have serious problems in their marriage.[9] While John was in Las Vegas working with a show, Carol called to inform him that she was looking into divorce proceedings. They would be separated five months. Distraught, John went out into the desert, on the advice of a friend, to "experience" the sunrise, thinking it would help him find peace.

On the way out to the desert, John began to cry un-controllably, and for the first time in his life felt the presence of Someone or Something. He pulled his car off the road and in anguish cried out, "If there is anyone there, help me!" Feeling suddenly ashamed of the foolishness of such a thought, he turned around and went back to the hotel.

When he returned, however, he found a message from Carol asking him to come and get her in LA. She wanted to give the marriage one more try. John knew how adamant Carol had been about the divorce and this sudden turn around was... well... miraculous. It had to have something to do with his prayer.
He thought to himself, "I'm in touch with the supernatural!" He jumped into the car and raced back to California to get his wife and three young sons.[10]

As John and Carol began to patch things up in Las Vegas, they talked about religion, and Carol suggested that they buy a Bible. John, who described himself as a fourth generation pagan, was at first surprised to find that God had a book out. Carol found a

Christian bookstore, and the owner assured her that the New English Bible New Testament was a good version.

As John was trying to read it at the hotel bar, the waiter said, "That's not a real Bible. A real Bible has a black cover and has HOLY BIBLE on the front in gold letters."

"I knew it!" John said.

The bartender wrote what to get and sent John and Carol back to the Bible bookstore. John got there at 3 AM but it wasn't open! When the clerk opened up at 8:30, they handed her the slip of paper It read, "King James Virgin." They finally had a real Bible and brought it home to read, only to find themselves more confused—it turned out that God was Jewish!

## FINDING GOD[11]

Realizing that Las Vegas was not the place to put one's marriage back together and raise a family, the Wimbers moved back to Orange County in LA in the summer of 1962 and started to check out religion. Carol had been brought up a Catholic, so John began to go through instruction about Catholicism. When the priest couldn't answer his questions, John dropped out.

In November of that year, two old friends suddenly reappeared in their lives. They had known Dick and Lynn Heying[12] for many years, Dick having played drums in some of John's bands. Dick and Lynn had some news to share they had become Christians and had lost their desire to party—they were even going to church!

## JOHN'S FIRST EXPERIENCE IN CHURCH

Dick and Lynn were desperate to get John and Carol to go to one of their church services. John's hilarious account (exaggerated to make a point) of that experience as a complete pagan is recorded on his *I'm a Fool for Christ* video. David Pytches does a great job summarizing it in his chapter, "A Man Called John," in *John Wimber*:

*Men he (John) took to be "bouncers," with flowers in their lapels, showed the Wimbers to the very front seats and one of them handed John a "menu" with a big smile and a*

*loud greeting. John studied the "menu" uncom-*
*prehendingly. "What does it say, dad?" asked one of the*
*boys. "Hell, I don't know, son," replied John, never*
*previously having been confronted by such pious*
*terminology. He needed to dispose of his cigarette but could*
*find no ashtrays in the pews. And so it went throughout*
*the service. Excitedly, the Heyings cornered John after the*
*service saying, "How did you like it, John?"*
*John: That was weird!*
*Dick: I was about to ask you to come again tonight.*
*John: How often do you do this?*
*Dick: We come every time they open the doors. We love it.*
*This is our church.* [13]

It was then that John knew that he might be in for a bumpy ride.

## THE FIRST BIBLE STUDY

The Heyings also wanted to know if John and Carol would come with them to a home Bible study led by Lawrence "Gunner" Payne. Gunner Payne was a man of God and personal evangelist who had gone through deep tragedy.[14] In 1952 his fifteen-year-old daughter had been brutally murdered, and the ensuing trial had captured national attention when it became a test case for capital punishment. Then in 1962, the year before meeting the Wimbers, his twenty-two-year-old son David had been incapacitated in a car accident. Through it all Gunner and his wife affirmed the love of God and gave their lives to telling others about him.

By April of 1963, John and Carol were ready to attend one of the Bible studies. John lit up a cigarette (he smoked five packs a day) on the first night and began to fire out questions. Gunner patiently tried to answer each one and became a living testimony of the grace of God to them as the weeks went on.

Suddenly, after three months, Carol announced one night at the Bible study that she was ready to do something about all that she had been learning about Jesus. Before John knew what was happening she was down on the floor weeping and repenting of her sins. This surprised John because she was the nicest person he knew. How could she say that she was a sinner? Then, in a moment of revelation he knew that he, too, was a sinner, and all that Gunner had been saying about the cross made sense. But get on the floor? He then realized that all the people in the room were looking at him. John had been on enough stages to know when it was his turn to go on, but he determined not to budge. John describes what happened next:

> To this day I cannot fully account for how I got out of that chair. All I know is that I ended upon the floor, sobbing, nose running, eyes watering, every square inch of my flesh perspiring profusely.[15]

He wrote that he tried to say the Sinner's Prayer but all he could get out was the sinner's blurb: "Oh God! Oh God! Oh God!"

While on the floor, he remembered a man he had once seen in Pershing Square in Los Angeles who had been walking with a sandwich sign that read, "I'm a fool for Christ," and on the back, "Whose fool are you?" John realized in that moment that he was going to become a fool for Christ, doing that which was foolish in the eyes of men for the honor of Jesus. As he prepared to enter his thirties, John had become a new man. The decade of his twenties had seen him rise to the top of the music business but almost lose his family. What would the next decade hold?

## THE PEARL[16]

In an earlier Bible study Gunner had taught on the parable of The Pearl of Great Price. John, suddenly grasping the implications, blurted out, "Are you saying that in order to become a Christian somebody might have to give up everything he has?" Gunner responded that one needed to be ready to give up anything, if that was what God was asking.

John's band was sky-rocketing to success. He thought to himself, "There is no way I am going to give that up."

But when John finally did get saved, he realized that he had found the pearl in the parable and that his career would have to go if God wanted it. Sure enough, he did! Within weeks John was out of the business and found a job in the real world in a factory.

One day when he was filthy from cleaning out an oil drum, he heard a familiar voice. It was an old partner in the music business with a contract worth a lot of money. Looking at John with oil all over him, he asked, "What are you doing here?" John remembers feeling like he had somehow missed the pearl. He said, "God did this to me." His ex-partner responded, "He's never going to do it to me" and drove away.

John was beginning to grasp something of what it meant to be a fool for Christ.

## INTRODUCTION TO THE HOLY SPIRIT'S MINISTRY

Shortly after their conversion, in the spring of 1964 John received the gift of tongues while outside praying.[17] He immediately went home to demonstrate his newfound gift only to find out from Carol that the devil had him. They hurried over to see their new pastor at the Friends church and found out, sure enough, demons had gotten hold of him. He was encouraged to repent and start getting "sound doctrine." John wondered, "That's funny. I've been walking with the devil a long time now, and that sure didn't feel like the devil." But as a new Christian, he complied, repented, and promised to stop praying in tongues.

A few weeks after the tongues incident, the Wimbers' three-year-old son, Sean, wandered away from their home in Yorba Linda, California.[18] When Carol noticed he was missing, she ran out and heard his screams coming from a neighbor's yard. He had walked into their beehives and was covered with stinging bees. John sprinted over, scooped up his body, and ran him home. He placed him on the bed and began to pray instinctively for his healing, even though he and Carol had recently been warned about Charismatic gifts and their divisiveness. Somehow Sean's condition superseded theological argumentation.

Not knowing how to pray, John opened his mouth to form

words, but instead of English he began to speak in a language he had not learned. The sentences in this unknown language were peppered with "Heal him, Jesus, heal him!" The more John prayed in the language, the more faith and confidence welled up inside of him. Within five minutes, they could see the welts going away and Sean fell peacefully asleep. When he awoke a few hours later, he had only one small red bump on his body and was completely well.

But because of the teaching they were getting that the gifts of the Spirit were no longer for today, John and Carol soon began to doubt the supernatural character of Sean's healing. One night they were invited to a Charismatic meeting, and they went to check it out. During the meeting someone spoke in tongues and another offered an interpretation that was couched as a prophecy to the people in the room. Something didn't seem right to Carol so she went home to study the issue on her own. She concluded from her research that tongues in the New Testament were always described as prayer to God. She reasoned that a legitimate inter-pretation of a tongue should be a prayer, not prophecy, and concluded, therefore, that the whole Charismatic experience was the result of a demon.

From that point on, John and Carol judged all supernatural activity of that sort, including healing, to be full of error. John became especially upset with healing evangelists like Kathryn Kuhlman, believing they manipulated people for material gains. He was critical not only of what they were doing but the style in which they did it. It all seemed so weird!

## EVANGELISM, 1964-1970

After "discovering" the divisive nature of Charismatic gifts, John turned his attention to what he knew was scriptural—personal evangelism. Gunner Payne had been in the practice of going door to door and telling people in Yorba Linda about Christ. John went with him so many times that personal evangelism was built into his spiritual genetic code. He said he could not go into the market or hardware store without evangelizing someone.[19]

During the period between 1964-1970, John estimated that he and Carol led hundreds to Christ.[20] By 1970 he was leading 11 Bible studies with over 500 people involved.[21] Many of the new converts joined their church, the Yorba Linda Friends Church, a Quaker congregation. John joined the staff of the church as the co-pastor in 1970. Carol's youngest sister, Penny, had recently married a young man named Bob Fulton and Bob had already gone on the staff of the church as the youth director. Before long Carol was an elder. It had become a family affair. During John's tenure on staff the church grew from 200 to 800 to become the largest church in the denomination.

Hungry for theological education, John at this time enrolled at Azusa Pacific University where he earned a two year degree in Biblical Studies. Because he never went on to seminary to receive a graduate degree, John, despite his brilliant mind and habits of self study, thereafter felt inferior to those with letters after their names. This is one of the few areas in which he could be intimidated and without good friends like theologian Don Williams supporting his risks for the gospel, he could have been taken advantage of more often than he was.

UNEXPLAINED PHENOMENA

Although John's cessationist theology disallowed Charismatic gifts in the present age, he remembered sometimes experiencing what he thought was intuition as he witnessed to people about Christ. While Carol maintained that the key was a logical, rational presentation of the gospel, John seemed to just know when someone was ready to receive Christ.[22] At times John would receive the details of people's lives, their deepest secrets and hurts. Hearing this information opened them right up and prepared them to hear the gospel.[23] He eventually learned to hold the rational and the trans-rational in unresolved tension.

Toward the end of this period, John decided to reopen the healing question when it was discovered that a close friend had brain cancer and only a short time to live.[24] After studying the issue in scripture, he concluded on the basis of James 5:13-16 that he should pray for her. Filled with faith, he prayed over his friend only to have her die. He became disillusioned with the healing ministry and decided to have nothing to do with it.

## THE CRISIS OF 1974

The years pastoring the Friends Church were a mixed blessing for John. On the one hand the church was growing so rapidly that they had to enlarge their facility. On the other, John felt a vague dissatisfaction that he couldn't put his finger on. It was as if something were missing…

### GOD CONFRONTS JOHN

In the corridor one Sunday in 1974, John met a young man who had been irregular in his church attendance.[25] John began to preach at him, telling him that if he would only go to church more, his life would improve.

As John was walking away, having read him the party line, the Lord spoke to his heart and said, "John, would you go to this church if you weren't paid to?"

John walked more slowly as he thought about the question. In a moment of profound personal revelation, he knew that even though his fingerprints were all over the church (he had picked out the curtains), even though he loved the people, his answer to the Lord had to be "No."

John rushed back to his office, lowered his head and asked, "God, what's wrong with me?"

The Lord immediately began to show him that in his desire to be a successful pastor he was using the flock to meet his own identity and security needs, rather than serving them in the love of Christ. He had built his success on the backs of his people rather than co-laboring with them.

As the horror of the picture became clearer before him, John again asked, "God, how did I get this way?"

God showed him that he had continually resisted the Holy Spirit over the years. Instances were brought to mind where John had refused to listen to God's inner prompting, opting rather to support the institution. He had been critical of anyone who had been touched by the Charismatic renewal and especially of those who prayed for the sick, all the while being ineffective himself in praying for people with deep needs. John concluded that he needed to leave the pastorate to sort it all out, but where was he to go?

## THE FULLER YEARS, 1974-78[26]

### WIMBER AND WAGNER JOIN FORCES

Peter Wagner, a disciple of the late Donald McGavran and former missionary in Bolivia, had come to Fuller Seminary in Pasadena, California, to teach on evangelism and church growth. In 1974, John Wimber signed up to take Wagner's Doctor of Ministry course in church growth.[27] Wagner knew of John's reputation for church growth in his denomination and realized by the end of the course that John's unusual aptitude for knowing how to grow churches qualified him for the new position he was creating at the seminary. Wagner was a theoretician in church growth. What he needed was a practitioner.

Two weeks after Wimber realized that he needed to leave the church, Wagner called and offered him a job to establish the Charles E. Fuller Institute of Evangelism and Church Growth. John took the position thinking it would be a good place to work out his problems. While he and his family remained members of the Yorba Linda Friends Church, he began to travel extensively as a church growth consultant for Fuller. During these years John worked with 27 denominations (none of them Pentecostal or Charismatic[28]), nine parachurch organizations and hundreds of local churches.[29] He met with some 40,000 pastors.[30]

He began to apply the findings from church growth research by men like Donald McGavran, Peter Wagner and Win Arn. In many cases his counsel led to dramatic evangelism and attendance increases in local churches.

It was also in 1974 that John Wimber met a young congregational pastor named John McClure. They hit it off right away, and Wimber hired McClure as his assistant at Fuller. They traveled together from 1975-78, and their friendship would endure for twenty-three years.

## FULLER INFLUENCES ON WIMBER

While at the seminary, John also had the privilege of working with other professors from Fuller such as Chuck Kraft, and Russell Spittler. In dialogues with these men, as well as through the testimony of students from third world countries, John began to encounter dramatic stories of healings and miracles that authenticated the preaching of the gospel and produced remarkable church growth in countries outside the Western world. John began to wonder if he had been wrong about taking a hard-line stance against spiritual gifts.

About this time John also discovered the Engel Scale, a model being developed by James Engel at Wheaton College, showing how people come to, and grow in, Christ.[31] The model demonstrates that some people are more ready than others and that conversion is more than just an issue of the right message but also one of timing. John began to assess his evangelistic success in light of being able to sense by the Holy Spirit's prompting when someone was ready to receive Christ. John had always been able to discern divine appointments and began to wonder if others could be trained to hear the Holy Spirit's voice in the work of evangelism.

He was also influenced at this time by the writings of men like Donald Gee, a British Pentecostal who wrote *Concerning Spiritual Gifts*, and the Catholic scholar, Morton Kelsey and his book *Healing and Christianity* which showed that signs and wonders had never ceased in the history of the church. Most influential, however, was the book *Jesus and the Kingdom* (now *The Presence of the Future*) by Fuller's own George Ladd. John McClure had introduced Wimber to the teaching of Ladd, and Wimber immediately sensed its implications for parish ministry. Ladd's understanding of the kingdom of God gave Wimber the theological ground he needed to explain the combination of evangelism and the miraculous that he was hearing from the missionaries at Fuller.[32]

Knowing that the kingdom was "already" gave him a basis for the in-break of the miraculous in the present. Knowing that the kingdom was "not yet" gave him a basis for explaining why not all people were healed and why there was still suffering in the world. He began to see that the Bible provided a theology of power as well as a theology of pain.

From his own study of the gospels and Acts, Wimber also began to see that the key to effectiveness was a combination of *proclamation* and *demonstration* of the gospel. Jesus himself had been a *word-worker*, preaching the word of the kingdom and doing its works. These works were summed up by Jesus in Luke 4:18-19: good news to the poor, liberty to the captives and sight to the blind.

## PETER WAGNER'S PARADIGM SHIFT

Wimber's boss, colleague, and friend, Peter Wagner, had, like Wimber, been a dispensational evangelical and was anti-Pentecostal, anti-spiritual gifts. By the time Wimber went on staff at Fuller, though, Wagner's worldview and theology were in transition. This transition, often called a "paradigm shift,"[33] had occurred in a number of stages.

The first stage in the shift came while Peter and his wife, Doris, were missionaries in Bolivia.[34] One night, against his better judgment, he went to hear the "liberal" Methodist missionary to India, E. Stanley Jones preach in a crusade. The night turned out to be an old-fashioned healing service ("Not very liberal," Peter thought), and Wagner received a healing for a nagging cyst on his neck that was going to require surgery. At this point his theological walls against healing began to crumble.

The next stage came after Wagner left the mission field to teach at Fuller. He had been a student of Donald McGavran in the late 1960s and now became his colleague as he continued to learn from McGavran how to study church growth. Wagner concentrated his research on the church in Latin America since he was fluent in Spanish and familiar with the culture. What he saw, he had never seen in all his years as a Christian—powerful preaching (beyond the normal), miracles and healings, sometimes explosive evangelism, and rapid church planting. His research culminated in the book *Look Out! The Pentecostals are Coming* published in 1973. This book is now updated as *Spiritual Power and Church Growth* due to the experiences Wagner would have with Wimber from 1982-1985 (more later).

Meanwhile, as Wimber was beginning to question his theology in light of this new data, his personal life was continuing to experience trauma. He had come on staff at Fuller to work on his problems, but he was so busy traveling, weeks at a time, that he never saw his young family. Eventually the traveling took its toll on their children, and John began to wonder where things had gone wrong.

His relationship with God had turned stale as well. He rarely prayed and read his Bible only when he had to teach from it. He was gradually becoming aware that he was spiritually bankrupt.

## CAROL WIMBER'S "PERSONALITY MELTDOWN"

While John was traveling so much for Fuller, Carol had what she called a "personality meltdown."

She describes her experience in the *Vineyard Newsletter*[35] saying that she went to God in 1976 to ask him what was wrong with their church. John had been gone from the pastorate two years, and it seemed that all they had worked for was crumbling. Instead of putting his finger on the church, God began to put his finger on Carol.

Carol and Margie McClure, both staunch evangelicals, began to read and debate books by people like Dennis Bennett and Arthur Blesset. During this period the Holy Spirit mightily touched both women.

In September, Carol had a disturbing dream. She saw herself on a soapbox preaching to a crowd about spiritual gifts, a subject on which she considered herself an expert. She was giving a seven-point sermon on why gifts were dangerous and divisive. When she got to the seventh point, however, she woke up speaking in tongues!

The experience so shocked her that her confidence and self-assurance began to drain away. She says she felt like "a bag of sand with a hole at the bottom." If what she had taught all those years had been wrong, then she realized that she had not known God as well as she had thought. God whispered into her heart, "You're right."

Carol was so devastated that she pulled out of all teaching, resigned as an elder at the church, and holed up at home weeping on and off for three weeks. God showed her how she had kept John time and time again from moving out in greater faith and power. She says, "My heart was broken. My tears were pleas for mercy as he showed me all that I had been responsible for John missing. He reminded me that 15 years previously, just after our conversions, John spoke in tongues and prayed for our son's healing, but I persuaded him that it was not from God. Turning away from those experiences wounded John, saddling him with a sense of loss. God had a pattern, a blueprint for renewal, and John was a key in what he wanted to do. But so far we had missed it, and I was responsible."[36]

This period of brokenness, left her profoundly changed. She was filled with an unquenchable hunger for God and began to long, also, for those of their church. Many had wandered away not receiving the healing they needed; others were gone because they had been kicked out for speaking in tongues and moving in spiritual gifts. God told Carol to make restitution with all those she had wronged. She went to over thirty people and asked for forgiveness. As she was reconciled with those she had sinned against, God lifted the weight of her guilt and her tears began to dry.

Not only did she receive a hunger for God and their local congregation, but she began to yearn for the whole church to be renewed. One day as she was sitting by their swimming pool, she saw in her mind's eye their flock being baptized in their pool. This was highly unusual because Quakers don't practice baptism in any form. It was then she knew that God was going to do something outside the boundaries of their denomination—he was going to do something new!

## A SMALL GROUP BEGINS IN YORBA LINDA, 1976-77

In October of 1976, some of the leaders from the Yorba Linda Friends Church started a home meeting to encourage one another in their teaching ministries.[37] Included in this group were Bob Fulton (Bob's wife, Penny, is Carol Wimber's sister) and Carl Tuttle. When Carol heard that they were meeting, the Lord revealed to her that this was the beginning of what he had shown her by the pool.

From the beginning the group had an intense hunger for God. They had been "Pharisees" but in their vulnerability were becoming learners again. As they met, they sang songs and then broke into small groups to pray for one another. The attendance grew from 12 to 50 in just a few weeks. People began coming back who had drifted away, an answer to one of the cries from Carol's shepherd heart. While they were not Charismatic in the exercise of spiritual gifts, their meetings were characterized by a vulnerable openness to God and a willingness to partner with God's Spirit.

### DISCOVERING WORSHIP

In the minds of those meeting, the word *worship* defined the hour on Sunday morning. They weren't prepared for God to redefine the term for them. Carl Tuttle was elected "song leader," because he was the only one who could play guitar.[38] Carl knew a few worship choruses from Calvary Chapel, and as he played them, the group would often experience a profound sense of the presence of God. Carl remembers those days saying, "I've never seen a group of people so hungry to meet with God."[39]

Carol Wimber describes her impressions in an article written by John in *Equipping the Saints* in 1987.[40] She says that shortly after the home group began to meet, the Lord impressed the word *worship* on her mind as clearly as a newspaper headline. She wasn't sure at the time what the Lord was referring to since all they did on Sunday morning was considered worship.

Soon, however, Carol began to recognize that as they sang

with Carl on Sunday nights, it was during the songs with words addressed directly to God that they experienced a more profound sense of his presence. She then began to realize that even though they talked of worship, they rarely ever did it, in the true sense of the word.

Those in the group, meanwhile, were beginning to worship at home. It turned out that effective corporate worship was partially the by-product of a healthy devotional life with God during the week. People were experiencing breakthroughs in posture, worshipping not only with their vocal chords but with the whole body—kneeling, bowing, lying prostrate, raising hands.

The most significant discovery was that worship wasn't for them at all, but a gift they gave to God. They learned that it didn't matter what they felt like; God was worthy and inhabited the praises of his people. When they gave him his gift, not as the warm-up for the teaching but as an end in itself, an interesting thing happened. God brought his presence and ministered to them. What an awesome time it was!

## Discovering the Gift of Healing![41]

One day as Carol was praying for John, the Lord brought back to her remembrance the incident of Sean's healing from bee stings so many years before. She began to wonder if John might not have the gift of healing, so she decided to try an experiment. She had a case of painful rheumatoid arthritis in one of her shoulders and wanted to see if John could lay hands on her and see her healed.

Since John at this time would have thought she had "gone off the deep end," she waited until he was asleep. She then took his arm and placed it on her shoulder and said, "Okay Lord, now do it." She suddenly felt a surge of heat go through her shoulder and the pain disappeared. John woke up wondering why his hand was hot. When Carol fessed up, John was glad that her pain was gone, but was still hardened to the idea of healing.

All these incidents put Carol in a time of personal renaissance. John, on the other hand, was continually out of town and wasn't having such a great time. One incident described by Kevin Springer[42] is especially important here.

On one occasion he was speaking at a camp in Northern California when a pastor friend named Ray told him that a lady from his church had a word for him. John resisted, having had "words" from strangers before, but Ray insisted. "I've known this woman for ten years," he said, "and she's never been wrong." John agreed to meet the woman in a quiet glen where she proceeded to cry, and cry, and cry some more. John became perturbed and said, "Listen Lady, your pastor said that you had a word from God for me, and I've got to be back down the hill in a few minutes to conduct this afternoon's session. What is it?"

The woman responded, "That's it," thus pointing out John's lack of patience.

John says, "It was like a gigantic blow to my solar plexus. I had figured if God was going to speak to me, he could have spoken about a hundred sins. I had a long list (and a rationale for each of them). But what God did bypassed all my barriers. I wandered out of the glen shaken. I knew that I had somehow wounded the Lord."

Later that evening the woman approached Wimber again saying, "God wants to know, 'When are you going to use your authority?'"

John replied, "Authority? What do you mean authority?

She retorted, "I don't know the meaning of the messages; I just get them."

Over the next three days of the conference the woman gave him four or five messages. One of them was that he was to return to the pastorate. That was interesting because Carol, who had originally been against this, had just told him that if he should ever decide to go back into the pastorate she would support him (John didn't know about what God was doing with her as yet).

## JOHN'S BREAKDOWN IN DETROIT, WINTER 1977[43]

Not too long after Carol's "meltdown," John's problems came to head on a plane en route to Detroit. In his destitution, John cried out to the Lord, "Oh God, what's the matter? What's wrong with me?" He felt like he was going to die. His weight had sky-rocketed; his blood pressure had elevated; he never saw his kids; his head constantly throbbed; he was tired of people; he rarely prayed and never found solace in personal Bible study. He wasn't sure if God was even listening anymore.

Still crying when he got off the plane, John found out that because of a flight mix-up due to a snowstorm he was stranded in the airport. He collapsed into a hotel room and for the first time in several years opened his Bible to read it for himself. He read from Psalm 61 that captured the cries of his heart. Asking God to show him what was wrong with his life, he fell asleep.

In the middle of the night God woke him up and said, "John, I've seen your ministry." I've heard John say that the Lord's tone of voice expressed the attitude "and I'm not very impressed." Then the Lord said to him, "And now I'm going to show you mine."

This pierced John like an arrow. He began to weep for joy saying, "Oh Lord, that's all I've ever wanted." This exchange marked the turning point in John's Christian life. God had brought him back to the point where he was once more open to the supernatural.

## STARTING THE CHURCH IN YORBA LINDA, MAY, 1977

### JOHN ATTENDS THE HOME GROUP

Carol had been excited about her home group since its inception, and she kept trying to get John to come. One night he gave in. He remembers being put off by the heat in the room (all those bodies and no air conditioner!), by having to sit on the floor at his size, and by people raising their hands now and then, and singing for what seemed like hours, joyfully sweating into the night.

Carol asked John later, "So, what did you think?"

John's response was that the group was leaderless and wasn't going anywhere. John admits that he was spiritually blind to what God wanted to do.[44]

## GOD SPEAKS

John has said on tape that it was during the period following his initial encounter at the home group that God spoke to him eighteen different times, mostly in ways he didn't believe in, to go home and start a church.

After the experience in Detroit a desire began to grow in John to see if the same church growth seen in developing countries could happen in America if a local church would open up to experiencing the healing power of God. Peter Wagner supported the idea, thinking that pastoring a little church would give John something to do on the weekends (!).

A few days after this John was in New York doing a seminar when a Lutheran pastor sheepishly came up to him and handed him a piece of paper on which, he said, was written a message from God. The paper read, "Go home."[45]

John did go home. He began attending the Yorba Linda home group regularly by January of 1977. By March so many adults came to worship each week that they spilled out onto the patio unable to all fit in the house.

## TROUBLE WITH THE YORBA LINDA, FRIENDS CHURCH

While all of these things had been transpiring, the leaders of the Wimbers' church in Yorba Linda had been having meetings to discuss the things that were going on in the Bible study.[46] The study met on Sunday nights after the evening service at the church. Cars used to flow out of the church parking lot down just a few blocks to Carl Tuttle's sister's house where they were gathering. It is easy to see why the leaders were concerned.

Before long the group was accused of speaking in tongues, a thought which had never occurred to them. Then it was said that they were casting out demons and falling on the floor. God was blessing them, so they made no attempt to defend themselves. Carol Wimber writes about their departure from the church:

*Everybody in that church, except the elders, believed that we had just coldly left them to start our own church. The elders knew the truth, of course, because they had asked us to leave in an effort to stop what was the beginning of the fire from heaven that for years we, along with them, had cried out to God for. The truth is, we would never have left that church. We loved those Quakers and they loved us, but they did not want an outbreak of "tongues" and asked us for our resignation. Our futile attempts to convince them that this was not about "tongues" ended with them agreeing to give us their blessing if we would just leave. We did and they did.*[47]

## THE CHURCH BEGINS

The group had grown to about 100 by April, and John had now become their leader. At this point the elders of the Friends Church had asked John and Carol to leave. They consented on condition that the leadership write a letter of release and give the young church their blessing. The elders agreed to this and encouraged the Wimbers to do what was in their hearts. Carol believes that this blessing has been very important in the history of the Vineyard. She has a theory that much of the shaking and supernatural phenomena that has characterized Vineyard meetings almost from the beginning is the result of the transfer of the anointing that was on George Fox. Fox and his followers were called "Quakers" by their detractors who were mocking the shaking that often accompanied the miraculous in their meetings.[48]

Since Carol had been attending the Calvary Chapel in Twin Peaks during the small group period, the pastor, Don McClure, John McClure's brother, suggested that they affiliate with Calvary.[49]

After Wimber had exhausted all the legitimate places in Yorba Linda to rent, the Masons charged the "outcasts" only $25 a week to use their building. Calvary Chapel of Yorba Linda had its inauspicious beginning on Mother's Day, May 8, 1977, in the Masonic Lodge. There were 150 in attendance. John was designated the pastor even though he continued at Fuller for the time being. He preached his first sermon from Luke on the stigma of illegitimate birth attached to Jesus. He made application to their alleged illegitimate beginnings as a split from the Friends

Church. They, like Jesus, had been born of the Spirit.

Immediately after starting the church John called together all the adult members and shared his vision for growth.[50] The price tag for this growth meant that the "inner circle" had to die to itself and break up into smaller groups to make way for new people. They called these groups *kinships*, borrowing a term coined by Lyle Schaller. In the smaller groups people began to find not only a new depth of relationship but a place for newcomers as well. Thus from the very beginning of the Vineyard, small groups were the heart of the infrastructure.

The following chart shows the journey and growth of the new church.[51]

| LOCATION | DATES | RESIDENCY (MONTHS) | GROWTH |
|---|---|---|---|
| Masonic Lodge | 5/77-7/77 | 1 1/2 | 200 |
| Bernardo Yorba Jr. High | 7/77-9/77 | 3 | 250 |
| El Dorado High School | 9/77-9/78 | 12 | 300 |
| Esperanza High School | 9/78-6/79 | 10 | 400 |
| Canyon High School | 6/79-9/83 | 63 | 2000 |

ଔ

NOTES:

[1] Gulford, Surrey England, Eagle Pub. House, 1998

[2] *Ibid.,* p. 10

[3] John was listed in *John Wimber* as being born in Peoria, Illinois (p. 10) but Todd Hunter called Carol Wimber for me to verify that he was, indeed, born in Kirksville, MO. Thanks Todd!

[4] A few years before his death, John found out that he had two half brothers, George and Bill, and had the incredible opportunity to meet them.

[5] John Wimber & Kevin Springer, *Power Points*, San Francisco, CA, Harper & Row, 1991, p. 60

[6] From John's personal testimony given at the first MC 510 course given in a public forum in 1984; the testimony can be viewed on the video *I'm a Fool for Christ. Whose Fool are You?*

[7] John White, in *When the Spirit Comes with Power* (Downers Grove, Illinois, InterVarsity Press, pp. 160-66), says he received some of the

following information from an unpublished manuscript written by John Wimber and Kevin Springer.

[8] "Worshipper and Musician," by Matt Redman in *John Wimber*, p. 63

[9] Wimber, *Power Points*, pp. 17-19.

[10] The Wimbers had three sons, Christopher (who died shortly after John of melanoma cancer), Timothy and Sean, and a daughter named Stephanie.

[11] *Ibid.,* pp. 21-25; 114-116

[12] Heying is pronounced "hine," thus the confusion in spelling in Donald Miller's *Reinventing American Protestantism*, Berkely, USC Press, 1997, p. 48

[13] Pp. 15-16

[14] *Ibid.,* p. 143

[15] *Ibid.*, p. 116

[16] *Ibid.*, pp. 117-120

[17] Kevin Springer, "Applying the Gifts to Everyday Life," *Charisma*, September, 1985, p. 30

[18] John Wimber, *Power Healing*, San Francisco, CA, Harper and Row, 1987, pp. 3-5

[19] Wimber, *Power Points*, p. 163

[20] Wimber, *Power Healing,* p.23

[21] Springer, *Charisma.*, September, 1985

[22] John Wimber, *Power Evangelism*, San Francisco, CA, Harper and Row, 1986, p. xvi

[23] Wimber, *Power Points*, p. 164

[24] Springer, *Charisma.*, September, 1985

[25] Wimber, *Power Healing*, p. 27ff

[26] It should be noted that there is a discrepancy between John Wimber and Peter Wagner as to the year the following events were initiated. In *Power Evangelism* Wimber said they occurred in 1974 (p. xvii) and Wagner in *How To Have a Healing Ministry Without Making Your Church Sick* (p. x) in 1975.

[27] C. Peter Wagner, *How to Have a Healing Ministry Without Making Your Church Sick*, Ventura, CA, Regal Books, 1988, p. 47

[28] Wimber, *Power Evangelism*, p. 41

[29] John Wimber, "Zip to 3,000 in 5 Years," *Signs & Wonders Today*, an

expanded edition of *Christian Life*, Wheaton, IL, 1983, p. 14

[30] *John Wimber*, p. 23

[31] *Contemporary Christian Communications*, New York, NY, Thomas Nelson, 1979, pp. 79ff.

[32] Wimber, *Power Evangelism*, pp. xix-xx

[33] Charles H. Kraft, *Christianity in Culture,* Maryknoll, NY, Orbis Books, 1979, p. 5

[34] Wagner, *How to Have a Healing Ministry*, pp. 42ff.

[35] "A Hunger for God - A Reflective Look a the Vineyard's Beginnings," *Vineyard Newsletter,* Vol. 2, No. 2, Fall 1987; cf. Wimber, *Power Healing*, pp. 30-32

[36] *Ibid.*, pp. 1-2

[37] *Ibid.,* p. 2

[38] Carl Tuttle, "Effective Worship Leading," *Worship Update*, Winter 1988, pp. 3-4

[39] *Ibid.,* p. 3

[40] John Wimber, "Worship: Intimacy with God," *Equipping the Saints,* Vol. 1, No. 1, pp. 4ff.

[41] Wimber, *Power Healing*, p. 32

[42] Springer, *Charisma*, September, 1985, pp. 31-2

[43] Wimber, *Power Healing*, pp. 32-34

[44] *Ibid.,* p. 44

[45] *Ibid.,* p. 45

[46] From an unpublished personal testimony by Carol Wimber as quoted by Nikolaus Kimla in a master's dissertation entitled *The Historical and Empirical, Social, and Practical Theological Aspects of the Vineyard Movement*, February, 1994, p. 35.

[47] *John Wimber*, pp. 290-91

[48] Wimber, *Vineyard Newsletter*, Vol. 2, No. 2, Fall 1987, p. 2

[49] It is interesting to note that right around this time period, John and Margie McClure resigned from their Plymouth Congregational Church and started Calvary Chapel in Whittier, California.

[50] Carol Wimber, "Hunger for God," in Kevin Springer ed., *Power Encounters in the Western World*, San Francisco, Harper & Row, 1988, p. 9

[51] Kimla, p. 36

# CHAPTER THREE

# POWER EVANGELISM

# POWER EVANGELISM

## LEARNING TO HEAL THE SICK[1]

Wimber continued to teach from the gospel of Luke on Sundays, and for all intents and purposes, the Calvary Chapel of Yorba Linda appeared to be a typical Bible church, teaching from the Word, praying, worshipping and enjoying fellowship. The only difference was that the worshipers used contemporary music, some of which they began writing themselves. John Amstutz, a professor from the Foursquare denomination's Life Bible College, taught Wednesday nights on spiritual gifts. Wimber had to be out of town with Fuller on most Wednesdays, so a number of his people began to jump out ahead of him in the things of the Spirit.

Teaching on Luke forced John to wrestle with the issue of healing. By August, four months into the series, he came to an impasse. Was healing supposed to be a regular part of church life? On one particular Wednesday night when John was able to attend the spiritual gifts study, he found his mind wondering off in dialogue with God about healing. God showed him four things from the story of the healing of the paralytic in Matthew 9:1-8:

- Christians had been called to heal the sick in the same way as they are called to evangelize. In the text it was almost impossible to separate the two.
- The lack of emphasis on the healing ministry was really an issue of people not understanding God's mercy for them.
- What John had always assumed were doctrinal differences were, in reality, a cover up for a pharisaical heart that was full of evil and unbelief.
- Not only was healing to be a normal part of church life, Christians had been *commissioned* to heal and to cast out demons.

## INITIAL FRUSTRATION

The next Sunday John gave an altar call to pray for the sick. It was humiliating. The people doing the praying caught the illnesses of those they were praying for, even their headaches! John didn't want to do another one, but God told him to do it again, and again—and not one person was healed. For the next six months almost every sermon John preached was on healing.

People now began to leave the church, not so much because of the concept of healing but because the act of doing it was too risky. John had seen this many times as a consultant. It was okay to talk about some things as long as no one actually tried to do them.

John became so upset with the Lord about healing that one week as he was preparing his sermon he slammed his Bible shut and said, "I will not teach about healing anymore!"

The Lord immediately replied, "Either preach my word or get out." John wondered what "get out" meant, but the Lord interrupted his thoughts saying, "Preach my word, not your experience."

This was another turning point for John. He continued to press into teaching and prayer for the sick even though people were still not being healed.

Realizing that he now needed to check out both past and present healing ministries, he began to read everything he could get his hands on. Especially helpful were two contemporaries: the Catholic Francis MacNutt who offered insights in his book *Healing* and Noel Weiss, one of the pastors at Melodyland Christian Center in Anaheim who had had great success praying for the sick. But still no one was healed in John's services.

One Sunday, after ten months of this, they prayed for yet another batch of people behind the curtain on the stage of the gymnasium where they met. John and a team prayed for two hours for a man with no results. When they finally did stop, John was so distraught that he threw himself on the floor and screamed, "It's not fair! You tell us to teach what your book says, but you don't back up our act. Here we are; we're doing the best we can do, and nothing happens. Oh God, it's not fair!" When he got up he saw that some of the other men had been on their faces too.

One of John's friends named Jim walked away saying, "I'm never going to go behind that damn curtain again!" When he got home Jim heard the Lord give him a Bible verse. He looked it up and read, "… the ark of the Lord dwelleth within the curtains" (2 Samuel 7:2). Jim repented hard that night.

## WE GOT ONE!

The next morning John was awakened by an early phone call from one of their newest church members. He said he was to start a much-needed job that morning, but his wife was sick with the flu, which meant that he would have to stay home with the kids. He wanted John to come over and pray for her healing. John said he'd be right there but then complained to the Lord, "This guy really believes this stuff. He's going to lose his job, or I'm going to have to take care of his kids today."

When he arrived, he was ushered into the bedroom. John has said it was obvious that she was *really* sick because otherwise no woman would let someone see her like that. He prayed a faithless prayer then turned around to explain to the husband why God doesn't always heal. As he rambled on, he noticed the man looking behind him. John turned to find that the wife was out of bed and combing her hair. She was completely well! He couldn't believe it. As he stumbled out the door jubilation suddenly filled him, and he shouted, "We got one!"

## THE VISION OF THE HONEYCOMB

In the euphoria of the drive home, he was jolted by a vision from the Lord. John wrote:

*Suddenly in my mind's eye there appeared to be a cloud bank superimposed across the sky. But I had never seen a cloud bank like this one, so I pulled my car over to the side of the road to take a closer look. Then I realized it was not a cloud bank; it was a honeycomb with honey dripping out on to people below. The people were in a variety of postures. Some were reverent; they were weeping and holding their hands out to catch the honey and taste it, even inviting others to take some of their honey. Others acted irritated, wiping the honey off themselves, complaining about the mess. I was awestruck. Not knowing what to think, I prayed, "Lord, what is it?" He said, "It's my mercy, John. For some people it's a blessing, but for others it's a hindrance. There's plenty for everyone. Don't beg me for healing again. The problem isn't on my end, John. It's down there."[2]*

This vision changed John. He never looked at healing ministry the same way again. God's mercy and compassion are available to all, but we need to learn how to receive it. We need to learn how to partner with the Holy Spirit. Once John and the church began to learn this, healing began to drop from heaven like honey.

## Anointed for Ministry

The next month, April of 1978, John started a home Bible study.[3] One evening he taught on the baptism and filling of the Holy Spirit. After the teaching, some of the people asked John to pray for them right there to be filled with the Holy Spirit. In response he went around the room praying for each one. As he did so, he felt spiritual power come out of his hands like electricity and people fell over. This was the first time anything like this had ever happened to him.

The next week John taught on the story of the healing of the invalid (John 5:1-15), and one of the girls who had had an accident resulting in an underdeveloped leg asked John to pray for her. They sat her in the middle of the room, and her leg began jerking and quivering during prayer. Suddenly her pants no longer fit. Her deformed leg had grown, and she was healed.

## Clinics Develop

On the way home, John and Carol discussed the relationship between teaching something and then modelling it. Carol said, "Instead of show and tell, this is tell and show."[4] Out of this experience grew John Wimber's model of having clinics where he would teach on a subject like healing or spiritual gifts from the Bible and then ask God to demonstrate the Word by his works, just as he had done on earth. In the gospels we see Jesus gathering disciples by teaching about the kingdom of God and then demonstrating its present power. In the same way, it has been watching the risen Jesus work in these clinics through the Holy Spirit that has put, as John says, "a hook in the jaws" of people all around the world to "do the stuff."

When John and Carol got home that night, he went to the refrigerator to get a glass of milk. Carol remembers,

> *As he was pouring the milk John said, 'It must be that when you teach the Word of God the Holy Spirit...' He never finished his sentence. As he started to say 'Holy Spirit,' his legs buckled and he caught himself on the counter, splashing milk all over in the process. He looked up at me with a surprised grin and said, "I think we're on to something here, Carol Kay.*[5]

He was right.

## LONNIE FRISBEE AND "COME, HOLY SPIRIT!"

### MOTHER'S DAY, 1980[6]

Two years after its beginning the church had grown to about 700 people. Lonnie Frisbee, having recently returned from ministering overseas, had now begun to attend their meetings in Canyon High School. During the Jesus Movement, Lonnie had been one of the most powerful evangelists, instrumental in the explosion of Calvary Chapel through his preaching on Wednesday nights. Scores of young people including drug addicts and runaways had come to Christ through his ministry. Now here he was attending the church in Yorba Linda. What was John to make of it?

Before long, John and Carol invited Lonnie over to dinner to get acquainted. Accompanied by his roommate, John Ruttkay, they fellowshipped together about all the things that God had done.[7] Shortly after that, God spoke to Wimber to ask Lonnie to speak at their service that night.[8] John at first balked at the idea because Lonnie's ministry style had a reputation for being controversial.

The Lord kept after him that morning, however, until he asked Lonnie to give his testimony. The young man readily agreed. John was in turmoil all afternoon, but as Lonnie spoke that night John wondered why he had been worried. It was great!

What happened next proved to be a watershed moment for the Vineyard. It has been talked about for years in private conversations, written about in books and retold in conferences. John wrote in *Power Evangelism* that when Lonnie got through with his talk he asked the people twenty-five and under to come forward. He then said that the church had been offending the for a long time so he was going to invite him to come and minister. He then said, "Holy Spirit, come."

A while back I was able to secure the tape of this night and listen for myself. As was typical of John, his recollections were more like reading the Cotton Patch translation of the New Testament than the Revised Standard Version.[9] John caught the essence but historians are like biblical interpreters—they want it a bit more literal. What actually happened was that after Lonnie had given his testimony, he opened up to Isaiah 60:1-3 and read about the glory of the Lord appearing over his people, causing them to shine in such a way that the nations of the earth would hear. He then prophesied over the young people saying that they would be going forth in under the anointing of the Lord. Those older than twenty-five were to extend their hands in blessing like the priests of old, thus showing the unity of the generations. Those under twenty-five (several hundred) were to hold their hands up to the Lord in a receiving posture. Everyone was to keep their eyes open because Lonnie said this was going to be the school of the Holy Spirit. He then asked a guitarist to sing a song from the recent revival in South Africa, "His Name Is Like Ointment Poured Forth."

While Lonnie did essentially say, "Holy Spirit, come," the context and wording was more like, "I see the Holy Spirit resting on this person in the blue shirt. Let the power and anointing of the Spirit fall!… I see the Lord on this group over here. Receive the power!"

The sounds that followed on the tape are now so familiar—the sobbing, bodies vibrating under God's power, loud commands to bless what God was doing, speaking in tongues. Lonnie's voice, trailing away from the microphone as he walked among the fallen youth, continued to invite the Spirit as the fire passed like a daisy chain from one to another. For me these are the sweet sounds of God visiting his people. They were the sounds that accompanied a John Wimber meeting—at least the Wimber meetings *after* 1980. I could hear John playing "Father We Adore You" on the synthe-sizer up on stage. He later described watching his people riffling out in tongues and falling under the power of God for the first time, and to him it looked like it was wrecking his church.

Carol Wimber, however, offers her recollections in her *The Vineyard Newsletter* article "A Hunger for God.":

> *the Holy Spirit came with great power on those young people. Suddenly kids were shaking and speaking in tongues. (While the church had been open to the movement of God and had seen a few people tremble and fall, they had never emphasized tongues.) One young man named Tim tangled in a cable as he fell and landed with the microphone right by his mouth as he called out praises to God in tongues. The sound went all over the auditorium. The place looked like a battlefield. Bodies were everywhere, falling, shaking, weeping, wailing, speaking in tongues— and poor Tim was unknowingly leading the charge.* [10]

John White, in his book *When the Spirit Comes in Power,*[11] adds some other details (probably received from talking with eye-witnesses when he was in Anaheim doing research). He says,

> *the young preacher became agitated and began shouting, "More Lord, more!" At one point he raised his hand and shouted, "Jesus is Lord!" and all those facing the palm of his hand fell untidily around the bleachers.*

John continued to stay seated behind the piano, playing softly, but was wide-eyed and angry. Some people began to leave. One man slammed his Bible shut and never returned.

Carol, on the other hand, was in shock, but elated. In her heart she knew that this was the visitation she had prayed for, though she was not prepared for how physical it was. She thought it would be an inner work like repentance or conviction, but instead God was shaking his people like rag dolls. She began to examine those who were lying on the floor and felt energy coming off their bodies. She asked one boy, "What's happening to you right now?"

He answered, "It's like electricity. I can't even move!"

## JOHN'S RESPONSE

John was up all night agonizing over his flock. He searched the Scriptures and couldn't find the prayer "Come, Holy Spirit" anywhere in the Bible. Was this God, or had he somehow been duped into letting the devil on the stage? He found some solace in that he did find some places in the Bible where people had fallen and trembled. He also poured over church history books that described accounts of revivals under men like George Whitefield and John Wesley. His search, however, did not yield any conclusive results.

Meanwhile, a thousand miles away, Tom Stipe was awakened about 5:00 AM from a peaceful slumber.[12]  Tom was a fellow Calvary Chapel pastor who was planting a church in Denver. He had been a key player in the heyday of the Jesus Movement and had experienced the very things that had just happened to Wimber. God prompted Tom to call John Wimber and encourage him. Tom tried to brush off the impression but couldn't get back to sleep. He finally decided to risk calling John. It was 6:30 AM California time.

By dawn John had gotten desperate. He cried out, "Lord, if this is you please tell me!"

Then the phone rang.

Surprised to hear Tom's voice, John proceeded to tell him the events of the previous evening and how he had been up all night trying to determine if it was God or not. Tom assured him that it was the Lord and recounted similar kinds of occurrences from the Jesus Movement.

That was all Wimber needed to know. John had only heard about these things; Tom had actually lived through them and was a credible witness. John didn't have to understand it. All he cared about was whether it was God.

## THE BIRTH OF POWER EVANGELISM

What happened the next few months they weren't prepared for. A revival broke out among the teenagers who had gotten "blasted" in the meeting, and they began to rove around in packs looking for other kids who needed to get saved. They witnessed and prayed for the sick on the streets seeing hundreds converted and healed.

Bob Fulton recalls that his daughter was in junior high at the time.[13] The young people at her school who belonged to their church began to witness with great power on the campus. Kids began repenting of their sins and some were so overcome by the Spirit's presence that they could no longer stand up. They began to sit on the grass in small circles talking about Jesus. The principal tried to break it up, but the kids were too filled with the Spirit. There were mass baptisms in swimming pools and Jacuzzis.

Between May and September, John and Carol baptized over seven hundred new converts in their swimming pool. This was exactly what Carol had seen in prayer some years before. John says that there might have been as many as seventeen hundred conversions in a three-and-a-half month period. He comments, "I was an expert on church growth, but I had never seen evangelism like that."[14] Suddenly they had a church with average attendance of about 1,800![15]

ଔ

NOTES:

[1] John wrote in some detail the events of the ensuing months in *Power Healing* (pp. 45-55). I will try to summarize the unfolding of what would become a worldwide renewal in healing the sick.

[2] Wimber, *Power Healing*, p. 52

[3] Springer, ed. *Power Encounters*, pp. 10-12

[4] *Ibid.*, p. 10

[5] *Ibid.*, p. 11

[6] It should be noted that the year of this event is disputed in the sources. 1979 has historically been the date most often given but research has now demonstrated that 1980 is the undisputed date. I have a tape of that night and it is dated 1980; cf. *Revival War: A Critique of Counterfeit Revival* by James Beverly (Evangelical Research Ministries, 1997, p. 80 note 6).

[7] From a personal interview with John Ruttkay

[8] Wimber, *Power Evangelism*, pp. 24-27

[9] The Cotton Patch version of the New Testament is an extremely loose paraphrase intended to communicate to those who live in the rural south in the USA. The eminent Revised Standard Version is an extremely literal translation of the entire Bible, thus reflecting the inflections and grammar of the Bible's original languages.

[10] Fall 1987, Vol. 2, No. 3, p. 1

[11] Pp. 158ff.

[12] Wimber, *Power Evangelism*, p. 25; cf. John White, *When the Spirit Comes in Power*, pp. 159-60. It should be noted that Hank Hanegraaff makes an issue out of this event in his book *Counterfeit Revival* (Word, Dallas, 1997, pp. 202-3). James Beverly responds to Hanegraaff's criticisms in *Revival Wars*, pp. 80-85.

[13] Recounted in a personal conversation

[14] Wimber, *Power Evangelism*, p. 26

[15] Neff, p. 10

# CHAPTER FOUR

# How John Wimber's Calvary Chapel Became a "Vineyard"

# HOW JOHN WIMBER'S CALVARY CHAPEL BECAME A "VINEYARD"

## KENN AND JOANIE GULLIKSEN PLANT THE FIRST VINEYARD[1]

Kenn and Joanie Gulliksen were a part of Calvary Chapel in Costa Mesa in the early 1970s during the boom years when thousands were saved and baptized in the Pacific Ocean. Kenn was ordained through Calvary in 1971, eventually moving to El Paso, Texas, where he and Joanie led a rapidly growing Calvary-style ministry called the Jesus Chapels. After returning to Costa Mesa for a brief period, the Gulliksens then moved to Los Angeles to plant a church. He fully intended to remain within the network of Calvary relationships, but he sensed the Lord doing something a bit different. He wasn't sure what he would call the new fellowship, but he felt they were moving in obedience to God.

Through a Calvary contact with Chuck Girard, the leader of the Christian rock group, Love Song, Kenn started a Bible study at Chuck's house in the San Fernando Valley. They began another one in Beverly Hills at the home of another musician, Larry Norman. In early 1975 they brought the groups together, thirteen in all, for a Sunday morning service at the Beverly Hills Women's club. They grew rapidly and began moving around from location to location, eventually winding up in "The Valley" meeting in a Lutheran school. At one point, they met for a year on the beach in Santa Monica at Lifeguard Station # 15. Kenn remembers having the tannest church in the country.[2] Jack Little recalls the power of those beach services.[3] One Sunday a man walked by the stage and mocked what was going on. Kenn stopped the service, engaged in dialogue with the man and led him to the Lord while everyone watched!

## HOW THE CHURCH GOT THE NAME "VINEYARD"

Early on the group wrestled with what to call themselves.[4] Someone suggested "Church of the Creator," another "Holy Ghost Fellowship." Kenn wasn't excited about either of these, to say the least. He asked God what he wanted it to be called. About a week later, Kenn was reading from Isaiah and the word *vineyard* jumped out at him. He realized that the Holy Spirit was speaking and saying, "You're the Vineyard. Everything the Father wants to do in the life of the church can be seen in a vineyard—ground preparation, sowing, husbandry, pruning, the production of the fruit, grafting, beauty, the joy of the wine..."

In looking back, Kenn realized years later (as he wrote in 1985) that God had, indeed, been a faithful gardener. Isaiah 27:3 says, "A Vineyard of wine, sing of it! I, the Lord, am its keeper; I water it every moment, lest anyone damage it, I guard it night and day." Even though Kenn knew that the verse was speaking of God's care for all of his flock, he somehow sensed that it had specific application for his church.

## WHAT THE VINEYARD WAS LIKE

I remember when my future wife and I were involved in Calvary Chapel in San Diego in 1977 and heard Keith Green play in our church. He was just getting started in his amazing ministry and was from a church in LA called the Vineyard.

Keith had come to Christ through Kenn and Joanie Gulliksen's Beverly Hills Bible study. In the biography of her husband's life, Melody Green tells that she and Keith were invited by musician Randy Stonehill to the Bible study at Larry Norman's house.[5]

She remembers the meeting, saying that about thirty-five people sat on couches, chairs, and the floor as the young leader got up and introduced himself. Kenn Gulliksen had "yellow-blond hair, a round friendly face, and his eyes were warm and smiling. He started speaking and his gentle manner immediately put me at ease... Kenn led the group in some songs we'd never heard before... "

81

Father we adore you,
Lay my life before you.
How I love you…

"The words just flowed over me. People broke into gentle harmonies that all seemed to weave in and out of each other. I felt a strange sense of peace start to wash over me."

After worship, Kenn got up to share from the Bible and his own life. Melody says,

*I'd never heard anybody talk like that before. It just sounded so down to earth. He made Jesus sound like his best friend or something. It didn't seem abstract or mystical at all…I gave Keith a sideways glance…he was totally absorbed.*

That night Keith gave his life to the Lord, Melody a week later. It was under Kenn's pastoring that Keith and Melody went on to found Last Days Ministries (more later).

While the Vineyard attracted other celebrities such as Bob Dylan, Debby Boone, and Hal Lindsey, it was not its people that made it distinctive. According to Bill Dwyer, who was involved at this time and later became a Vineyard pastor the Vineyard "offered an expression of Christ that was magnetic in its simplicity and intimacy."[6] From Kenn's perspective, the Vineyard was very similar to Calvary Chapel at this point except that there was more emphasis on intimacy in worship, the gifts of the Spirit, and relationships. Kenn's hallmark purpose throughout his ministry has always been 1 Timothy 1:6 "The goal of our instruction is love from a pure heart, a good conscience and a sincere faith."

## GULLIKSEN "ACCIDENTALLY" PLANTS OTHER VINEYARDS

### LANCASTER/BIG BEAR

Kenn had no big plans to start a movement, but by 1977 Brent Rue and his wife Happy had planted two more Vineyard churches (at the same time!). Brent flew up to the mountain area of Big Bear twice a month and started a church there.

He also drove into the desert to Lancaster and planted there. The Lord finally spoke to them that the church in Lancaster was where they were to go (even though Happy hated the desert at the time). They found a pastor for the work in Big Bear and moved their family to Lancaster where they grew the church up to as many as 1,000 people.[7]

## San Luis Obispo

In 1978, twenty-three-year-old Jack Little and his wife Susan had just graduated from Azusa Pacific University and were attending the Vineyard in San Fernando Valley.[8] They had a home group of fifty people, so it appeared to be time for them to come on staff.

But the Lord spoke to both Kenn and the Littles that it was not to be. Jack was feeling drawn to plant a church up the coast in San Luis Obispo. The Littles moved there and after some initial rejection were handed a core of people who had been gathered by another pastor. Jack grew this core into a church of over a thousand in a year's time. And so another Vineyard was born.

## Vineyard "East"

Also in 1978, Craig and Sue Mechler planted a church in New Bedford, Massachusetts, called Vineyard East since it was so far from the others. It still exists today as the Vineyard in Dartmouth (Massachusetts).

## Santa Monica

In 1979, Kenn had a traffic accident and ended up on his back for almost two months with a broken leg.[9] During his convalescence he had time to seek the Lord about the church and felt that God was calling him to relocate from its meeting place in Tarxana in the Valley back to the west side of Los Angeles where they had originally felt called. So Kenn and Joanie took most of the church (which had grown to over 400 by then) and moved it out near Santa Monica.

Bill Dwyer was the church administrator at the time and lived in the Valley. Kenn left Bill and his wife, Christy with about 80 adults who became the Valley Vineyard. And then there were six.

## FAILURES AND TRAGEDIES

The church in Big Bear died, as did another attempt in Prescott, Arizona. Even more shocking were some deaths that rocked the young movement and showed them that church planting was a form of spiritual warfare.

In 1982, John and Dede Smalley, converted in the early days of the Vineyard and married by Kenn, were leaving Simi Valley in Los Angeles to plant a Vineyard in Connecticut. John had been on staff with Kenn from 1977-79. On the way they stopped by Last Days Ministries in Tyler, Texas, to see their old friends, Keith and Melody Green. On a whim John and Keith decided to go up in the Last Days airplane for a bird's-eye view of the property. In the small plane were the Smalleys, their six children, Keith, two of his children and the pilot. All twelve died as the plane went down due to having too much weight. The story is recounted in *No Compromise*.[10]

In 1983, John Odean and a team of nine people left California to plant a Vineyard in Annapolis, Maryland.[11] As they traveled caravan-style, the big U-Haul truck went out of control in Colorado, fell on its side, skidded, and ignited in flames killing the two kids in the cab of the truck. Sobered to the bone, the team eventually did make it to Annapolis where John still pastors.

## JOHN WIMBER'S CHURCH LEAVES
## CALVARY CHAPEL

John Wimber had started his church wanting to field-test the discoveries he had made at Fuller on the correlation between signs and wonders and the growth of the church. He had originally aligned himself with Calvary Chapel because he assumed that it would be open to his desire to seek the ministry of the Spirit. Calvary Chapel had been birthed in revival and had seen many supernatural phenomena, as Tom Stipe had reported to Wimber in 1980. Both my wife and I can attest to the miracle flavor of those earlier days. When I met my wife, Betsy, at Calvary in San Diego, she was one of the worship leaders not only in their evangelistic Sunday morning services, but also in their "afterglow" services where gifts of the Spirit were welcomed.[12] Before we were married Betsy's roommate, Sherrie, continually wore a bandana, in style at the time, to hide her almost completely bald head. She had lost all but three strands of hair due to a bout with rheumatic fever as a child. She went forward one Sunday to get prayer for an unrelated issue and the next day woke up with a complete head of curly, red hair a few inches long! Betsy says that her memories of Calvary Chapel in San Diego in those days were filled with demonstrations of the power of God.

Chuck Smith, founder of Calvary Chapel, was originally from the Foursquare Gospel denomination, the church movement that had grown out of Aimee Semple McPherson's ministry in Los Angeles. While McPherson had been an evangelist who moved in healing and spiritual gifts, she downplayed them in her meetings wanting nothing to distract from evangelism. As Calvary's ministry progressed, Chuck Smith adopted a similar policy of moderation toward the gifts, because he had, in Kenn Gulliksen's opinion, an aversion to the hype and manipulation that he had experienced in the Foursquare churches of his generation.[13]

Consequently, when John Wimber began to promote in the front room what Calvary was only doing in the back room, tension began to mount. Wimber's church was looking less and less like a Calvary congregation. Some of the pastors who had come from backgrounds with no emphasis on the Holy Spirit were attracted to what John was doing, but for others, it created concerns.

In April of 1982, Chuck Smith invited pastors from the larger Calvary Chapels to Lake Arrowhead, California, for a time of fellowship and prayer.[14] Among those present during the meeting were Calvary leaders such as Chuck Smith, Mike MacIntosh, Greg Laurie, Jeff Johnson and Raul Reis as well as Wimber and Gulliksen. During that meeting it became apparent that some were upset with John's new emphasis on the Holy Spirit and his use of church growth principles that seemed to contradict Chuck's teaching on the sovereignty of God in the expansion of the church. As a solution, it was suggested that Wimber's church align with the Vineyard churches that had formed under Gulliksen's leadership. John agreed to this, and he and Kenn began to make plans to affiliate.

It is important to note that from Gulliksen's perspective it had never occurred to Chuck Smith that the Vineyard would become a separate movement from Calvary. [15] During this period ('74-'82), all the Vineyards had participated in the Calvary movement as full partners. Chuck later told Kenn that he just assumed that the Vineyards would continue as a part of the movement but with a different flavor.

As far as Wimber was concerned, the animosity he felt in Lake Arrowhead, not so much from Chuck but from some of the other Calvary pastors, was deeply wounding. He realized then that with the theological convictions he had it would not be possible to co-labor in the Calvary system. [16]

Kenn Gulliksen had met John Wimber a few years earlier in about 1979. [17] From Bill Dwyer's vantagepoint, the partnering of these two was perfectly timed. Kenn, a man of genuine vision, knew that the Lord had great plans for the Vineyard, but he also knew his own limitations. John, with all his experience in church growth had the skills and willingness to pastor and train leaders. Kenn, therefore, felt led of the Lord to submit the Vineyard to John's leadership.

Sensing the potential for a mutually beneficial relationship, both Wimber and Gulliksen joined in alignment together and Wimber's church became Vineyard Christian Fellowship of Anaheim with Chuck's blessing in May of 1982. Along with Kenn at this time, a handful of Vineyard and Calvary pastors such as Brent Rue, Jack Little, Bill Dwyer, Craig Mechler and John McClure began to relate to John as well. The Vineyard, now seven churches in all, had a new leader. [18] What they didn't anticipate was that within a short time, thirty Calvary Chapels would join the new Vineyard movement. From Gulliksen's perspective, the Calvarys that joined the Vineyard at this time "were pastored by people who were hungry for more of the Holy Spirit in their own churches, in their own lives. They were more risk takers, possibly more pioneering, and they were people who had previous relationship with John."[19] The point of demarcation was clearly differing perspectives on the gifts of the Holy Spirit. The churches jumping ship put a deep wedge between Calvarys and Vineyards that I have felt often throughout the years.

## Historic tensions with Calvary Chapel

While Chuck Smith did bless John Wimber in their parting, there has unfortunately been an historic tension between Calvary and Vineyard churches. Many have conjectured about this; I will cite some reasons I see for that tension.

When Kenn stepped out to start the church that would become the Vineyard, he had desired to emphasize certain things that made it slightly different from Calvary. Kenn wanted to pursue intimacy with Christ, and Vineyard worship reflected this more intimate approach. Over time, Vineyard worship began to look less and less like Calvary worship.

Kenn's gift of compassion also saw him begin to delve into inner healing, an area Wimber would later explore as well. As a movement Calvary Chapel has not embraced this ministry.

While these things were happening, the Calvary pastoral network reflected the unplanned nature of their rapid growth as well as Chuck's hesitancy to be intentional about structuring for growth. Kenn, desirous of developing churches that were highly relational in collegiality, felt the need to plan in addition to trusting God.

Chuck Smith's philosophy on church growth was simple. He believed in trusting the sovereignty of God, worshipping, and teaching the Bible. He believed the church would grow naturally from there. Some of the Calvary pastors, however, were not experiencing the growth that Chuck had experienced. These began to be helped by relating to John Wimber who had been willing to teach them how to develop their church infrastructure to enable growth. Thus John began to gain an unintentional following among some of the Calvary pastors.

When John became a Vineyard, it wasn't long before about thirty of the Calvary guys who had relationship with John changed their affiliation and became Vineyards. One of those to do so was Tom Stipe, a long-standing Calvary pastor. My perception is that one sources of hurt can be traced to feelings of betrayal that occurred during this time.

These feelings were exacerbated when, as the Vineyard began to grow, many of those who joined were Evangelicals looking for the power of the Holy Spirit in their lives and ministries. This made the Vineyard's early expansion very different from Calvary's which had come from an explosion of evangelism among the counter-culture.

This trend was indicative of a basic confusion in the Vineyard between the call on the Vineyard to both church renewal and to church planting through evangelism. Calvary pastors tended to view the Vineyard's transfer growth as illegitimate. This criticism was, in some ways, valid and reflected the immaturity of young pastors enamored with the healing ministry and not having a clear picture of biblical church planting through conversion growth.

Another factor concerned eschatology. The pre-tribulational, imminent return of Christ is a central doctrine in the Calvary system. When I was attending Calvary Chapel in San Diego we used to hear messages on his soon return. My wife recalls that it was repeatedly said that Christ would surely return at the end of such-and-such a year. Chuck Smith himself predicted the rapture in 1981. While I loved our church, I wasn't sure I believed in a pre-tribulational rapture and after a period of intensive study adopted a different end times position. While provisionally satisfied for having worked through the biblical texts on my own, I was also saddened because I knew that holding a different position excluded me from the potential of pastoring among the Calvary network of churches.

The influence of George Ladd is reflected in Wimber's post-tribulation position, but in contrast to Calvary, he has not made eschatology a part of Vineyard culture. Also because of the influence of Ladd's *New Testament Theology* on many of us who went to seminary, the post-tribulational position is common among Vineyard pastors, thus creating another divide with Calvary.

Perhaps the most central issue is that Calvary has never embraced the signs and wonders movement as popularized by John Wimber in Fuller's MC 510 course and the ensuing book, *Power Evangelism*. (We will soon see how John developed his thinking on this subject.) Chuck Smith has written his views in *Charisma vs. Charismania*.[20] While he aims the book at the whole of the Charismatic spectrum, his positions reflect a clear distancing from the Vineyard. As was said before, Calvary has taken what Chuck feels to be a more biblical, low-key approach to spiritual gifts. He had seen the trouble things like shaking and being "slain in the Spirit" had caused in his Pentecostal past and wanted no part of it.

Probably the strongest stance Calvary has taken has been over the issue of whether Christians can be affected by a demon. While the Vineyard began to minister to demonized believers, Chuck Smith maintains that no Christian will ever be in need of deliverance.

The tensions with Calvary have caused my wife and me great pain, as is the case with many others in the Vineyard who have come from the Calvary movement. Even though we see many issues through different theological and philosophical lenses, even though we have both made mistakes, it is our prayer that Calvary would forgive the Vineyard for past wounds and that we would agree to disagree for the sake of unity in the Body of Christ. Betsy was one of the original converts from Calvary, San Diego (now called Horizon), and was in their first Bible study. She and I have fond memories of our days there, pastored my Mike MacIntosh. We have much to thank them for I don't agree with infant baptism or with praying to the Virgin Mary, but I choose to bless those Catholics, or Baptists, or whatever if they love the Lord and are bearing genuine fruit. In the words of the apostle Paul, at least Christ is being proclaimed (Phil. 1:18). Neither side has done everything right, but as brothers I hope we can forgive one another and bless what the Father is doing in each.

ભ

NOTES:

[1] I am indebted to Bill Dwyer, pastor of the Valley Vineyard, for his insights here. He was there from the beginning of the Vineyard and graciously offered to lend me his perceptions of what transpired.

[2] Kimla, p. 14

[3] Related in a personal conversation

[4] Kenn Gulliksen, "Birthing a Vineyard," *First Fruits,* July, 1985

[5] Melody Green and David Hazard, *No Compromise, the Life Story of Keith Green*, Eugene, OR, Harvest House, 1996, pp. 115-120

[6] Personal facsimile from Bill Dwyer, May 7, 1996

[7] Personal facsimile from Bill Dwyer, May 8, 1996

[8] Jack Little, "The Risk of Belonging to God," *First Fruits*, October, 1984

[9] Bill Dwyer, "Confessions of a Church Planter," *First Fruits*, May/June, 1985

[10] Pp., 349ff.

[11] "Risk Takers," *Vineyard Newsletter*, Summer 1987

[12] Jesus Movement historian, David Di Sabatino, told me that these afterglow services were developed at Calvary to control Lonnie Frisbee's Pentecostal style of ministry.

[13] The following information comes from a personal letter from Kenn Gulliksen, August 13, 1996.

[14] *Ibid.*

[15] *Ibid.*

[16] Communicated to me in a letter from Margie McClure, August 28, 1998

[17] Personal Facsimile from Bill Dwyer, May 7, 1996

[18] Sam Thompson, "A Vineyard Overview," *Vineyard Newsletter*, Winter 1988

[19] Donald Miller, *Reinventing American Protestantism*, Berkeley CA, USC Press, 1998, p. 49

[20] Costa Mesa, The Word for Today, 1992

# CHAPTER FIVE

# A
# CHURCH
# PLANTING
# MOVEMENT IS
# BORN

# A CHURCH PLANTING MOVEMENT IS BORN

### A CHURCH FUNERAL

When John Wimber worked for Fuller, he attended a funeral that had a great impact on his life.[1] He relates that this funeral was unique in a number of ways.

First, it was quite large and lasted all day. About 20,000 people, mostly Puerto Rican, representing 56 churches, attended in groups of 1,000. As they paid their last respects, they wept and laughed in honoring the deceased.

Second, what had died was a church. Those who attended the funeral were the spiritual descendants of those who had been sent out from this mother church to plant other churches. One pastor stood up and shared that in the last year alone, the mother had planted eleven churches and was like an old bitch dog that had given birth one too many times.

Third, those who had come back from the funeral had nothing but good to say about the church that had given them birth. There had been no splits, no fights. The members had been saved, discipled, and sent out to do it all over again... and again.

Wimber remembered the pastor of the church weeping throughout the day as his dream to plant churches had become a reality. Church growth research has clearly demonstrated that the best way to evangelize the lost is to plant new churches. This man had understood that and had literally spent himself to win the lost. The pastor felt he could now go home a fulfilled man, having done what God had put him on the earth to do.

Wimber was profoundly touched and reflected later, "That day God burned a passion into my soul for renewal and growth. I knew that whatever God called me to do, it had to be marked by a willingness to give everything away. I prayed, 'Lord, if you ever call me to minister in another church, I promise it will be a sending church.'"

## A VISION FOR CHURCH PLANTING

Shortly after becoming the leader of the Vineyard, John had an incredible experience with God in answer to the prayer he had prayed after the church funeral. He described the vision in the premiere issue of *First Fruits* magazine.

*Several years ago God spoke to me in a vision concerning the planting of 10,000 fellowships. In this vision I saw a map of the United States with thousands of little lights all across the country. Some in the Mid-West, Denver, Chicago, Kansas City, etc.; a large number across the Sun-Belt from Los Angeles to Phoenix to Houston and on into Florida. The New England states from Maine to New York City were covered as well as the Pacific Northwest clear down to Southern California. Thousands of little flashing lights! I asked God what this meant. He told me that each light represented a new fellowship that He wanted to start. I thought I had gone berserk. It must be me. I'm only making this up. As usual, God was persistent and patient and I was slow and resistant. I am now convinced that God has called me to encourage the planting of these 10,000 fellowships.*

*Where will they come from? Some we will adopt (i.e., existing churches who wish to become Vineyards). To some we will be foster parents to (i.e., they will stay who they are, and we will provide assistance as requested). Others we will give birth to. It is in this later grouping that most fellowships will be planted. God has initiated; now it is up to us to follow.[2]*

Looking back, one can now clearly see how God had prepared Wimber step by step for the role of leading the Vineyard:

- John had been trained by a personal evangelist, so he could train others.
- John had been gifted in how to help churches get started

and grow. While he was with the Quakers, he helped plant or strategize the planting of hundreds of churches in almost every state.[3] He now had the theory, practical experience, and materials to help church planters.

- John was introduced to the field of church growth research while he was at Fuller and learned more about how churches were growing around the world, especially when evangelism and church planting were accompanied by signs and wonders.
- John had a profound experience at a church funeral that gave him a vision for pastoring a mother church.
- God sovereignly started that mother church in 1977, grew it, and empowered it to evangelize.
- God joined John with the Vineyard and gave him catalytic church planters like Kenn Gulliksen, Jack Little, and Todd Hunter (more below) as his early leaders.

After preparing him for years, God now had commissioned John Wimber to start a church planting movement. The pieces of the Vineyard were beginning to fall into place.

## TODD AND DEBBIE HUNTER: THE FIRST CHURCH PLANTERS OUT OF WIMBER'S CHURCH[4]

Todd and Debbie Hunter were newly married and had just graduated from college. Born and raised in Southern California and saved in the Jesus Movement, they were deeply impacted by their experience in Calvary Chapel, especially in John Wimber's Calvary in Yorba Linda. They wanted to share that experience with other Baby Boomers, so they approached John about planting a church. What started out as nothing more than an impression that they were to go "east," eventually became a specific call to Wheeling, West Virginia.

John tried to persuade them not to go to Wheeling, arguing in favor of a large, growing city like Houston or Kansas City. But Todd was so convinced they were to go to Wheeling that in the fall of 1979 the Hunters and another young couple naively journeyed to a completely foreign culture, found a place to live, got jobs in the community and proceeded to plant the Calvary Chapel of Wheeling. (Todd later changed the name to Vineyard Christian Fellowship after John joined Gulliksen).

As Todd wondered why Wheeling, he later wrote, "We now realize that coming to Wheeling opened our eyes to the great needs of the urbanized areas of the Mideastern United States."

The Vineyards that would eventually be planted out of Todd's vision all had a sovereign call to minister to what might be called the "new poor" who had fallen victim to urban needs in the bread-basket of America.

## THE FORMATION OF VMI (1983)[5]

After the outpouring of the Holy Spirit at Wimber's church in 1980, their rapid growth began to attract worldwide attention. By 1981, through John's visibility and his evangelical credentials at Fuller, as well as the unusual nature of the growth of his church, he began to get invitations from around the world.[6] This would shortly accelerate to "warp speed" when he was invited to teach the course at Fuller Seminary called MC 510, Signs, Wonders and Church Growth (more following). The Vineyard would then get extensive media coverage. At this point John saw the need to organize around what was happening. One of his fundamental axioms has always been that organization must follow organism to aid its growth.

In the April 1982 meeting of Calvary Chapel pastors, the tensions had come out regarding what was happening at Wimber's church. It was then that John's formal association with Kenn Gulliksen and the Vineyards had begun. That decision was first shared publicly a few weeks later, in May, in Morro Bay, California. The pastors of the Vineyards as well as a number of the Calvary pastors who had been relating to John attended this meeting. It was here that Kenn stood up and recognized Wimber's leadership over the Vineyard. While John wanted to honor Chuck in all that was to follow, he also saw the need to provide structure to bless and support what God was doing. In this meeting he first began to share his vision for developing a pastoral network of collegiality and support.

A short time later, seven Vineyard pastors met in John's office to discuss the formation of such a network that would be separate from the Calvary movement.[7]  In attendance at that meeting were John Wimber, Kenn Gulliksen, Bob Fulton, Jack Little, Bill Dwyer, Brent Rue, and John McClure.

A year later, in May of 1983, the Vineyard pastors along with a handful of Calvary pastors again met in Morro Bay to formalize the new organization. They had to put some kind of structure in place because a church with cult-like tendencies had adopted the name *Vineyard,* and it became apparent that the name had to be legally service marked quickly.

The structure that emerged from this meeting was given the name *Vineyard Ministries International* (VMI).  VMI was designed to do four things:

- Facilitate John's international conference activity
- Be a distributing company for John's and the Vineyard's music, for a teaching tape ministry, and for printed material
- Facilitate conferences by other Vineyard pastors and/or associates of John's
- Oversee Vineyard church planting in the United States
  It was also in this year that John's church moved to Anaheim and became known as the Anaheim Vineyard.

Shortly after the second Morro Bay meeting, the first Vineyard pastors' conference was held. John wanted this conference, called "Building the Church from the Bottom Up," to give the new churches a common foundation on which to build.

## THE FORMATION OF AVC (1986)[8]

To this point, the Vineyard had been small and relatively unknown. In those first years they saw only limited growth, primarily in Southern California where they multiplied to about 50 churches. But when publicity from the MC 510 course (see chapter 7) began to go out all over the world, VMI, now doing double duty by channeling renewal *and* by church planting, quickly lost the ability to oversee the church planting arm. There were also legal complications in giving oversight to pastors. VMI could not license or ordain, nor could it help with the incorporation process.

In January 1985, the Vineyard movement was centered in Southern California and Colorado and numbered about 70 churches.[9] By December of that same year it had spread to the East Coast, through the South, Midwest, into the Northwest and numbered 139 churches. It was clear that something had to be done. Projections into 1986 indicated the possibility of doubling the number of churches again.

To enable continued growth in church planting, the solution was to form, in 1986, a new organization called *The Association of Vineyard Churches* (AVC). While VMI would continue to handle Wimber's renewal ministry, AVC was designed to do the following:

- Provide a legal covering for the expanding movement and its joint activities
- Facilitate church planting
- License and ordain pastors
- Raise and release funds for church planting
- Oversee existing fellowships

John Wimber was named International Director of AVC, and Sam Thompson, the executive pastor at Anaheim, became the National Coordinator. The country was broken up into regions, each one with a Regional Overseer and Area Pastoral Co-ordinators. These were the Regional Overseers at that time.

- Southern California—John McClure
- California Central Coast—Bob Craine
- Central California and the Northwest—Brent Rue
- Rocky Mountains and the South—Tom Stipe
- Midwest and North Central—Todd Hunter
- East Coast—Kenn Gulliksen

My wife and I, newly arrived in Indianapolis to plant a Vineyard, were at the first meeting of the Midwest Region. Todd Hunter, who was then still in Wheeling, convened a small group pastors interested in the Vineyard in February 1985, at the La Quinta Inn by the airport in Indy. There I first met

Todd, Steve Sjogren, Randy Clark, Jim Bricker, and Ben Hoerr, all Vineyard pastors today. As a Vineyard pastor in the Midwest during those years, it was amazing to see the growth. The states represented in that room within a few years multiplied into five independent regions encompassing over 80 churches. It seemed we were on our way to "10,000 blinking lights" by the grace and sovereign call of God.

ℭℬ

NOTES:

[1] John Wimber, "Sent into the Harvest Field," *Equipping the Saints*, September/October, 1987

[2] John Wimber, "Do You Know?" *First Fruits,* May, 1984

[3] John Wimber, *Expanding the Kingdom Now*, September, 1984

[4] Todd Hunter, "Culture Shock," *First Fruits*, May, 1984; "Church Planting: Listen and Obey," *First Fruits*, June, 1984

[5] Sam Thompson, "A Vineyard Overview," *The Vineyard Newsletter*, Winter 1988

[6] John Wimber, "Season of New Beginnings," *Vineyard Reflections*, May/June, 1994

[7] Communicated in a personal conversation with Jack Little

[8] Sam Thompson, "A Vineyard Overview," *The Vineyard Newsletter*, Winter 1988

[9] Dave Taylor, *First Fruits*, March/April, 1986

# CHAPTER SIX

# THE
# VINEYARD
# GENETIC CODE

# THE VINEYARD GENETIC CODE

## LOOKING FOR PEOPLE LIKE US

In 1983 when I was graduating from Gordon-Conwell Seminary north of Boston, and we had had our first baby, my wife and I couldn't find a group to partner with in our desire to plant a church. God had created us in a generation that was opting out of the traditional church, and we wanted to reach them in a more contemporary form. He had also built into us a set of non-negotiable values:

- Putting into practice the kingdom theology of George Ladd: its implications were awesome!
- Intimate worship that focused on God and a style that was honest and natural as opposed to hyped and formal.
- Wanting to be us, casual, rock 'n roll boomers.

We didn't want to do it alone, but we couldn't find anyone to do it with either. We were stuck until we met John Wimber.

Invited by a friend to a healing seminar in Melrose, Massachusetts, at a little church called The Chapel (now a Vineyard), I sang Vineyard music for the first time, heard a Ladd-inspired lecture on the kingdom of God by Wimber, and watched a deaf lady receive her hearing while John gently tried to explain what was happening to her. When it was done, I went back to the apartment and told my wife, "I think we found what we've been looking for."

There is a saying in our movement: "The Vineyard is not something you join but something you find out you are." Betsy and I were "Vineyard" long before we met John, but what John did, not only for us, but for many others, was give language for what was already in us.

John Dawson of YWAM once called the Vineyard a tribe. That's what we are, one of the tribes of the new Israel of God, complete with our own banner. We are only one part of the whole, but we like the part we are. We are a family joined together with the church universal by a common experience of salvation and

100

historic doctrine, and joined together as a tribe, or family, by a set of common values and mission. What these are I will try now to share.

In the pastors' conferences in 1983 and 1984, John articulated the Vineyard's basic genetic code. We affirm these things to this day. They serve as our boundaries to keep us on track. I was not at either of these conferences since we were not part of the Vineyard yet, but I have heard John go through this material on other occasions and have heard the 1984 conference on tape.

## BUILDING THE CHURCH FROM THE BOTTOM UP, 1983

### THE PASTOR'S JOB

In the 1983 conference about building the church from the bottom up, John said that the church is in the people-processing business. He told us that our goal is to catch 'em, clean 'em, and send 'em out, more like Jesus than we got them.

The pastor's job is to build the infrastructure of the church so that this is able to happen. John likened the infrastructure to the skeleton of the body. The true church is the 25% who are committed in time, energy and money and who serve as the workforce. They hold the body together. John estimated that for every part of skeleton there would be three parts flesh. This 75% are the crowd out of which we seek disciples who will serve Christ and become a part of the infrastructure.

The pastor's job, then, is to identify, recruit, train, deploy, monitor, feed, and reproduce workers and leaders. In short, it is to disciple people who will in turn disciple others (2 Timothy 2:2). Jesus modeled this; Wimber called it the "discipleship loop."

- The leader does it.
- The leader does it while a disciple watches.
- The disciple does it while the leader watches.
- The leader leaves the disciple doing it.

John said if we focused on quality by using the discipleship loop, we would get the quantity.

John wanted the Vineyard to plant churches from the bottom up by concentrating on building the infrastructure from the very beginning. This was accomplished by starting and multiplying small groups of people newly saved through evangelistic efforts of various kinds. The small group leaders and key task leaders would then become the core leadership of the church.

John counseled that it was not time to go public as a church on a Sunday morning until the infrastructure was in place and there were somewhere between 50 and 100 committed adults. He said the two biggest mistakes a new church could make were to go to Sunday services too soon or to commit to a facility before achieving financial stability.

## BIRTHING, NURTURING, AND BALANCING

John also taught about the different phases of the Spirit's activity in a church. Just like in birthing a baby, there is a gestation stage where something new is introduced into the life of the church. For a period of time this is the main item of concentration, of teaching, of modeling. From the outside it might appear as if the church is myopic, but the period of gestation requires this to birth the value into the body. At some point this baby is birthed into the life of the fellowship and needs to be nurtured until it can function on its own. An example of this was when God birthed healing at the Anaheim Vineyard. For a number of years this is what they focused on. Now it is firmly entrenched as a core value and only needs some occasional attention to nurture it.

When I was planting our church the first thing I hoped to birth was worship. I taught on it for quite a while, and then one night "they got it." It only needed vitamins after that. I also realized that along with birthing and nurturing one needs to add balancing. In order to offer the whole council of God we need to pay attention occasionally to issues that have not been birthed and, therefore, cannot be nurtured. If, for instance, God had not led a young church into ministry to the poor, since it didn't exist as yet, it could not be nurtured. What the church must do, however, is balance this gap by occasionally teaching on God's heart for the poor to plant the seed in preparation for the day of God's divine initiation of that ministry.

## WRITING A FIVE-YEAR PLAN, 1984

Having directed how to jump-start the church-planting division of the Vineyard, Wimber next concentrated on renewal, teaching ex-hippies from the Jesus Movement how to plan. John said that the Jesus movement saw as many as 3½ million young people saved from 1968-78, but because those in leadership failed to organize and plan, it ran its course. The prevailing eschatology that looked for the any-minute return of Christ contributed to this. Why plan for the future when we may not be here at year's end? He saw this thinking as shortsighted and likened it to the irresponsibility of letting the grain lie in the fields because there are not enough silos in which to store it.

John first laid down the biblical basis for Spirit-led planning. The job of church leadership is to pray, find the mind of the Lord, and then organize "the parade." Organization allows the organism to continue to grow.

At the 1984 conference pastors were given tools for what John called "writing our history in advance." (this material is available from VMI under the same title.) Once we have the mind of the Lord for the future, we conceptualize with God how to get where he wants us to go and then pray that he would create what we have planned as we move forward with implementation. Adjustments are made along the way.

John gave the following process to work through:

- Determine the biblical **purpose** of the church.
- Make a list of all our **values**, the things we think are important.
- Out of this list, determine the most important values; these are our **priorities**, those things we give our time, energy and money to. These priorities serve as red and green lights telling us what to say yes to and what to say no to.
- Our **practices** are those sets of behaviors that demonstrate our priorities. We may *say* we value something, but in reality, we only *do* what we value. What we do the

most determines our priorities.

- Our **programs** are like jets on a rocket—they get us where we want to go. We develop programs as environments to model and impart our practices.
- Our **personnel** are people who model our practices and run our programs.
- Our **philosophy** is our approach to how we do all of the above. It is our style and is determined both by who we are, what we value, and who we are trying to reach.
- Our **plans** enable us to fulfill our purpose by running programs with personnel who model our practices because they have our priorities and values.

In order to give an overview of our genetic code, I will now give an overview of our purpose, our values, and our priorities. John likened this to putting the sign on the front of the bus. People need to know where the bus is going so they can decide whether or not they should get on.

## THE PURPOSE OF THE CHURCH

The Vineyard's understanding of the church is based on our understanding of the kingdom of God. We believe the purpose of the church is to advance the rule of God on the earth by continuing the ministry of Jesus in word, deed, and life through the power of the Holy Spirit.

We have a theology of power that affirms the present day ministry of Jesus through spiritual gifts given to the church to win the lost, heal the sick, care for the poor, cast out demons, and disciple our people as we live according to the fruit of the Spirit.

We also have a theology of pain knowing that the kingdom will be consummated only at the return of Christ. We teach our people how to suffer in Christ's name but never to befriend our sickness. Our call is to participate with Jesus in destroying the works of the devil (1 John 3:8), and, like Jesus, our desire is to do what the Father is doing (John 5:19) at any given time.

## Our Values

First we affirm orthodox, evangelical doctrine as seen, for instance, in a statement such as the Westminster Creed. John Wimber, John McClure, and Dr. Don Williams, all pastors in the Vineyard, have worked for a number of years to develop AVC's *Theological and Philosophical Statements* (January, 1995). This comprehensive statement of theology and praxis is available from the AVC office.

In addition to our theology as stated in *Theological and Philosophical Statements*, we have a number of other core values. These include:

- The pursuit of God
- Christlikeness
- Being Spirit-led
- Prayer
- Discipleship
- The kingdom of God
- The mercy of God
- Integrity
- Servant leadership
- The individual, single or married
- Unity and reconciliation
- Collegiate relationships
- Living in reality affirming both the natural and the supernatural in our worldview
- Simplicity (a non-hyped approach)
- Being culture current so as to contextualize the gospel for our culture

## Our Priorities

**Worship**: Worshipping God is our highest value. It is an end, not a means. We want to give God that which is due him as we are led by the Word and the Spirit. We want to worship with our whole beings through the culture-current music God has given us. We also worship him through the sacrifice of our time, energy and resources.

**WORD**: In the Vineyard we value the Word of God as central to all of life. We believe in expounding the Word for our people for the purpose of living and doing the Bible. Ours is not an accumulation-of-knowledge approach, nor do we desire to filter out parts we do not like. Our desire is to demonstrate a true evangelical commitment to the whole counsel of the inerrant Word of God.

**FELLOWSHIP**: We believe that Christians are called to serve, and our first area of service is to Christ's body, the Church. Relationships with other believers, therefore, are a priority for us. We want our movement to be characterized by walking together in unity and honesty and are committed to resolving conflict in a healthy way. We pray that the Vineyard way would be the way of love.

**MINISTRY**: We believe that Christians are called to serve Christ, secondly, by serving the world.

Our highest ministry to the world is through **evangelism**. We don't want our churches to grow through transfer growth (although that can happen) but through winning the lost.

We also are committed to Jesus' ministry of **healing** the sick. We believe the New Testament understanding of salvation is wholeness: Jesus brought salvation for the whole person. This includes healing for the body, deliverance from demons, the healing of damaged emotions, the healing of creation gone awry, repairing broken relationships, and raising the dead.

We believe that Jesus has also commissioned us to **care for the poor** of the earth, be it to feed, clothe, house, or teach people to read.

**TRAINING**: The apostle Paul explains that the job of church leadership is to equip the saints to serve. Jesus had already modeled this through the discipleship loop. The Vineyard believes, therefore, that the church should be taught how to minister. The job of the leader is to give ministry away by teaching people how to move in the gifts of the Holy Spirit as they live their daily lives through the fruit of the Spirit. The value of equipping is one of the Vineyard distinctives. Wimber has built his entire renewal ministry around it, and the banner publication of the movement bears the name *Equipping the Saints*.

SENDING: The Vineyard sees the priority of sending through three different lenses.

**Church renewal** is the call to bless the whole body of Christ. Jesus loves his bride in all of her expressions, and we want to participate in his efforts to bring new life to her in any way we can. We believe that one of the calls on John Wimber's life, and therefore on the movement as a whole, is to bring renewal to the existing church through the way of love and through a willingness to receive reciprocally from others in return. In doing so, we work to promote the unity of the Spirit in the bond of peace. This can be seen in our willingness to pray with other pastors, join for mutual services and teach in each other's churches.

We also believe the Vineyard has been called to the work of **church planting**. We believe God has called us to raise up 10,000 Vineyard or Vineyard affinity churches. Most of these will come through the work of church planting in metropolitan areas. This is the New Testament model for making disciples through evangelism and nurture.

We aim to plant these churches not only in our culture but in other cultures as well. We embrace the world mission of the church to see the kingdom advance in every ethnic group on earth that the end might come (Matthew 24:14). The Vineyard, then, is also committed to **cross cultural church planting**.

OTHER THINGS TO NOTE

We value a **common mission to rock 'n roll culture**. The Boomers cut their teeth on rock 'n roll and grew up in denim. Our mission is to reach Boomers, Busters, and their kids by offering church life they can relate to.

STYLE: The style of our church life in the Vineyard is to be characterized by a **casual, non-hyped, non-religious atmosphere**. We value being casual, not for the sake of casualness but because it typifies who we are.

SPIRITUAL GIFTS: We are also committed to **welcoming the**

**gifts of the Holy Spirit** in our gatherings and on the streets. Some Vineyards are quite free in the Spirit on Sunday mornings; others adopt more of the seeker approach by focusing on teaching and evangelism on Sunday mornings; but all are committed to the healing ministry and the present day move of the Holy Spirit as a part of who they are.

POLITY: When I worked through the five year plan material for the church I planted, I added an extra category starting with the letter *P*: **Polity**. Vineyard churches are governed in a manner that represents a hybrid of historic forms of government. We believe that the New Testament church was governed by a plurality of elders. We also see the gift of leadership operating in the early church, so we affirm the need for one among the elders to take the lead in showing the way and in making directional decisions. This person we call the senior pastor. We do value the input of the congregation even though we see no biblical basis for including them in government. John Wimber believed that women are to be affirmed in every aspect of ministry except the governance of the church. In the New Testament he saw this as belonging to men. Some in the Vineyard define "governance" as excluding women from eldership while others ordain women as elders but retain a man as the senior pastor.

☙

# CHAPTER SEVEN

# MC 510,
# SIGNS, WONDERS
# AND CHURCH
# GROWTH

# MC 510, SIGNS, WONDERS AND CHURCH GROWTH

## How the Course Got Started

Robert Meye Dean of Fuller Seminary School of Theology, said at a joint faculty meeting, "I know of only two seminary courses that have become famous, One was the course on dogmatics taught by Karl Barth and the other is MC 510 taught by John Wimber here at Fuller."[1] Let's now take a look at the MC 510 phenomenon and how it factored into the growth of the Vineyard movement.[2]

As Wimber was learning about the role of the miraculous in evangelism, he began to accumulate a lot of material and one day proposed to Peter Wagner that he do a lecture in the Church Growth II class about the relationship between signs and wonders and the growth of the church. The dean of the School of World Mission at Fuller, Dr. Paul Pierson, sat in on the class.[3] The material was new to both Wagner and Pierson, but they were impressed with what they heard.

Wimber then suggested that they offer a whole course on the subject with the material he had collected. The School of World Mission debated the issue for a while and, with the blessing of the president of Fuller, Dr. David A. Hubbard, decided to go ahead with the experiment.

Beginning in January 1982, the course MC 510, Signs, Wonders and Church Growth, convened for ten Monday evenings in a Fuller classroom. Peter Wagner was the professor of record, but, Wimber, in the role of adjunct professor, did most of the teaching. Three hours of lecture were to be followed by an optional hour of clinic, with no predetermined format, where students could get an opportunity to pray for others in the class.

During these clinics, John would invite the Holy Spirit to come and minister, and from there the Spirit would take over. Sometimes the prayer would begin with "words of knowledge" from

John, other times with words from class members, and other times with student requests for prayer.

As students were being prayed for, John took an objective approach and attempted to explain what he felt he saw the Spirit doing. He would say, "Can you see this? This is the presence of the Spirit on this person." He wanted to teach people how to discern God's healing presence in order to partner with the Spirit in a more effective way.

## PARTICIPANTS IN THE FIRST CLASS

According to Charles Hummel,[4] of the 90 or so in the first course, theology students predominated. Psychology majors formed the second largest group, followed by older men and one woman from developing countries. He says that many of those present had come with considerable pastoral experience and were avid learners.

Later on, Wimber's detractors would claim that the record numbers who attended from 1982-1985 were skewed because many from Wimber's church took the course without intending to enroll in any degree program at Fuller.[5] There were people from the church that attended but they were in the great minority and were only there to help model healing prayer.

## THE BASIC COURSE CONTENT

The content of MC 510 is essentially found in the book *Power Evangelism,* published in 1986. While the authors are stated to be John Wimber and Kevin Springer, it was Springer who actually wrote the book from John's lecture notes and tapes. Kevin Springer played a key role during that period, getting Wimber's theses into the hands of people around the world. Springer would go on to become the editor of *Equipping the Saints* magazine and later a Vineyard pastor. Wimber's role in the writing process was to be in continual contact with Springer and to revise each chapter as he saw fit.[6] The book was so revolutionary that I will briefly give an overview of Wimber's thesis.

## PROGRAM VS. POWER EVANGELISM

Working with statistics gleaned from his years at Fuller, Wimber shows that not many converts had been grafted into the body through recent efforts to catalyze whole churches to reach the lost. He contrasts these approaches with what he terms power evangelism, which seeks to find out what God is doing through the gifts of the Holy Spirit. These divine appointments are more like a well-placed bullet than a shotgun shell. There is greater effect as well as an economy of motion.

After the first publication, Wimber was highly criticized by some because it appeared he was saying that all evangelistic efforts were subservient to power evangelism. In the 1993 revision of the book, the hard contrast is dropped for an affirmation of the value of *all* evangelistic effort. Power evangelism is defined as a *conscious* attempt to cooperate with the Holy Spirit's anointing, gifting, and leading.[7]

## THE KINGDOM OF GOD

As said previously, Wimber received his theological framework of the kingdom of God from George Ladd. He also benefited from the work of the Lutheran theologian James Kallas.[8]

Ladd understood the kingdom to be the dynamic rule of God, its present reality seen in Jesus' ministry through various signs. Some of these include:

- The forgiveness of sins
- Care for the poor
- Healing for the sick
- Deliverance of the demonized
- Miracles over nature
- Raising the dead

The gospel records show that the kingdom is here but not here yet. Jesus inaugurated the rule of God by destroying the works of the devil through his own life, death and resurrection. But Satan's defeat was only initiated. It will not be completed until the return of Christ. Only then will all tears be dried. As was said above, this gives us a theology of power and pain, a way of believing that healing will happen and a way of explaining why it does not always happen.

## How Did Jesus Do What He did?

Rich Nathan, pastor of VCF of Columbus, Ohio, makes a good observation in *John Wimber*.[9] Rich notes that historic evangelicalism has based its doctrine mainly off the epistles in the New Testament. Historic Pentecostalism has tended to focus on Acts for support of its Spirit-baptism doctrine. What Wimber did for empowered evangelicalism was to take us back to the gospels. It was there that Jesus commanded his disciples to pray "Thy kingdom come." In doing so he is, in effect, commissioning the church universal to pray that the kingdom come as in his ministry. But how can we do what Jesus did? He was God!

Basic to Wimber's thesis is that while Jesus never gave up any aspect of his deity while on earth, he chose not to use some of them in order to live as a man, anointed by the Holy Spirit. In regard to his omniscience, for instance, it was clear that he did not know everything in his earthly ministry and had to ask questions and learn the way others did (e.g., Mark 5:30-33 where Jesus wanted to know who had touched him). In doing so he was becoming the prototype for a new race of people called *Christians*, who would live as he lived, speak as he spoke, and do as he did through the same Holy Spirit he would pour out on the day of Pentecost.

The record of Jesus in the gospels is not, then, the story of an unreachable ideal, nor is Jesus to be separated into the moral Jesus (who is for today) and the miracle Jesus (who was for yesterday). All of Jesus is for today! Wimber gave us a new look at the Christ as someone who could show us how to move in the gifts of the Spirit and do the kinds of things he did (even though the gospel writers do not use the later Pauline language about spiritual gifts).

## Power Encounters[10]

Borrowing from the field of missiology and especially the work of Alan Tippett, Wimber describes divine appointments with people as power encounters with the enemy. Just as Elijah battled the prophets of Baal, so we battle the devil over the lives of people. We do spiritual warfare as we evangelize the lost, heal the sick and cast out demons. With every attack against the kingdom of darkness, asserts Wimber there will be a counter attack against the kingdom of light. Kingdom ministry is war!

## WORLDVIEW PROBLEMS[11]

Wimber believed that the primary reason Americans do not take readily to moving in the supernatural is that we have inherited our worldview (basic assumptions about how the world works) from the rationalism of the Enlightenment. He quotes the work of missiologist Paul Hiebert[12] who demonstrates that every society since the Enlightenment has had a category in its belief system for supernatural activity through divine intervention, angels, demons and such—every society that is except Western culture.

He also notes that the worldview of the Bible not only allows for it, but is filled with supernatural activity. Western theology, working off the Enlightenment worldview, filters supernatural parts of the Bible right out of the equation.

The answer is for Westerners to go through a "paradigm shift" in which they recognize the flaw in their worldview and adopt one that is more in line with the Bible. Doing so will allow a Christian to embrace the present day ministry of the Holy Spirit and open the door to learning how to minister in power.

## THE GIFTS OF THE HOLY SPIRIT

In Wimber's understanding of the Holy Spirit, any Christian can move in any of the gifts as the Spirit enables. In the first list of spiritual gifts in 1 Corinthians 12, Paul appears to say that a believer will only have one or two gifts and that no one will experience them all. Wimber points out that this is an argument from silence because the interpretive key to the passage is the context given to us in chapter 11, verse 18. In chapters 12-14 Paul is addressing problems when the church comes together for worship. When Paul asks if all have this and all have that, he is only referring to the church service. It cannot be proven, therefore, that God could not give one of these gifts to any believer at any time if he so chose. Indeed, Wimber proposed that God could empower a believer in any situation with any of the gifts. He calls this situational gifting. Gifts that the believer regularly receives to pass on to others he calls constitutional gifts.

Of the four main New Testament gift lists (1 Cor. 12:7-11; 27-31; Rom. 12:6-8; Eph. 4:7-13), only the first one appears to involve situational gifting. But if Wimber's interpretation of the earthly Christ is correct, Jesus is the ultimate model for moving in any gift in any situation. The other lists refer to those gifts which occur so regularly in a believer that they constitute that person's job description in the church. Wimber did not believe that we "have" the gifts in the sense of ownership. They are always given to us for someone else and never truly ours. To say we have the gift of evangelism, for instance, means that this gift is given so regularly that it begins to describe our basic function in the body.

Wimber also believed that one does not have to have a "baptism in the Spirit" experience to begin to move in spiritual power. The baptism of the Spirit technically takes place at conversion, and any subsequent and repeatable experiences with the Spirit can be labeled as fillings. Because of this any believer can begin to "do the stuff," i.e., the works of Jesus.

Wimber was often asked if he fasted or prayed long hours before a meeting in order to move in spiritual power. He used to jokingly respond that he drank a Diet Coke. What he meant was that he was no more spiritual than anyone else. He did what he did not because of who he was but because of who Jesus is and what he has called Christians to be and to do as he gives his Spirit to them. As Todd Hunter has said, "This isn't even about us. It's about Jesus."

Contrary to the classic Reformed view that the gifts of the Spirit ceased after the writing of the New Testament, MC 510 included historical research which showed that even though there were ebbs and flows of the Spirit's presence, signs and wonders never ceased. In the appendix to *Power Evangelism* a compendium of quotes from all historical periods shows the miracles of God.

## A Healing Model We Can All Relate To

One of the evangelicals' objections to the healing ministry has been that the Pentecostal models of healing have appeared either too dramatic (e.g., Kathryn Kuhlman) or one-man centered (e.g., Oral Roberts). John researched healers from the last century finding their similarities and differences in both theology and style. He then offered a simple five-step model designed to give ministry to church. The assumption is that Jesus has called us—even commissioned us—to heal the sick as we win the lost. As a matter of fact, healing the sick was Jesus' *modus operandi* for winning the lost in the gospels.

These five steps are not a model in the sense of a formula, but rather a logical path to hearing from God to know what he wants to do in a prayer engagement.

- Interview (Where does it hurt?)
- Diagnostic decision (What has caused this condition?)
- Prayer selection (What kind of prayer do I pray?)
- Prayer engagement (How are you doing?)
- Post prayer direction (i.e., offering not advice but simple direction on what to do next)

This simple model is, in my opinion, John's greatest practical gift to the body of Christ. It has helped countless numbers in over 50 countries of the world get started in "doin' the stuff" as they evangelize.

## The Early Effects of MC 510

### Peter Wagner's Experience[13]

When the MC 510 course was approved, Peter Wagner looked forward to attending every class to learn as much as he could. His interest in healing had begun while a missionary in Bolivia when he was healed through the ministry of E. Stanley Jones. He was healed again, this time of high blood pressure, on the first night of MC 510. He describes sensing the presence of the Holy Spirit and vaguely hearing Wimber in the background helping to explain what the Spirit was doing with him. When

Wagner later visited his doctor, he was surprised to see that his blood pressure had fallen considerably. The doctor reduced the medication gradually and a few months later discontinued it. When Wagner received a clean bill of health, he says it completed his paradigm shift.

He was so excited about learning to minister in the gifts of the Spirit that Wagner later approached his pastor, Dr. Paul Cedar of Lake Avenue Congregational Church, about starting an experimental Sunday School class to study these issues and learn to pray for each other. Cedar complied, and Wagner started the 120 Fellowship. What this class learned about prayer for the sick is the subject of Wagner's book, *How to Have a Healing Ministry Without Making Your Church Sick*. My wife and I attended the 120 Fellowship during our Pasadena years and found it to be a delightful time of learning and fellowship. This class commissioned us with the laying on of hands when we went off to plant our first Vineyard church in 1985.

## CHUCK KRAFT'S EXPERIENCE

Author of the groundbreaking *Christianity and Culture* (1979), Dr. Charles Kraft is a missionary anthropologist who taught at Fuller. He sat in on every class of the first session of MC 510 to listen to John Wimber whom he saw as a credible witness to the healing ministry. He too had come from a conservative evangelical background and had, like Wagner, been on the mission field. He and his wife had served in Nigeria and had been frustrated that their Western approach only touched the surface of the Nigerians' hearts. In this world filled with spirits and spells, sickness came not from germs but from curses or the like. The Nigerians worshipped the God of the Americans for his morality, but when they needed power, they turned back to the witch doctor.

During MC 510, Dr. Kraft went through his paradigm shift and while retaining his evangelical theology, began to move in God's power. The experience so impacted him that he later challenged the powerlessness of the Western worldview in his book *Christianity With Power*.[14]

### JOHN WHITE'S EXPERIENCE

In the winter of 1984, Dr. and Mrs. John White took a three-month leave of absence and attended MC 510 where their lives were changed as well. John White is a noted evangelical psychiatrist and describes his experience with the class in *First Fruits* magazine.

In Dr. White's typically honest and objective style, he makes the following assessment of what he saw:

> *During the laboratories, healing would take place...a few of the healings were dramatic and did not admit to any "psychological" or psychosomatic mechanism known to me personally...I cannot describe even all that I saw, or affirm a supernatural healing in every case...Some healings were instantaneous and attended by no dramatic manifestations. Others were real but progressive, that is to say healing took place in stages during several prayer sessions. Sometimes healing would not happen during a prayer session, only to follow during the hours and days succeeding the session. At other times, no healing would take place at all. Sometimes the healing could have been explained on a psychological basis, that is to say that they were similar to healings carried out using hypnosis or suggestion. At other times no such explanation would suffice.[15]*

Like Wagner and Kraft, Dr. White also went on to write in this area producing *When the Spirit Comes in Power: Signs and Wonders among God's People* (1988).

### "CHRISTIAN LIFE" MAGAZINE

MC 510 had been inaugurated with a good bit of fanfare. Invited to observe, *Christian Life* magazine, a journal that has tried to chronicle the Charismatic movement since the 1960s, became so excited they devoted a whole issue to the course (October, 1982). This issue was republished in a form edited by Peter Wagner in 1987 called *Signs and Wonders Today.*[16]

With the publication by *Christian Life*, the Vineyard received international publicity, and the movement shifted into another gear. Shortly after the Vineyard moved to its new warehouse location on Cerritos Street in Anaheim, it began to play host to the world.

## MC 511, SIGNS, WONDERS AND CHURCH GROWTH II

Because the course was so popular, a follow-up was developed called MC 511. It went into more depth on the healing ministry, delving into specifics of praying for the physically sick, healing deep emotional wounds, and praying for deliverance from demons.

John also tackled a number of the tougher questions such as the problem of suffering, when people are not healed, and whether or not healing is in the atonement. John's view of the latter is that healing is not available in the atonement at the same level as salvation. It is better to say that healing is "provided for" in the atonement and move the theological basis off the atonement and onto the New Testament revelation of the kingdom of God. Taking this position put Wimber outside historic Pentecostalism which has always seen healing as guaranteed in the atonement.

The basic content of MC 511 is found in Wimber and Springer's book *Power Healing* (1987).

### PETER WAGNER AND THE THIRD WAVE

Peter Wagner was deeply impacted during these years. He believed that God was doing a new work among a stratum of Christendom heretofore resistant to the ministry of the Holy Spirit: the evangelicals. Wagner coined the phrase "Third Wave" to describe the phenomenon.[17]

Wagner's thesis was that there had been two historic waves of the Spirit in the twentieth century. The first, at the turn of the century, birthed Pentecostalism; the second, begun in the late 1950s, birthed the Charismatic movement. Wagner saw the present move of the Spirit as distinct from the other two—thus the term "Third Wave."

David Barrett, the pre-eminent demographer of the Christian world, agrees with Wagner and defines the Third Wave:

*These are Evangelicals and other Christians who, unrelated to Pentecostalism or the Charismatic movement, have recently become filled (or empowered, energized) with the Spirit and are experiencing the Spirit's supernatural and miraculous ministry (though usually without recognizing a baptism in the Spirit separate from conversion), who exercise gifts of the Spirit (with much less emphasis on tongues, as optional or even absent or unnecessary), and emphasizes signs and wonders, supernatural miracles and power encounters, but who remain within their mainline non-Pentecostal denominations and who do not identify as either Pentecostals or Charismatics.*[18]

Wimber, himself, did not see what is happening as a distinct wave but simply another stage in the development of the Charismatic movement.[19] He believed that conservative Evangelicals, a subset among the larger evangelical camp, will begin to align themselves experientially with historic Pentecostalism while retaining evangelical doctrine.

Pentecostals have often misunderstood the Third Wave. Wimber, for example, had Pentecostals ask him if he had had a "visitation." The assumption was that he could not experience the supernatural as he did if he had not had some kind of extraordinary experience with God. Wimber's response was to tell them that he got started by reading the gospel of Luke. In other words, he started where any evangelical would start with Scripture. He then tried to go out and live the Book.

## THE DISTINCTIVES OF THE THIRD WAVE

Pentecostal doctrine has seen the baptism of the Holy Spirit as a distinct event subsequent from salvation and initiated by speaking in tongues. This doctrine has kept evangelicals at bay for the better part of a century. The Third Wave has all but removed that barrier by affirming that a second experience and speaking in tongues are not necessary to move in the gifts of the Spirit. It sees experiences with the Spirit as moments of empowerment for ministry and available throughout a believer's life. The gifts then are released by the believer simply "going for it," but also can be imparted in sovereign seasons of empowerment.

Wimber wrote, "When I pray for Evangelicals, I ask them if they are born again and if they received the Spirit when they received Christ. If they answer 'yes,' I tell them that all that remains is for them to actualize that which the Spirit has—all that is required is for them to release the gifts. I then lay hands on them and say, 'Speak in tongues or prophesy'—and they do. I always use those two gifts as initiatory because that seems to be the pattern in the New Testament."[20]

One cannot prove biblically that one has to speak in tongues or that everyone can speak in tongues. While many in the Third Wave do speak in tongues, it has not received the central (and some would say divisive) place it has had in Pentecostalism. On the other hand, as Wimber had noted, speaking in tongues and prophesying were normal New Testament activity.

Probably the best statement of the Third Wave position is found in Charles Hummel's *Fire in the Fireplace* which calls for the balance between Word (the fireplace) and Spirit (the fire). Wimber desired the Vineyard to be just such a synthesis of Word and Spirit. His vision was that the Vineyard would build on the best of experiential Pentecostalism and the best of doctrinal Evangelicalism.

Hummel does not see the Vineyard as defining the Third Wave movement but as part of it. Wimber agreed and wrote in the preface to the revised edition of *Power Evangelism* (1992) that the Third Wave is now an accepted historical fact, even for those who disagree with what it stands for.[21]

## MC 510 GOES PUBLIC

Because of the publicity of MC 510, people from all over the world began to make requests for the teaching. So in June of 1984, 2,000 of us filled the Vineyard facility in Anaheim for the first public version of MC 510. It was a week that changed my life. Right before my eyes I saw things I had only dreamed were possible as I read my Bible.

I was impacted by the teaching itself, but had already been through much of it and come to many of the same conclusions studying with Pentecostal scholar Gordon D. Fee at Gordon-Conwell Theological Seminary in Boston. What was new, however, was *doing* it. I had theologized about spiritual gifts and had experienced them from time to time, but never as a lifestyle and never to the degree we saw them in action that week. In the clinic times I watched intently as the awesome presence of the Holy Spirit could be felt and seen. John's associate, Blaine Cook seemed to sense consistently what the Spirit was going to do. I once saw him say to a section of the audience, "Here comes the Holy Spirit," and before people had time to even think about it, the whole group slumped down in their seats and onto the floor under the power of the Holy Spirit.

During one of the ministry times, I stood in the back of the room and just watched. I could see people weeping, some being healed of illnesses, some receiving deliverance from evil spirits and even a former dancer get up out of a wheelchair and began to run around the auditorium. I felt for the first time in my life that I was actually living the gospels. This must have been what a typical day in the life of Jesus was like!

One time I felt heat on the back of my neck that was so sudden and so intense that I immediately looked up to see if a spotlight was shining on me. It wasn't. God was showing me his power and teaching me to hear from him. Shortly thereafter I began to receive words of knowledge for people I was praying for. I saw a pronounced increase in my ability to move in the gifts of the Holy Spirit and pray for the sick.

Learning to get these words of knowledge was one of the most amazing things about MC 510. [22] John taught us that subtle impressions, pictures in the mind or feelings in the body could be information from God as to who to pray for and what the root cause of the sickness was. I remember opening myself up to receive these "words" for the first time ("Am I crazy?" I thought to myself). I had trouble at first distinguishing them from the effects of the pizza at lunch. Over time, however, I began to catch on. I am not always right (sometimes it is the pizza), but more often than not, these subtle pictures that appear on my inner screen have led to a dramatic rise of healing in those I pray for.

I am often asked, "How do you know that it's God?" My answer is, "The only way is through trial and error." The prospect of being wrong leaves people aghast, but John taught us that we learn to heal the sick and cast out demons the same way we learn to preach, evangelize and counsel—by taking risks.

The day after the course was over, my wife and I were with some friends, and the wife had a fever. We prayed for her and saw her fever break as we watched sweat marks literally move up through her body. Eventually the fever left out the top of her head. She then felt completely well, and we went out for ice cream. The kingdom of God had drawn near.

## THE PASTORS REPENT

Without a doubt, the most significant thing that happened to me that week occurred when someone stood up during a ministry session in the morning and said he felt that God was giving the pastors an opportunity to repent. At the time I was teaching Bible at William Carey International University in Pasadena and planning to go on for my doctorate in New Testament at Fuller. The top half of my body knew I was a teacher and was relieved that I didn't have to repent with the pastors. The bottom half of my body apparently didn't agree. Against my better judgment, I suddenly found myself running down the aisle. I kept rebuking my legs, but they weren't stopping!

All of a sudden I was standing on stage like a fool in front of 2,000 people. What was I doing there? The next thing I knew, I was down on the floor weeping uncontrollably in repentance for my hardness of heart and my lack of love for the flock of God. When I eventually did get up, after blubbering all over the carpet, I was surprised to find out that there were 200 other pastors up there with me.

I look back on that day as my ordination to the pastoral ministry. God had supernaturally asked me to throw my lot in with the church. Within eight months, my family and I would go off to plant a Vineyard, and I am still pastoring to this day.

## FULLER STOPS MC 510

MC 510/511 caused so much controversy at Fuller that the School of World Mission called a moratorium on the course in March of 1986, pending a faculty review. Just because the course broke all enrollment records did not mean the faculty unanimously supported it. The professors from the School of Theology, especially, had not been in favor of the course from the beginning. The highly valued consensus among the faculty was being threatened.

Later in the year, a faculty task force reported its findings which were then published as *Ministry and the Miraculous: A Case Study at Fuller Theological Seminary.*[23] The book raised a number of issues, the primary objection being the concept of healing clinics in an academic environment. The faculty felt that a seminary was set aside for academic pursuits and that things like healing clinics belonged in the local church.

They concluded that any future course of like nature be conducted by one of Fuller's full-time professors and that any practical ministry component be held off campus in the context of the church under the supervision of a pastor. A substitute course was introduced in the spring of 1987 called MC 550, The Ministry of Healing in World Evangelization. Peter Wagner taught it (although Wimber continued to lecture in part of the course).[24] To develop his own thinking on the subject, Wagner published *The Third Wave of the Holy Spirit* in 1988.

While at the surface level *Ministry and the Miraculous* was a philosophical discussion about the place of healing clinics in the world of academia, not far below the surface was a clear bias against Wimber's thesis that the church is called to move in the miraculous as a part of everyday life. The position being taken by Fuller was essentially, "We're not against it, but we're not for it either." I would refer the reader to Charles Hummel's excellent critique of the book in *Fire in the Fireplace*. He believes that Fuller's task force was guilty of arguing from silence, offering undeveloped conclusions, misrepresenting a theology of suffering to include sickness, perpetuating a false dichotomy of body and spirit, and a reductionism that denies the multi-faceted meaning of Jesus' healing ministry.

While the split with Fuller was probably inevitable, it caused Wimber incredible pain. In talking with former Vineyard pastor, Ken Blue, who was close to John during this period, Ken thinks John never fully recovered from the hurt. Wimber had dreamed of applying the kingdom theology of Dr. Ladd to the lives of real people, and the MC 510 course was a way to give that away to future pastors. While the course only lasted a few years, its impact was enduring and lived on at Fuller through men like Peter Wagner and Chuck Kraft who developed alternate courses.

## THE NUMINOUS OF GOD

We will leave this chapter with one final thought. When I try to extract the pure essence of what it was that Wimber taught us in MC 510, I would have to say that it was to build our faith for the *numinous* of God. Writers like C.S. Lewis use this term (normally an adjective meaning supernatural, mysterious or holy) as a noun to describe the manifest Presence of God. God is everywhere, of course, but we are not used to the removal of the veil. That removal allows us to experience him more fully.

Encounters with the numinous of God are replete in the Scriptures. Whether it was Moses at the burning bush, Samuel hearing a summons in the night, Elijah calling down fire from heaven, or the priests weighted down by the glory filling the temple, the omnipresent God allowed himself to be experienced from time to time by mere mortals. In the New Testament the word became flesh and dwelt among us, and the apostles beheld his glory—but even then his glory was veiled. It was lifted briefly on the mount of transfiguration when the disciples saw Jesus dazzling white. After the resurrection his glory was revealed in his walking through walls. In the book of Acts the numinous was seen in everything from shaking buildings to Ananias and Sapphira dropping dead under the power of the Spirit.

In the Western rationalism of our scientific age, our society has ruled out the possibility of the numinous of God. New Testament theology, a la George Ladd, demonstrates that Jesus' intent was to teach his disciples to believe and demonstrate the kingdom presence of God that could break in to present circumstances at any given moment. To pray "thy kingdom come" and then to actually wait to see how the kingdom is coming—this is what John Wimber reclaimed for the church.

We had been raking leaves in a poor neighborhood in Indianapolis, and before we left I asked the elderly homeowner if there was anything we could pray for him. He mentioned his poor eyesight. Probing a bit I found out that one of his eyes was actually blind. I put on kingdom theology and prayed for the eye. Nothing happened, so I turned to walk away, consoling myself with the fact that the kingdom is "not yet." As I was leaving I began to sense the numinous of God. Faith buoyed up in me, and I turned and sheepishly asked the man if we could pray again. Being polite, he let me pray. Again nothing happened. "Must not have been the numinous after all," I thought. As I was walking away the second time, I sensed the clear prompting of the Lord to go pray again. This time the guy was some distance from us and to go back was going to be embarrassing. But God was in this. My spirit discerned the numinous, ever so faintly. I gathered my courage and went to him to pray one more time. He let me pray, and to my amazement this time when he opened his eyes—I will never forget the look on his face—he could see out of his blind eye! The presence is the power.

That is what I learned in MC 510.

ൠ

NOTES:

[1] C. Peter Wagner, *The Third Wave of the Holy Spirit*, Ann Arbor, MI, Servant Books, 1988, p. 25

[2] The letters MC stood for "Mission Class" since the course was offered through the School of World Mission, and 510 was the course number.

[3] Wagner, *How to Have a Healing Ministry*, p. 49

[4] *Fire in the Fireplace*, Downers Grove, IL, InterVarsity, pp. 206ff.

[5] James R. Coggins and Paul G. Hiebert, *Wonders and the Word, An Examination of Issues Raised by John Wimber and the Vineyard Movement*, Winnipeg, MB, Canada, Kindred Press, 1989, p. 20

[6] Wayne Grudem, *Power & Truth: AVC Position Paper #4*, 1993, p. 31

[7] Hummel, *Fire in the Fireplace,* p. 203

[8] James Kallas, *Jesus and the Power of Satan*, Philadelphia, PA, Westminster, 1968; *The Real Satan*, Minneapolis, MN, Augsburg Pub. House, 1975

[9] Pp. 95-6

[10] See *Power Encounters Among Christians in the Western World*, ed. Kevin Springer, San Francisco, Harper & Row, 1988

[11] See Charles H. Kraft, *Christianity with Power: Your Worldview and Your Experience of the Supernatural,* Ann Arbor, MI, Vine Books, 1989

[12] "The Flaw of the Excluded Middle," *Missiology: An International Review*, vol. 10, no. 1, January, 1982, pp. 35-47

[13] Wagner has described this experience in a number of places, e.g., *How to Have a Healing Ministry*, pp. 37-64.

[14] Ann Arbor, MI, Servant Pub., 1989

[15] "MC 510: A Look Inside, Part I" July, 1985; "MC 510: A Look Inside, Part II," September/October, 1985

[16] Wheaton, IL, Christian Life Missions, 1983

[17] C. Peter Wagner, *The Third Wave of the Holy Spirit*

[18] Stanley M. Burgess, Gary McGee and Patrick Alexander, eds., *Dictionary of Pentecostal and Charismatic Movements*, Grand Rapids, Zondervan, 1988, p. 820

[19] *Power Evangelism*, p. 122; this is something of an inconsistency in Wimber because he, at times, disassociated himself from the Third Wave label but here identified with it.

[20] John Wimber with Kevin Springer, "John Wimber Calls it Power Evangelism," *Charisma*, September, 1985, p. 35

[21] *Idid.,* p. 16

[22] It has been debated whether what has been called in the Pentecostal tradition a word of knowledge is what the apostle Paul meant by that term in 1 Corinthians 12.8. It is possible that the gift he was referring to was the ability to receive insight into the meaning of Scripture. This is common during preaching when, in a moment, the preacher suddenly and spontaneously receives insight from the Holy Spirit as to the meaning or application of a passage (cf. Gordon D. Fee, *The First Epistle to the Corinthians*, Grand Rapids, MI, Eerdmans, *ad. loc. 1987*) If this is true then what is currently called a word of knowledge would then be a subset of the gift of prophecy, or perhaps referred to as "a revelation" (1 Corinthians 14.30).

[23] Ed. Lewis B. Smedes, Pasadena, CA, Fuller Theological Seminary, 1987

[24] Cf. Wayne Grudem, *Power and Truth*, p. 31

# CHAPTER EIGHT

# LAUNCHING THE MOVEMENT 1984-1987

# LAUNCHING THE MOVEMENT
# 1984-1987

## 1984

As was said earlier, a loose association of Vineyard churches had been formed by this time. Due to the visibility of the MC 510 course and the hunger of the church all around the world, John Wimber's materials, in the areas of both church renewal and church planting, were increasingly in demand from VMI. The tape sets and accompanying booklets, especially on subjects such as healing, spiritual gifts, and deliverance, became crucial to sowing these things back into the church.

These were some of the more important tape sets:

- Healing I-IV
- Spiritual Gifts
- Spiritual Warfare
- Kingdom of God I-II

"The Healing I" seminar has been taught so often by so many that it is now common property in the church at large. Each one who taught it personalized it and tweaked it, but it was still basically John's material. Ken Blue taught it so many times he finally published it![1]

Three important seminars were offered during this year that would become standard tape sets for the Vineyard.

### WIMBER ON WAGNER

Called "Wimber on Wagner" the pastors' conference for '84 was held in September in Costa Mesa. Peter Wagner presented his basic church growth concepts from the standpoint of a theoretician, and John Wimber commented on each point as a practitioner. I have referred to this material many times over the years.

### CHURCH PLANTING

John Wimber and Bob Fulton put on a seminar in Anaheim to teach and empower all the would-be church planters who had presented themselves to the Vineyard.[2] I was one of the 150 present and took notes that I would soon refer to like a textbook. The main approach was to move to a city, get a job (the Vineyard offered help with moving expenses), and share the gospel via power evangelism. When people got saved, they were to be gathered into small groups. As previously stated, when two or three kinship groups were gathered, a Sunday night service was started. When that service reached 50-100 adults, it was time to move to Sunday mornings.

This is exactly how my wife Betsy and I started our church in the Midwest. When she was eight months pregnant, we moved from California with our two-year-old son. After a rocky start with an existing church, I found a job at a factory, and Bets started a day-care business out of our apartment. No one seemed to respond to the gospel, and we became desperate. One day I almost gave up and didn't want to get out of bed, but my blessed wife pulled my legs onto the floor and said, "You are going to work!"

Only a few weeks later the machinist at the factory walked by my station, and I heard the words "carpal tunnel" in my head. I went up to him and asked what it meant. He explained that it was a wrist ailment and that he was going to have an operation for it the following week. Clueing in now, I asked his permission and mumbled a simple prayer for healing over the roar of the machinery. He was completely healed and did not need the operation. I led him to the Lord the next week, and that night he went home and led his girlfriend to the Lord praying the same prayer I had prayed. Adding his brother and sister-in-law and another young man from the factory, we started the small group that eventually became our church.

WORSHIP

Besides healing, worship has been the biggest contribution the Vineyard has made to the church. Vineyard worship songs are sung all over the world.

The Lord had spoken to John in a vision in 1978 telling him that a fresh, new worship was coming.[3] In the vision John saw many garage bands made up of amateur musicians. God would sovereignly use rock 'n roll, John was told, and he was going to raise up garage band musicians to touch the heart of the generation that had cut its teeth on rock music.

It is not surprising, then, that Wimber's church was birthed in a revival of worship. Jack Little reported to me that very early, shortly after the forming of VMI, a tape of John's church in worship was widely distributed and used by the Lord to spread the new worship fire. This homemade tape was the precursor of worship tapes that would soon be sent throughout the world.

The theology, values and philosophy of Vineyard worship were first introduced publicly at a conference I attended in 1984 in Los Osos, California. Carl Tuttle put together the initial set of notes. Many worship leaders took those notes back home and began to do with them what had been done with Wimber's "Healing I" notes.

## THE BASIC VALUES OF VINEYARD WORSHIP

According to the Scriptures, worship is the church's highest priority and is a voluntary offering to God. In 1984 worship was returning to those roots, being redefined to mean "time devoted to telling God that we love him." Worship is for God! He is an audience of one, and the congregation is the choir. Most of the words to our songs, therefore, were, and still are, written *to* God and not about him.

Worship involves the whole body. Carl graphed worship expressions on a chart with the quiet activities such as kneeling and meditating on one side, singing and lifting hands in the middle, and shouting and dancing on the other. In a Vineyard service, depending on what God was doing at that moment, one could be kneeling, another lying prostrate, yet another speaking silently in tongues. In the context of celebration, one could be dancing, another clapping. Whatever God is leading each to do is okay as long as it is a "string in tune."

The worshipper is to come with an expectation of meeting God. The number one goal in worship on God's end is to receive our love; on our end it is to become, intellectually and experientially, intimate with God.

## THE PHASES OF WORSHIP

To get refreshing water out of a garden hose in the summer, we let the stream run awhile until the hose has been cleared of warm, stagnant water. So it is in worship: intimacy with God is not achieved instantly. John taught that there were five basic phases in worship.[4]

THE CALL TO WORSHIP: Songs like "Come Let Us Worship and Bow Down" or "Don't You Know It's Time to Praise the Lord?" call the body to worship.

ENGAGEMENT: In this phase, we connect personally with God through expressions of love, adoration, praise, thanksgiving, confession, intercession, petition—all dynamics of prayer interlocked with worship.

EXPRESSION: As our worship becomes more intimate we begin to express ourselves more and more freely to God. Our minds spin off into intimate meditations of the wonder of him.

VISITATION: Expression moves to a zenith where God begins to respond to us, to our prayers and to our worship. His visitation is a by-product of worship.

GIVING: The natural next phase is to make ourselves living sacrifices by offering up our time, energy and resources to God as an act of worship. Taking the offering after worship in a service is an extension of our worship.

## OTHER SIGNIFICANT EVENTS IN 1984

For almost two years *First Fruits* magazine did double duty serving both the renewal and church planting arenas. Then two magazines, *Equipping the Saints* and *The Vineyard Newsletter*, were developed to replace it (more below). In its day, *First Fruits* was a great piece that published some classic articles articulating the genetic code of the Vineyard and chronicling early church planting efforts.

A number of things happened in 1984 that were inklings of things to come. In 12 months the church in Anaheim added

133

1,500 new people and reached an average attendance of 6,000 per Sunday. But also in that year they gave away over 600 people to Bob and Penny Fulton to start a Vineyard in Yorba Linda. The thinking was that this church would accommodate those who had participated from the beginning, but who did not want to drive to Anaheim.[5] The agony of being separated from long-standing friends had an affect on Carol Wimber that she had not anticipated.

She discovered a lump on her breast and later realized that it was related to the straining of these relationships. She went through a season of emotional healing, and the lump disappeared. This experience launched John and Carol into a deeper level of healing for the emotionally wounded.

Other church planting efforts this year would see Kenn and Joanie Gulliksen starting the Vineyard in Framingham, Massachusetts, Lance and Cheryl Pittluck the Vineyard at Rockville Center in New York City, and Steve and Janie Sjogren planting what is now the Vineyard Community Church on the north side of Cincinnati, Ohio.

One final note is that God spoke to John during this year that He was going to begin to judge leaders in the church in the United States.[6] While John didn't understand it at the time, God showed both him and Carol that many US pastors were involved in immorality, pornography and all kinds of sexual sin. He was shortly going to judge it, and told John and Carol to watch their private lives and to exhort the pastors under their care to do the same. In just a few short years the Bakker/Swaggart affairs would come out into the open.

# 1985

ASSOCIATE SEMINARS

The speaking invitations were far too many now for John to handle alone, and many seminars by his associates were being held. While some began as early as 1982-84, it was in 1985 that the number of associate seminars began to explode. Here are some of those listed in *First Fruits* magazine who did a lot of traveling for the Vineyard during this period:

- John McClure
- Blaine Cook
- Todd Hunter
- Brent Rue
- Jack Little
- Kenn Gulliksen
- Randy Larson
- Lance Pittluck
- Randy Clark
- Gary Weins

## TODD HUNTER, "HEALING I," INDIANAPOLIS, 1985

I attended an associate seminar with Todd Hunter on the south side of Indianapolis in 1985. Everything was going along fine until Todd, using the discipleship loop, asked me to do the last session. Not only had I never led a Vineyard seminar before, but my two kids were both at home with chicken pox. Because of my understanding of the kingdom as already/not yet, however, I had no tension with teaching healing when my kids were sick. In fear and trepidation I decided to go for it. I personalized Wimber's "Healing I," lecture 4, and made it through okay. But then it was clinic time.

I invited the Holy Spirit to come and waited for what seemed like hours. Nothing. I was a rookie and felt completely helpless. I didn't know then that the veterans often felt the same way and that we only "sort of" get over that feeling. But then, suddenly, I heard myself say, "Speak in tongues!" Surprised, I wondered why I said that, but before I could react, people began to riffle out in tongues. Some fell on the floor. Demons began to manifest in people (in church no less), and the room took on the general feel of a battlefield. I didn't know what to do next, so I walked around on the stage until I felt foolish and stepped down, thus ending my first Vineyard seminar. I've done many since then, but I will never forget that first one.

## OTHER EVENTS IN 1985

Church planting really accelerated during 1985. As stated earlier, at the beginning of that year there were 70 Vineyards; by its end there were 139, some of them overseas. Since Bob Fulton had gone to pastor the church in Yorba Linda, the church-planting arm of the Vineyard was turned over to Dave Taylor. It was Dave who commissioned my wife and me to plant in the Midwest.

## WIMBER'S ANGINA

The explosion of church growth added to the stress that was already on Wimber. While he was in England in '85, it came out that he had been having angina pains off and on since 1983.[7] He was overweight and overworked, and he was now the president of three organizations—a growing church, an exploding renewal organization, and a burgeoning church planting movement. One wonders how he did it at all.

Tests showed that his heart had a small blockage in one artery and that he had three small duodenal ulcers. Doctors put him on blood pressure medication, started him on an exercise program, regulated his eating, and tried to get him to cut back from his exhausting conference schedule. But it was to no avail. He was out forty weeks in 1985.[8]

I have heard John say that for a number of years during this period he felt that he could have died at any minute. Sometimes he thought he was going to fall over while he was speaking. The fact that men in Wimber's family tended to die before the age of fifty exacerbated this concern. He felt his days were numbered, and he became emotionally distant from the church and from the movement. Attendance in the church fell 30% during those years, the first drop in their history.

During 1985, John taught about 100 messages on prayer. He was trying to birth prayer in the church, but it never seemed to take. The church in Anaheim had become prideful and was riding on the grace of God. He knew during those years that they were charging on someone else's credit card (i.e., somebody out there was praying!) and that at some point God was going to show up at their door to collect the bill.[9]

## "TEACH US TO PRAY," SAN DIEGO, SEPTEMBER 1985

John's emphasis on prayer that year was evidenced in the annual pastors' conference. Overall, this was a good conference (God sure met me there), but it will be remembered in the movement more for the line that was drawn in the sand than for the content of the week.

In the workshop that I attended, the teaching pastor shared a fascinating story about being influenced by the revival in South America, where certain men would go lock themselves in a room to fast and pray until the demon spirits who controlled the area would reveal themselves. At that point they would duke it out with the demons in prayer until the victory was achieved. They then went out and preached with great results.

This Vineyard pastor then shared how he and his elders had done the same thing: they had locked themselves in a hotel room and fasted and prayed. At some point (a week or so later as I recall) a major demon presented itself to challenge them. They were literally thrown around the room, but felt they had had a breakthrough. Before long the drug traffic in their city took a severe blow, and they saw results in the church. As might be expected, those of us who were at the workshop were excited about the possibilities in what he was saying. We had no idea that John Wimber did not know what was being shared, and we had no idea how he felt about it.

The next plenary session we came ready to plod through our notes on prayer, but John came out with both barrels blazing. We knew in about thirty seconds how he felt about it! He exhorted with some volume that there was no biblical model for taking on demons over areas.[10] The model we had been given was for casting out demons that were either afflicting or inhabiting people. In regards to Satan he showed us that not even the archangel Michael spoke to him; rather he said, "The Lord rebuke you" (Jude 9).

137

The Vineyard had already caused a stir in what was called spiritual warfare by teaching that Christians can be "demonized." Many, such as those in Calvary Chapel churches, were theologically opposed to this concept, but even though the biblical data is inconclusive, John had developed an implicit case for it in Scripture.[11] Experientially, though, demonic spirits had been manifesting and been cast out of Christians since the beginning of the Vineyard.

This issue of speaking to principalities and powers, however, was different. John felt strongly that the "strong man" had already been bound in the ministry of Jesus; we have now been commissioned to go out and plunder his house. We do spiritual warfare over areas by winning the lost, healing the sick, casting out demons, and caring for the poor. There is no need, nor is there a model, for praying against regional powers.

At this point, Wimber's relationship with Peter Wagner began to cool off, not because of a broken fellowship, but because they came to a collegial divide. They had fundamental disagreements over two key areas. The *first* was the issue of spiritual gifts. Wagner had slightly different views and language than did Wimber.

The *second*, and the greater issue between them, would come over praying against territorial spirits (or what became known as "strategic level spiritual warfare"). Wagner is fascinated by anything that makes the church grow, and since he had been a missionary in Latin America, he was intrigued by these South American men who were having such amazing results praying this way. Wimber, however, had pastoral responsibility over a young movement, and he was deeply concerned over the serious nature of immature believers taking on powerful demons in their innocent presumption without even implicit biblical ground. While Wagner went on to do extensive research in this area and write several books on the subject,[12] Wimber steered the Vineyard away from it.

## "CHURCH GROWTH LEADERSHIP AND THE KINGDOM OF GOD IN THE '90s," ASHLAND, OHIO, 1985

Wimber had taught his pastors how to plant churches and develop a five-year plan. Out of his interaction with Peter Wagner on church growth principles, he now began to focus on leadership issues in a new seminar that he did with Wagner in conjunction with Don Williams and John White.

I went to this conference when it was held in Ashland, Ohio. Leaders from churches all over the Midwest were there. One was a young man named Steve Nicholson, senior pastor of Christ Church in Evanston, Illinois. When I first saw Steve, he was on the floor, "resting" in the Spirit, and I remember wondering what God was doing in his life. Steve would go on to lead his independent church into association with the Vineyard and would, himself, become the American task force leader for church planting in AVC. He would also become a good friend and mentor to me. I look back at some of these early conferences and see the hand of God drawing us all together.

Here's a final note on this year: at this point two new companies were started that have had a tremendous ministry to the body of Christ.

*Mercy Media* was started under the leadership of Steve Zarit to handle the production of teaching materials.

*Mercy Records* was started under the leadership of Randy Rigby to produce the worship music for the new movement. God had put a divine deposit on Vineyard worship, and *Mercy Records* would go on to produce many tapes and eventually CDs that would go all over the world.

Up to this point VMI had produced two tapes, *All the Earth Shall Worship* and *He's Worthy to Be Praised*. *Mercy Records* now produced two more, *Just Like You Promised* and *You Are Here*.

# 1986

## CHURCH PLANTING

In 1986 the Vineyard grew to about 200 churches. New starts numbered 64, but 20 were closed, the latter comprised mostly of church plants.

Todd Hunter, still in Wheeling, was intrigued by this and decided to conduct a survey of church planters who had been successful and those who had failed. He wanted to see if there were any common denominators. He started by informally talking to pastors but could not get any solid data. He eventually tried a more scientific approach and developed a survey based on the writings of Donald McGavran and Peter Wagner. He also drew from one of Wimber's lectures in the church-planting seminar called "A Church Planter's Profile." He only surveyed factors related to the church planter and his family and did not try to develop a church profile.

Todd conducted the first part of the survey in early 1986 and started with 22 church plants that had failed. His results were passed out at the AVC Council meeting in December. In the winter of 1987 he conducted the second part of the survey by asking 20 successful church planters the same questions. These results were handed out at the AVC board meeting in April of 1987. The spring 1988 issue of *Equipping the Saints* published the results called "Successful Pastors: Are They Really Different?" The survey was helpful in years to follow as the movement endeavored to become better at selecting church planters and coaching church plants.

Characteristics of **unsuccessful** pastors rated in order of importance:

- They do not have the ability to identify, recruit, train, deploy, monitor, feed, and reproduce workers and leaders (95%).
- They use ineffective methods of evangelism, and are unwilling to be ruthless at evaluating the results of those methods (77%).
- They have no clear plan and goals, which results in working hard at the wrong things or lack of focus (77%).
- They have no proven track record under supervision or authority (73%).
- They emphasize being a nurturer/enabler/facilitator rather than an assertive leader and equipper (68%).
- They fail to adequately research and understand the community in which they try to build a church (64%).
- They have no local or extra-local support and encouragement

from other leaders (64%).
- They are unsure about the Holy Spirit's leading for the church (59%).
- They are not willing to take responsibility for church growth (55%).
- They have ego strength problems; success or failure of the church is tied to the planter's self-image (55 %).
- They are unsure of their call (50%).

Characteristics of **successful** pastors rated in order of importance:
- They are hard workers (100%).
- They have a proven track record under supervision or authority (95%).
- They are sure of their call (95%).
- They have an attitude of optimism and faith (95%).
- They have good social skills, are friendly, easily liked (95%).
- They take responsibility for church growth (95%).
- They, both husband and wife, feel called to the church (90%).
- They hold values, priorities, and philosophy of the Vineyard (90%).
- They have indigenous or extra-local support from other leaders (80%).
- They have a strong marriage (80%).

OTHER SIGNIFICANT EVENTS DURING 1986

By July the Vineyard had grown to 233 churches with the pastors' conference being attended by 1200 adults and 600 children.[13]

Wimber and Springer's book *Power Evangelism* came out. Its initial printing of 20,000 copies was sold out in a week, and it was soon translated into Dutch, Swedish, Norwegian and German. A woman behind the iron curtain translated it into Czech and hand typed copies for underground circulation in the churches.[14]

*First Fruits* gave way to two new publications:
- *Equipping the Saints*, edited by Kevin Springer, would

now handle the renewal side of the ministry and would lead the charge until it ran its course in 1996.

- *The Vineyard Newsletter*, edited by Suzanne Springer, was started to feed the church-planting arm in the Vineyard. Al though it only lasted about two years, this great magazine contained some priceless articles and council for church planters. Its most popular feature was called "Works of the Father" which was a listing of testimonies to the power of God at work in our churches.

Another associate seminar that began to circulate around this time was Lenny and Tracy LaGuardia's *Bringing the Kingdom to the Kids*. Lenny was the children's pastor at Tom Stipe's large Vineyard in Denver and brought a fresh vision for seeing children as equal partners in advancing the kingdom. He traveled all over and sowed this vision around the country.

Jack Deere, then a professor at Dallas Theological Seminary, was introduced at this time to John Wimber through a contact with John White. Jack would eventually change his theology to affirm the present-day ministry of the Holy Spirit and begin to attend the Vineyard in Anaheim. Jack was a theologian and would become a valuable addition to the Vineyard team at a crucial point in its history.

Wimber continued to expand his international ministry doing conferences in Brighton, Wembley, and Harrowgate, England, and Frankfurt, West Germany, where over 1,000 attended. He also went to Auckland, New Zealand, where he and four teams totaling 130 people ministered to over 6,000 "down under." All told, Wimber and his teams did thirteen major conferences in '86 with an attendance exceeding 76,000.[15]

*Mercy Records* produced *Hosanna*.

New tape sets were produced.

- The Gift of Prophecy
- Power Points
- What the Holy Spirit is Saying to the Church Today
- Kinships
- Inner Healing

# 1987

By 1987 John was worn out and began to co-pastor the Anaheim Vineyard with Sam Thompson who was then also the director of AVC. Sam and his wife, Gloria, accented Kenn Gulliksen's original emphasis on love and relationships in the Vineyard and produced a number of tapes called *The Christian Life Series*:

- Communion in Marriage
- Premarital Training
- Developing Family Relationships
- Parents of Teens
- Personal Growth

Under the leadership of Carl Tuttle, who had by then planted a church in Santa Maria, California, the *Worship Resource Center* was started to minister to the growing number of worship leaders in the Vineyard. Joining the Worship Resource Center for an annual fee entitled the subscriber to a quarterly tape of new songs, as well as *Worship Update*, a magazine for worship leaders. As a kick off, they put on a conference called "Worship '87."

In order to nurture the healing ministry, John did a conference called "Healing '87" with Francis MacNutt, a Catholic who was known for his success with "soaking prayer" (i.e., praying for someone continuously for some length of time).

Wimber continued to expand his international ministry going to Belfast, Northern Ireland, and Dublin, Ireland. He also made another trip down under, this time to Canberra, Australia. This connection with Australia would lead to major conferences there that would become the eye of an Australian storm.

Of all the events of this year, however, the exposure of sin was foremost. The Jim and Tammy Bakker scandal followed by the debacle with Jimmy Swaggart the next year brought the moral issues that John and Carol Wimber had seen some years earlier to the surface. God brought judgment in the Vineyard as well. Two of John's key associates were caught in sexual sin, and there was some disagreement over the kind of discipline and restoration process that was needed. This resulted in tension in Anaheim's infrastructure that would surface later.

143

STEVE SJOGREN, SERVANT EVANGELISM, AND THE
SEEKER MOVEMENT IN THE VINEYARD

A significant Vineyard church in Cincinnati had, by 1987, been underway for about two years. Todd Hunter had bought airtime on a Cincinnati radio station. With a band, he traveled over from Wheeling once a month to gather people who had listened to the show. Meanwhile, Steve and Janie Sjogren, from Kenn Gulliksen's Vineyard in California, had recently returned from planting a church in Norway. They were helping a new church near Washington D.C. when Todd convinced them to move to Cincinnati and take the group. Early on Steve and Janie were joined by Dave and Anita Workman. Dave was easy going, a musical and technical genius, and the perfect complement to Steve, a hard-driving but fun-loving evangelist.

Steve tried many things to gather people back then, but one day he took a group out to minister to the poor. Such a sense of God's presence accompanied them into impoverished areas that they began to take out food, and eventually clothes, regularly. Since then, Saturday mornings at the Cinci Vineyard have become sacred as the troops gather to go out. They bought an old bus and renovated it so people could enter the front, select clothes from racks on either side, and grab a bag of groceries on the way out the back. Vineyard workers would share the message of God's love as they helped their guests down the foldout back steps.

Before long Steve began to do other simple acts of kindness for people. He washed cars and windows, raked leaves, and wrapped presents at the mall at Christmas, among other projects. His "Servant Evangelism"[16] turned pew sitters into power evangelists. I was close to Steve in those days, as I was planting my church in Indianapolis around the same time, and remember him telling me stories of God touching lives in a powerful way.

After talking with Steve, I felt God was telling me to start a ministry to the poor too. Todd Hunter's assistant pastor, Fred Grewe, had moved to Indy to help me, and one morning we met to pray about how to minister to the poor. As we prayed, I saw the picture of a house in my mind. Fred said he got the strong impression that we were supposed to find a certain street. We looked on a map, and sure enough, that street was in a poor area. We bought some groceries, found the street and started driving down it from the north. We hadn't gone but a few blocks when I saw the house I had seen in prayer. A couple with a new baby stood on the porch talking about what to do because the young man was out of a job and they had run out of food that morning. God had just started our ministry to the poor.

Within three or four years, Steve's church was busting at the seams. They moved from an old square dance barn, where they had started, to a school. About this time Sjogren began to realize that the non-Christians who had been touched by the servant evangelism projects could not relate well to the Sunday morning services. In an effort to reach them, the church shortened the worship time and began to target these seekers in its messages. They fed their core people into a mid-week service for believers.

This seeker approach was new in the Vineyard. Vineyard services had traditionally been for the saints and not the sinners. But Steve was having so much success with his approach that many Vineyards began to do regular servant evangelism projects, and some began to orient their Sunday morning services to reach seekers as well. This change in philosophy of ministry caused quite a stir in the movement, but eventually leveled out as one of the workable approaches in the system.

145

## NOTES:

[1] *Authority to Heal*, Downers Grove, InterVarsity, 1988

[2] This tape set was originally put out by AVC under the title *Advancing the Kingdom Now* but was later changed to *Church Planting: God's Heart for Expansion.*

[3] This was conveyed to me in a personal conversation with Bob Fulton.

[4] For a summary of these principles see John Wimber, "Worship: Intimacy with God," *Equipping the Saints*, January/February, 1987, Vol. 1 No. 1, pp. 4-5, 13.

[5] Neff, *An Accurate Picture of Vineyard Christian Fellowship, Anaheim, CA*, 1993, p. 11; but cf. John Wimber, *Power Healing* (p. 77) who says that the average attendance during this period was 4,000 and that they sent 600 people to Yorba Linda.

[6] John Wimber, "As I See It," *The Vineyard Newsletter*, Spring 1988, Vol. 3, No. 2, p. 2

[7] John Wimber, *Power Healing*, pp. xv ff.; cf. John Wimber, "In My Opinion," *First Fruits*, July/August 1986, p. 3

[8] Neff, *An Accurate Picture*, p. 11

[9] John Wimber, "Get Ready!" *Equipping the Saints*, Spring 1989, Vol. 3, No. 2, p. 20-21

[10] Unsuspecting listeners to the tape series *Teach Us To Pray* must be surprised when suddenly Wimber comes out so strongly against these things. There is no context for it in the notes.

[11] In 1996 this would again become an issue when Randy Clark, the Vineyard pastor used to spark the Toronto Blessing (see the chapter on this topic), began to develop a relationship with the men in the revival in Argentina. Randy told me that through their South American paradigm they do see biblical data to support strategic level spiritual warfare.

[12] *Wrestling with Dark Angels*, C. Peter Wagner and F. Douglas Pennoyer, eds., Ventura, Regal Books, 1990; *Engaging the Enemy: How to Fight and Defeat Territorial Spirits*, C. Peter Wagner, ed., Ventura, Regal Books, 1991; *Breaking Strongholds in Your City*, Ventura, Regal Books, 1993; *Confronting the Powers*, Ventura, Regal Books, 1996; cf. John Dawson, *Taking Our Cities for God*, Lake Mary, FL, Creation House, 1989; Francis Frangipane, *The Three Battlegrounds*, Cedar Rapids, IA, Arrow Pub., 1989

[13] Notes from Vineyard pastor, Les Yoder, off the internet

[14] *Equipping the Saints*, "Renewal News," January/February, 1987, p. 14

[15] *Equipping the Saints*, "Renewal News," Spring 1988, p. 22
[16] Steve Sjogren has written his ideas in *Conspiracy of Kindness*, Ann Arbor, Servant, 1993.

# CHAPTER NINE

# COMING UNDER SEVERE ATTACK

# COMING UNDER SEVERE ATTACK

## VIA DOLOROSA

Jesus said that whoever would come after him would need to pick up his cross and follow him (Matthew 16:24). It was so with John Wimber. Being a fool for Christ was *via dolorosa*, the way of the cross. John and Carol knew from the beginning that the quest for the radical middle would be fraught with peril. The evangelicals would criticize them for being too Pentecostal and the charismatics would mistake the laid-back style as quenching the Spirit. John knew he was called to be an agent of change and that true pioneers can always be recognized by the knives sticking out their backs.[1]

It had been that way when the Quakers had asked them to leave. It was that way when Calvary asked them to change their name. It was that way when trusted intimates betrayed him and then blamed him for the breech in the relationship.[2] It was that way when people would make threats on John's life. Carol wrote that one time in a restaurant a man who had just come back from a Dave Hunt[3] seminar started screaming at him that he was the antichrist![4]

The very nature of the call of God on the Vineyard opened it up to attack. John would later write that:

*The Vineyard is a church planting movement that actively seeks to discern what God is currently doing wherever we find His working in the Body of Christ. This philosophy of ministry exposes Vineyard churches to many different beliefs from various streams of thought within the church. On the one hand, this keeps us honed, because we are continually driven back to the Word of God as interpreted by the Spirit of God, and to the historic church to ask, "Is this consistent with God's written Word, and its historical expression through the centuries?" On the other hand, this openness can lead to a temporary drifting from the anchor of our historical beliefs and practices, and even a short-term distortion, while the "fresh wind" is sorted through.*[5]

These attacks would stay with John until the day he died. Carol wrote:

*That's how I remember it most of the time. The controversy going on, but John just ignoring it all and not allowing it to slow us down. But sometimes I remember the ache that went along with the lies written about him, when it was impossible to avoid reading them, the misquotes, the misunderstandings, the constant harangue against John by the "Bible Answer Man"[6] on his radio program. It was one thing for me to deal with it when he was young and strong, but as the years of illness came with the painful cancer treatments that left him deaf and with a dry mouth so he could never sing again and the debilitating stroke with the "forever" pain and the loss of his left hand so he couldn't go to the piano and sing songs to Jesus anymore, and the constant dizziness and weakness as his poor used-up body gave out, and still the lies, the misquotes, the meanness by the press, the jealousy, the never-ending attacks, were sometimes almost unendurable for me. They were still nipping at his heels when he was too weak to even walk down the hallway without help. I wanted to pick him up in my arms and carry him away to some safe place where he wouldn't hurt anymore. I couldn't do that, of course, but Jesus finally did.*[7]

## THE PUBLIC ATTACKS BEGIN

For the sake of our story I will take this chapter and try to outline the more public criticisms of John Wimber and the Vineyard. As you will recall, when the MC 510 course was eliminated from the catalogue, a Fuller faculty task force published *Ministry and the Miraculous* in which Wimber's ministry had come under attack. The negative criticism did not stop here, however. Over the next years more bad press ensued.

In 1985, Dave Hunt and T.A. McMahon wrote *The Seduction of Christianity: Spiritual Discernment in the Last Days.*[8] In the book the authors attempt to isolate those ministries that have been tainted with what they feel are New Age views and practices. In the chapter on inner healing Hunt and McMahon accuse Wimber of drawing on extra-biblical sources and being influenced by suspect authors like Agnes Sanford and Dennis and Matthew Linn.[9]

Wimber never responded to these allegations, but in his book *Fire in the Fireplace* Charles Hummel has an excellent critique of this chapter from *Seduction.*[10] He points out that the authors base their sweeping conclusions on only a handful of quotes taken out of context. He also accuses Hunt and McMahon of using flawed logic and errant linguistic methodology.

In August of 1986, *Christianity Today* appeared with a weird caricature of Wimber on the cover and a lead article by Tim Stafford entitled, "Testing the Wine from John Wimber's Vineyard."[11] Stafford tried to be objective, but he was not short on giving Wimber's critics space in the article. In response to the question of whether the Vineyard was the latest fad from LA, Stafford writes, "No one can be sure."

Written by scholars, a 1989 book, *Wonders and the Word: An Examination of Issues Raised by John Wimber and the Vineyard Movement* was a more direct attack.[12] One of its editors was Paul Hiebert, the professor from Fuller's School of World Mission who published the article "The Flaw of the Excluded Middle"[13] that Wimber used to support his paradigm shift toward the miraculous in ministry.

## WIMBER REFUSES TO RESPOND TO CRITICISM

Interestingly, Wimber did not respond to any of these public challenges during this period. Some of his critics thought he was hiding and was not open to criticism. These incorrect assessments eventually caused him to write, in *Equipping the Saints,* "Why I Don't Respond to Criticism"[14]

In that article John explained that because of the controversial nature of his ministry and his worldwide visibility, rarely a week went by that he did not receive an article, book, or tape in which he was critiqued. He wrote that he was grateful that the majority were "generous, fair, and helpful." He did, however, receive negative assessments and gave two reasons for not responding to these, one biblical and the other prophetic.[15]

He based his biblical rationale on passages like Matthew 18: 15-17, Galatians 6:1 and 1 Timothy 5:1 which call for one brother to go to another brother when he has something against him. This can be done either in person or by letter but not in a book or magazine or on radio or television. John, on this basis, refused to deal with his critics in these arenas.

The prophetic rationale he based on a word given him in 1977 when a woman prophesied that he would have a worldwide ministry and that he was not to defend himself when he was criticized. She said, "Your brother and sister are never your enemies, even when they act like it. Learn to turn the other cheek."

John said in the article that he was not saying that one could not defend himself or herself when attacked. Indeed, the Bible is full of examples of God's people doing so. It is just that in his case, he explained, God told him not to, even though his personality was such that he liked to "jump into a good scrap."

Choosing not to defend himself against attack did not preclude addressing valid constructive criticism, however. John related that he had benefited greatly from helpful correction.

It should be noted that at the time when some of these criticisms were being leveled, the Charismatic element of the church at large was being judged. In 1987, the year that *Ministry and the Miraculous* was published, the scandal involving Jim and Tammy Bakker came into the open. It was a time when John, I'm sure, would have wanted to defend himself against false accusation. I am sure that the passive objector stance of his Quaker heritage was a factor in his non-retaliatory philosophy.

THE QUEST FOR THE RADICAL MIDDLE

From Carol Wimber's perspective, they were, from the beginning, working against time. She writes:

*It was my understanding (from God) that we would have enough grace to do the job God gave us to do, and no more. Therefore, if we stopped to defend ourselves or fight back, we wouldn't have enough grace to finish the race. We would get bogged down forever explaining and defending. Consequently, there was the sense of fixing our eyes on Jesus...with blinders on so that we wouldn't get distracted and stop because of all the hassle we were causing the church.*[16]

Before long, however, issues of such a serious nature were raised that John had no choice but to respond. His defenses are published by AVC as a series of position papers. At the time of this writing (1996) there are five of them with the first being John's rationale for changing his "no response" policy. I will briefly give the history of these attacks and the various apologies that were penned by John's defenders.

## THE BRIEFING, 1990

In March of 1990 I had the privilege of being with John and a team from VMI during a four-day Sydney, Australia, conference called *What the Holy Spirit is Saying to the Church Today*. John had been invited by a large group of evangelical churches from Sydney who valued his ministry. Not all were so excited, however.

John became aware before the conference started that a group of men were going to attend who were hostile toward the Vineyard.[17] Furthermore, these men wanted to meet with John up-front. Compliant with their request, on the day before the conference John, his new associate Jack Deere and Paul Cain, a prophetic minister, met with Philip Jensen, pastor of St. Matthias Anglican Church in Sydney, John Woodhouse and David Cook. What John, Jack and Paul assumed would be a discussion of their theological differences, was rather an attack. The meeting began with the Australians saying, "We do not want you here. We would like you to go back home."[18] Deere thinks that Jensen had come to the conclusion that Wimber was a deceived person before talking with him, so there was no point in dialogue

The tenor during the meeting carried over into the conference with these men looking for ammunition against the Vineyard. In one of Deere's workshops, he had a caustic encounter with a man named Graham Bannister, who demanded his time, broke his word about off-the-record comments, and was rude and belligerent during the presentation.

The next month there appeared a double issue of a journal, *The Briefing,* produced by Philip Jensen's church.[19] On the basis of Paul's prayer in Galatians 1:8 that those who preached a different gospel be "eternally condemned" (NIV), and believing Wimber and his associates to be deceived, the authors openly wrote that they wished Wimber *et. al.* would go to hell (!).[20] As well as other allegations *The Briefing* proceeded to accuse John, Jack, Paul and others of lying, being double-tongued, devaluing the Bible, misconstruing key biblical texts and blasphemy by "demanding" the Holy Spirit to come. John had been attacked before but never as seriously as this. Church leaders began to ask John for some kind of response because the confidence of the people in Australia had been severely damaged.

## "WHY I RESPOND TO CRITICISM"[21]

In May of 1992, AVC published *Why I Respond to Criticism,* John's explanation of why he now would defend himself in certain situations after having said in 1988 that he would not do so. He confessed that although he held the prophetic word he received in 1977 as still valid, he came to believe that the application of this word had changed. In regard to the prophetic word, John thought that the Lord was saying that while the cheek must still be turned to personal attack, it is important that the message be clarified and defended against unjust criticism to prevent people from being confused. In regard to the biblical texts, John saw that some occasions warrant—even require—a public response.

John said that as a general rule, public response is appropriate when attempts at personal reconciliation have failed and the false criticism meets these criteria:

- It is believed by a significant number of Christians.
- It seriously misrepresents Vineyard views and practices.
- It hinders significantly the work of God.

## "THE VINEYARD'S RESPONSE TO THE BRIEFING," MAY 1992[22]

Coinciding with Wimber's position paper, Jack Deere published his response to the accusations in Australia. He defends not only the attacks against Wimber but also the serious accusations leveled against his own integrity. Dr. Deere writes that there were four major issues on the table.

- *Continuing revelation*: The authors of *The Briefing* interpreted any incident of receiving a "word" from the Lord in a form other than through the written pages of the Bible to be a rejection of what they called "the sufficiency of Scripture."
- *The use of Scripture*: According to *The Briefing*, any interpretation of Scripture that allowed for the possibility of God's gifts being in operation today was a false interpretation.
- *Whether any real healings take place in Vineyard meetings*
- *Whether Christians can be demonized*

*The Briefing* also pointed out that the Vineyard song list for the conference was short on songs about the cross. They also pointed out that John Wimber did not make the substitutionary atonement clear enough in his evangelistic appeal on the Thursday night evangelistic meeting. *The Briefing* concluded, therefore, that Wimber did not value the atonement.

Deere points out what he thinks were four errors in the methodology used by *The Briefing*.

- The refusal to grant legitimate differences in interpretation.
- The scarcity of appeal to the Scriptures for the contentions and criticisms.

- Basing accusations on summaries of what they heard the Vineyard speakers say rather that using direct quotes.
- The refusal of any of the authors of *The Briefing* to contact Vineyard speakers to ensure that they had represented their views accurately.

Dr. Deere's paper is a thorough refutation of each of these allegations. While he also makes a defense for John's views on the centrality of the cross, the Vineyard did acknowledge the validity of *The Briefing's* observation that the message of the cross was not emphasized enough. Both John and Jack went home and did a teaching series on the subject, even though John had already put out a tape series called "The Cross" and had devoted a whole issue of *Equipping the Saints* to it.[23] John also called the Vineyard's main songwriters together to confess his shortcoming to them and to exhort them to study the cross and to begin to write more songs demonstrating the centrality of the atonement. In both his books *Power Points* (1991) and the revision of *Power Evangelism* (1992) John's high value on the blood of Jesus is very clear.

## THE STANDARD, 1990-91

In May of 1990, John Armstrong, a Baptist General Conference pastor from Wheaton, Illinois, attended a John Wimber conference in the Chicago suburb of Villa Park. Also attending was Wayne Grudem, a professor of theology at Trinity Evangelical Divinity School located in Deerfield, and a member of the Vineyard in Evanston. These two men had radically different responses.

Starting the following October and running for ten months until July of 1991, John Armstrong wrote about John Wimber and the Vineyard in the Baptist General Conference journal called *The Standard*. With the exception of the issue in May of 1991 which listed a few positive aspects to the Vineyard, all the articles were extremely critical. In response, Dr. Grudem, a former member of the Baptist General Conference, penned an article entitled, "The Vineyard and John Wimber: A More Positive View." He sent it to *The Standard,* but they declined to publish it. Rather, the editor, Don Anderson, sent a four-page letter and a thirty-four-page rebuttal to Kevin Springer, the editor of Vineyard's *Equipping the Saints.*

## "THE VINEYARD'S RESPONSE TO THE STANDARD," JUNE 1992

AVC did publish Grudem's article, along with his response to Anderson's rebuttal, as *The Vineyard's Response to The Standard* (Position Paper #3) in June of 1992. Dr. Grudem summarizes Armstrong's criticism as follows:

- The Vineyard does not understand or preach a biblical gospel, or preach the cross of Christ.
- John Wimber, the leader of the Vineyard, refuses to listen to or respond to his critics.
- The Vineyard exalts experience over Scripture and reason.
- It teaches unorthodox doctrine.
- It encourages strange, highly emotional experience in worship.
- It endorses a kind of contemporary prophecy that will lead people astray.
- It overemphasizes encounters with demonic forces.
- Its healing ministry is not effective.

The first part of Grudem's apologetic is a point by point refutation quoting Wimber's own writings. He starts with the most serious charge that Wimber and his movement need to return to the gospel[24] and then moves to the lesser charges. In a style that is gracious yet to the point, Grudem points out with impeccable reasoning that the accusations of *The Standard* are based on inaccurate information and convoluted logic.

Secondly, he expresses dismay at the tone of the articles. He notes that the Baptist General Conference has heretofore not been a polemical, contentious group and laments that he does not know of any denomination within evangelicalism to have issued such a sustained attack on another denomination or organization within Christendom through its official journal.

Thirdly, he believes the articles oppose a genuine and powerful

work of the Holy Spirit in the world today. He cites th
wide impact that Wimber has had, as well as the V
remarkable growth.

After finishing with Armstrong's arguments against the
Vineyard, Grudem then takes up Don Anderson's lengthy rebuttal
of his article that *The Standard* refused to publish. He
categorizes Anderson's charges thus:

- Charges of doctrinal error without any quotations of error
- Charges of doctrinal error by logical deduction instead
  of quotation
- Charges of duplicity against John Wimber
- New charges of heresy against John Wimber
- Rebuttals to Grudem's charges that *The Standard* had been
  inaccurate and misrepresentative.

Grudem takes up each of these issues point by point as well.

1.He begins by noting the methodological error of drawing
conclusions based not on what an author has actually said but on
the basis of what someone had said Wimber had said.

2.The same point was made regarding *The Standard's* use
of "mistaken inference." Because Wimber believes something
*The Standard* doesn't believe (e.g., healing), they concluded
that Wimber does not believe other things *The Standard* does
believe (e.g., the cross). Grudem reduces their logic to the
following syllogism:

- Wimber teaches doctrine A (the cross)
- But *The Standard* disagrees with Wimber's doctrine B (healing)
- Therefore *The Standard* will tell people that Wimber does
  not teach doctrine A (the cross) and will feel justified in
  doing so.

3.After refuting the arguments of both Armstrong and Anderson,
Grudem calls *The Standard* to issue a public retraction and
apology, not only for what they had said, or for the methodology
they used, but for the less-than-Christian tone in which they spoke.

## POWER RELIGION, 1992

In 1992, another book was published severely criticizing John Wimber and the Vineyard. *Power Religion: The Selling Out of the Evangelical Church?* was edited by Michael Scott Horton.[25] While the title of the book has a question mark in it, there was no question mark in the accusations by the three authors, John Armstrong, D.A. Carson, and James M. Boice.

Two of these authors, Carson and Boice, have widespread credibility in the evangelical world, and their writings have significant weight in a large portion of the church. The gravity of these charges called for a rebuttal, so Wayne Grudem once again picked up his pen.

### "POWER & TRUTH: A RESPONSE TO THE CRITIQUES OF VINEYARD TEACHING AND PRACTICE," *MARCH 1993*[26]

Grudem knows each of the authors personally: Armstrong because of their relationship through the Baptist General Conference and previous joust over the Vineyard, Carson because his office as professor of New Testament at Trinity was across the hall from Grudem's, and Boice because of their mutual efforts in connection with the Biblical Council on Inerrancy.

Grudem's overall assessment of the book is that the authors:

*have been uncharacteristically careless and surprisingly inaccurate in gathering and assessing information about the Vineyard movement. All three attribute to Wimber views he does not hold and practices he does not endorse. In addition, I think their exegesis of key Scripture passages has been uncharacteristically insensitive to context, and they have used Scripture to paint a much more negative view of miracles today than the Bible warrants.*[27]

The three authors each wrote a section of the book Dr. Grudem takes up each author's section and critiques it point by point for 63 pages. Grudem belabours his points because of the influence these men have on the church and because their criticisms were, in a sense, a summary of most of what had been said before.

A good rebuttal, therefore, would function as an overall apologetic for the basic criticisms.

## GRUDEM'S CRITIQUE OF D.A. CARSON

*Demonic healings and preaching a false Christ*: Carson accuses the Vineyard of being associated with demonic healings and infers that it preaches a false Jesus on a par with the Mormons, Muslims and Jehovah's Witnesses. Grudem points out that Carson's logic can be reduced to the following:

- False Christs work miracles
- Miracles are occurring in church A
- Therefore I will stay away from church A just to be safe
  (I really couldn't discern the falsehood anyway because I need men like Dr. Carson to discern it for me)

Grudem shows that it is actually Carson's reasoning that is false and that this most serious charge has no foundation whatsoever.

*Not having all the facts*: Carson makes sweeping judgments about the Vineyard but does not quote Wimber or other Vineyard leaders in making these assessments. Neither does he give evidence of having been to a Vineyard church or having talked with any responsible Vineyard leader. Grudem takes each allegation and shows from Vineyard writings that the charges are unfounded.

*No real healings occur in Vineyard meetings*: In regard to the common criticism that no genuine healings occur at Vineyard meetings, Grudem refers the reader to the book *Healing: Fiction, Fantasy, or Fact* by anthropologist David C. Lewis.[28] In 1986 Lewis attended a Wimber conference in Harrogate, England, for the specific purpose of researching all alleged instances of healing. Of 862 cases of prayer for physical healing, 32% (279) reported a great deal of healing or total healing. Another 26% (222) reported a fair amount of healing. Several case studies are presented with medical verification.

*The Vineyard makes too much of the miracles of Jesus*: Dr. Carson, being a non-cessationist, accepts miracles today, but he is not comfortable with the emphasis he thinks the Vineyard puts on them. His response is to downplay their role in New Testament evangelism and church-life. Grudem takes up each of the passages used here and challenges Dr. Carson's exegesis.

In the end he says,

> *Perhaps Dr. Carson and I have a difference on whether Christians ought to seek miraculous answers to prayer today. But even if we do, it would seem that he needs some Scripture passages saying that believers should not seek them today before he gives such a negative overview of their use in Scripture. Whether he intends it or not, I think the overall force of his article will discourage Christians from seeking miraculous answers to prayer today—it will not increase their faith.*[29]

Grudem says that it is not enough to believe that God worked in the past. The Scriptures clearly imply that God wants to work in the present as well.

*The best conversion is one that is not associated with the miraculous:* Grudem begins this section by evaluating Carson's assertion that the best conversion is one that is not accompanied by signs and wonders, because it is accompanied by a more pure faith. Grudem says that the New Testament does not bear this out; the pattern in the early church is to preach the gospel with signs and wonders following.

He wonders, given Dr. Carson's narrow perspective, whether any denomination or movement could do it "right." Grudem feels that Carson is putting the Vineyard in a no-win situation:

> *If people in the Vineyard take care to compile and report what God is doing among them, he says that they are exaggerating and distorting what is happening. If they don't report what is happening then someone would quickly criticize them for giving no evidence and showing no results for their views.*[30]

### GRUDEM'S CRITIQUE OF JAMES MONTGOMERY BOICE

*Doctrinal concerns:* After clearing up some incorrect facts Boice had written about the Vineyard, Grudem begins to address the more serious issue of misconstruing Vineyard doctrine. Implicit in Boice's arguments is that the Vineyard is a false religion and should be avoided. Boice writes that Wimber was preaching a message of signs and neglecting the gospel. Nothing could be further from the truth, and Grudem proves this by quoting the source. Wimber's motive had always been to make the presentation of the gospel more effective by including the possibility of the miraculous. He had *never* taught that miracles save. He wrote in *Power Evangelism*, "Signs and wonders do not save; only Jesus and his substitutionary work on the cross saves."[31]

*Downplaying the role of suffering*: Boice also asserts that Wimber downplayed the role of suffering in the Christian's life. This too is an error as Dr. Grudem shows from Wimber's writings and Vineyard publications. Wimber affirmed that the kingdom is both already and not yet. It is a question of which aspect is to be our starting point for ministry. Boice seems to clearly default to the not yet; Wimber, to the already. It would seem that, given the New Testament evidence, the burden of proof falls on Dr. Boice's shoulders because the New Testament is full of miracles accompanying the preaching the gospel.[32]

*The role of miracles in the New Testament and giving glory to the Holy Spirit*: Dr. Boice writes that "a desire for further (i.e., present day) signs and wonders is sinful and unbelieving."[33] Grudem takes up this premise and challenges it biblically saying that if this is true then it is hard to explain the activity of the early church where they actually prayed for God to stretch out his hand to perform miraculous signs and wonders (Acts 4:30). As to the criticism that the Vineyard glorifies the Holy Spirit, Grudem is puzzled. Is not the Holy Spirit fully God, and has not the church throughout the ages glorified him in the historic creeds? While conceding that the Spirit's role is to glorify Jesus, it is pointed out that it is also one of the Spirit's jobs in the age of the church to manifest his (the Holy Spirit's) presence in order to make God more fully known. In this the Spirit is glorified in the present age.

*Forcing the reader to make either/or choices the Bible is not asking us to make*: To the assertion that the Spirit's

163

weapon is not additional revelation, nor power encounters, but only Scripture, Grudem asks, "But why can't the Holy Spirit use both Scripture, *and* gifts of prophecy *and* the authority to cast out demons?"[34]

*The miraculous cheapens the gospel*: Boice says that preaching the miraculous cheapens the gospel by "reducing its promises to shrinking goiters, straightening backs, and lengthening legs." To this Grudem points out that the neither the Bible nor the Vineyard pits the new birth against healing, as if one had to choose. Is not the biblical position to win the lost *and* heal the sick *and* feed the poor? Are these not all part of destroying the works of the devil (1 John 3:8)?

*Concluding concerns about Dr. Boice's section*: Dr. Grudem affirms that he and Dr. Boice have differing interpretations of Scripture at key points. He also realizes that the same was true about Wimber's theology in regards to the emphasis on miracles today, the value of miracles in evangelism, and the nature and use of spiritual gifts. This kind of dialogue is healthy, says Grudem, and is to be expected within the Christian community.

The main concern, however, is not over the validity of different interpretations of Scripture but over the serious charges of false teaching brought forth without proper documentation. This is a grave and troubling error and Grudem asks if Dr. Boice would want his treatment of John Wimber to be used as a model for Christians to follow when they speak and write about those with whom they disagree.

### GRUDEM'S CRITIQUE OF JOHN H. ARMSTRONG

In regard to the section by John Armstrong, Grudem says that after reading early proofs of the book he noted that Armstrong's writing was a rehash of his early criticisms in *The Standard* (to which Grudem had already responded). Grudem wrote him to point this out. When the book came out, Armstrong had abandoned his older arguments for new ones. Unfortunately he had retained the shoddy methodology. He quotes non-Vineyard sources on Vineyard doctrine and continues to make inaccurate statements about what Wimber believed. One wonders why he doesn't just read Wimber's books. Grudem is puzzled why Armstrong has continued his apparent crusade to prove that the Vineyard teaches things it does not teach.

*Grudem's conclusions on both* Power Religion *and* The Standard: Grudem sums up his arguments by counting 38 negative criticisms in both *Power Religion* and *The Standard*. His two position papers see him taking on each of these points showing that they are based on different interpretations of Scripture and inaccurate information.

He pauses here and asks a question that is actually a powerful indictment on the "edge" that he discerns in these writings. In asking what the real motive is for this vendetta, he wonders if it doesn't come from a desire to see the Vineyard become quiet and go away.

*If that happened, if the Vineyard just stopped teaching and doing these things, then no one would say that it is proud or that it distorts stories of miracles, or that it doesn't emphasize suffering enough, or that it is argumentative or power hungry, or that it preaches miracles instead of the gospel, or any of the things that have been said, because then it would simply be like the rest of Evangelicalism, not only in doctrine but also in practice. Then it would not be different, and there would be no cause for alarm.[35]*

Grudem thinks (as did Wimber) that constructive criticism of the Vineyard is healthy, but says that before it can receive the positive input it needs from the Christian community, "the kind of misrepresentation found in *Power Religion* has to come to an end."

## CHARISMATIC CHAOS, 1992

John F. MacArthur Jr. began his attack on the Charismatic element in the church in 1978 with his book *The Charismatics*.[36] He continued that attack in 1992 with *Charismatic Chaos*[37] in which he is highly critical of John Wimber and the Vineyard. Because of MacArthur's worldwide visibility and influence as

165

one of the chief spokesmen for fundamentalism, AVC commissioned Dr. Rich Nathan, former professor of law at Ohio State University and now pastor of the Vineyard in Columbus, Ohio, to write a rebuttal.

## A RESPONSE TO CHARISMATIC CHAOS[38]

In his introduction to *A Response to Charismatic Chaos*, Dr. Nathan notes that MacArthur's general approach is to consistently exaggerate his opponents' faults by concentrating on the bizarre rather than issues representative of the mainstream of the Charismatic movement. His excessive dogmatism blinds him to the legitimacy of differing biblical viewpoints; it's MacArthur's way or the highway, and those who aren't travelling his road are treated as outsiders needing to be eliminated. With this tone, MacArthur attempts to get the leaven out of the lump and rid the world of the Charismatic disease.

The critique begins with the need to straighten out MacArthur's facts regarding the Vineyard. As with the authors already mentioned, MacArthur is guilty of making judgments without having done his homework.

*The Vineyard has no doctrinal statement*: MacArthur accuses the Vineyard of having no doctrinal statement. At the time the book was published in 1992, all Vineyard pastors had to affirm the Vineyard doctrinal statement. This statement has recently been updated after 2-3 years of work, hardly demonstrating a low value on doctrine. MacArthur also believes that the Vineyard pursues personal piety through ecstatic experiences and devalues the traditional disciplines. This is also untrue. Nathan demonstrates that the classic disciplines have always been a part of the Vineyard genetic code.

*Signs and Wonders save*: MacArthur shares concerns with the previously mentioned critics over Wimber's concept of power evangelism. He accuses Wimber of having taught that signs and wonders save, a fallacy that has already been addressed in the other papers. To make this assertion, MacArthur tries to prove that there is no connection between signs and wonders, and conversion in the New Testament. Nathan shows the data negating this thesis to be so overwhelming that one is left to ponder how an otherwise faithful exegete could become so blinded to the very texts he has spent a lifetime studying. Nathan concludes, "Proclamation *and* demonstration were the normal way that the gospel proceeded in Jesus' ministry and in the ministry of the New Testament church as recorded in the book of Acts."[39]

*Wimber denied the deity of Christ*: Because Wimber tried to wrestle with Jesus' humanity, MacArthur accuses him of having denied the deity of Christ. Rather than reading *Power Points* where Wimber clearly stated his affirmation of the full deity of Christ, MacArthur, again like some of the other authors, derives his views from statements made by Wimber on unpublished tapes (those of us who preach and teach, know about moments when we wish we would have said things another way!). One wonders why he would do this when finely honed theological writings are available for this purpose. Nathan believes he may be misleading his readers to "portray Wimber as a heretic."

*Wimber associated with liberals*: Wimber's ecumenism: Fundamentalism has scorned ecumenism since mid-century, and MacArthur is consistent in his concerns about Wimber's influence among more liberal denominations. Nathan says that Wimber ministered among the Catholics, Lutherans, and Anglicans not because he agreed with every point of doctrine, but because these brothers in Christ want to learn to do what Jesus did. He preached where God told him, as long as he was not asked to compromise his core beliefs.

*The Vineyard's healings are not verifiable*: To this charge Nathan refers the reader to David C. Lewis' book *Healing: Fiction, Fantasy, or Fact* as was mentioned by Grudem in "Position Paper #4."

*The Third Wave is a marketing technique*: MacArthur accuses Wimber of being a Third Wave leader (a label Wimber would vacillate on; see *MC 510: Signs and Wonders and Church Growth*, footnote #16) and says that the movement markets itself as non-Charismatic so it will sell better. Here MacArthur moves from verifiable criterion to judging the heart motives of John Wimber and other Third Wave leaders, very serious ground indeed. Nathan denies such a motive saying, "One of the observations that has been repeatedly made about John Wimber by friends and foes alike, is his unfailing willingness to confess mistakes, to display weakness, to admit to failures, to be, in general, ruthlessly honest, especially about himself."[40]

*Conclusion*: Nathan's basic assessment of *Charismatic Chaos* is that it is written in the same spirit of lovelessness that has characterized fundamentalism since it took on its modern forms in the 1940s. He quotes Carl Henry saying that the fighting spirit of fundamentalism "stands discredited as a perversion of the biblical spirit."[41]

## DOING IT THE RIGHT WAY

It is interesting to note that just prior to this period when Wimber came under attack for heresy and was criticized in public forums for refusing critique, he was invited by **Kenneth Kantzer**, dean of the *Christianity Today Institute*, to take part in a behind-closed-doors meeting with evangelical leaders to explore common ground in regard to the power of the Holy Spirit. In addition to Wimber, Kantzer invited the following leaders to participate:

- **Charles Ryrie**, author of the *Ryrie Study Bible* and professor at Dallas Theological Seminary for 26 years;
- **James I. Packer**, professor of theology at Regent College and senior editor of *Christianity Today* ;
- **Stuart Briscoe**, pastor of Elmbrook Church in Waukesha, Wisconsin, and author of several books;
- **Timothy Warner**, former missionary to Africa and professor of missiology at Trinity Evangelical Divinity School;
- **Russell P. Spittler**, a Pentecostal and professor at Fuller Theological Seminary; and
- Timothy Smith, professor of history at Johns Hopkins University

The meeting convened with Kantzer serving as moderator. The record of their discussion appears as a ten-page article published in the March 19, 1990, issue of *Christianity Today*.[42]

Wimber wrote at the conclusion of the discussion:

*When I first accepted this invitation I had some reservations. I have been misrepresented many times and I was not about to enter a situation that might have contributed to that. But the Lord clearly said that he wanted me here, and now I understand why. We've gone a long way toward clearing up misunderstandings, and that, I think, will be a major contribution to the body of Christ.*[43]

In a conversation I had with John in Australia, he told me that at the conclusion of this meeting the men gathered around, laid hands on him, and prayed for him. He was deeply touched and ministered to. It could be that the Lord gave him this genuine affirmation from major evangelical leaders to get him ready for the storm that was about to begin in Australia.

 C3

NOTES:

[1] "The Leader" by Todd Hunter in *John Wimber*, p. 184

[2] "Coping with Controversy and Suffering," by Carol Wimber in *John Wimber*, ed. David Pytches, Guilford, Surrey England, Eagle Pub. House, 1998, p. 292

[3] See next paragraph

[4] *John Wmiber*, p. 292

[5] *Reflections*, August 1997, p. 1

[6] Hank Hannegraff; see the chapter entitled "The Lions Roar".

[7] *John Wimber*, pp. 296-7

[8] Eugene, OR, Harvest House

[9] "Psychological Salvation," pp. 171-188

[10] "Inner Healing," pp. 159-177; Agnes Sanford is considered by Hunt and McMahon as the primogenitor of the inner healing movement through her book entitled *The Healing Light* (originally published in 1947 by Macalester Park Publishing Co. and reprinted in a revised edition in Watchung, NJ, by Charisma Books in 1972). Hunt and McMahon see *The Healing Light* as the beginning of using the technique of visualization in healing emotional wounds. They also cite the work of Dennis and Matthew Linn, brothers and Catholic Priests who have written on this subject (e.g., *Healing Life's Hurts*, New York,

New York, Paulist Press, 1978).

[11] August 8, pp. 17-22

[12] James R. Coggins and Paul G. Hiebert, ed., Winnipeg, MB, Kindred Press, 1989

[13] *Missiology: An International Review*, vol. 10, no. 1, Jan. 1982, pp. 35-47

[14] Vol. 2, No. 3, Summer 1988, pp. 15-16

[15] John would later add two more reasons: the first is that he avoided using valuable time and energy on anything but the work of the gospel; the other had to do with his personal pacifism resulting from his Quaker roots; cf. John Wimber, *Why I Respond to Criticism*, Vineyard Position Paper #1, May 1992, p. 2, 6.

[16] "Coping with Controversy and Suffering," *John Wimber*, pp. 289-90

[17] Jack Deere, *The Vineyard's Response to The Briefing*, Vineyard Position Paper #2, May 1992, pp. 3-4

[18] *Ibid.*, p. 3

[19] April 24, 1990, pp. 45-46

[20] Deere, p. 1

[21] Vineyard Position Paper #1

[22] Vineyard Position Paper #2

[23] Spring 1988, Vol. 2, No. 2

[24] *Ibid.*, p. 3

[25] Chicago, IL, Moody Press

[26] Wayne Grudem, Vineyard Position Paper #4

[27] Grudem, Position Paper #4, p. 1

[28] London, Hodder and Stoughton, 1989

[29] *Ibid.*, p. 20

[30] *Ibid.*, p. 29

[31] P. 78

[32] Gordon D. Fee would agree. In a recent *Christianity Today* article ("Father, Son, and…" June 17, 1996), Fee says that after a year of research on the doctrine of the Holy Spirit in the Pauline writings that led to his book *God's Empowering Presence* (Peabody, Hendrickson, 1994), it is clear that despite Paul's affirmation of the tension between the kingdom as already and not yet, his understanding of the Christian life is "living the life of heaven *now*" (p. 20).

[33] Grudem, *Power and Truth*, p. 38

[34] *Ibid.*, p. 44

[35] *Ibid.*, p. 61

[36] Grand Rapids, Zondervan

[37] Grand Rapids, Zondervan

[38] Position Paper #5

[39] *Ibid.*, p. 28

[40] *Ibid.*, p. 35

[41] *Ibid.*, p. 37

[42] Pp. 24-35; note that this is the same month that Wimber *et. al.* were under attack in Australia

[43] *Ibid.*, p. 35

# CHAPTER TEN

# INTRODUCING
# THE
# PROPHETS

# INTRODUCING
# THE PROPHETS

## SETTING THE STAGE

The next phase of Vineyard history takes a remarkable turn. A number of things began to happen all at the same time. In 1987 John Wimber began to hear reports that some Vineyard pastors were involved in various kinds of carnality and pride. John went before the Lord about these things and God showed him that the Vineyard was in desperate condition.[1] The nature of some of these things would begin to come out at our pastors' conference in 1988 in Anaheim.

During that conference, John Wimber also had a remarkable encounter with a "prophet" that would embroil the Vineyard in a stormy controversy over the next three years. This event would initiate what has been called the prophetic period in the Vineyard's history.

While the prophetic storm was swirling out among the average Vineyard churches, the greater issues for the movement were taking place behind closed doors at the board level. The decision-making core of the Vineyard was embroiled in a controversy over the direction of the movement. The watershed came at a board meeting in 1991.

I will take the next few chapters and try to outline this incredible period of history, but it should be noted that in doing so, I have had to make a philosophical choice. In the larger scope of things, the prophetic themes would never be incorporated into the movement. Should I then report what happened in brief or in full? In light of the international visibility the events received and the fact that some of the materials that record these events are now out of print, I have decided to write about what happened in some detail. The story that follows is primarily reconstructed from literature disseminating from either Anaheim or Kansas City during this period.

Despite the criticism of those who will say that these chapters seem more like the history of Kansas City Fellowship than the Vineyard, for at least two years their history was integrally related to ours. I know some, perhaps many Vineyard churches weren't swept up into the turbulent waters. What is important though is that John was. Todd Hunter told me that at one point that he was ready to turn the whole movement over to Mike Bickle (soon to be introduced into our story). I don't want us to be guilty of rewriting history according to what we want to remember. The only way I can give someone who wasn't there the flavor of the period is to immerse him or her in it—and that is what I am about to do.

I must confess before going on with the story that these chapters have been the hardest to write. They have been through numerous drafts as I have accumulated more and more information. I have had a few conversations with Mike Bickle who was kind enough to interact with various drafts of the manuscript. I have also talked to Vineyard pastors who were key players during this period. In their responses and counter-responses, I have found clarity to be evasive. In the end I threw up my hands and resolved to do the best I could to report what went on, offering differing perspectives where it seemed appropriate.

It should also be noted that those Vineyard leaders who had to deal with problems related to instances of prophetic abuse have called the credibility of many of these stories into question. Their opinion is that some of the prophecies were bogus and that the stories that were communicated at the popular level were often sensationalized; the real issues never really being dealt with. They also think that when prophecies didn't come true, disclaimers were given to explain the discrepancies. Only as I began to do the research for these chapters was I made aware of a lot of the things that transpired. I was not privy to many of the overt abuses and don't have firsthand knowledge of the inner workings of the prophetic stream. I will tell the stories as they came down to us at the time and will, at times, bring in the perspectives of Vineyard pastors who were closer to the action. Buckle your seatbelts. The turn in our history began at the pastors' conference in Anaheim in the summer of 1988.

## THE PASTORS' CONFERENCE, ANAHEIM, 1988

When we went to Anaheim in 1988, the primary agenda was to consider becoming a denomination. We had called ourselves a movement up until then but all our churches had the name Vineyard in them and we were united under a common set of values, priorities and leadership structures. For all intents and purposes we were a denomination, so why not acknowledge it?

Todd Hunter believes that the pastors who had come out of Calvary Chapel saw the prospect of organizing into a denomination to be a violation of a core Vineyard value. Calvary Chapel has never seen itself as a denomination and the original group of Vineyard pastors had agreed, under John's leadership, that they would not organize for future generations. From John's years as a church growth expert he had seen that churches and movements only retain their vitality for about forty years. An original assumption, then, of those that had founded VMI at Morro Bay had been to stay relational and stay loose. John was now, however, driving autocratically toward what to many felt like institutionalism.

### SHOULD WE BECOME A DENOMINATION?

All week long we debated this and other issues before an open microphone. By Friday, those of us who could were going to sign a statement of commitment to the constitution and bylaws of the new organization. What we didn't know was that on the first day of the conference, Carol Wimber had had a disturbing dream.[2] John later wrote:

*In the dream Carol was on a house with a back porch. She came out through the back porch into the backyard. The house was a comfortable home, and the back porch was substantial, built of stones and mortar. From the backyard she noticed Evan, one of our grandsons, following her. She called Evan out onto the porch to come and see Grandma, and when he came, the porch collapsed. Then she woke up.[3]*

The interpretation of the dream was that Evan represented the Vineyard movement that by that time had grown to 233 churches. The house was the structure that had been built to house the movement (AVC) but the porch was the new part of the structure that we were trying to add on that week - the constitution and bylaws. If we were to call the Vineyard out onto the porch, it would collapse and kill the child.

John at first ignored the word but in his heart he knew it was the Lord. That afternoon he went into the AVC board meeting not intending to share the dream because he felt it would be a misuse of prophecy. During the course of the meeting, however, Bob Craine, one of the board members, gave a prophecy admonishing John not to be afraid to make hard decisions and act on them even if they were unpopular or caused temporary confusion.

John chose wisely to wait on the words and see how the week unfolded. As the week progressed, it became clear to John that while the values and priorities of the movement were in place, the organizational structure that we were considering was not what God wanted at that time. On the eve of our signing the commitment statement, all of these things came out in a closed session with the board. The next day many of us came with our pens ready only to find out about the dream and the prophetic word. We went home just as Bob Craine had prophesied, a bit confused but trusting that God had worked through John and the board. In the long run, I look back on it and am glad that it came down the way it did. None of us knew what was just over the horizon.

## A LEADERSHIP CRISIS

The second issue involved a leadership struggle in John's inner circle. During the conference John was contacted by Jack Deere who told him that there was a prophet named Paul Cain who had a message for him. While John believed in the gift of prophecy, he would normally have been hesitant to receive a word from an unknown, but because of Deere's credibility as well as what he felt was the prompting of the Lord, he allowed Paul to contact him.

What was communicated through the prophet was, at the time, helpful to John in regards to his leadership problems and opened him up to receive further contact with Cain in the future. Years later, in retrospect, some view this as the beginning of a devastating period in Vineyard history; for others it is remembered as the initiation of a period of renewal.

## THE CONFERENCE AFTERMATH

In the weeks following the pastors' conference, John became very depressed. He had a lot of things on his plate:

- He was tired, overweight, overworked and not feeling like he was leading any of his three organizations well.
- He had leadership problems in the church and the movement.
- There was sin in his life, his church, and the movement that he did not know how to deal with.
- One of his sons was not following the Lord and it was causing John and Carol great heartache.
- John felt like he was going to die at any time because of his physical problems.
- He was regularly receiving negative critiques from somewhere around the world.
- He was running against the wind in light of the Bakker/ Swaggert scandals.

In his depressed state he watched TV, and in general, opted out of life for a season. Enter Mike Bickle and Paul Cain.

## WIMBER AND BICKLE, SCOTLAND, FALL 1988

John Wimber had met Mike Bickle in 1985. Mike was the pastor of a church called Kansas City Fellowship and had a message about passion for Jesus and the rise of a victorious church at the end of the age. He and his people were committed to night and day intercession for the revival they felt was coming, believed strongly in the prophetic ministry to guide the revival, and were committed to generous giving to the poor. John's initial contacts with Mike were positive, and, as with Cain, he was open to more contact with the young pastor.

A prophetic minister named Bob Jones who was part of Kansas City Fellowship told Mike Bickle early in 1988 that John Wimber would be calling him and that this would open up a door for future ministry with John and the Vineyard.[4] John did call five days later, and in the fall of 1988, John and Mike ministered together in the United Kingdom.

While they were there, Mike began to exhort John (John thought he was "pestering" him[5]) from Psalm 89, a Psalm about God's sovereign choice of David as the leader over his people. Mike was saying that God had made John a sovereign vessel and that he needed to rise up and embrace his leadership over new things God was going to do in the Vineyard. John felt chastised by Mike in these exchanges but was somehow also reassured. John thought, "Maybe God had a plan for the Vineyard after all..."

## PAUL CAIN - THE FIRST ENCOUNTER

That same fall, John got another phone call from Jack Deere. Paul Cain wanted to make an appointment to see him. John had received Paul's ministry in the summer during the conference, but was now busy and reluctant. In the end, though, he agreed to the meeting and arranged dates with Deere. Later it was written that Jack finished by saying, "By the way, so that you will know that God has a strategic purpose in this for Paul and the Vineyard movement, Paul says there will be an earthquake that day."

The story of Paul Cain's earthquake prophecy was recounted in the winter 1990 issue of *Equipping the Saints*. While Wimber wrote the account as coming before the fact, he later doubted his memory when he re-examined the prophetic. He would later wonder privately if it hadn't really come after the fact.[6] This is a very important distinction to make because the prediction of the earthquake was recorded by Deere as coming before the fact and was used to validate Paul Cain's message to the Vineyard. In a phone conversation with Jack Deere, Deere recounted to me in vivid detail the facts surrounding this prophecy, verifying that it did come before the earthquake.[7]

In the prophecy, it was said that Paul had added, that although it was not going to be the "big one," there was going to be a big earthquake that would occur elsewhere in the world on the day after he left.[8] On the day Paul arrived in Anaheim, on December 5, 1988, there was an earthquake in Pasadena under the Rose Bowl at 3:38 A.M. Paul believed that the time of the earthquake was significant and felt directed to give John Jeremiah 33:8: "I will cleanse them from all the sin they have committed against me and will forgive all their sins of rebellion against me."

Paul reassured John in the privacy of the Wimber's own living room with a three-word prophecy saying, "God has told me to tell you in the Vineyard, 'Grace, grace, grace.'" He went on to explain that John had come close to committing the sins of Eli with his spiritual sons (letting them get away with "murder") and that as a result they were on the verge of being judged as a movement.[9] Paul told John that he was to discipline his leaders and not offer them what John later called "unsanctified mercy."[10] Paul felt that the sins of a few leaders had contaminated the whole movement and it was time to get the leaven out of the loaf. Paul encouraged John to deal with these sins so God would no longer be robbed of glory and judge the Vineyard. John's repentance and obedience would result in God's blessing instead.[11] If John complied with the Lord's direction, then the Lord would change the Vineyard by the next time that John addressed the movement. That date had already been fixed. The next pastors' conference was to be in August, 1989.

In addition to this, Cain had another, more personal word for the Wimbers. If John would issue the call to holiness, the Lord would deliver their son, Sean, from years of rebellion and drug addiction—and he would do it within the next nine months i.e. before the pastors' conference.[12]

The evening of Paul's leaving on December 7, there was a major earthquake in Armenia at 10:51 P.M. PST. Mike Bickle would later write that from his perspective,

*The prophetic symbolism seemed clear—God was speaking to the Vineyard churches through these events that He was*

*going to shake the Anaheim Vineyard over the next season by prophetic ministry like the local earthquake shook Pasadena. The prophetic shaking would not merely be local, but would eventually cause a shaking internationally. This was pictured by the internationally known earthquake in Soviet Armenia.[13]*

These events sobered John and propelled him out of his depression and into action. Before we go on to outline what happened, let's pause to find out some things about Paul Cain.

## THE LIFE OF PAUL CAIN[14]

Paul Cain was born in 1929 to his mother Anna who was 45 years old. Anna was pregnant and had inoperable cancer that had eaten away one of her breasts; the doctors sent her home to die. In the throes of death she vowed to offer her child to God, as Hannah had done with Samuel, if the Lord would spare her life. A short time later the Lord spoke to her through an angel and promised her that she would live and bear a son. She was to name him Paul since he would preach the gospel as Paul of old. She was immediately healed, her breast grew back and she suckled her new baby as a medical miracle.

Paul says that the Lord appeared to him when he was eight years old and told him that he would preach the gospel through healing if he would keep himself pure. Before that time his mother had kept the details of his birth from him, but now informed him about the call on his life. He quickly became a boy preacher and was something of a phenomenon because of his ability to receive words of knowledge and heal the sick.

By the time Paul was eighteen, he had a regular radio ministry and was conducting healing services in a small tent. It was at this point, in the years following the Second World War, that God began to move sovereignly in various revivals. There were moves among the Evangelicals in such things as Youth for Christ, Billy Graham, and revivals on many college campuses. On the Pentecostal side, God began to raise up healing evangelists. The premier healer of that era was William Branham. Branham was famous for his detailed words of knowledge and the healings that occurred in his meetings. Before long Paul Cain became something of an understudy to Branham and would often finish meetings that the frail Branham couldn't finish.

Paul was on the verge of a stellar career in the early 1950s. He had, by this time, received a call to celibacy and became something of a recluse, desiring to be alone with God. In 1954 his manager purchased the world's largest tent to conduct Paul's crusades. Everywhere Paul went God filled the tents and great miracles and salvations followed his ministry.

Before long, however, he became disillusioned with not only the pressures of running a big organization, but also with the carnality he began to see around him among the healing evangelists. He eventually left the "sawdust" trail and watched in agony as he saw many of these men fall in the next few years through moral failures involving money, sex, and power.

Since Paul Cain was so closely associated with William Branham, he has often been charged with holding to doctrinal errors that Branham embraced later in his ministry. Paul's confinement would seal him from these errors, but he would have to defend himself against these kinds of allegations many times.[15]

In the midst of this, Paul says that God spoke to him and told him that if he kept himself from corruption and became content with living a humble life, given to Scripture reading and obedience, one day he would be allowed to stand before a new breed of men and women who would be serious about holiness and the things of the Lord. This new breed would be a "faceless" generation wanting nothing for itself and giving God all the glory. God added that this new generation would be used to usher in a great revival and he would see them before his mother died. At that time Anna was 73 years old.

Paul assumed that this word would be fulfilled within a few short years but he spent the next 25 years living in a two-bedroom home in Phoenix, Arizona, where he took care of his mother with the help of family members. He spent most of those years reading Scripture and occasionally preaching. He refused to take offerings and trusted the Lord for his income. He briefly pastored two churches and was a help to many leaders during the Charismatic movement.

## THE LATTER RAIN MOVEMENT

Before we go on to finish the story of Paul Cain, we need to add some information about one of the other revivals that occurred during the post war period. Even though Paul Cain and William Branham were not really a part of this revival, many of the driving assumptions of what was called "The New Order of the Latter Rain" no doubt touched them. Indeed, knowing something about the "new truths" that were emerging will give us a basis for evaluating much of what is to follow in the history of the Vineyard. Indeed, Todd Hunter pointed out to me that the guys who didn't buy the prophetic teachings were primarily those who had had experience with the Latter Rain and said, "Been there—done that—don't want to do it again."

The Latter Rain revival began out of Pentecostalism at a Bible school in North Saskatchewan, Canada. The Spirit of God fell on the students through words of prophecy and the laying on of hands. These were second generation Pentecostals who had not experienced the Holy Spirit in the way their forebears had; it was in their theology but not their experience. Word of this new move of God quickly began to spread and people began to be touched all over the world.

The revival was powerful but short-lived. It ran aground because of some of the new doctrines, an authoritarian leadership structure, and an elitist attitude driven by apocalyptic assumptions that they were the true churches ushering in the last great move of God. Most of Pentecostalism rejected the Latter Rain and it eventually waned as a movement. But the theology of the movement did not disappear and went underground fueling many of the independent Charismatic churches and informing the Charismatic movement that exploded in the 1960s. Just what the Latter Rain taught will be examined briefly.

## THE THEOLOGY OF THE LATTER RAIN[16]

The driving assumption of the Latter Rain was that God was pouring out the last great worldwide revival that would usher in the consummation of the kingdom of God.

The term "latter rain" was used by the early Pentecostals and was based on the prophecy of Joel that God would pour out his Spirit in the last days in a way that paralleled the rainy seasons in Palestine (Joel 2:23). The former rains occurred in the fall to help the newly sown seeds to germinate. The latter rains in the spring were greater than the former rains and helped the crops mature for harvest. Pentecostals believed that the outpouring of the Spirit at Pentecost in Acts chapter 2 was the promised former rain that began the last days and helped the seeds of the gospel take root. They believed that the outpouring that birthed the Azusa Street revival that lasted from 1906-1909 was the latter rain and would catalyze world evangelization and usher in the return of Christ.

Because Christ hadn't returned within the first generation of Pentecostalism, it was assumed by those involved, that when the Spirit broke out in Canada, the end of the age was upon them and that they had been chosen to usher it in.

The Latter Rain leaders believed that just as in revivals past when forgotten biblical truths were rediscovered—Luther and justification by faith, Wesley and sanctification, the Brethren and premillennialism, the Christian and Missionary Alliance and healing, the Pentecostals and the Holy Spirit—so now another truth was being dusted off. What was coming into preeminence was the RESTORATION OF THE CHURCH, the glorious bride that Christ would come back to redeem. All the "discoveries" that were made during this time had to do with various aspects of ecclesiology, the doctrine of the church. Faupel says that Latter Rain leaders believed that there were four areas of the church that were being restored.

### 1. ITS NATURE

- **Fasting and prayer** were seen as integral to the churches moving in power.

- The Baptism and gifts of the Spirit were imparted not through "tarrying," as with the first generation of Pentecostals, but through **the laying on of hands**. The Pentecostals saw this as a cheapened "baptism" disassociated from deep soul searching and a heart for holiness.
- The Latter Rain saw the passage from Ephesians 4:18-19 as pivotal to the restoration of the church. God had given **the fivefold ministry**[17] to the church to equip the saints for works of service so the church would grow up into maturity. It was obvious that there were evangelists, pastors, and teachers in the church, but where were the apostles and prophets? These were the two gifts that Paul said would lay the foundation for the church (Ephesians 2:20). It was no wonder the church was not all that she had been designed to be, because these gifts had been stolen. God was now going to restore the offices of apostle and prophet to lay the foundation for a new and glorious church.

2. ITS MISSION

- The main message of the gift of tongues was that God wanted to **finish the great commission** that every nation should hear the gospel.
- In order for world evangelization to take place, the world would have to see the **unity of the church** (John 17:23). The concept of city churches was introduced as in the first three chapters of the book of Revelation. When God looks at our cities he does not see the Baptist, Presbyterian, and pentecostal church but, rather, sees the church at Ephesus or Thessalonica. City churches would begin to emerge as God raised up his apostolic government. All the churches would recognize the new order and the true church would unify.
- The doctrine that became the most heretical was called **"The Manifested Sons of God."** It was believed that an invitation was being given to a group of "overcomers," who would be the true church and usher in the millennial kingdom after much suffering. These Manifest Sons of

God would play a key role in getting the world ready for the return of Christ. Some Latter Rain leaders argued that not only is it possible to experience justification and sanctification in this life, it is possible to overcome mortality as well. Some of the faithful one day would receive their heavenly bodies and would move at will from country to country and from city to city. Through the Spirit of Wisdom they would have the answer to every conceivable problem. Their physical forms would be able to change and they would be able to speak any language. All things would be restored to the prefallen state. This teaching created an elitist mentality and caused division rather than the unity that was sought.

### 3. ITS WORSHIP

- The chief metaphor for the church used during the Latter Rain was **the Temple model** from the Old Testament. God has been looking for a people in whom he can dwell. He is looking for a resting-place and he will one day find it in a people that finally get serious about the things of God. He is looking for his end-time bride.
- The key to Latter Rain worship was **praise**. Since God inhabited the praises of his people and God was looking for a habitation, the end-time church would learn to praise the Lord. If they would learn to praise the Lord they would experience his awesome presence of habitation.
- The Psalms were put to music thus creating a **new hymnody** that would give the Charismatic movement the prototype for a new kind worship that would sweep the world.

### 4. ITS AUTHORITY

- The source of authority for the Latter Rain was **an allegorical interpretation of Scripture**, especially the Old Testament. They reasoned that because the New Testament writers took Old Testament passages out of context at times, they could too. Old Testament

186

passages were thus interpreted apart from their historical setting and the author's original intent. Latter Rain leaders assumed that they had been authorized by God (because of the revival) to interpret the Bible to match the new truths that were being taught.

- **The key to their interpretations was prophecy**. It had been prophecy that had started the revival in the first place and it was prophecy that opened up the new interpretations. All of human history had climaxed at the Latter Rain revival that would usher in the final move of God before the return of Christ. This prophetic/apocalyptic worldview colored all that they did.

- The undoing of the Latter Rain had to do with their teaching on **submission to authority**. Because of their apocalypticism, the leaders of the Latter Rain assumed that they were the new apostles and prophets that God was raising up. It doesn't take a rocket scientist to see what was going to happen. Almost all of Pentecostalism rejected the Latter Rain and forty years later, George Hawtin, one of the fathers of the movement, wrote to repent of his authoritarianism and elitist pride.

It should be noted that the basic premise here is Arminian rather than Reformed. Reformed doctrine says, "God has... therefore I will." An Arminian paradigm says, "If I... then God will. The question posed by the Latter Rain had to do with the role of human obedience in helping or hindering the sovereign plan of God. On what basis or for what motive do we serve him? How does revival come?

## BACK TO PAUL CAIN

I have included this brief look at the Latter Rain because the parallels between Paul Cain's message to the Vineyard are so striking. It has been hard for me to decide how much of Paul's message has been shaped by his history and how much has come through things he has thought the Lord has told him.

It should also be noted that while the thesis of Restorationism is at the center of Paul Cain's and Mike Bickle's theology, they don't appear to have ever embraced the more heretical doctrines of the Latter Rain such as the Manifested Sons of God.

As the years of seclusion were coming to an end, Paul felt the Lord told him that he would soon see some of the new breed that he had so often seen in the prophetic realm. His mother was 102 years old when he met Mike Bickle and others from Kansas City Fellowship in 1987. He said God spoke to him that these were some of the people He had shown him in repeated prophetic experiences over the years. Kansas City Fellowship embraced Paul and loved him. As they interceded for him, he said his strength and confidence began to return.

A couple of years before this, Paul says that God had told him to look for a man that would act a certain way when approached. God would use this leader to give the prophetic ministry a platform to be restored to the church. Paul then traveled widely at his own expense and visited some of the prominent Pentecostal and evangelical leaders in the world, but none of them responded as the Lord had said. Paul never even considered John Wimber as an option until he was in the room with John delivering a prophetic word to him on December 5, 1988. It was then that he said God whispered to him that John was the man he had been looking for.

Before going on to the next phase of the story, we need to learn more about Mike Bickle, a prophet named Bob Jones, and Kansas City Fellowship because they are all integrally linked to what happens next in the history of the Vineyard.

 C3

## Notes:

1 John Wimber, "Introducing Prophetic Ministry," *Equipping the Saints*, Vol. 3, No. 4, Fall 1989, p. 4

2 This story is recounted in John Wimber's article "Where is God Taking Us as a Movement?" in the last issue of *The Vineyard Newsletter*, Fall 1988.

3 *Ibid.*, p. 1

4 David Pytches, *Some Said It Thundered: A Personal Encounter with the Kansas City Prophets*, Nashville, Thomas Nelson, 1991, pp. 135ff

5 John Wimber, "Introducing the Prophetic Ministry," *Equipping the Saints*, Vol. 3, No. 4, Fall 1989, p. 4

6 From a personal conversation with Todd Hunter

7 Recounted to me in a phone conversation, April 2, 1999

8 *Ibid.*, p. 5; The article states that the Armenian earthquake occurred not the day after Paul Cain left but the evening of the day he left. When Jack Deere realized the error he said he remembered that Paul had not said "the day after I leave" but "after I leave," thus leaving the timing ambiguous. He apologized for the misquote. It was these kinds of disclaimers that raised the ire of many toward the prophetic because it seemed like backpedaling.

9 John Wimber, "The Way of Holiness," *Equipping the Saints*, Fall 1989, p. 29

10 John Wimber, "Pure Hearts," *Equipping the Saints*, Summer 1989, p. 11

11 Wimber, "Introducing the Prophetic Ministry," p. 5

12 "The Prophet," by Jack Deere in *John Wimber*, p. 111

13 Bickle and Sullivant, *Growing in the Prophetic*, Orlando, FL, Creation House, 1996, p. 40

14 For the life of Paul Cain see Pytches, *Some Said it Thundered*; Kevin Springer, "Paul Cain: A New Breed of Man," *Equipping the Saints*, Fall 1989, pp. 11-13

15 Cf. Kevin Springer's article, "Paul Cain," in *Equipping the Saints* (Fall 1990, pp. 9-14) where Paul lists the distinctions between he and Branham in an interview

16 The following is taken from an unpublished Ph.D. thesis by D. William Faupel entitled *The Everlasting Gospel: The Significance of Eschatology in the Development of Pentecostal Thought* (The University of Birmingham, England, 1989, chapter seven, "The New Order of the Latter Rain," pp. 394-518).

17 There is a possibility in the original language that "pastor" and "teacher" were a hyphenated concept (pastor-teacher). This "fourfold" office wasn't apparently taken into consideration.

# CHAPTER ELEVEN

# MIKE BICKLE, BOB JONES AND KANSAS CITY FELLOWSHIP

# MIKE BICKLE, BOB JONES AND KANSAS CITY FELLOWSHIP

## MIKE BICKLE AND THE START OF KANSAS CITY FELLOWSHIP[1]

In 1979, Mike Bickle became the pastor of a church plant in St. Louis Missouri called South County Christian Fellowship. As the church began to grow, he and his wife, Diane, assumed they would be there for a long time. God had other plans. In June of 1982, Mike had his first encounter with the gift of prophecy at the level it is being described in these chapters. An itinerant prophetic minister named Augustine Alcala stood up in his church during a meeting and prophesied that Mike and his wife Diane were going to leave St. Louis and plant a new church in Kansas City. Before long this word was confirmed in their hearts and, after releasing the leadership of the church, they began to prepare to move to Kansas City with another couple.

### CAIRO, EGYPT, 1982[2]

In the interim, Mike accepted a speaking engagement in India in September of 1982. Since he had one of those fly-anywhere-for-thirty-days tickets, he decided to visit some of the third world's most impoverished cities to receive God's heart for the poor. While he was in Cairo, Egypt, he says that God spoke to him in what he describes as an "internal audible voice." He was terrified, but the Lord said, "I am inviting you to be a part of a work that will reach to the ends of the earth. I have invited many people to do this thing and many have said yes."

Mike by this time was sobbing in both terror and awe and found himself saying, "Yes, Lord, yes!"

He says that the Lord went on to give him a fourfold plan to build his new church on the foundation of Jesus. It was to be built with:

- night and day prayer.
- holiness of heart.
- unwavering faith.
- extravagant giving to the poor.

After warning him to take heed "lest your brothers steal these things from your heart,"[3] the Lord added one more thing, Mike says, that shook him to the core. He said, "I will change the understanding and expression of the church in one generation." Which generation God was referring to was not clear, but Mike believes that it is the one in which we now live. In *Growing in the Prophetic*[4] Mike explains what he thinks this last sentence means.

The phrase "the understanding of Christianity" refers to the way Christianity is perceived by unbelievers. Christians will be feared and respected by the world, even if hated, because of the power of God in our midst. It will be as the book of Acts says, "No one else dared join them, even though they were highly regarded by the people" (5:13).

The phrase "the expression of Christianity" refers to the way the church expresses its corporate life. He thinks we are in for a major change in wineskins as God pours out the new wine of his Spirit. Paul Cain has preached that the emerging church will be unparalleled in power, purity, unity and intimacy.

KCF would come to believe that the intensity of night and day would be stirred by the encouragement of the prophets and their "words" gave something for the intercessors to "pray in." Bickle was later criticized because such a system seemed to make intercession dependent on prophecy rather than on simple love for the lost. This was not Mike's intent—he has a great love for the lost—but at the practical level it seemed to pit the work of evangelism *now,* against waiting for a great revival that would come *later*. Former staff member at KCF, David Parker, told me in a phone conversation that most of their growth during this time came from Christians who had transferred their membership from other churches. They had come to KCF to be a part of the great end times revival, a day in which God would *then* win the lost. Bickle would later see the lack of balance here and pull back on some of the intercession to include evangelism as a part of their regular ministry.[5]

Even with the inclusion of evangelism, Mike's core belief is that God is getting ready for a massive outpouring of the Holy Spirit in a future day. That move of God will bring about a reformation in the church that will be integrally linked to the restoration of a mature apostolic and prophetic ministry. His belief is consistent with the restorationist thesis that began in the Latter Rain. These values would later be called the four "banner themes" of KCF and are known by the acronym IHOP.

- I - intercession
- H - holiness
- O - offerings (i.e., giving to the poor)
- P - prophetic

After Mike came back to St. Louis, the prophet who had first spoken to him about going to Kansas City gave a second word.[6] He said that God was going to give Mike three things.

1. Multitudes of young people, thousands, will be rallied to you.

2. In the days to come there will be a full manifestation of the gifts of the Spirit, but it will be for an appointed time.

3. There will be a false prophet in your midst from the very beginning. If you are patient and discern him you will save the church great heartache. If you do not, you will suffer many, many problems.

## MEETING BOB JONES[7]

After arriving in Kansas City in November of 1982, Mike gathered a small core of people and immediately began night and day prayer. Within a short time God also miraculously gave them a huge building before they had people to fill it. Things were looking up!

In January of 1983, a brother informed Mike that a Kansas City prophet named Bob Jones had been saying for ten years that a young man of 27 (Mike's age) was going to plant a church on the south side of Kansas City (their building location) that would be based on intercession for revival (the two things Mike was teaching). Bob wanted to meet Mike, but Mike was wary of the false prophet warning and kept him at arm's length. Before long, another brother exhorted him in the same direction, so Mike reluctantly agreed.

Bob came to Mike's office on March 7, 1983, a fifty-three year old man in a winter coat—it was 70 degrees. He delivered a prophetic word to Mike. This work, he said, was going to become worldwide and would touch the nations of the earth with such power and glory that it would go far beyond the book of Acts. In his heart Mike was thinking "false prophet," but Bob, sensing this, finished by saying, "The Lord tells me that on the first day of spring when the snows melts we will sit around the table and they will accept me." (This prophecy about the snow was the reason for the winter coat.)

As Bob was turning to leave, he said in passing, "The Lord says there are four things you already know. One, thousands of young people will be rallied to you. Two, you will see a full manifestation of the gifts of the Spirit among you. Three, there will be a false prophet in your midst from the beginning.[8] Lastly, there will be major resistance to you and misunderstanding but you are not to lose heart."

Mike was stunned. He wondered, as Wimber would later with Paul Cain, "Who is this guy?"

## THE LIFE OF BOB JONES[9]

Bob Jones grew up as a poor sharecropper in the hills of Arkansas in the 1930s. He says he had his first spiritual visitation at the age of nine, seeing an angel on a white charger coming right toward him. It stopped and blew a trumpet, as if to announce something and then disappeared. The Lord appeared to him two more times in his youth, but he never responded to God's call.

Bob became a drinker and fighter while he was a Marine in the Korean War. He and his wife later moved to the "dry" state of Oklahoma and ran an illegal liquor store. His dream of owning a big bar didn't pan out, and at the age of thirty-nine he checked himself into a hospital thinking he was losing his mind. He became hooked on the painkillers prescribed when doctors could find nothing wrong with him.

Having moved to Kansas City with his family while in his teens, Bob next tried another hospital, this one in Topeka. The doctor gave him a prescription of sweeping the floors, and he began to slowly get better. The real change came when a friend read the Psalms to him. One night a demon appeared to try to get him to exact revenge on all those who hurt him, but Bob quoted the Psalms and cried out to the Lord. The Lord was faithful and spoke to Bob telling him to forgive those who had hurt him rather than getting revenge. He did so and was shortly discharged from the hospital.

His doctor invited Bob to church, and before long he was saved, baptized, filled with the Holy Spirit, and speaking in tongues. Almost immediately Bob began to have prophetic insight into people and situations, regularly seeing visions and having dreams. Those in his church tried to work with him, but when he began to prophesy against abortion and homosexuality, the warfare against him became intense. Bob experienced rejection on many occasions. One night a demon told him that if he didn't stop prophesying against homosexuality, the devil would kill him. Bob refused to comply and became so ill he died.

While he was out of his body, he says the Lord spoke to him and said, "You go back and teach the leaders of the latter-day church that the old leadership is coming to an end. A new quality of leadership across the earth with a deep commitment to the Word of God, a passion for Jesus, and a burden for holiness is coming into being to bring forth the bride of Christ."[10]

After his full recovery, the Lord spoke to him again saying that he was going to raise up a group of young people in the south of Kansas City who would not reject him nor God. They would be there by the spring of 1983 and before the snow melted on the first day of spring they would accept him. They would be on the south side of the city; they would be speaking about intercession and revival and would be led by a twenty-seven year old man.

Bob and his wife, Viola, joined a church in the meantime with the understanding that in 1983 they would be leaving to be with the group God had spoken about.

## BACK TO BICKLE AND KANSAS CITY FELLOWSHIP

In March of 1983, Bob and Viola Jones began to attend Kansas City Fellowship, but Mike Bickle still thought Bob was the false prophet God had spoken about. One Sunday, Art Katz, a Jewish Christian author came to fellowship with the young church. After the service Bob Jones told Art the secrets of his heart, and Art declared to Mike, "This is a true prophet of God!"

That night Art felt strongly that he needed to see Bob one more time before he left, so Art, Mike, and some others went over to Bob's house. Bob then told Mike something that only Mike knew, thus finally confirming that he was a true prophet. As the group sat around the table, in full acceptance of Bob, they looked out the window and realized that it was snowing. The date was March 21, the first day of spring.[11] As if this weren't enough, in April Mike says that God spoke to him in another internal audible voice and told him to call Kansas City to a solemn season of prayer and fasting before the Lord. Mike wrestled with this, realizing that he had no credibility in the city yet, but when Bob Jones told him the exact words that God had spoken into his heart, Mike decided to go ahead with it.

Bob had already predicted that an unknown comet would be discovered by scientists as proof that God wanted to visit Kansas City and the nation with revival. In the paper that came out on May 7, 1983, the first day of the solemn twenty-one day fast, there was an article about a completely unforeseen comet that had been discovered by astronomers.[12]

## A TWENTY-ONE DAY FAST

Despite being rebuked by some local pastors for his presumption, the fast began on May 7, and on the first night 700 people showed up. Encouraged by the appearance of the comet, for three weeks they prayed for revival from 6:00 A.M. to 12 midnight with an average attendance of 200 daily and 500 nightly.[13] Mike remembers it as an agonizing time of feeling weak and barren.

On the last day of the fast, Bob Jones stood up and prophesied

197

that there would be a drought for three months because the people (in Kansas City) had rejected the call to fast—they had mocked God. The drought began in late June and lasted until the end of September, a full three months. Local records show that it was the second worst drought in the history of Kansas City.[14]

In the midst of the drought, Bob predicted that God would also send rain on August 23, a prophetic sign that they should not grow weary in waiting for the precise timing of the spiritual drought over the nation to end. Just as the natural drought over Kansas City was to be divinely interrupted on a predetermined day, the spiritual drought would also be divinely interrupted precisely at the appointed time. The intercession that God was raising up all over the country in various groups was not in vain. At 6:00 P.M. on August 23 it poured for an hour before their evening meeting. There was loud rejoicing that night.

One more phase of the prophecy was that as God had humiliated the city, so now he would humiliate their church because God resists the proud. They were going to experience three years of dryness as God showed them their poverty. An extravagant humility would be required before God would pour out his blessings on them. Mike Bickle almost immediately contracted a serious throat condition that lasted for three years. By May of 1986, the three years ended, and Mike's throat condition cleared up within a month.

OTHER SIGNIFICANT PROPHETIC EVENTS

Bob Jones says that in 1979 God spoke to him about a group located 40 miles southeast of Los Angeles that the Lord called "worship and compassion." He also told Bob that the group he would meet in 1983 would be called "prophetic and intercession" and that he would cause these two groups to "cross-pollinate." In January of 1984, Bob told Mike about the "worship and compassion" group, and in June, Mike and some others from KCF attended the first MC 510 course taught publicly by John Wimber (after the moratorium from Fuller). While there they felt the Lord confirmed to them that the Vineyard was the group they were to cross-pollinate with.

In September of 1984, Mike Bickle was driving with Augustine, the prophet from St. Louis who had prophesied to Mike originally. They were going from Phoenix to Los Angeles to attend a Vineyard conference. As they were driving, Augustine was telling Mike about Paul Cain and his miraculous birth. Mike mentioned that he wanted to meet him. Shortly thereafter they stopped at McDonalds to eat, and in the restaurant was a man Augustine knew named Reid Grafke. After chatting for a minute they discovered that Reid now worked for a prophetic minister from Dallas—Paul Cain. Mike felt encouraged that one day he would meet Paul, but resigned himself to letting the Lord arrange it.

Three years later, in April of 1987, Mike took some of his prophetic ministers to Birmingham, Alabama, where he was booked as the main speaker at a conference. Paul Cain had heard that Mike would be there and went to meet him. The conference host recognized Paul and at one point invited him to come forward to say a few words. Paul spoke prophetically to the team from Kansas City Fellowship, and by the time he was done, they were all on the floor weeping. The words seemed to confirm many of the things they felt the Lord had already shown them.

Paul paid his first visit to KCF the next month. He would now begin a long-term relationship with them, returning often to preach and minister. With each visit he seemed to gain strength. The first time Paul saw their building he says it shook him. KCF was in its new Grandview location, and Paul was taken back to a vision he had seen many times over the years. In the vision this precise building had a sign on it that read "Joel's army in training." Paul felt that the Joel 2 prophecy about a powerful army referred to a group that God would raise up in the last days. This interpretation is foreign to biblical scholarship and raised the very important question of whether receiving interpretations of tough biblical texts through prophetic means is valid. Contrary to our evangelical convictions, many of us went along with the new interpretation, aided by a tape series on it by Jack Deere who used his tools and expertise as an Old Testament scholar to support it.

Because of his visions, Paul believed that God was showing him that Joel's army was about to be raised up. It was not going to be a destructive army but a deliverance army. God would not work anymore through superstars, but through ordinary soldiers, who would respond in obedience to his voice. They would be led by a new breed of leaders and teachers who would work only for the glory of God. It is interesting that even as the vision was shared that God wasn't going to use superstars any more, the entire restorationist premise was built on God raising up end-time apostles and prophets. The basic thesis, when framed this way, could seem contradictory.

John and Margie McClure wrote,

*Almost from the beginning there were tremendous problems...problems which, we believe, violated the values of the Vineyard such as our emphasis and core value of lay ministry. Probably what the Vineyard and John Wimber contributed most in church renewal was giving the work of the ministry into the hands of the laity—equipping the saints. With the inflow of prophetic personalities, the focus of lay ministry changed to "up front" ministry by an elite—a tragic change in our view—and one which eventually cut off all our renewal influence.*[15]

Again, to Mike's credit, he would eventually see the need for balance here and now is committed to an equipping ministry while retaining his restorationist views.

In October of that year, 1987, Bob Jones prophesied that the cross-pollination between the Vineyard and KCF would begin in January of 1988. In January, three months later, John Wimber felt suddenly impressed to call Mike Bickle. In the fall of '88, Mike would minister with Wimber in Scotland and in December Paul Cain would visit Anaheim with predictions about two earthquakes and the grace of God for the Vineyard.

One more word is worth noting here. In April, 1984, it was reported to Mike that the Lord spoke separately to two prophetic team members at KCF in an audible voice. They said he told them that in ten years (1994) he would begin to release the wine of his Spirit.[16] The releasing of wine appeared to symbolize a wave of the Spirit to refresh and renew his people in the midst of their weariness. It was ten years later that the Toronto Blessing began, even though the ministry of Rodney Howard-Browne was in full swing some years before.

CZ

NOTES:

[1] This story is recounted in Pytches, *Some Said It Thundered* (pp. 60-62) and Mike Bickle and Michael Sullivant's *Growing in the Prophetic*, pp. 29-31. It should be noted that James A. Beverly in *Holy Laughter & the Toronto Blessing* (Grand Rapids, Zondervan, 1995, pp. 212-133) criticizes Pytches' account for its "uncritical" acceptance of the Kansas City recollection of the facts.

[2] The following is Pytches' rendition.

[3] This wording was given to me by Mike Bickle in phone conversation.

[4] P. 30

[5] *Growing in the Prophetic*, p. 25

[6] *Ibid.*, p. 35ff.

[7] *Ibid.*

[8] The false prophet was eventually discerned and appropriate measures taken

[9] Bob's story is recounted in *Some Said It Thundered*, pp. 69-79

[10] *Ibid.*, p. 77

[11] Bickle and Sullivant reference an article by Marquis Shepherd in the *Kansas City Times* (March 21, 1983) entitled, "Gentlest of Winters Goes Out with a Blast of Snow, Cold."

[12] For an excerpt of this article, "Comet's Path to Give Close View" from *The Examiner* (Independence, Missouri) see *Growing in the Prophetic*, p. 39.

[13] Pytches, *Some Said It Thundered*, p. 89

[14] *Ibid.*, p. 91

[15] A personal letter, August 28, 1998

[16] *Growing in the Prophetic*, p. 26

# CHAPTER TWELVE

# THE VINEYARD MEETS THE KANSAS CITY PROPHETS

# THE VINEYARD MEETS THE KANSAS CITY PROPHETS

## THE SPIRITUAL WARFARE CONFERENCE, FEBRUARY 1989

In February 1989, John Wimber hosted a conference on spiritual warfare in Anaheim. It was to be a typical Vineyard conference—work through the notes and minister as the Lord directed. What made these meetings different was that Wimber, who had just had his initial encounter with Paul Cain in December, invited Paul to speak at one or two of the sessions. No one was ready for what happened. It was so intense that the seminar was held over for two extra days.

In essence, Paul Cain told conference registrants that God had given him a torch with which to initiate the "last days" ministry. What is more, God had instructed him to offer that torch to the Vineyard. The symbolism appeared to be the image of the Olympic runner lighting the fire that initiates the games. Paul had run his leg of the marathon and now was passing the flame to the final runner who would light the vessel in the stadium, thus officially initiating a significant era in the countdown of human history. John Wimber was, as would be imagined, stunned and didn't know how to respond. It sounded so presumptuous!

Paul Cain then proceeded to minister prophetically giving what appeared to be accurate words of knowledge for people. It was said that there were power surges in the building that first blew out a battery-operated video camera and second short-circuited the phone system. I talked to a secretary who was there at the time and she doesn't remember the phones going out. Todd Hunter, then executive pastor of the Vineyard in Anaheim, says that there is really no way to prove any correlation between the prophetic ministry and the video camera blowing out, but, at the time, that's what we believed.

204

## THE PASTORS' CONFERENCE, DENVER, 1989[1]

By the time of the pastors' conference that summer, the Vineyard was stirred up. Some came with great anticipation, others with concerns that we would get off track. The previous summer we had tried to sign the constitution and by-laws, but had been prevented by the Lord from doing so. We had left that conference confused and during the course of the next year had heard wide-eyed stories about Paul Cain, Bob Jones and the prophets. As we gathered in Tom Stipe's Vineyard in Denver we wondered what was going to transpire.

During this week we put what was called Vineyard I on Isaac's altar, not knowing if our movement would make it through the fire of God's judgment. It was said of Vineyard I that:

- It was sovereignly raised up by God.
- It was called by God "worship" and "compassion."
- It did not persist in pursuing God's presence but became enamored with God's power (we sought his hand and not his face). God saved us by lifting his anointing because power without purity would kill us.
- It was laced with immorality that was not dealt with by leadership ("unsanctified mercy").
- It was a relatively prayer-less movement drawing spiritual power from the intercession of others.
- It had been saved by God the summer before from becoming tied to a governmental system.

Some believed the Lord had given the opportunity through Paul Cain in February to re-ante with a new heart posture. Cain's life was seen as a kind of parable for the movement—a faceless man who had stepped out of the limelight in humility only now to be reinstated by God in a significant way. In that same year, God had used Mike Bickle to help John repent and believe that he had been called sovereignly to lead the movement.

We believed at the time that we put Vineyard I to death on August 8 through corporate repentance and a recommitment to seeking God's face and not his hand. John McClure gave a classic talk on covering the father's nakedness taken from the text about Noah's sons in Genesis 9. We then chose to cover John Wimber's nakedness, thus affirming him as our leader and committing ourselves to honoring him, even though he had made mistakes.

We did not know if there would be a Vineyard II, and if there were, what it would look like. We were instructed to go home, seek the face of God and do the work of the ministry. The new character and structure would perhaps emerge in God's time. We were even open to not having the name Vineyard—the name not being the issue, but heart postures.

### CORPORATE PROPHETIC WORDS

The prophetic people were filled with many words that week, some for the Vineyard and some regarding what they felt would be coming in the future. To many, these words were preposterous, to others, the words of the Lord. I will try to give a brief overview of what was prophesied over us:[2]

- God was going to raise up a faceless generation, a new breed, dread champions who would think only of righteousness and the glory of God on the earth. They would cause the enemy to tremble.
- It was not the parents' generation but the children's that would be the chosen generation. Our highest level of anointing and wisdom was where they would begin. Children's ministry was to be top priority.
- God had not given the Vineyard permission to fail. Leaders could opt out, but the movement had been sovereignly raised up by God.
- God was about the business of offending the mind to reveal the heart. God would use the reproach and rejection of the larger church to prepare the faceless generation.
- The enemy had stolen the foundational ministries of apostle and prophet from the church, but God was now restoring them. We were seeing the emergence of the prophetic in the '80s, and they would come to maturity in the '90s. We would begin to see a new wave of apostolic men in the

'90s who would come to maturity after the turn of the millennium.

- God was raising up Joel's army, and the church would become the pure and spotless bride that Jesus would come soon to redeem.
- God was raising up city churches that would relate governmentally to apostolic teams raised up for each city.
- Twelve major streams would emerge and cross-pollinate. Each had a revelation of the truth, and they would need each other. The first to emerge was the Vineyard with worship and compassion. It would cross-pollinate with KCF, representing prophetic and intercession.
- God would be raising up worldwide movements of prayer that would go on day and night.
- A sudden impartation of the power of the Holy Spirit would be given to the church to enable power evangelism. No one knew when this impartation would be, but it would come suddenly and would move the church a quantum leap forward in power.
- God would give more signs in the heavens as the highest form of verification that all this was true.
- A sword of judgment was coming to the church. All those who were not abased in their hearts would be chopped down. God was showing up to say how serious he was about holiness.
- In the last days ministry God was requiring an extravagant humility that would be connected to prayer and generous giving to the poor.
- God had given John Wimber David's harp that had been lost. This referred to the worship God had given to the movement.
- The Vineyard was going to receive a tenfold increase. This increase was to get the leaders ready for the great move of God.
- God had raised up prophets who were not in the Vineyard to say these things because no one in the Vineyard would have been presumptuous enough to have said them.
- In the end, this had nothing to do with the Vineyard—it was

for the whole body of Christ and had to do with Jesus. He raises up, and he lowers down anyone or anything according to his sovereignty.

## INDIVIDUAL PROPHETIC WORDS

After some of the sessions, the prophetic men gave words for Vineyard pastors. The most remarkable were those by Paul Cain. He knew names and details about people's lives. He called my wife and me out by our given names (which no one ever uses) and told us where we ministered and things that would supposedly happen there. We sat there shocked and glad for all we thought God would do. Many of us went home full of hope for the future and awed to be part of a sovereign move of God. Little did Betsy and I know that none of these things would come to pass, at least not at this time and in our understanding.

## PAUL CAIN'S WORD TO JOHN MUMFORD[3]

A significant word came from Paul Cain during the evening session on August 5. He had called out John and Eleanor Mumford (whom he did not know), the pastors of the S.W. London Vineyard in England. In the context of prophesying to them he closed saying, "and I believe that revival will probably find its starting point somewhere in October there [in England], when the Lord will just start to move throughout London and throughout England."

Mumford assumed from the word that revival would break out in London in October 1989. When October 1989 came and went, he wondered if Paul had missed the date. He withheld judgment on the word, however, because of Paul's track record of accuracy. In January of 1990, David Parker, one of Bickle's teammates, visited London and listened to the transcript of the tape. He pointed out that Paul never mentioned the year of the revival. For many this was an example of the kind of back-peddling that would take place when prophecies did not come to pass.

Also in January, Mike Bickle records that five prophetic people in the space of a week independently received the word that God would strategically visit London and that the Holy Spirit would move to Germany and then to all of Europe.[4] This appeared to agree with the word that Paul Cain had had.

In March of 1990, Mumford recounted his experience to a group at St. Andrew's Anglican Church in Chorleywood. He believed that he had received an accurate *revelation* from Paul Cain, but he (Mumford) had added a false *interpretation* (that revival was coming to London in October 1989) and *application* (if it didn't happen, it wasn't a true word). Unknown to Mumford, this tape was widely distributed in the U.K. and would have a bearing later.

I am going into this case study in some depth for a couple of reasons. First, the prophecy about revival in London will have tremendous bearing on Vineyard history. Second, it illustrates the massive problem that pastors who received words would have with not being prepared for the fine but incredibly weighty distinctions between the three phases of prophecy:

- **Revelation** is the word the prophetic person receives (be it picture, vision, dream, audible voice, etc.).
- **Interpretation** is what the word means. It requires just as much supernatural gifting as getting the word. Interpreting genuine words in a wrong way would create massive problems for those who received them.
- **Application** is knowing what to do with a word. This also requires wisdom from God.

Wimber went on to schedule conferences in the U.K. for October of 1990, not because of the prophecy, but because he regularly ministered there in October. He brought Paul Cain to London in July of 1990 to introduce British leaders to the prophetic and prepare them for the October meetings. On July 14, the Saturday after the conference, Wimber, Cain, Mumford and several others met with some leaders who had expressed severe reservations over the upcoming conference. During the course of the meeting one of the detractors brought up Mumford's teaching in Chorleywood and wondered if he had not attempted to rationalize a word that was, in fact, wrong.

Wimber records what happened next:

*Before Mumford could respond, Paul Cain said, "I stand by every word I prophesied to John Mumford on August 5th." Almost as an afterthought, he added, "Thus saith the Lord: Revival will be released in England in October of 1990...Tokens of revival will come in October 1990." I was stunned. I had never before heard Paul introduce a word with the phrase "Thus saith the Lord," and I assumed—correctly—that he was speaking with great authority. Suddenly the words that he had spoken in February took on greater urgency and importance. "Paul," I said, "what do you mean by that? Do you mean revived people or revived churches? Or both? Paul responded, "I mean both." [5]*

In summary, Paul Cain prophesied

- That the "first shot" of revival would come to England in October 1990
- That "tokens" of revival would be the first fruits of a greater revival
- That it would affect individuals and whole churches

Wimber was deeply impacted by this word and the gravity with which Cain had said it. He became convinced that revival would, in fact, break out in London, and impact the world. He then made some crucial decisions that would affect the next series of events. What these were we will take up after we talk about the prophetic honeymoon that swept up the movement and the ensuing controversy that broke out in January of 1990.

## THE PROPHETIC HONEYMOON

The aftermath of the 1989 pastors' conference was a general renewal in the movement and in individual lives. I remember coming home and pursuing God more ardently than at any other time in my life.

John Wimber attested that the prophetic ministry had a major effect on his personal life. He had new hope for his church and movement. His health eventually improved, and most of all, God had indeed used one of the prophetic ministers before the conference to bring his backslidden son, Sean, to repentance. This is a powerful story of the grace of God and had a dramatic impact on John. One day Bob Jones showed up at Wimber's house and told him that he was there to see his estranged son. John told him that he didn't understand. The boy didn't live there and wouldn't be coming anytime soon. But then, suddenly, there he was—out of the blue. Bob had specific words for the boy that broke his heart and opened him up to repent before the Lord and become reconciled with his family. It was a miracle that John and Carol would never forget and that would underlie all the struggles he would have with the prophetic ministry in the future, thus creating great tension for him.

This period set off a wave of interest in the prophetic, holiness, and intercession in the Vineyard. In the fall of 1989 there was a big conference on prophecy, and in January of 1990 a massive conference called "Holiness" ran two separate weeks with 5000 registrants each week. John Wimber now began to share the platform regularly with Paul Cain and Mike Bickle. Some of the other KCF prophets like Bob Jones, John Paul Jackson, Jim Goll, and Larry Randolf began to travel extensively in the Vineyard. We also began to see non-KCF men such as Leonard Ravenhill, Rick Joyner and Francis Frangipane incorporated into the conferences. It should be noted here that from Mike's perspective, while all these men were in relationship to one another, they were often wrongly linked in the literature and labeled "the Kansas City Prophets" as if Mike was their pastor. Mike says that much of the heat he took was in relation to men over whom he had no governing authority.

One of the vehicles for introducing these new people into the Vineyard was the annual June conference in Kansas City sponsored by Grace Ministries, which was KCF's equivalent of VMI. These conferences had a Charismatic flavor to them, and many of the evangelicals in the Vineyard were introduced to a radically different style. People wondered what cross-pollination was going to look like, many saying, "This isn't what I signed up for."

Mike Bickle now began to teach around the movement on the things they had learned about administrating prophetic giftings and about corporate intercession. This was helpful for two reasons, first because Vineyard pastors began to lead their congregations in prayer and second because prophetic people in their churches started to come out of the closet at all different levels of maturity.

By the fall of 1989, *Equipping the Saints* began the prophetic rollout with an issue called "Introducing Prophetic Ministry." It started with Wimber telling all that had transpired in the last year—the condition of the Vineyard, Paul Cain, the earthquakes, John's sin, the word of grace, the Spiritual Warfare Conference—the whole incredible story. The second article introduced Wayne Grudem to the Vineyard. Grudem was, at that time, a professor of the department of Biblical and Systematic Theology at Trinity Evangelical Divinity School in Deerfield, Illinois. He now chairs the department. In 1988 he published *The Gift of Prophecy in the New Testament and Today*.[6] This book was one of the guiding lights during this period. Dr. Grudem was able to use his expertise to help John set biblical parameters for governing the prophetic. Dr. Grudem would subsequently align himself with the movement and, along with Jack Deere, become a valuable addition to the team. This was a period of severe criticism, and God used these men as apologists to give people confidence that the gift of prophecy had a biblical foundation, even if the movement didn't always know how to process what it was going through.

The winter 1990 issue of *Equipping the Saints* was devoted to holiness, with spring covering intercession. Wimber had said in the conference on holiness that his highest priority was to give broad acceptance to the issues of the prophetic, holiness and intercession for revival. Many of us embraced these new emphases and tried to incorporate them into the standard Vineyard values.

People in Wimber's church began to ask him where the prophetic move would take them. He wrote, "I believe that, like worship and healing earlier, it will end in the appropriate balance as presented in the New Testament."[7]

He was saying that God was birthing the prophetic like he had birthed worship and healing in earlier times. Back then there was almost a myopic concentration on those subjects until they were firmly a part of the genetic code. After that they only had to be occasionally nurtured.

A new wave of worship rose up at this time as well. Kevin Prosch had been one of the worship leaders at KCF, and his songs began to be played all over the world. A British songwriter named Graham Kendrick also had songs that seemed to catch the heart of what God was doing. His song "Shine, Jesus, Shine!" was sung everywhere with the cry "fill the nations with grace and mercy" ringing around the globe.

ೞ

NOTES:

[1] The information from this section is from my own notes from this conference.

[2] These prophecies were recorded in my conference notes.

[3] The whole story of what happened with this prophecy is recounted by John Wimber in "Revival Fire," *Equipping the Saints*, Winter 1991.

[4] Bickle and Sullivant, *Growing in the Prophetic*, p. 26

[5] *Equipping the Saints*, Winter 1991, p. 11

[6] Crossway, Westchester, IL, 1988

[7] Wimber, "Introducing Prophetic Ministry," *Equipping the Saints*, Fall 1989, p. 6

CHAPTER THIRTEEN

# THE
# KANSAS CITY
# PROPHETS MEET
# THE VINEYARD

# THE KANSAS CITY PROPHETS MEET THE VINEYARD

## THE HONEYMOON IS OVER

The first shot in the prophetic wars was fired on January 21, 1990. In his Sunday morning message entitled, "Do We Keep on Smiling and Say Nothing?" an influential Charismatic pastor named Ernie Gruen accused Kansas City Fellowship of a whole series of abuses with the prophetic ministry. There were three or four meetings in the late '80s where Gruen confronted KCF with the goal of correction. The issue had appeared settled when Gruen wrote them in 1989 saying the "differences between us were resolved."[1] The next exchange between them, however, came through the sermon tape that was sent around the world as a warning against false prophecy (especially by Bob Jones) and a new "Charismatic heresy." He believed Satan had deceived Mike and that the prophets were prophesying by a "familiar spirit."[2]

Bickle's response to Gruen came in the form of an open letter to him on January 29, 1990.[3] Wimber says that in the letter Mike declined to question Gruen's motives or sincerity, claiming instead that their accusations were based on misinformation. Mike took responsibility for not communicating clearly enough in earlier attempts to resolve their differences and declined a public response to avoid further confusion and pain in the churches. He said he was willing to meet privately with Gruen, but he never replied.

Instead, in May, Pastor Gruen escalated his charges by distributing a 233-page paper entitled, "Documentation of the Aberrant Practices and Teachings of Kansas City Fellowship (Grace Ministries)." In it, Gruen's staff had documented with transcriptions of KCF teaching tapes, letters, and other written materials, more charges of abuse and heresy. Paul Cain was also indicted along with John Paul Jackson. The document was widely distributed in the United States and abroad.

Pastors in Kansas City began to take sides at this point, a number rallying to support Gruen. Even Pat Robertson and the 700 Club were behind him. Even though it would later come out that Gruen himself was involved with immorality at this time, the affair escalated when the so-called cult watchers jumped on board and declared open season on the prophetic ministry. Wimber now had an international mess on his hands. Interestingly, the KCF storm reached its peak right at the point that the controversies in Australia came out. It was a bittersweet season.

In the midst of all this, Bickle and Gruen counseled with a group of Christian leaders trying to resolve the problems. Efforts were made to engage a panel of respected Charismatic leaders to review the charges. The two men ultimately agreed to a meeting in July with 12 "presbyters" of the Network of Christian Ministries (NCM), men like Dick Iverson, Earl Paulk, Charles Simpson and Ken Sumrall.[4]

In a surprise move, however, John Wimber stepped in during the month of May to cut off the controversy's momentum. He announced that Kansas City Fellowship was going to become a part of the Association of Vineyard Churches and come under Wimber's oversight (Mike Bickle had approached Wimber about becoming a Vineyard in May of 1989). On May 12, 1990, the Kansas City Fellowship became Metro Vineyard Christian Fellowship of Kansas City (henceforth MVF). Contrary to the widespread perception that MVF joined the Vineyard for protection from the prophetic storms, Mike Bickle later explained that they joined for four reasons:

1. A divine call to cross-pollinate with a group called "worship and compassion"
2. The excitement of joining the banner themes of prophetic and intercession with worship and compassion
3. The need for a spiritual covering
4. A personal connection with John Wimber

Wimber made it clear at that time that he both supported the validity of the prophetic ministry, yet acknowledged that AVC's initial investigation found some excesses. Wimber and Cain had

217

met with Gruen as early as April to try to resolve some of the differences. It was then agreed that Wimber's associate, Jack Deere, would meet with Gruen and his staff and consider all the charges. That meeting took place on June 12th. On June 28th, Wimber, Cain, and Deere delivered their response to Gruen and after several hours of discussion, Gruen agreed to stop his attacks on MVF and Paul Cain.

Gruen wrote on July 1 that he realized that he had been wrong about Paul Cain and exonerated him from all wrongdoing. He released the whole controversy into Wimber's hands feeling that he had done what his conscience had dictated. He said it was not his responsibility to provide either correction or approval.

Wimber had written in *Equipping the Saints* in the summer of 1988 explaining why he did not respond to criticism. The problems of 1990 with both MVF and Australia caused him to reverse that policy, and he published the results of AVC's investigation in *Equipping the Saints* in the fall of 1990. After taking up each of the major charges, Wimber concluded:

> *After reading every line of Pastor Gruen's document, listening to his tape, and interviewing as many people involved as possible, my staff and I are convinced that the accusations against the Metro Vineyard of Kansas City and Paul Cain are untrue. I find no evidence that they teach heresy; have an occultic spirit; have unethical practices; promote bizarre, unscriptural experiences; have cult-like tendencies or teachings; or use prophetic gifting to take over churches. I do not believe that the Metro Vineyard Fellowship of Kansas City is a fully mature church; nor do I believe that their prophetic ministry is perfect. However, they have brought great blessing to me, and I welcome them into the Vineyard family.*[5]

Wimber did, however, find MVF guilty of a number of errors and released a statement of those errors, which were also published in the fall 1990 issue of *Equipping the Saints*. Some of these included:

- A lack of accountability for prophecy
- Allowing prophetic men to teach who were not gifted to do so
- The attempt by some prophetic men to establish doctrine on the basis of prophecy
- Dogmatic assertions in the delivery of prophetic words
- Using jargon from groups that the Vineyard was trying to distance itself from
- Manifesting an attitude of superiority through the information gained in prophecy

It is incredible to note here that it later became public knowledge that Ernie Gruen was in an immoral relationship at the time of these proceedings and that his ministry was eventually discredited. Jack Deere thinks that Gruen was jealous of Mike and used his influence to try to destroy him.[6]

It should be noted that James A. Beverly would later point out that his research indicated that Wimber's article was really the report of Jack Deere who was openly sympathetic toward Bickle.[6] A source close to Wimber also reported to me that Wimber later came to believe that the facts in the case had been somewhat biased toward KCF and, while never acknowledging it publicly, privately apologized to Gruen for being careless and unbalanced.

Bickle responded with deep humility and brokenness, despite the fact that he had inside knowledge of what was going on in Gruen's life. To Bickle's credit, he never cried "foul," choosing rather to let the Lord bring judgment.

As the controversy wound down, Wimber said that God had told him that the way he dealt with Mike would set a precedent for disciplining leaders in the future. In obedience to 1 Timothy 5:20 where Paul counsels Timothy to publicly rebuke an elder who sins, Wimber disciplined Bickle before 7,000 people at MVF's annual conference in June of 1991. Bickle responded with deep humility and brokenness.

Lee Grady, the associate editor of *National & International Religion Report*, asked Mike Bickle what he had learned through this process. He responded that God had used Gruen to expose "pride, impatience and defensiveness" in his own spirit. Mike outlined four immediate adjustments occurring at MVF.[7]

1.  The "City Church" teaching: Bickle and his leadership team had been advocating unity among pastors in a geographic area. He realized that he should rather have emphasized unity through relational lines rather than through governmental structure.

2.  The "New Order" teaching: Mike and his team had taught that God was raising up a new order of church leadership that would help the church advance beyond anything previously known in the history of the church. Mike admitted that could have sounded elitist even though this was never in his heart. He realized the need to change the way they communicate their convictions.

3.  The ministry of Bob Jones: Almost 75% of Gruen's charges had to do with Bob Jones. While Bickle supported Jones both in terms of gifting and character, he realized the error of putting Bob in a teaching role and put a stop to it.

4.  The ministry of John Paul Jackson: Bickle acknowledged that Jackson had given some wrong prophecies and supported his move to Anaheim for a period of instruction.

## GO BUMP IN THE NIGHT: A HOPEFUL SIGN

In August of 1990, a paper began to circulate: "Go Bump in the Night: The Merging of Kansas City Fellowship with Vineyard Christian Fellowship" was written by the late George Mallone, pastor of the Arlington, Texas, Vineyard. In it Mallone did an excellent job articulating the differences between the classic evangelical presuppositions of his own worldview and those of the more charismatic/prophetic worldview he perceived in Kansas City. Mallone wrote in his introduction:

*Whenever two streams merge, rough waters can be expected for a distance. So it is with the entrance and influence of Kansas City Fellowship in the Vineyard. Some have received this merger with open arms and little conflict. Others, being more cautious, have held back endorsement, taking a wait and see attitude. Still others are convinced the merger is dangerous and are planning to manifest their convictions by leaving the Association of Vineyard Churches.*

*During the last two years I have been tempted with all three positions. Today, I find myself comfortable with the merger and the directions we are headed. This does not mean the tensions are gone, for they are not. But today I have an interpretive grid for viewing the event which gives me consolation.*

Mallone then listed the five areas of tension which form his interpretive grid.

1. *Indicatives and imperatives*

The Vineyard has put the weight on what are called "indicatives" in the New Testament—statements of fact i.e., Christ died for your sins. KCF was putting the weight on the imperatives—commands i.e., repent. Mallone asked which is the better motivator of Christians to pursue the things of God. In the New Testament, indicatives always come before the imperatives i.e., Christ died for your sins; therefore repent.

The result of the Vineyard approach is that we have been a movement resting in grace and slothful in behavior. The result of the KCF side has been a church serious about holiness but tending toward legalism.

2. *Pastor, teacher and prophet*

Our giftedness determines whether we use indicatives or imperatives to motivate people. A pastor's motivational method will be relational, a teacher's will be informational, and a prophet's will be revelational.

The Vineyard is a movement of pastors and teachers. KCF is a church with many prophets and a prophetic message. Both messages are needed for proper balance in the body of Christ, but revelational guidance must always be supplementary to scripture.

3. *Historical-grammatical and allegorical hermeneutics*

The Vineyard is a branch from the evangelical tree. Many

221

of its leaders were trained to interpret the Bible in context, a discipline that calls for sensitivity to culture, grammar, and authorial intent. KCF, due to the influence of the prophets, uses not only this method but also an allegorical interpretation. Allegory looks beyond the plain meaning of the text to a hidden or deeper meaning, often from the Old Testament.[8]

The merging of the two streams presents a conflict in hermeneutics. The prophets often urge New Testament concepts (e.g., deeper intimacy with Christ) by using and interpreting an Old Testament text allegorically (e.g., Christ is looking for a temple to dwell in). To teachers trained in the historical-grammatical method, this is a false application of the text (Christ already dwells in the temple), even if we know what the prophets mean. Interpreting the Bible in context is foundational for evangelicals, even if the allegorical theologian's heart is right.

4. *Process and crisis*

In the New Testament, the writers describe the Christian life in terms of process ("I am finding it") and crisis ("I've found it!"). The difference is seen in the two words "renewal" and "revival." The appeal for renewal is an appeal to process, and the appeal for revival is for a sudden intervention by God, a crisis.

In church history, the Reformed tradition has endeavored to go forward because of what Christ has done. In the Arminian tradition, revival has been viewed as something to wait for in prayer because of what Christ will do.

The Vineyard was built on the premise that the strongman was bound in the Christ event, and we now have been commissioned to go out and plunder his house. KCF, in its earlier days, had prayed and waited for the "big bang." Now, they have pulled back on many of their prayer meetings to allow more time for evangelism and outreach though they are still committed to praying for a great end-time revival.

5. *Wholeness and holiness*

After the pursuit of wholeness in the '80s, the church had gotten more healthy, but lazy. The prophets began to call us back to holy living and classic disciplines such as fasting and prayer.

There's truth in both positions. We cannot get well until we rest in the indicatives of Scripture, but neither should we sin that grace should abound. Wholeness and holiness are both important, but true holiness comes out of greater trust in God produced in people who are becoming whole.

Mallone concluded that as an evangelical he was inclined to:

- Indicatives
- Pastors and teachers
- Historical-grammatical interpretations
- Process
- Wholeness

*But he recognized the value of:*

- Imperatives
- Prophets
- Allegorical insights
- Crisis
- Holiness

At this point in the story, it appeared that the difficulties were over. Men like George Mallone were hopeful that the emphases of MVF could be incorporated into the life of the Vineyard. We would continue to be "us"—winning the lost, caring for the poor, healing the sick, worshipping God, planting churches—but at the same time we would receive the word of the Lord about holiness and begin to intercede for a visitation from God and worldwide revival. The prophets would learn to be healthy members of local churches, learn the value of interpreting Scripture in context, adjust their styles to be better communicators, and travel around the Vineyard encouraging the body. We, on the other hand, would learn the art of weighing revelation, interpretation and application. But there was yet one more obstacle on the horizon that would greatly affect what ultimately happened.

## REVIVAL (?) IN ENGLAND, OCTOBER 1990

After Paul Cain had predicted that "revival, tokens of revival," would break out in London in October 1990, Wimber began to ask himself whether he *really* believed it. Did he believe it enough to rally the troops to be ready for it?

During this period he read *The Puritan Hope*[9] by Ian Murray, which changed his eschatology to embrace the message of the rise of a victorious church at the end of the age. Murray chronicles the impact of the Puritan postmillennial belief that the church would one day rise victorious. Even though Wimber himself was a premillennialist, he believed the church would go through the great tribulation. According to this view, the Bible predicts a massive harvest among the Jews; the church will finish the task of world evangelization as it is purified by intense persecution. While reading about the impact eschatology had on his Reformed forebears, Wimber was given faith to believe for the rise of the last day church.

Once he had embraced the vision for revival in London, he scheduled a conference back in Anaheim for January 1991, thinking that he and the team would bring some of the revival back home with them. Brochures were printed up and sent out all over the world. Wimber was committed.

The conferences in the U.K. in October 1990, centered in London, but meetings all over England, Wales, and Scotland were powerful indeed, the sessions in Edinburgh seeing many signs and wonders. I brought a team from our church and preached one weekend at one of the satellite conferences in the highlands of Scotland. To this day I have never experienced preaching under the anointing of God as I did at the end of my final sermon. As I started my conclusion, I suddenly felt taken to a new level of power. It is incredible to think about it even now. I gave an invitation, and the people who responded fell on top of each other in the aisles, slain by the Spirit as they came forward for prayer I don't know whether the meetings produced any long-term change or not, but they were amazing experiences for me.

I will never forget the look in John Wimber's eyes and the

speech he gave the team before the conference began. He had brought his entire family to England to experience this conference, convinced that something significant would happen. Happy Leman, senior pastor of the Vineyard in Champaign, Illinois, recorded Wimber's comments to their team at the Docklands in London. John told them:

*This week is the most crucial moment in the Vineyard. It is the most important task in VCF history. If we have success here, it will give us momentum for the next two decades. Our future could pivot on this meeting...All we have done in the last ten years has been preliminary for this very moment. We have been setting the stage for this week since we began. This is the time for each of us to do our jobs!* [10]

Happy added that Wimber believed that this could be a turning point in history. He stated that he had come to announce that Jesus was about to unleash a move on the face of the earth that would be called a worldwide revival.[11]

## DID REVIVAL COME?

The meetings in London were powerful. But did revival come? Many thought not. Happy wrote, "The trip was not as many of us had expected it to be—one with awesome creative signs and wonders, spectacular revival, and unloosing of the Holy Spirit to the degree that we have never seen previously. Yet we all agreed it was a very powerful meeting."[12] Steve Nicholson conveyed to me that these meetings were disappointing to him in light of the meetings in 1984-86 that, in his opinion, were much more powerful. Wimber himself said after the conference, "I think we won, but it will take four months to know for sure."[13]

At the conference Mike Bickle tried to clear up what Paul Cain had actually said. Cain had been quoted as saying that revival would break out in London in October 1990. But Paul had qualified what he meant by adding that "tokens" of revival would come forth. What Paul said and what was communicated

225

were different. The whole affair set up many for disillusionment. Mike Bickle told me that Paul was shocked when the brochures came out for the Revival Fires conference in Anaheim in January 1991, because Paul was quoted as saying "revival" and not "tokens of revival." Mike told me that Paul realized then that he would eventually have to pay the bill on this one. On the other hand, some Vineyard leaders think the prophecy had simply been wrong and the tokens thing was an attempt to back-peddle.

## IN THE MONTHS AFTER LONDON...

At a pastors' conference in the Midwest the next month (November 1990), Wimber shared with us that in England we had ministered to 50-65,000 people in five major conferences, 38 satellite conferences, and 26 more churches on Sundays. They believed there were 6,000 at the pastors' meetings. The ministry was similar to what the Vineyard experienced in 1983 to 1985— tremendous power, but few creative miracles. Nevertheless, John believed that many hearts were captured and that revival may, indeed, have broken out in England. He cautioned us that the beginning of revival is never as clear cut as we, and/or the historians, try to make it.

He was still on board with the themes of the end-time revival and intercession at this point but shared with us that he had come to a disagreement with Paul Cain concerning Paul's message regarding "coming outside the camp." By this Paul meant that those who were suffering reproach from evangelicals for their Charismatic convictions were to "come outside the camp" (i.e., the evangelical church) to rally together. John, however, had based his entire renewal ministry on his call *to* the church, not outside of it. John shared that Paul had prayed about it and realized that it was a true word, but out of season. There was nothing outside the camp to rally to at this point, nor was there a need.

In the same context, John shared that he was concerned about what might be called the "big bang" theory of revival. The Vineyard was built on the assumption that even though we wait for the confirmation of the kingdom of God at the end of the age, Jesus taught and modeled that the kingdom had, at the same time, come *now*! While we should pray for revival, the strong man was bound during the earthly ministry of Jesus, and we have been commissioned to go out and plunder his house. Paul Cain had already delivered this word to MVF, and they were making adjustments. John wanted to make sure that "occupy until he comes" remained the standard operating procedure in the Vineyard.

## WIMBER VISITS THE VINEYARD 1990-91

At the pastors' conference in 1989, we had set Vineyard I on the altar. What Vineyard II would look like, no one knew. Wimber was busy traveling with the prophetic men, overseeing the problems in Kansas City and dealing with his detractors in Australia. He did not have a vision for where the movement was to go. In the spring of 1990, however, someone he trusted gave him a word that if he would spend less time with the prophets and more time with the Vineyard, he would get direction for the movement. Subsequently, he began visiting each of the regions, listening to what the guys were saying and trying to help them process the season of the prophets. As he traveled, he had observed that approximately

- 25% were for the prophetic
- 50% were neutral
- 25 % were against

He was also surprised to discover how little uniformity there was. It was not a matter of saying, "I go to a Vineyard." One had to ask, "What kind?" This led him to ask two key questions: "What is a Vineyard?" and "Who decides?" Wimber attempted to answer these questions at the pastors' conference the next summer, but at this point, he listed ten things he was looking for in a Vineyard church.

- The Bible taught as a standard for living
- Ministry toward the poor, widows, orphans, etc.
- Evangelism tied to these social concerns
- A strong emphasis on physical healing, signs and wonders

- Effective small groups with a reasonable proportion of adults attending
- Effective training and discipling our people in the area of organizing their financial lives
- Interaction with other local churches
- Good worship
- Intercessory prayer
- Openness to prophetic ministry

One of John's other comments at Revival Fires is worth noting. In his travels around the regions of the Vineyard that year, he saw that some of the churches were no longer willing to pay the price they had originally paid to "do the stuff." [14] There was a definite move away from encouraging a full display of the Charismatic gifts, not only on Sunday mornings to be more inviting to visitors, but in the overall philosophy of ministry of the churches. The quest for the radical middle was indeed hard to sustain. It seemed very difficult to remain open to spiritual gifts while, at the same time, being effective in evangelism.

## THE AVC COUNCIL MEETING, DECEMBER 1990

The Vineyard's new direction was formulated at the council meeting in December of 1990. We were going to enter into major reorganization. Kenn Gulliksen, who was now the National Coordinator, and Happy Leman, a board member, were assigned the job of being the architects of the new structure.

Evangelism and church planting values were going to be revisited and the vision to plant 10,000 churches in the coming decades rekindled. There were now over 300 churches, a number of them overseas, especially in Europe. The decision was also made to birth world missions. These new courses of action would play themselves out in the pastors' conference the following summer.

## REVIVAL FIRES CONFERENCE, ANAHEIM, 1991

The Revival Fire conferences that went on in many locations in 1991 were good conferences, but revival did not break out in them either. In the winter 91 issue of *Equipping the Saints*,

Wimber addressed revival. He exonerated Paul by getting the quote right and then tried to define the meaning of revival. He wrote that revival came in two stages, first internally to the church and second to the world in the form of conversions and social reform. He said that tokens of revival did come to the church and that we were on schedule. He summed it up saying:

*Signs and wonders were experienced at all five of the major conferences and many of the regional conferences. However, London stands out from the rest. In the Wednesday evening session my staff estimates that over 4,000 (out of 6,000) came forward to be empowered by the Holy Spirit. In my entire ministry I have never seen a greater response to the word of God from Christians.* [15]

## SNOQUALMIE FALLS, WASHINGTON, MAY 1991 [16]

Just prior to the 1991 national pastors' conference, the board held their biannual council meeting in Snoqualmie Falls, Washington, in May. It was an important meeting for a number of reasons. First of all, there was a consensus on the board to make a distinct move away from the prophetic. Secondly, they decided to "get back on track" as a movement; the Vineyard had been called to plant churches, and it was time to get back to business. Part of that process would involve a concerted effort to plant churches cross-culturally. Most importantly, a long-standing tension regarding the future of the movement was resolved at this council meeting and a changing of the guard was initiated on the board.

Coming out of these decisions, it became clear that the current organizational structure was no longer adequate for what God was calling the movement to, and changes were in order in that realm as well.

### RECONSIDERING THE PROPHETIC ERA

A shift away from the prophetic emphasis had been in the works for some time, but it was in Snoqualmie Falls that John addressed the issues with the board. John admitted that he had not screened the prophetic closely enough and that in an attempt to bless and honor them, he probably gave them more publicity and reinforcement than was wise. Because of this, the problems were of greater magnitude and would take longer to clean up. He stressed that the newcomers did not represent the Vineyard. While he was at this time appreciative of men like Mike Bickle, Paul Cain, Bob Jones, John Paul Jackson, and Jack Deere, he was not willing to give over who we were and where we were headed to them. Just because he had not spoken plainly about his reservations in the last two years did not mean that he agreed with all the things they taught.

Even at this stage stories of prophecies that had been wrong were beginning to circulate. Many of us had, to varying degrees, gotten caught up in some of the elitist tendencies and apocalyptic fervor that were common immature responses to the prophetic messages that were given at this time. In fact, we were often so caught up in looking for the fantastic and extraordinary, the big bang, that it became harder to deal with the merely mundane events of everyday life.

This would become more and more of a problem in the next few years. Bob Fulton told me that at this point John realized that he had been intimidated by the prophets' gifting and had not realized that he had the authority to pastor them. As more and more lives were affected, either by prophecies that did not come to pass or by immature responses to prophecies, it became clear to Wimber that in the same way that the Vineyard had met the prophetic, it was now time for the prophetic to meet the Vineyard. And some of the prophetic men did not like to be governed.

### PHILOSOPHY OF MINISTRY CHANGES

There had also been, in the board's mind, a dramatic shift away from the Vineyard's Reformed foundation. Wimber had always believed that renewal and ministry were under the sovereignty of God. He was just a "fat man trying to get to heaven," precious treasure in a jar of clay. If God had used him, it wasn't because he had prayed harder than other men. It had been God's sovereign choice.

230

The prophetic emphasis had shifted the center to a much more Arminian emphasis on fasting, intercession, and holiness in order to usher in the coming revival. Ministry was in the hands of the new breed and dread champions. John had always taught us that everyone gets to play—we just have to play nice and share our toys. Dread champions we were not.

## A Pioneer/Homesteader Conflict on the Board

A pioneer/homesteader conflict is a predictable barrier that growing teams need to work through. Those who pay the price to pioneer the land grow close to one another. They bond at a deep level through a shared history. Those who come in to homestead that land are not relationally in the club and are often perceived as not having paid their dues. In order for the organization to get to the next level of growth, however, the pioneers, who have formed a primary group, have to concede to the inevitable—the homesteaders are here to stay, and the old gang has to break up to give birth to something new. This transition period is a hard one for pioneers, and they often don't make it.

At Snoqualmie Falls the core leadership of the Vineyard went through their pioneer/homesteader test. While prophetic issues were capturing international attention, a battle of greater consequence for the Vineyard was being waged between some of the original Vineyard pastors who had come out the Calvary movement and those who had joined later.

The issue on the table was whether the Vineyard would choose to become an organized, cohesive movement which would make room for and take pastoral responsibility over hundreds, even thousands of new churches, or whether it would become a completely loose fellowship of churches with no organizational ties or structures for church planting, missions, and pastoring.

Steve Nicholson, one of the homesteaders from the Midwest, wrote me that he felt that the position of the old Calvary men was best articulated by one pastor who asked, "Why do we have to have an organization at all? Why can't we just be friends?" This approach was reflective of Calvary's deeply held conviction against quenching the Spirit and a latent distrust of anything that hinted of a methodology.

According to Todd Hunter, at this point the Calvary guys felt betrayed by John who had promised when they had started that the Vineyard would not become a denomination. In Snoqualmie Falls, John emphatically stated that they *were* a denomination and that all Vineyard churches needed to change their names to So-and So Vineyard Christian Fellowship or Vineyard Christian Fellowship of So-and-So. The Calvary guys blew a cork. Chuck Smith had never cared what a church was called, and this felt controlling to them.

Nicholson told me that he felt that the West Coast group needed to give way to the new thing God was trying to create. He argued that an organization had to be built for the children and for the younger pastors who were coming on board, sometimes at the expense of their evangelical reputations.

## BOARD FALLOUT

The meetings at Snoqualmie Falls were intense, and within a year, four pioneers resigned from the board: Kenn Gulliksen, Tom Stipe, Lee Bennett and Jack Little. They were replaced by a new wave of homesteaders. Nicholson wrote, "The long-standing division and paralysis that had plagued the board was broken, and we were finally able to go forward with a high degree of consensus."[17]

John and Margie McClure's perspective saw the lack of consensus as the result of the prophetic years. They remember with fondness the intense love, mutual admiration, powerful ministry and fun the board had had before those years, a period of time the homesteaders weren't around to enjoy.

Kenn Gulliksen wrote me that he resigned his position as national director in 1992 because he felt an increasing tension with John's leadership style and with the general direction of the Vineyard. Kenn said that he didn't want to undermine the Vineyard by being in open conflict with John and felt the need to retain his own integrity by pursuing what he felt was the Lord's direction for his life. He felt called to return to West Los Angeles where he and Joanie began to plant a new church in affiliation with Calvary Chapel.[18]

After Tom Stipe's resignation, he also returned his church to its Calvary Chapel roots, believing the Vineyard to have left its biblical moorings. Tom has since taken a very negative stance toward the Vineyard and has written the introduction to Hank Hanegraaff's *Counterfeit Revival* where he comes out against the Vineyard.

Lee Bennett went on to pastor in the Northwest.

Jack Little would not leave the Vineyard until 1994. While the rumor floated around at that time that Jack had left because he was upset with the Toronto Blessing (see chapter 17), Jack told me in a personal interview the real reason why they left. While on a trip to Hawaii to scout out the potential for planting Vineyards there, the Lord spoke the same word to Jack and his wife, Susan, independently. He told them that they "had grown up in the house called Vineyard." They were now to leave to start their own "house." They went back and met with John Wimber and some other leaders in John's office. John affirmed that it was the Lord, and in tears blessed Jack and Susan to start an unaffiliated church in Oceanside, California, called Grace Chapel of the Coast. Jack now has a number of other pastors who relate to him.

## THE FALL OF BOB JONES

In the fall of 1991, the tragic news that Bob Jones had become involved in sexual sin broke over the wires. After the accusations by Ernie Gruen, most of which involved concerns with Bob's ministry, this news seemed to put the final nail in the prophetic coffin for many. Bob had effectively ministered to both my wife and me on more than one occasion, and we were deeply saddened by the news.

Bob was put under the care of a pastor outside the Vineyard named Larry Alberts and was eventually released by Alberts to minister at large again in 1994. The Vineyard board, on the other hand, has not (as of 1999) recognized that release due to a lack of trust and still prohibits Bob from ministering in the movement.

## WIMBER WOULD EVENTUALLY APOLOGIZE FOR THE PROPHETIC ERA

At the pastors' conference in the Vineyard's new facility in Anaheim Hills in 1995, Wimber told the movement that he regretted leading the Vineyard into the prophetic era, saying that it did, indeed, get us off track. Behind closed doors it became apparent that John had been deeply hurt by the lack of a significant revival in London and had become disillusioned.

The prophetic period could have been considered all but over except for one more factor—the presence of Metro Vineyard Fellowship in Kansas City.

## MIKE BICKLE PULLS OUT OF THE VINEYARD

One has to wonder with all that had gone on how Mike Bickle and the churches under him in Kansas City were faring. Essentially they remained under the Vineyard covering, but it was generally acknowledged that while there were similarities between Mike's churches and most Vineyards, the two represented different streams. Most felt that at some point Metro would be freed up to follow their convictions. This would not ultimately come to pass until the summer of 1996 and will be covered in a later chapter.

While the values of prophetic ministry and intercessory prayer had always been a part of the Vineyard, the board felt that these values would never be expressed in the Vineyard in the way that Mike had always hoped. In the end there was very little cross-pollination, and there certainly had never been a merger as George Mallone was suggesting in his paper.

## IN RETROSPECT

Given all the different opinions here, I want to pause at this point to address some of the issues raised by the prophetic era. None of us, John Wimber included, were prepared for what came down—stories of earthquakes, comets, droughts, names and dates. These things seemed so validating. On the other hand, what was one to do with the prophecies that had not come true?

The first time something comes at me, I seldom get it all right. Knowing this, ought to impart grace for mistakes. If we were John Wimber or Mike Bickle, given all that has happened to them, how would we have fared?

The first question that must be asked is whether the prophets were from God or not. Some within the Vineyard are now very skeptical, even to the point of thinking that some of the prophets are dangerous. I have never held that position, but hearing some of the stories of prophetic abuse and methodology while doing this research, I have come to realize that I was never in the eye of the storm. Even though I was hurt by prophecies that seemed not to come true, I always thought men like Mike Bickle and Paul Cain were sincere, genuine servants of God. While I am not personally convinced by their restorationist thesis, I still, to this day, withhold judgments in my heart about the meaning of comets and earthquakes.

My experience with some of the prophetic, especially with Paul Cain's ministry, was that it was presented in such a way that the prophet could not be wrong. When I went to Kansas City to hear Paul Cain for the first time it was clearly inferred that his words "never fell to the ground." I remember dropping to my knees and sensing the holy presence of God during that experience. Looking back, if it was God I was sensing, I certainly responded to his presence in an immature manner. I went home and told my church that everything was going to be different from that point on. The last days events were beginning. I now deeply regret getting caught up in that apocalyptic fervor and wish I had been more even-handed. It was not at all healthy for our church.

TAKING RESPONSIBILITY

What we have seen through these prophetic ministers is typical of New Testament (NT) prophecy. I refer the reader to Wayne Grudem's book, *The Gift of Prophecy in the New Testament and Today* for an in-depth biblical study on the subject of prophecy, especially pp. 32ff for explaining the differences between Old and New Testament prophecy.[19]

Dr. Grudem points out that in the OT, the test of a true prophet was 100% accuracy (Deuteronomy 18:21-22). Prophesying either in error or in the name of another god was a crime punishable by death (Deuteronomy 18:20). When we turn to the NT, those who were considered prophets were not subject to the same stringent standards (e.g., there is no indication in 1 Corinthians 12-14 that a prophetic error was a crime punishable by death). By the time of the NT the word "prophet" meant spokesman in a general way and was used to refer to prophecy that was not held to the 100% accuracy test. In other words, the NT allows the local church to be a place for people to learn how to prophesy. It was a gift they had to grow in (i.e., they could make mistakes as they learned).

The NT equivalent to the OT prophets were the apostles. Theirs were the only words that were considered fully authoritative and have been recorded for us as the New Testament Scriptures. The difference between the utterances and writings of the NT apostles and the NT prophets was not in kind (they were both giving forth revelation) but in authority. The words of the apostles were fully authoritative and 100% accurate, the words of the NT prophets were not. They needed to be weighed in the context of community. They grew in their gift just as one grows in teaching and evangelism.

Here then, is perhaps the crucial issue for our study. Since NT prophesy is to be weighed, what does that look like in the context of the NT church? My mentor in seminary, Dr. Gordon D. Fee, told me one time that the Charismatic movement would be judged for two great sins, the so-called "health and wealth" gospel and the failure to weigh prophecy. It is on this latter count that I think we have failed greatly.

The prophetic ministry was often introduced in our meetings in a way that reflected OT prophecy (inerrant) rather than NT prophecy (needing to be weighed). This packaging created an invincible aura around the prophetic ministers, and some of them did not want to be held accountable for prophecy that did not come true. The answer is not to "stone" the prophets, as the cult-watchers would have us believe. There is a vast difference between a person who is learning to prophesy and a false prophet. False prophets were severely disciplined by God in the OT and were treated just as harshly by Jesus and the apostles in the NT (Matthew 24:10; 1 John 4:1).

I think that our problem with the prophetic was both with the prophecies themselves (some were clearly wrong) and with our inability to weigh them. Learning to weigh prophecy involves evaluating all three phases of the prophetic experience: revelation, interpretation, and application.

## THE RESPONSIBILITIES OF THE PROPHET

*Firstly*, the prophetic person has a responsibility before God and men to learn to receive *accurate* prophetic words and to communicate them in a way that edifies the church. Prophets must not go beyond their revelation and add their own "stuff." This just muddies the waters.

*Secondly*, the *language* that is used to communicate prophetic revelation has tremendous bearing on what the hearer receives. Most of the prophecies were communicated as though they were going to come true, and later, when they didn't happen, it was explained to us that they weren't guarantees but rather invitations into God's intent that were contingent on our or others' obedience. When a prophet says that such-and-such is going to happen and it doesn't, this is errant prophecy. If it is a prophecy contingent on other factors, then the one who is prophesying is responsible for saying so, lest the person being ministered to be set up for disappointment. "God says" is very dangerous language.

*Thirdly*, the *setting* in which a word is given is important. The words given the Vineyard during the prophetic era were often in front of thousands of people. This kind of setting put the recipients of the words under great pressure. There was generally no personal time with the prophets to help process the words, and people were left to go home to study the transcripts with local leadership teams who wanted to take the ball and run with it. NT prophecy is to come in the context of the body of Christ and usually in conjunction with pastoral ministry (1 Corinthians 14:26ff). The process has to be relational; if prophetic words are spoken in larger contexts, I think time should be carved out with the prophet and a pastor to help people process the word's interpretation and application.

*Lastly*, as was said above, the prophetic person has to be able to risk the potential rejection of having his/her prophecies *weighed* either by the elders or by the community. They have to come into their ministry knowing that they are not always going to be right and that they will have to admit when they are wrong. The church, on the other hand, has to be careful to weigh prophetic words in an atmosphere of love so as not to damage the prophetic person.

### THE RESPONSIBILITIES OF THE COMMUNITY

Not only do the prophets have a part to own, but so do the people receiving the word. I think interpreting and applying a word correctly takes just as much gifting and wisdom as does the revelation itself.

One of the trickiest problems in interpreting prophecy is to determine whether the prophetic person is getting revelation of what God intends, what the devil intends, or what the person wants. The prophet, as was said above, must not interpret the revelation unless he or she is sure God is giving that interpretation. This is a crucial distinction and requires the gift of discernment.

On more than one occasion John Wimber was given the word that he was going to die. It was explained to us later that the prophetic person was receiving information on the devil's plan for John and misinterpreted the word as a guarantee on the future. An accurate revelation wrongly interpreted can be destructive.[20]

On other occasions prophets received words about such and such happening, but what they were reading was what the person wanted and not what God was saying would happen. This kind of misinterpretation could lead to prophecies that do not come true.

When a prophecy is given and I, not the prophet, interpret its meaning or timing incorrectly, this is not a problem with the revelation, nor with the one who gave it—it is now mine to interpret correctly with the help of wise counsel in the context of relationship. If it is misinterpreted or misapplied, we have to own it as our problem and not make prophetic ministers the lightening rods for our unresolved issues. We need to weigh a prophetic word carefully to spot any theological or eschatological agendas that may be clouding accurate revelation. If it doesn't fit what we believe biblically, we do not have to receive the word. We should not party to any "Charismatic witchcraft" that would violate our freedom to disagree with a word.

## SOME FINAL THOUGHTS

We should embrace the gifts and outpouring of the Holy Spirit but refrain from any kind of apocalyptic exegesis and fervor other than prayers for the Lord to come (maranatha, "Lord come!"; 1 Corinthians 16:22).

We need not to get so caught up in a particular interpretation that we lose sight of the fact that we could be wrong.

We should never try to establish doctrine from prophecy. Doctrine is derived from the exegesis of Scripture. In the same vein, even though NT writers at times used an allegorical method in interpreting OT texts, they were doing so under the inspiration of the Holy Spirit. We have no such license, and our hermeneutical method should be grounded on ascertaining the author's intended meaning in a text.

We should beware of any kind of elitist attitude in connection with prophetic ministry. I am no better than my brother and our bond is our faith in Jesus Christ and an inspired Bible, not whether we believe a particular prophecy.

We need to affirm that our pastoral call is to equip the saints for the work of ministry; our people are to be active in ministry, not passive, not needing to wait either for the anointed apostles or prophets or for the coming revival. People are dying now, and we are the ones Jesus is sending to them.

We need to be careful about our motives in pursuing prophecy. I am a teacher by gifting and often travel to other

Vineyard churches. When I do seminars on the biblical text, the attendance is usually lower than when I do seminars that have the promise of the supernatural and prophetic revelation. This is a disturbing trend. Would we rather have a "word" from God than do the work of building our lives on his word, the Bible, and believing what it says by faith? I don't need a prophetic word to know that God loves me. That was communicated very clearly in a historical event 2,000 years ago. If God wants to confirm what I already know through a prophetic word, then I praise Him—but I don't need it to replace faith. While we are to encourage prophecy in the local church, let us beware of fostering a climate that is no different than why people pursue astrologers in the secular world—because they don't have faith in a sovereign God who has all enemies under his feet.

As we leave the subject of prophecy, we need to reaffirm the importance of this gift in both the New Testament (1 Corinthians 14) and in our local churches. When Joel prophesied in his second chapter (as quoted by Peter in Acts 2) about the coming of the Spirit in the last days, he wrote that our sons and daughters would prophecy, that our young men would dream dreams. Prophetic revelation is a very important part of life in the local church. It does help to fuel intercession and quickens us to what God is doing. It builds our faith and opens a path to the power of the Holy Spirit. I think that in the sovereignty of God he brought Vineyard through the prophetic period to teach us both the possibilities and the pitfalls. Like two ends of a continuum, John Wimber and Mike Bickle both struggled to bring us to the radical middle.

CB

NOTES:

[1] Wimber, "A Response to Ernie Gruen's Controversy with Kansas City Fellowship," *Equipping the Saints*, Fall 1990, p. 4

[2] Lee Grady, "Resolving the Kansas City Prophecy Controversy," *Ministries Today*, September/October, 1990, p. 49; note that a "familiar spirit" is a term from the Charismatic movement which means that when two parties prophecy the same erroneous thing it is because the

demonic spirits that are inspiring them are familiar with each other, thus offering the same word to their human victims.

[3] *Wimber*, "A Response to Ernie Gruen," *Equipping the Saints*, Fall 1990, p. 5

[4] Lee Grady, "Resolving the Kansas City Prophecy Controversy, *Ministries Today*, September/October, p. 51

[5] Wimber, "A Response to Ernie Gruen," *Equipping the Saints*, Fall 1990, p. 14

[6] *Holy Laughter &the Toronto Blessing*, Grand Rapids, Zondervan, pp. 124-126

[7] *Ibid.*, p. 7; Bickle and Sullivant go into greater depth on the things God taught them in *Growing in the Prophetic*, pp. 47-49, 88-92.

[8] When I talked to Mike Bickle about Mallone's view, Mike wanted it stated that the only place where he uses an allegorical hermeneutic is in the Old Testament book Song of Songs.

[9] Carlisle, Pennsylvania, Banner of Truth, 1971

[10] Happy Leman has been on the national board of the Vineyard since 1989 and has written summaries of these and other significant meetings in the Vineyard that are distributed around the country. They are called *Happy Notes* and are Happy's views and perceptions and not necessarily those held by John Wimber, the board, or individuals on the board; *Happy Notes*, October 31, 1990, p. 2.

[11] *Ibid.*, p. 7

[12] *Ibid.*, p. 9

[13] *Ibid.*, p. 10

[14] *Happy Notes*, February 8, 1991, p. 2

[15] Wimber, "Revival Fire," *Equipping the Saints*, Winter 1991, p. 13

[16] This information was taken from a confidential set of *Happy Notes* (May 7, 1991) and used with Happy's permission.

[17] Personal e-mail message

[18] Fax, August 6, 1998

[19] Westchester, IL, Crossway Books, 1988

[20] Some now think that Wimber's "death words" were attempts to control him because he was beginning to withdraw his endorsement from the prophetic.

# CHAPTER FOURTEEN

# GETTING BACK TO OUR ROOTS

# GETTING BACK TO OUR ROOTS

## THE DENVER PASTORS' CONFERENCE, 1991

T he 1991 pastors' conference in Denver was the largest yet, with almost all the movement's families represented. Pastor Tom Stipe was still with the Vineyard and Lenny LaGuardia, the children's pastor, hosted a tremendous program for the kids of participants. In comparison to the last two conferences, the atmosphere was festive with a strong sense of "getting back on track."

Some felt that we had been off track the last two years, while others had received the experience with the prophets as a positive and important learning curve. Whatever the individual pastor's response to the prophetic era, everyone was thrilled with the direction and the tone set during this week. What happened in Denver in 1991 set the rudder that still guides the movement as I finish this in 1999.

## A *"CENTERED SET"* MOVEMENT

In 1988 we had considered becoming a denomination with delineated boundaries defined by a constitution and by-laws. God had clearly said no. Now, in 1989, John attempted to explain why we had not gone in this direction. He lectured from his training as a sociologist and gave us the philosophical grid and language to understand what we were attempting to do.[1] In the lecture John borrowed from what is called Social Set Theory which seeks to describe the dynamics between individuals in three basic kinds of groups (here called *sets*).

1. **Fuzzy sets** describe groups that have no organizational center. A group of little league parents might perceive themselves as a group in that they have a common interest, but no core values define their existence.

2. **Centered sets** describe groups that have joined together around a common center articulated by core values. People in

a centered set want to go the same place and generally agree on how they will get there and who will lead them. There is a lot of latitude for collegial disagreement on non-core issues and flexibility in forms.

3. **Bounded sets** describe groups that not only have banded together around a common center, but that have also clearly defined rules about beliefs and practices. The number of people who can get in the group becomes narrower because the parameters are more defined.

John explained that from the beginning he intended that the Vineyard be a centered set of like-minded churches. There was enough latitude in the system to allow for differences on what were considered to be peripheral doctrines, such as the mode of baptism. Anyone could be a Vineyard who could prescribe to the genetic code articulated earlier.

John also taught that historically groups couldn't remain centered sets forever because the rules that determine the insiders and outsiders will eventually have to be defined. His desire, however, was to keep the Vineyard a centered set movement for as long as he could.

## TRIMMING BACK THE BUSH

John's highest value in leading the movement was always to obey God within the confines of Scripture as determined by an evangelical hermeneutic. His *modus operandi* had been to do whatever the Father was doing within those parameters. In order to evaluate trends and views emerging in the movement, he generally chose to let them alone until they could be studied biblically and examined for long-term fruit. In describing this philosophy he used the analogy of *growing a bush*. It is a temptation to trim a bush back too soon before a gardener knows what he has. This means letting the thing go for awhile, thus having to endure a period when the bush looks messy and untrimmed. Then, when the course the branches are taking is clear, that which is unwanted is trimmed back. This allows for more growth in the rest of the plant. In this way the boundaries of our centered set were being defined.

Earlier John had taken a stand on the issue of praying against territorial spirits because he saw no biblical model for it. He'd also established that no Vineyard could have a woman as a senior pastor. In like manner he now explained to us that after two years of traveling with the prophetic men, while affirming the value of their ministry and their message on holiness, he could endorse neither the "come outside the camp" message, which he felt promoted elitism, nor the message heralding the "new thing" that God was doing. God was not doing anything new, only drawing new attention to facets of the old.

In taking these stands, John was defining the "rules" of Vineyard protocol, tightening the edges of the set around what he thought were biblical lines.

## RE-ARTICULATING CORE VALUES

The heart of the Denver conference was reaffirming who we were and where we were going. Two years prior we had laid Vineyard I on the altar in the very same auditorium in which we now reconvened to affirm that Vineyard II was alive and well and somewhere in process. John Wimber and other leaders reiterated the Vineyard genetic code. He gave a list of ten things he was looking for in a Vineyard church. These ten things were the values that centered the movement:[2]

- The Bible taught as the Word of God
- Ministry to the poor, orphans, widows, etc.
- Evangelism tied to social concerns if possible
- Healing the sick and casting out demons
- Commitment to small groups
- Equipping the saints in things such as serving, giving, doctrine, family, finances, etc.
- Interaction with other pastors and churches
- Worship that reflects the values God had given us such as intimacy, being natural, etc.
- The exercise of spiritual gifts
- Commitment to missions

The values of evangelism and church planting were nurtured all

246

week long. In the two years since we had supposedly put Vineyard I to death, our church planting had been minimal compared to earlier years. The immature way we had responded to prophetic ministry had all but halted our forward progress. We now called up our common center from our past and talked about how we were going to fulfill the mission that God had given us.

John also reiterated the values of being low key, doing only what the Father is doing, and our commitment to planning with God in prayer. On this last point John felt we needed to be much more intentional about how we were going to plant 10,000 churches.

The afternoon sessions by Vineyard leaders dealt with the major themes of the week:

- Gary Best from VCF Langley in Vancouver taught on evangelism;
- Jack Little from VCF North Coast in California taught on church planting; and
- Brent Rue from VCF Lancaster in California taught on missions.

BIRTHING MISSIONS

The highlight of Denver '91 for me was seeing God birth a new emphasis in the Vineyard: missions. Many of us had been involved in missions, some heavily, but God had not directed us into it as a movement. The reasoning had been that at the early stages of our development most of the churches were young, getting into their first buildings and hiring staff. To get heavily involved in missions at this point would have been premature. Within the preceding year God had indicated to John that Vineyard fellowships had reached a level of maturity that warranted a denominational missions thrust.

Part of this shift was precipitated in the natural realm because a large church-planting movement in Brazil called PAZ (Project Amazon) had approached us about becoming a Vineyard. God had used their overture as an indicator of his timing. That week I had the privilege of doing a half-hour Bible study each morning on God's heart for missions. From Genesis to Revelation I traced the missions thread and had a wonderful response.

After the final plenary session we had a powerful time of blessing for all our missionaries. It seemed that God was endorsing our new direction.

Bob Fulton was made the coordinator of the International arm of AVC thus giving church planting overseas top priority, especially in three areas/cultures:

- Hispanic
- Asian
- Eastern European

## PROCESSING THE PROPHETIC

In addition to our forward thrust, John also took some time to affirm some of the prophetic themes from the past years. While he no longer believed all that had been prophesied about the Vineyard in 1989, he did believe that God planned to use the Vineyard as a change-agent in the Western world. John believed that an expansion was coming to the Vineyard and that this would involve a wave of young people. He said that the Holy Spirit had told him that he would get to disciple 20,000 young people before he died.[3]

John said that week that his theology was essentially the same as it had always been except that the prophetic had forced him to re-evaluate his thoughts in two areas.[4] First, he now believed that prophetic ministry is valid and much more available than he had originally thought. Second, his eschatology had changed to embrace the fact that we were in the greatest move of God in history.

He explained that Paul Cain was a "revivalist," and that John and the Vineyard tended to be equippers. John said it was hard to get the messages to dovetail, and that he and Paul were not going to be traveling together much anymore. God had used Wimber to give Paul and the prophetic a worldwide platform, and that job was done. Paul Cain has rarely ministered in Vineyard churches since then (with the exception of Bickle's congregation before his withdrawal from the Vineyard and some conferences at the Anaheim Vineyard in 1998-99).

John also embraced the prophetic message on holiness but believed their language in communicating it tended to lead toward legalism. He exhorted us to receive the word even if we had trouble with the packaging.

In one session, John explained some of the reasons prophetic words go unfulfilled. This session was intended for those who, during the prophetic period, had received words that had not come to pass.

- First, sometimes the ministry comes from false prophets. Wimber was quick to point out that he did not feel that this was true in our case.
- Second, the message is misinterpreted by either the person giving the word or the person receiving it. He went on to address the three phases of revelation, interpretation and application.
- Third, the person receiving the word either responded with a lack of faith or encountered conditions that altered the word's fulfillment. He explained that most prophetic words are contingent on the choices of people. If people make the wrong choices, the word might go unfulfilled.
- Fourth, not enough time had passed since the prophecy was given (misinterpretation of timing).
- Fifth, there might be factors we can't see or don't understand.

RE-ORGANIZING THE VINEYARD

Kenn Gulliksen, the National Director of AVC, addressed the new structure that would become the framework for the emerging Vineyard II. The philosophy of the new structure as proposed by Kenn and Happy Leman, was based on recognizing two types of leaders:

1. **Overseers:** those with the gifting to oversee and govern.
2. **Specialists:** those who are gifted in a specialized area such as church planting, evangelism, missions, children's ministry, training, administration, etc.

The new structure would take these two types of leaders into account, thus forming a council of overseers getting input from task forces geared around areas of specialization. The overseers were broken down into Regional Overseers (ROs) and

Area Pastoral Coordinators (APCs).

*THE SENIOR LEADERS*

- John Wimber - International Leader
- Kenn Gulliksen - National Coordinator
- Bob Fulton - International Coordinator

*THE REGIONAL OVERSEERS*

- Southern California - John McClure
- Northern California - Bob Craine
- Northwest - Lee Bennett
- Rocky Plains - Rick Olmstead
- Midwest - Happy Leman
- Ohio Valley - Ron Allen
- Northeast - Lance Pittluck
- Southeast - Todd Hunter

*TASK FORCES*

(THREE PRELIMINARY TASK FORCES WERE SET IN PLACE)

- Evangelism - Jack Little
- Church Planting - Steve Nicholson
- World Missions - Bert Waggoner

గ్రహ

NOTES:

[1] John outlined this lecture in "Staying Focused: The Vineyard as a Centered Set," *Vineyard Reflections*, July 1995 - February 1996.

[2] *Happy Notes*, August 26, 1991, p. 3-4. What is fascinating about this list is that it is exactly the same as the list given to the Vineyard board in December of the previous year except for the last two items. In December's list the last two items were prayer and openness to the prophetic. In the list that is given here, the last two items are spiritual gifts and missions. There has been, by this time, an open move away from the themes introduced by Metro Vineyard Fellowship in Kansas City.

[3] *Ibid.*, p. 5

[4] Many had wondered if the events of the last two years meant that John had moved theologically.

# CHAPTER FIFTEEN

# BIRTHING
# MISSIONS
# IN
# THE VINEYARD

# BIRTHING MISSIONS IN THE VINEYARD[1]

## INTRODUCTION

I was hooked on missions the first time I heard a lecture on the "hidden peoples" by Dr. Christie Wilson at Gordon-Conwell Seminary. While pastoring our first Vineyard, we began to become involved in laying the groundwork for mission efforts in Papua New Guinea and India. We brought in Rick Love, a missionary sent out by the Vineyard in Oxnard, California,[2] to do a conference in our area. Rick was successfully planting churches among Muslims. To find out what other churches were doing cross-culturally, I produced the prototype of *Nations Network*, a newsletter I hoped would chronicle missions in the Vineyard. In it I included a survey to gather statistics on our global activity. Before I sent the newsletter out to the churches, however, I sent it to John Wimber to get his approval. To my surprise he sent it back saying that it was not time for missions in the Vineyard and asking me to scrap the project.

While I obeyed his request, I must confess being confused by what he meant. I knew that there was plenty of mission activity in our churches. I didn't understand his wisdom until a few years later. A vision for missions was birthed in the Vineyard in God's time at the pastors' conference in Denver in 1991, and I was allowed to be a part of that process. But before that seminal event, God had been sowing cross-cultural ministry into the Vineyard in sovereign ways. Like a vine, it had to grow down before it could grow up.

The history of missions in the Vineyard actually began through the ministry of Lonnie Frisbee. In the same way that God had used Lonnie to spark the Calvary Chapel revival, and would shortly use him in similar ways in the Vineyard, so also did Lonnie play a significant role in getting the cross-cultural ball rolling.

## THE FIRE GOES TO SOUTH AFRICA[3]

Early in 1979 an American missionary called a South African pastor named David Owen who had started a church in Johannesburg. David's church was part of a church planting movement in that country called "The Invisible Church" which was led by Nelson Nurse. The network of invisible churches was comprised of young people seeking God with a vision for a contemporary wineskin for a new generation. This wineskin would be characterized by the fullness of God's power.

Based on the missionary's recommendation, David brought Lonnie, who was then attending Wimber's Calvary Chapel, over to South Africa that same year. On the first night of meetings, the Spirit of God visited David's congregation mightily. They started at six o'clock and were still going strong at eleven. People were being healed, saved, delivered, shaken, and empowered. David says that the presence of God was awesome. He was so touched that he went over to America to spend some time in Wimber's church in March of 1980 and left to return to South Africa at the end of April. Just before he left, he spoke at the church, which numbered about 500 people at the time. It was the very next week that Lonnie Frisbee gave his testimony at the evening service at Canyon High School and Wimber's church was catapulted into revival.

When David came back to Anaheim in July, the church had mushroomed in attendance. Wimber writes in *Power Evangelism* that between May and September they baptized over 700 new converts with estimates that there may have been as many as 1,700 that prayed to receive Christ.[11] During this period David Owen's church officially aligned with John's.

John and Carol Wimber went to South Africa in October 1980 and brought with them a team comprised of Lonnie, Kenn Gulliksen, John and Margie McClure, and two laymen. They did a series of meetings on church growth for pastors during the day and had open meetings at night. The power of God was visibly evident.

David remembers one incident in particular. It was late, and Lonnie was very tired, having prayed for people all night. He stopped to pray for one last woman in her fifties who was completely blind. Her sight was restored instantly, and she began shouting in jubilation, telling everyone what clothes they were wearing. The woman worked for an important company associated with the mining industry, and the story was written up in their company newsletter. The *Sunday Times*, the largest newspaper in the country, also did a spread on her, thus giving God glory and Wimber instant credibility.

## THE FIRE SPREADS TO ENGLAND

Wimber's ministry in England began in 1981 when Eddie Gibbs, a church growth professor at Fuller Seminary, spoke to the late Canon David Watson from the Anglican church in England. David was going to California to lecture at Fuller and Dr. Gibbs told him he needed to visit a church near Anaheim called Calvary Chapel. While David was there he did contact the Vineyard and Bob Fulton went to pick him up. He seemed out of place in his three-piece suit but sat through what was a delightful service. It was what happened at the end of the service that was destined to have a tremendous impact on the nation of Britain.

During the ministry time at the end of the service a teenage girl in blue jeans had a word of knowledge for someone with a bronchial condition. No one responded but afterwards, David Watson leaned over to Wimber and said, "I have that condition. What am I supposed to do?" Wimber promptly called over the girl and some other youth to pray for him. Through their prayer David received profound improvement in his condition. If it had been Wimber or the church elders doing the ministry it would have been different, but what was this?—a teenage girl in blue jeans (and chewing gum for that matter!). David clearly sensed the presence of the Lord in that exchange and was so taken aback that, when he got back to England he invited Wimber to minister to his church in York.

### TEAMS GO TO ENGLAND

Wimber took a team of thirty over to England in 1981. It was a significant event because it initiated the model of taking lay people from churches aligned with John's and training them not only for power ministry but also for cross-cultural evangelism.

Power was released during this trip in unprecedented measures as they blessed another people group with the kingdom of God. The emerging movement was discovering a principle articulated by missiologist William Shenk:

> *the Christian faith has been saved repeatedly in nearly two thousand years of history by moving from an established heartland to a new environment. Apparently the process of cross-cultural transmission has been critical to the survival of the faith.[4]*

When the team arrived, they went first not to Watson's church, but to St. Andrews Anglican in Chorleywood pastored by David Pytches. God turned St. Andrews topsy-turvy, and a long-standing love affair began between Wimber and many of the churches in England.

The meetings in Chorleywood saw some incredible miracles. Bob Fulton prayed for an elderly lady with a cataract in one eye. As he prayed, he saw a picture in his mind of her optic nerve with a black spot on it. As he spoke healing to the optic nerve, she cried out that she could see. As it turned out, God didn't heal her cataract but opened up her other eye that had been blind! Bob didn't even know she had a blind eye. The next year when the Vineyard team went back to Chorleywood, Blaine Cook prayed for her cataract, and it was healed. John Wimber also prayed for a lady with multiple sclerosis, and she got out of her wheelchair and began to push it around.

During one of the meetings, there were five young men standing in the back mocking what was going on. The Holy Spirit fell on them and knocked them to the ground where they repented and turned their lives over to God's control. One of those men was a descendant of George Fox, the father of the Quakers, and four out of the five are in the ministry today.

After Chorleywood, the team visited Watson's church in York. Attending the meeting was a chief surgeon and some other doctors.

They watched God touch a girl with braces and could hear her bones cracking as God straightened them out. The miracle came as a group of children prayed for her.

## BACK TO SOUTH AFRICA

Without returning to the states, the team, now numbering about 30, then traveled to South Africa for meetings in Johannesburg that were attended by 300 pastors during the day and over 2,000 people in open meetings at night. The news of what had happened in the Anglican churches in England had already traveled to South Africa, and there were many Anglicans there.

David Owen remembers these meetings being characterized by extraordinary miracles. Conditions of every kind were healed resulting in a jubilation in worship that was nothing short of awesome. Teams fanned out on the weekends and ministered in local churches with great effect. Owen recalls one incident involving a colored[5] Methodist minister in Johannesburg who had a high profile in the political arena. He had received literature on the meetings and had thrown it away, but his wife dug the brochure out of the trash and encouraged him to go. He was so impressed at the first meeting that he came back with about fifty young people ranging in age from about four to sixteen. The Spirit of God fell on these young people so powerfully that some of them had to be carried home by their parents. David says the whole experience had such purity and holiness about it that everyone left stunned.

John Wimber writes in *Power Evangelism* about a Zulu boy they met who, when he was seven, had been a runner for his aunt who was a witch doctor. At that time, the boy's mother had made plans to move to another area. Unbeknown to anyone, the witch doctor had placed a curse on the child in retribution for losing his services. From that point on the boy had been reduced to a degenerated, animal-like condition. At the time of the encounter with Wimber's team, the boy was fourteen. He had not grown an inch since the curse had been placed on him, his toes partially missing, he suffered from a cleft palate and had ruined teeth. His mother had carried him to the meeting. As Wimber got down on his hands and knees, the young boy slobbered, mumbled and growled, the demons causing him to shrink back at the name of Jesus.

Wimber and some team members took him aside and began to minister to him. I was able to confirm what happened with Susie Hartman (then Hansen) who was on this prayer team. Team member, Becky Cook discerned the curse through a word of knowledge and they broke its power in the name of Jesus. Several demons manifest which they cast out. Within two days the boy returned to the meetings, able to recognize John. When they left South Africa other Christians continued to pray for the boy and at the four-month mark he was able to return home from the institution where he lived and he enrolled in school. He advanced several grade levels within several months.[6]

As the impact of the ministry began to grow, other South African pastors now began to be brought into the picture, men such as Costa Mitchell, Derek Morphew, "Bushie" Venter and Samuel Kisten, a man of Indian origin.

John went back to South Africa in 1982 with 72 people from all over the United States. The separation with Calvary had now taken place, so they came representing the Vineyard. Their express purpose was to birth Vineyard churches in South Africa. David Owen had turned his "Invisible Church" in Johannesburg over to Costa Mitchell (now the National Director of the Vineyard in South Africa) and had gathered fifty people as the core of a new Vineyard church in anticipation of the team's arrival.

The team in Johannesburg hit the streets during the day to witness and pray for the sick. They invited anyone they could to the meetings at night and the power of God fell. Marwan Bahu, one of Lonnie Frisbee's old roommates, was on this trip, and remembers one evening when Lonnie prayed for God to come and every one of the 500 or so people (excluding the ministry team) fell out under the power of God. The ministry team left the building because God was apparently doing quite well without them.

By the time that the team left after the second week they had baptized 65 new converts and the core of the new church grew to about 130-150, thus birthing the first truly Vineyard church in that country. Other churches were added as well. By 1998 there were 38 Vineyards in South Africa.

## A Growing Ministry in Europe

John went back to England every year. In the vision of the blinking lights that served as the basis of the Vineyard's church-planting thrust, the light in the States jumped over the ocean and landed in the U.K. From there it went all over the world. Because of this vision, John felt a divine connection with England, and in October of 1984, he took a team of two hundred people from Vineyards all over the U.S. to conduct a major campaign that touched some four hundred churches.

Unfortunately this was also the year that Wimber's good friend, David Watson, died of cancer. Watson tells this poignant story himself in his last book, *Fear No Evil*,[7] which he wrote during the ups and downs of that final year. In the book he describes being prayed for by John Wimber, Blaine Cook, and John McClure who flew over to England for that purpose. God was powerfully present during repeated prayer, but he died nonetheless. Watson's death was one of great heartache for Wimber, and was a test of his theology of the kingdom (ala George Ladd) that the kingdom was here but not here yet, thus allowing for pain as well as power. It said to the world that the Vineyard was not part of the faith movement. It allowed for tragedy as well as signs and wonders.

It was inevitable that the Vineyard would eventually break the language barrier. Up to this point Wimber's ministry had been to the English-speaking world. Vineyard associate, Brent Rue, had been going to Scandinavia, but after the events in South Africa, Wimber was invited to Germany where he met a translator named Martin Buehlmann. Buehlmann was a German-speaking pastor of an independent church in Bern, Switzerland, and is now one of the key leaders among the Vineyards in Europe. As he had in

South Africa, God was giving the Vineyard the global leadership it would need at an early stage.

When the Iron Curtain fell, the ground had now been laid for Vineyard church planting efforts in places like Russia, Romania, Bulgaria, and Hungary.

## THE MORATORIUM ON CHURCH PLANTING

Before the first team went to England in 1981, they had prayer meetings at Bob and Penny Fulton's house. During that time Bob had a dream about ministering in the streets in England and saw a whole series of churches popping up. Bob knew that the dream meant that the Vineyard would be planting churches in foreign countries.

When they arrived in the U.K., they told David Watson about the dream, but his response was, "No—that is not what this is about at all." He asked Wimber to make a commitment that he would not plant churches in England, but would equip the churches there to move in power. The churches in England would do the rest. Wimber agreed.

Many of the Vineyard's cross-cultural invitations had come through contacts with Watson, and he had ensured his Anglican friends that Wimber would not plant churches in their countries. Thus, a number of countries became off-limits for church planting efforts from the start.

The rules were broken fairly early, however. John and Eleanor Mumford were Anglican curates (associate pastors) who had been touched in the Vineyard meetings in England. Even though Watson's plan had been for Wimber to equip the Anglican churches, Mumford became convinced that England needed Vineyard churches. Consequently, he moved his family over to the U.S. to "hang out" at the Vineyard and learn from John. Wimber had always figured that Mumford would go back into the Anglican Church, but as he and Eleanor planned to return, they explained to John that they were now Vineyard and no longer Anglicans. Consequently, when they returned to England, they planted what is now a large Vineyard church in London.

Other curates now began to come over such as Rick Williams, Martyn Smith, and Chris Lane. All three went back to England and planted Vineyards that in turn began to plant other Vineyards. In this way the Vineyard movement in England was established, thus putting tension between Wimber's love and respect for Watson and the call of God on the Vineyard to plant churches. David Pytches, on the other hand, always felt that Watson's view was wrong and encouraged the young churches.

## 1989-1991: A TIME OF TRANSITION

Meanwhile, John Mumford and others had gone back to the U.K. as early as 1986 to plant Vineyards there, despite the moratorium on church planting. Wimber loved and respected David Watson, and so stayed true to Watson's desires even after David was gone. A strategic turn, however, began at the AVC board meeting in 1989 in Palm Springs.

It must be pointed out that up until this point there had never been any official encouragement toward foreign missions in the movement. John would address his reasoning for this two years later in the *Equipping the Saints* released during the Denver pastor's conference in the summer of 1991. In his article entitled "The Vineyard's Call to Missions,"[8] Wimber came out clearly in alignment with an evangelical call to bring the gospel to every ethnic people. He then gave two reasons why he had not led the movement into missions up to that point (thus helping me understand why he vetoed my newsletter).

The *first* was that the movement was too young. The churches were new and would need resources to renovate and build buildings. A deep financial commitment to missions, he felt, was premature. He likened it to teaching a three year old how to read.

The *second* was that he wanted God to initiate the timing on a unified missions effort. At the 1989 board meeting in Palm Springs, the leaders began to sense God's voice. John appointed Bob Fulton to become the overseer of missions in AVC. John had also invited two men from Europe to the meetings: Martin Buehlman, pastor of the church in Bern, and another man who had a vision

260

for planting American expatriate churches in foreign cities. Their presence precipitated a sharing time about all the ways Vineyard churches were involved in missions. God had been quietly initiating missions at the grass roots level since the first trip to South Africa. Now it became clear just how involved we were. We were scattered all over the world!

Another factor in the equation was that Wimber, whose church had outgrown their Anaheim facility, had been offered an incredible deal on a piece of property in Anaheim Hills, right next Bob Fulton's church. That year Bob had seen about seventy people come to Christ, so the prospect of having Wimber's church move next to his created tremendous tension. Bob intuitively knew that his church was going to have to die and be absorbed back into John's, and as God spoke to John about world missions in Palm Springs, John knew instantly that Bob's purpose was for missions. Bob was going to become the Director of Missions in the Vineyard.

Out of that meeting in 1989, catalyzed also by a desire to get on with our call to plant churches, the theme for the next pastors' conference (Denver '91) was conceived. That event would launch us officially into the "missions business." Bob Fulton was to be set in place as the Director of Missions, and the movement would feel a full release to plant churches at the leading of the Lord with the exception of those countries affected by the moratorium.

## THE MORATORIUM IS LIFTED

While John was in Australia in 1993, the Lord told him that the commitment to avoid church planting was "illegal." Bob had already known this and was lobbying to lift the ban. David Pytches, consistent with his views, aided him.

Bob convinced John that planting churches was part of our genetic code. It was part of who God had called us to be. He likened it to being married, but not being allowed to have children.

Furthermore, John's renewal ministry, which was supposed to equip the existing churches to win the lost and multiply local congregations, was not resulting in evangelism. He then realized that if the state churches were not going to "take it to the streets," then the Vineyard had to.

John and Bob went to each of the key church leaders affected in countries under the ban and apologetically communicated their new stance. The Vineyard was now going to begin to plant churches at the leading of the Lord.

## MISSIONS STRATEGY

The ultimate goal of missions is to reach every ethnic people with the gospel of the kingdom. When that happens, Jesus said that the end would come (Matthew 24:14). How should the Vineyard approach this awesome task? John and Bob developed their strategy by observing what the Holy Spirit had already been doing in places like Spain and India.

The world is broken up into thousands of ethnic peoples, some of which are so culturally distant that it would take years to raise up and train missionaries to go into those countries. But even then, the language barrier would make even the best presentation of the gospel seem foreign due to the inability of the missionary to speak without an accent. The best way to reach a culturally distant people was to reach a people linguistically and culturally in-between. By establishing beach-heads in these countries, they would be the best candidates to win indigenous evangelists who would then, in turn, reach their own people.

To reach into the more culturally distant European nations such as Germany with its language barrier, the Holy Spirit had led sovereignly over to Britain. It was from this European beach-head that the doors were opened to language barrier countries.

I saw the same phenomena in Australia. As the Vineyard reached out to this nation in 1990, I watched one evening as a group of Aborigines sat on the fringes, not entering in but very interested. By establishing an Australian base the ground had been laid for a potential outreach to a culturally distant people by a people that were culturally in-between.

Bob Fulton told me that he is confident that this strategy will eventually see doors opening supernaturally to peoples even more culturally distant (we will go into this in greater detail in a later chapter). It is in this way that the Holy Spirit has prompted an intentional strategy for the Vineyard to do its part in reaching all the nations of the earth so that the end might come.

## MISSIONS SUMMIT, 1993

Two years after the conference in Denver, in the summer of 1993, John Wimber and Bob Fulton hosted a conference that I attended in Kansas City called *Missions Summit*. It wasn't a conference to convince people to get involved in missions; it was an attempt to get those people together who were already involved and say, "This is what the Vineyard is currently thinking about our global task," and then to solicit feedback. The key concept that was presented was what Bob called "local church-based missions." I will try to summarize Bob's main points below.

Throughout most of church history, the missionary movement had been based in the local church. Even the Catholic orders were supported from within the church. With the advent of the student volunteer movement, however, the emphasis shifted away from the local church to parachurch organizations as the sending base for mission efforts. Instead of churches planting churches, parachurch organizations were now doing it.

Mission vision, therefore, waned in the pulpits and had to be maintained through parachurch structures, even though the local church still remained the money base for all mission endeavors.

The issues of training, sending, and pastoring the missionary were now largely out of the hands of the churches. This resulted in lonely missionaries on the field who weren't being pastored and often produced the same unfruitfulness they had at home. Furlough was a labored process of traveling all over to their support churches, showing slides and trying to keep the enthusiasm going. Often no one had ever visited the missionaries in the field to see firsthand what was happening.

The New Testament model shows the sending base for Paul and Barnabas to be a local church. Their furlough was not a frenzied tour of Palestine but real R&R in Syria.

263

### PARTNERSHIP

Bob's main concern was to get churches to partner together to reach peoples and countries. At one point he had all the people working with or burdened for specific peoples to gather together in cluster groups to meet each other and synergize. These groups resulted in many fruitful cooperative efforts.

- Phil Strout, a former missionary from Chile and now a Vineyard pastor in Maine, spearheaded a unified thrust with the churches in the Northeast to reach the Basque people in Spain. Together the churches raised up the team, provided the funding, and did the training. Now, they continue to provide the pastoral care. These local churches are personally involved as "senders."
- A group of churches in the deep South began to go to Colombia and Costa Rica. They recently hosted a crusade at which they anticipated 10,000 attendees.
- The churches in the Midwest and Phoenix are still partnering in Mexico.
- A group of churches in South Florida are beginning to go to Venezuela and Cuba.
- Churches from the Northwest have focused on the Shingu River in Brazil.
- Churches in Colorado are reaching out to Romania, Hungary, and Bulgaria.
- A Russian cluster is beginning to form as this is being written and so is a group focused on India.

Questions remain about the relationship between local Vineyard churches and parachurch organizations that offer specialized training and support not possible through local churches, but the signs are encouraging, and there is a general feeling that we are on the right track.

## WIMBER AND FULTON RELEASED
## TO GO TO THE NATIONS

In October of 1994, Vineyard missions was catapulted into warp speed. In a board meeting in Houston, Texas, John asked the board to die to their power over the Vineyard in other nations. It was not right for the U.S. to govern the world. He asked them to release Bob and him from the development of the Vineyard in the U.S. to a global expansion. To the board's credit they recognized that the spontaneous expansion of the church had to belong to the Holy Spirit and that they had to take their hands off. Now it was only John as the International Director and Bob as the International Coordinator who had to be convinced that God was opening doors in a new country, not a whole board. This paved the way for rapid movement.

## CASE STUDIES IN MISSIONS[9]

Bob Fulton could write a full account of all the amazing things God has done to open doors for us in missions, but he and I agreed to present a few case studies to give a flavor for how God has worked. A full study of what God has done in the Vineyard's worldwide expansion is beyond the scope of this work.

### LEBANON

While all these things were going on in England, South Africa, and Europe, God was moving in sovereign ways in other countries as well. One of these directly affected our church. In the summer of 1989 a group of five young people suddenly showed up at our church in Indianapolis from war-torn Beirut, Lebanon. They said that God had told them to come to the U.S. for training and specifically told them to come to Indy. Through a series of circumstances, they wound up at our church. As it turned out, they were one of only two Christian rock 'n roll bands in the whole country of Lebanon, and God had set them on our doorstep for training.

Meanwhile, God was speaking to Carl Madearis in the Vineyard in Colorado Springs to move to Beirut as a missionary. By the time Carl and his family arrived in Lebanon, an indigenous worship team with Vineyard values had already been trained and was engaged in prayer, fasting, and evangelism.

## MEXICO

### Fred and Debbie Collom[10]

Fred Collom was one of the thousands of young people affected by the Jesus Movement in the early seventies. He was something of a real estate tycoon in Peoria, Illinois, and at the age of twenty was buying, renovating, and selling rental properties. Shortly after he gave his life to Christ, God called him to sell all of his assets and he began to make trips into Mexico with the gospel. Knowing no Spanish, Fred began going over the border to boldly share Christ.

He took his guitar and linked up with Bible school students fluent in Spanish. He began to make trips into towns and villages to play Jesus rock 'n roll and preach the gospel. The people had never heard anything like this, and God's favor was with Fred. He planted churches and turned them over to pastors from various denominations in places Protestant churches had been unable to penetrate. Fred's life was threatened many times, and it is a miracle that he is still alive.

Along the way Fred married his wife, Debbie, and they settled in Fresnillo in the hardened interior of Mexico to raise a family and plant a solid, indigenous Mexican church.

Some of the churches he planted remained under Fred's authority through a tight bond with the pastors he had trained and released. The churches needed names, but for some reason Fred never felt led of the Lord to give them any. He waited on the Lord until the mid-1980s and then came into contact with the Vineyard. That was it. The reason his churches didn't have names was because he had been planting Vineyards!

### God Brings Fred and Dennis Bourns Together

After the meeting in Denver in 1991, Fred was set in place as the director of the Vineyards in Mexico. At the pastor's conference, a Vineyard pastor from Phoenix named Dennis Bourns began to tell Fred about a harvest in Mazatlan, a major city on the western coast of Mexico. After a number of evangelistic trips there, Dennis had seen first hand how responsive the people were. Fred, however, being used to the hardened Catholic ground of the interior of Mexico, never really believed him. Then, in 1995, Fred decided to take Dennis up on his offer to come over to Mazatlan and put on his own crusade. He took his associate pastor and worship leader, Mario Santillan, with him. Larry and Marji Larson, then pastors of the Vineyard in Bloominton, Illinois, joined them. Larry preached for twenty-one days straight while Fred interpreted and Mario led worship. Larry recorded that experience in his journal and in a conversation with me recalled that about 125 people made confessions of faith to Christ. After the crusade was over Fred remembers that about 50 people remained as a part of the new church plant.

Fred and Mario went back and processed this with the team in Fresnillo, concluding that God was calling them to plant a church there. With the blessing and laying on of hands of both the church in Fresnillo and the local pastors in Mazatlan, Fred and Mario moved their families to this coastal city and planted the first *La Viña* there.

INDIA

John and Carol Christian were natives of India and while working for a Christian organization there, became disillusioned. They decided to move to the States and settled in San Jose, California. Before they moved, however, a friend told them to check out a church there called the Vineyard. John went to one of the Vineyard meetings and the power of God fell on him. He was overcome by the Holy Spirit and was deeply ministered to, thus causing him to reconsider the reality of the kingdom of God and the power of the Holy Spirit.

Before long Dave Shaw, the pastor of the Vineyard in San Jose, approached John about going with him on a trip to India. At first Dave had no interest, but before long the Lord began to prompt his heart to go back to his native land. A small team, including a worship band, went to Madras where they had a connection at one of the universities. They plastered the campus with signs that a rock 'n roll band from the United States was going to be playing that night. To their complete surprise about 500 students showed up, many of them making decisions to follow Jesus. To follow up they had an interest meeting to see how many of them would be interested in forming a new church. Again they were shocked when about 200 students expressed interest. The team from San Jose was not in any position to start a church in India at that point, so they did their best to give initial follow-up and then traveled, somewhat in shock, back to the states. On subsequent trips to Madras and then to Delhi, they tried to maintain contact with as many of the students as possible, most remaining in the cities rather than returning to their villages after college.

God used the these experiences to capture John and Carol Christian's heart again for their people and within two years they were ready to go back. In October of 1997 the Christians took a team of eight people to Madras to plant a church. A number of the college students who had been reached earlier were waiting for them, so the new church began quickly with about 30 people.

Bob Fulton visited the church in October of 1998 and by then they had grown to 200, many being new converts gained either through servant evangelism or through the medium of music. MTV had started to be broadcast on Indian television shortly before the arrival of the team. To capitalize on the open door in the culture they began to do rock 'n roll worship concerts and crowds of people began showing up. In each one they explained how to become a follower of Jesus Christ and people began to investigate Christianity out of either the Hindu or Islamic faiths.

In January of 1999 Bob Fulton received an e-mail from the new church that informed him that they had been praying about planting churches (they were only a year and a half old). Two things have occurred since then. *First*, someone in the fellowship had a connection in a town called Shalong. They rented a stadium there on faith, spread posters throughout the area that a rock 'n roll band was going to be doing a concert, and then waited and prayed. They wondered who would show up. The local newspaper would report the next morning that the traffic was backed up for miles as about 5,000 people found themselves the lucky ones who were able to buy a ticket (free events in India are considered unimportant). John's team did worship, gave testimonies and invited people to accept Christ.

The *second* thing that has occurred is that a couple of John's new leaders moved back to their hometown about five hours north of Madras and have gathered a nucleus for another new church. Under the sovereignty of God the church is spontaneously expanding as God has touched indigenous leaders to reach their own people.

CB

NOTES:

[1] The data for this chapter came out of talks with Bob Fulton unless otherwise noted.

[2] Rick is now the national director of Frontiers, an organization reaching Muslims.

[3] The information on the events in South Africa has come from phone conversations with David Owen, Marwan Bahu and Susan Hartman. After reading the chapter, Alexander Venter was able to add valuable insight as well.

[4] "Missionary Encounter with Culture," *International Bulletin of Missionary Research*, July, 1991, pp. 104-109.

[5] The term "colored" is a technical term in South Africa referring to someone part white and part black.

[6] P.p. 175-6

[7] Published by his wife, Ann, after his death on February 18, 1984 (Wheaton, Harold Shaw Pub., 1984)

[8] Vol. 5, No. 3, pp. 26-28

[9] Many more stories could be told but these will suffice.

[10] Fred told me his story in a recent trip to Mexico.

# CHAPTER SIXTEEN

# GOING
# FORWARD
# 1992-93

# GOING FORWARD, 1992-93

T he Vineyard began to get back on track in the two-year period following the 1991 Denver conference. The dual call on John Wimber's life, for both church planting (as seen in AVC) and renewal (as seen in VMI), had created an identity crisis in our history. Up until the period under consideration, we were much more renewal-based as a movement. AVC was acting as if it was really VMI; expectations were that Vineyard Sunday services would look like the conferences, and pastors needed to be gifted in the ministry of signs and wonders like John.

## THE ROLE OF THE TASK FORCES

After 1991 the AVC task forces began to redefine our identity to align with our mission. Truly renewed churches would be involved in evangelism, church planting, caring for the poor, and world missions. Housed in the Vineyard's new facility in Anaheim, the ship began to move forward with new wind in its sails.

Steve Sjogren, the leader of the task force on evangelism, began to travel into the regions, along with other task force members, to sow the importance of evangelism into the churches. Steve's church had been inundated with seekers after being challenged to find God's "friends."

The task force endeavored to raise awareness of how our meetings were attracting seekers. Sjogren asked questions such as, "How long do we worship before we've alienated the seekers in our midst?" In developing a seeker model on Sunday mornings, Steve was raising the greater question, "What is Vineyard?" Steve was trying to keep us on center with what God had called us to be and do—win and disciple the lost. If our VMI conference model was keeping us from fulfilling our calling, then we needed to rethink our model without compromising our biblical thesis.

## CHURCH PLANTING

Steve Nicholson, the leader of the church planting task force, began to develop an intentional track for church planters. He and his team developed a standardized process that included being trained at approved regional churches that had the resources needed to equip church planters. Training was also taken on the road in the form of modular courses that potential church planters could attend. Coaching systems were set in place to help planters on the field.

Since Steve has taken over the directorship of church planting, we have seen a significant rise in the number of churches planted. By as early as 1992, 30 churches were planted and 105 more were preparing to go out. Churches giving two percent of their income to AVC to fund our expansion and oversight financed the process.

## EDUCATION

John Wimber had always felt that since we were evangelicals, we could use existing seminaries and Bible schools to train our leaders. He never wanted to develop our own institutions. Under the vision of Bob Fulton, however, the *Vineyard Bible Institute* was developed to serve the needs of the advanced lay-level person or the Vineyard pastor who had not had any formalized theological education.

Various other schools began to emerge focused on training and releasing church planters and missionaries. The Lancaster Vineyard had run a school for a number of years, and others like it began to take shape. Some of these included Tri Robinson's in Boise, Rich Nathan's in Columbus, and Steve Nicholson's in Evanston. Most of these put the emphasis on practical training and not on theology, leaving that to standard evangelical institutions at John Wimber's request.

## BUSTER VINEYARDS

The rise of Buster Vineyards was another phenomena that began to emerge in '92. The age of the average Baby Boom

Vineyard pastor was about 40, and we began to joke about the "graying" of the movement. Todd Hunter led the charge to recruit a whole new generation of twenty-something leaders to plant Vineyard churches. The first "Doin' the Stuff" youth conference was also held in 1992. New churches soon began to be planted that had almost no one over thirty. They had a different look and feel to them, but they were based on core Vineyard priorities and practices.

## BLOOD 'N FIRE

Though it would not actually start until 1994, the groundwork for another church planting effort was being laid during this time as well. Under the auspices of the Atlanta Vineyard, Dave Van Cronkite, an entrepreneurial businessman with a six-figure income, began to take food to the poor in the inner city. Before long he was given the opportunity to buy a building that took up an entire city block and was located across from a housing project. The building was worth over two million dollars, but David got it for under $500,000 with a deferred-payment, interest-free, two-year loan. On the day that the first balloon payment was due, they had no money until a man walked in the door with a check for $50,000, the exact amount of the payment.

The Lord spoke to Van Cronkite to call the ministry Blood 'n Fire. The Vineyard grapes didn't cut it in the ghetto! Later they found out that the same words appear on the Salvation Army flag, a ministry they closely resemble.

During the summer Olympics in Atlanta, I went down with our church youth group for Blood 'n Fire's "summer of service." We had a marvelous week ministering in the projects and dodging raindrops through the leaky roof in that old building. We saw many lives touched that week, but none more than those of our own kids!

## PROMISE KEEPERS

Another major ministry that would have its genesis during this period was Promise Keepers. Bill McCartney, former coach of the University of Colorado Buffaloes, founded Promise Keepers in 1990 with the goal of calling men to Christ and family. The first conference attracted 4,200 men, but soon men were filling football stadiums all over the country. In 1997 more than one million men gathered for prayer in the nation's capital, the largest gathering in the history of America.

In 1996, Promise Keepers gathered pastors in Atlanta for the largest meeting of pastors in American church history. It was an awesome experience as pastors from all different denominations took communion together. American Indian pastors representing 75 different tribes filled an entire section of the stadium. Coach McCartney was then a member of James Ryle's Vineyard in Boulder, Colorado. The Vineyard's value of loving the whole body of Christ is exemplified in the spirit of Promise Keepers in that many denominations have taken part. It has had a massive impact on the men of the United States as it has attempted to turn the hearts of the fathers back to their wives and families.

## VINEYARD REFLECTIONS

The year began with John Wimber's first issue of *Vineyard Reflections*. It was intended to be a quarterly newsletter where John could communicate his views on issues touching Vineyard pastors, communicate the values and vision of the Vineyard, and comment on trends affecting the worldwide church.[1] In my opinion, *Reflections* was the most significant aid to Vineyard pastors produced up to that pont. It was a fine effort.

## JOHN WIMBER GETS CANCER

Just as the first issue of *Reflections* was being distributed (and, though we didn't know it, just as worldwide renewal was about to break out), John Wimber was diagnosed with cancer. In April doctors found a small (3.2 centimeters) undifferentiated carcinomatous tumor located in the left side of John's nasal pharynx.[2] He began X-ray and proton radiation immediately and finished just before the international pastors' conference in the new facility in Anaheim in July. As a result of the treatments, he lost tons of weight and the ability to produce saliva in his mouth. From then on he had to use "spray spit" when he spoke, and, as usual, showed us how to laugh in the face of tragedy. He never had the same stamina after that and began to slowly fade into the background as he gave more and more authority to the international board.

On the eve of the pastors' conference, the Vineyard received more tragic news. On May 16, Brent Rue, our beloved brother who had planted the first Vineyard out of Kenn Gulliksen's church in West LA, passed away from cancer at the age of forty-eight. We missed him terribly.

The National Pastors' Conference convened in July 1993 to help chart the new course. It had the feeling of a family reunion as the movement began to celebrate the victories of its new direction.

## A SEASON OF NEW BEGINNINGS

### RANDY CLARK

While all of this was going on, there was a Vineyard pastor in St. Louis who did not share this sense of going forward.[3] Randy and DeAnn Clark had planted their church in St. Louis at the same time that we were planting ours in Indianapolis. Randy had been the pastor of an American Baptist church in the rural community of Spillertown, Illinois, when he was filled with the Holy Spirit in 1984 at a James Robinson conference. John Wimber was one of the speakers there and prophesied over Randy at a pastors' meeting, telling him that he was a "Prince in God's kingdom" and was being called to an apostolic ministry. By "apostolic" John meant "translocal."[4] John would prophecy this again in 1985.

Shortly after this conference, Blaine Cook took a team from Wimber's church to do a healing seminar in Spillertown. The move of God was so strong during that weekend that it became known as the "Spillertown revival." Ben Hoerr, the executive pastor of the Champaign Vineyard, was there and describes one ministry time when the Spirit of God came in through the back door and proceeded to move up the church one aisle at a time. Ben said you could actually see him move up the rows by the effects on peoples bodies. There were many powerful healings.

After the "revival," Randy tried his best to lead his Baptist church into the things of the Spirit, but met much opposition. On a twenty-day fast, he felt the Lord speak to him that he was supposed to be in the Vineyard. He eventually sensed a call to plant a church in St. Louis and began to commute there from Southern Illinois. He worked frying donuts while he planted the church.

Randy would later say that God chose him to spark the Toronto Blessing (more on that later) because he was an ordinary man and a relatively unsuccessful pastor. I have known Randy since his donut days and can vouch for his unassuming, humble character. He is a man ardent for God, and his zeal after the Lord has been a model for me over the years. He has never had any pretense. He is also right in saying that he has had struggles as a pastor. Early on Randy couldn't find a worship leader. He even had our worship team from Indy come out and do a conference hoping that it would spark their worship. Years later God would give him a fabulous worship team led by Gary Shelton, but those initial years were tough for him.

Despite the powerful work of the Spirit in his life and ministry in Illinois, Randy wrote that it seemed to him as if the "Holy Spirit stayed in Illinois."[5] His efforts to make the church grow were largely for naught, and Randy began to move away from power-based ministry, and more toward church growth principles. Randy concedes that there is nothing wrong with church growth principles, but he knows in his heart that he was looking to the wisdom of men and not to God.

By July of 1993 he was close to a nervous breakdown and felt like he was barely hanging on. "Job's counselors" were telling him that he needed to pray more and read his Bible more, but he couldn't; he was broken and didn't know what to do to fix it.

In the midst of his brokenness, he got a call from a friend named Jeff from Illinois who asked how it was going. Randy lied, as pastors often do when asked this question, and told him that everything was going great. Jeff, however, was honest and proceeded

277

to tell him about his struggles and how he had been helped by going to a meeting led by a South African man named Rodney Howard-Browne  Jeff exhorted Randy to go to one of his meetings in Tulsa at Rhema Bible Church. Randy didn't want to go because he had had trouble with the "word of faith" teaching, but eventually went out of sheer desperation.

At the meetings Randy was exposed to people being massively slain in the Spirit and laughing hysterically. He found himself skeptical, but the Lord nailed him on his bitterness toward the word of faith movement. He opened himself up for ministry from Rodney Howard-Browne and got in line again and again, being slain in the Spirit repeatedly.[6] He began to follow Rodney around to watch what he was doing so he could learn.

Randy felt wonderfully renewed and came home with his children's pastor, Bill Mares, to share with the church what had happened. The first Sunday back, the same phenomena accompanying the renewal were released at his church. The sanctuary resembled a battlefield with slain bodies everywhere. And so it happened week after week.

Soon after, Randy and his staff were scheduled to go to the Vineyard's regional meeting led by Happy Leman. Randy called Hap and asked to share what had happened. Hap gave him five minutes, but it turned into several hours when pastors from our region received a radical touch from God. The same phenomena broke out there as had been breaking out in the other places.

The next month, Hap attended the annual Vineyard board meeting and there spoke with John Arnott, a Vineyard pastor in Toronto, Canada, and told John about the outpouring of the Spirit at the regional meeting. John had been on his own spiritual search, having just returned from the revival in Argentina. John had wanted to have a set of meetings to bring renewal to his own congregation and sensed from his dialogue with Hap that Randy was just the guy to come and do the meetings. Randy got a call from Arnott as soon as John got home and reluctantly agreed to go to Toronto in January.

Randy was a bit nervous about the meetings, but Anni Shelton, his worship leader's wife, had a powerful vision in which she saw a map of Toronto being set on fire. She sensed that something was going to start there and go all over North America.

## A Season of New Beginnings in Anaheim[7]

On the night before the pastors' conference in July, the Lord spoke to Carol Wimber and told her that John was to go to the nations. John and Carol would later understand this to mean going to the church in the nations, thus stirring up renewal and revival. Carol responded, "Lord, my husband is sleeping 20-22 hours a day. He has no voice. Tomorrow pastors from all over the world are going to be here, and he won't even be able to participate. If this is indeed your will, touch him tonight. Please give him his voice back, so that he may minister." And that's exactly what the Lord did. When John woke up, he was able to speak and had just enough energy to go and participate in the conference.

By October 1993, the same month that Randy Clark was releasing the Spirit at the regional conference in the Midwest, God had spoken to John twenty-seven times confirming that he should go to the nations. Seventeen of these confirmations had come in the context of the Lord speaking that this would be a season of new beginnings. God had told John, "I'm going to start it all over again."

What the Lord appeared to mean was that the same anointing that fell on the church in 1980 was going to start all over again. Since that time there had been ebbs and flows of the Spirit's presence. Now the Lord was saying that he was going to pour out his Spirit as he had done in the beginning.

As John sat in the sanctuary during worship, he identified with Abraham and Sarah after the angelic announcement that they would have a son. John told the Lord that he was out of energy and asked the Lord as Sarah had done, "Shall I have this pleasure in my old age?" The Lord assured him that he would, and this reassurance gave life to John. John gave this word at the AVC board meeting in November, the same board meeting where Happy Leman shared with John Arnott about the Midwest regional meeting.

On December 5, the Lord told John Wimber to stir up the gifts of the Spirit that the people might have a greater hunger for the Giver. Consequently, throughout the months of December and January, the Anaheim Vineyard set aside Sunday nights to give the Holy Spirit an opportunity to move with freedom.

As 1993 drew to a close, all the signs indicated that God was setting up the Vineyard for a new wave of the Holy Spirit's power. But, as Richard Riss points out in his internet book - *A History of the Awakening of 1992-1995*,[8] this season of new beginnings was not a Vineyard phenomenon, but something that God had been doing in the greater church as well and was planning to send all over the world. That the Vineyard would play a role was a great honor indeed.

◌◈

NOTES:

[1] These are the three goals as stated in the first issue of *Vineyard Reflections*, April/May, 1993.

[2] *Vineyard Reflections*, June/July, 1993, p. 1

[3] The information on Randy Clark is taken largely from his unpublished manuscript, *Lighting the Fire* and from my own recollections of conversations I have had with Randy over the years.

[4] For a clarification of John Wimber's views on the "fivefold" ministry of Ephesians 4 see his last issue of *Reflections*, August, 1997.

[5] *Lighting the Fire*, p. 87

[6] Rodney Howard Browne's model was that it was he that was the prayer so the pray-ees lined up in long lines waiting to be prayed for. This model was very different from the Vineyard model where everyone was trained to pray.

[7] For this account see *Vineyard Reflections*, May/June, 1994 and *Equipping the Saints*, Fall 1994.

[8] Eleventh Edition, October 15, 1995 (See Richard's web page at http://www.grmi.org/renewal/Richard_Riss/). Riss shows how the renewal had already been breaking out in Argentina and in men like Rodney Howard Browne, Kenneth Copeland, Karl Strader, Bud Williams, Oral Roberts, Charles and Francis Hunter, Ray Sell, Mona and Paul Jonian, and Jerry Gaffney.

# CHAPTER SEVENTEEN

# THE
# TORONTO
# BLESSING

# THE TORONTO BLESSING

## INTRODUCTION

As I write on the "Toronto Blessing," a name that the British media gave the phenomenon I am going to describe, I am reminded of a fabulous quote from Annie Dillard in her book *Teaching a Stone to Talk*.[1] Lamenting her dull experiences in church, Dillard writes:

*Why do people in churches seem like cheerful, brainless tourists on a packaged tour of the Absolute?...On the whole, I do not find Christians, outside of the catacombs, sufficiently sensible of conditions. Does anyone have the foggiest idea what sort of power we so blithely invoke? Or, as I suspect, does no one believe a word of it? The churches are children playing on the floor with their chemistry sets, mixing up a batch of TNT to kill a Sunday morning. It is madness to wear ladies' straw hats and velvet hats to church; we should all be wearing crash helmets. Ushers should issue life preservers and signal flares; they should lash us to our pews. For the sleeping god [sic] may wake someday and take offense, or the waking god [sic] may draw us out to where we can never return.*

The events that are about to be described seem worthy of crash helmets and life preservers. Any attempt to summarize them seems trivial, but for the sake of our purpose, I will try.

## GETTING READY

On the afternoon of Sunday, January 16, 1994, the Holy Spirit spoke the word "Pentecost" to John Wimber.[2] The season of new beginnings had already begun, so he asked the Lord what it meant. Not sensing any answer, he went off to the Sunday night service at the Vineyard in Anaheim. During the service, the Lord gave him a vision of young people in a certain order. During the ministry time, John asked the young people to come forward. The Lord came and consumed them with his love and power. That night began an overflow of power in the church that lasted for months.

Just a few days later, Randy Clark was nervously getting his team ready for the trip to Toronto. He was very afraid that they would go there and nothing would happen. On the night before they were due to leave, Randy received a call from a friend named Richard Holcomb who called once or twice a year with a prophetic word. Randy had always appreciated Richard's words but admits being cautious, and at times skeptical, about prophecy in general.

This time Richard's words became very pointed: "The Lord says to you, Randy, 'Test me now. Test me now. Test me now. Do not be afraid. I will back you up! I want your eyes to be opened as Elisha prayed for Gehazi, that you can see into the heavenlies and see my resources for you. And do not become anxious because when you become anxious, you can't hear me.'"[3]

Randy would later write, "It was this prophetic word that did much to change my life. It gave me the faith to move in the anointing I had received when Rodney had prayed for me.' "[4]

As the team left for Toronto for a four-day conference, Randy was filled with faith. But even he had no idea that they would be there from January 20 to March 26!

## THE TORONTO BLESSING BEGINS

As Randy and his team drove into the Airport Vineyard in Mississauga, Ontario, they saw where it got its name. It lay just at the end of one of the runways leading to the Toronto airport. The church was in a little, nondescript strip mall and certainly didn't seem like the future home of a worldwide move of God.

About 160 people attended the first meeting. Randy gave his testimony, and many people were slain in the Spirit during ministry time. What was surprising was that people were getting "drunk" in the Holy Spirit and were going into fits of laughter. These patterns continued for the next four days.

On Sunday, Randy gave Anni Shelton permission to share some words of knowledge, and as she did, a stocky man with long hair and tattoos stood up in the back and challenged her saying, "Did you get my name? Did you get my name? Taz, the Tasmanian Devil. I will show you my power." Sensing the Lord's presence in it, Randy responded, "No, I will show you power, the power of God." Randy then exhorted the congregation to focus on God and invited those who felt the power of God to come forward. As they did, the power of God fell on the church, filling the people with the Holy Spirit. Many began to fall, shake, weep, laugh, or just rest in deep peace. Some men took "Taz" into a back office and led him to Christ. It was an electrifying service, and Randy estimates that almost four hundred people were slain in the Spirit.

As the conference came to an end, John Arnott told Randy that he couldn't go home. He believed that they were experiencing an unusual outpouring of the Spirit and they had to stay with it. Randy agreed to another couple of days. After those days, John asked if he could extend the stay again. Randy was constantly on the phone with DeAnne in dialogue about it. In nineteen years of marriage, they had almost never been apart, and she was home alone caring for four children. Finally, the Lord himself gave her assurance through the Scriptures. He told DeAnne that it was all in his hands and that he would be sending Randy to the nations of the earth. In her heart she agreed to let Randy stay out under the parameters of the Lord. The church also gave its blessing, not realizing that it would take Randy out of town for 175 days per year.

During the second week, Randy felt like they needed to have a meeting for pastors. Among the 28 pastors and spouses there that first day, twenty were Baptist, three were Presbyterian, two were Nazarene, and one was Pentecostal. Randy doesn't remember the affiliation of the others.[5] After lunch and a time of worship, they gave the pastors an opportunity to receive prayer. To their amazement, they almost all fell to the floor and were mightily touched by the Holy Spirit.

Because of the openness of the pastors, alternate meetings began in other churches in the area. In addition to the services going on six nights a week at the Airport Vineyard, averaging over 800 per night by February, there were 600 per night in Cambridge, 300 in Stratford, 250 in Barrie, and 250 in Hamilton.[6]

By the third week of the renewal, Randy became distraught over the lack of healing in the services. He went before the Lord about it and even called his intercessors back in St. Louis to pray for a release. Soon afterwards, he began to feel excruciating pain in his back. Finally realizing that it was the Lord giving a word of knowledge, he called people up that night with pain in that exact location in their backs. The first person Randy prayed for was healed not only of scoliosis but also of asthma. From that time on, healing became a normal part of the renewal.

## RON ALLEN

Vineyard leaders began to arrive early in the process to check out what was going on. Ron Allen, at the time one of the national leaders in AVC, had an encounter with the Lord as he prepared to go. The Lord told him, as he was packing a notebook, "If you go to criticize, I will lift my anointing. You go to receive."[7] Ron put away the notebook. He was filled so powerfully with the Holy Spirit that he could barely talk for quite a while and brought renewal home to his church in Ft. Wayne, Indiana, where they had meetings nightly for nine weeks.

After the seventh week, the Lord led them to set up a large tent. More than a thousand people came per night as God poured out his power. Instructed by the Lord to take the tent into the inner city, they saw fifty-five gang members receive Christ. Before long Ron and his associates were inundated with calls to do renewal meetings.

## MARION, ILLINOIS

Because I was on staff during this period with Happy Leman, Randy's Vineyard Regional Overseer, we got first-hand accounts of what was going on in Toronto almost immediately. One night I got a call from my friend, Jeff Stoner, from Indianapolis. He was in Toronto because Ron Allen's wife, Carolyn, had called him and told him that he had to get up there as quickly as possible. Jeff tried to describe to me what was going on, but it didn't really register. Suddenly Randy appeared in the lobby and Jeff handed him the phone. After getting some more background I perked up a bit. I learned that Randy was scheduled to do a meeting in March in Marion, Illinois, near his old church in Spillertown. I told him I'd think about coming.

In my personal life, I had gone through a two-year *"dark night of the soul"* where God had gotten my attention about things in my life and ministry that had needed to change. This process had been initiated, interestingly enough, two years previous when a prophetic minister named Marc Dupont suggested that I go up to spend some time with John Arnott in Toronto, Canada. I had only met John a couple of times and had never met his wife Carol. Sensing the hand of the Lord in it, I went up to Toronto. John and Carol took me into their home and were incredibly gracious hosts and ministers. While there, I had a life-changing encounter with the love of the heavenly Father. I resigned from ministry shortly after that under the direction of the Lord and worked in secular employment for about a year and a half as God brought repentance and healing to my heart.

As I heard about the initial events in Toronto, I was just entering back into ministry and had only been on staff in Champaign for about a month. As I prayed about the meetings in Marion, I began to sense that the Lord was going to meet me there. And did he! When ministry time came, I was so filled with faith that I almost ran down the aisle. The power of God hit me almost immediately, and I wound up shaking violently under the unction of the Holy Spirit. People said I was actually bouncing on the floor. Jeff and his family had come along and the Lord mightily ministered to his young boys. Jeff's son, Aaron, described his experience with the Holy Spirit like being inside Nintendo and going to the next warp level. For me, this event began a period of sovereign initiation back into ministry. I told Jeff, "I think I'm back."

## TORONTO COMES TO CHAMPAIGN

When I got back from the meeting, I shared my experience on a Sunday morning in church, and the blessing began to break out at the Champaign Vineyard. I remember seeing the Lord move on someone in the congregation about five rows back, and I pointed at him and said, "The Holy Spirit's moving on you right now." To my surprise the person fell right to the floor, slain in the Spirit. I thought to myself, "What in the world is this?"

I spent the next couple of weeks thinking about what all this might be and wound up putting out a draft of notes I called *What in the World is Happening to Us? A Biblical Perspective on Renewal.* It was my initial thoughts on the subject and was intended for our church. As I look back on it now, God gave me wisdom to write about only those phenomena that had biblical and historical precedent. I decided to leave the inexplicable unexplained. It was not a scholarly paper since I was using secondary historical sources and was writing for the average lay person. When I was done, I showed it to a few people to get their thoughts to see if I was on track. What I didn't realize was how hungry people were for some kind of precedent for the things that were going on.

Before I knew it, John Arnott got a copy of the notes and started giving them out in Toronto. As people started arriving there from all over the world almost immediately, I soon began to get letters from places like Lebanon, Fiji, Israel, and South Africa. The paper was put on our web page and was getting 800 to 1,000 hits a day from every place imaginable. To this day I can't believe it. If I had known what was going to happen, I would have been a lot more careful in writing it![8]

Toronto came to Champaign four times. Both Randy Clark and John Arnott did two meetings each in our facility, and they were powerful meetings indeed. People were marvelously touched. One of my friends, Dave Neukomm, had a marvelous healing in his relationship with his father. Two of his family members who had come out of a cessationist theology had their lives turned topsy-turvy. Both families have had long-lasting, fruitful ministries ever since.

287

## BRIEF SUMMARY

Randy Clark was in Toronto from January 20 to March 26, 1994, a total of 42 days. Since that time Randy has been established as a renewal evangelist bringing the Holy Spirit's presence all over the world. God has especially opened doors for him among the Pentecostals.

John Arnott has demonstrated an apostolic anointing and was rapidly becoming a worldwide leader of churches touched by the renewal even before the events described in the next chapter.

The internet home page of the Toronto Airport Christian Fellowship (formerly the Airport Vineyard) reported that:

> *In early September of 1995, cumulative attendance at what was later to become known as the Airport Christian Fellowship was about 600,000, including approximately 20,000 Christian leaders and 200,000 first time visitors from virtually every country and denomination.*
>
> *Attendance at evening services now numbers in the thousands, and ministry is carried out by a trained, 45-member team. Within twenty months of the beginning of this outpouring of the Holy Spirit, 9,000 people had made a first-time commitment to Christ at the Toronto Airport Vineyard. Church membership tripled in size to about 1,000 regular members from 360 in early 1994.*

## A TYPICAL RENEWAL MEETING[9]

Renewal meetings were long! But I think they were long because God doesn't tire out very easily. After an extended time of worship, people were allowed to give testimonies of things that God had been doing in their lives. These people were prayed for right there on stage after their testimony and often fell in a heap, sometimes lying there for the duration of the service. I was one of the pray-ees one time and was resting in the Spirit off to the side of the pulpit. My whole body began to come up off the floor and fall back down, over and over. People later told me that it was physically impossible to do what I was doing. It certainly wasn't me wanting to do that in front of all of those people, especially while John Arnott was talking! But, bless his heart, he just went on as if nothing was happening.

After testimonies, someone would preach, usually for 30-40 minutes. One of the criticisms of the Toronto Blessing was the lack of biblical exposition. James A. Beverly, in his book *Holy Laughter & The Toronto Blessing,*[10] says that weak biblical preaching was one of the most common criticisms of the meetings. He writes that the messages usually consisted of story-telling about manifestations or about the latest developments in the renewal. John Arnott would probably not call himself a Bible teacher (he is certainly a pastor and apostolic in his vision), but it cannot be said that he has not valued the Bible in the renewal. Indeed, John's desire has been to build around him a team of men and women who are gifted in ways that he is not.

MINISTRY TIME

Ministry time was the finale of the evening and could go on into the wee hours of the morning. As the worship team began to play again, the leaders waited on the Lord for direction. They moved forward under the Lord's direction, often with a call to those who wanted to be filled or refreshed by the Holy Spirit. Each night there was a call for salvation and rededication to the Lord.

In a personal reflection paper after a visit to Toronto, William J. Abraham, professor of theology at Southern Methodist University, described his experience during ministry time:

*The atmosphere remained totally calm, even casual. For individuals the situation was totally different. Scores ended up on the floor and would lie there for up to and well beyond a half an hour. I walked across the room...and had to pick my way carefully through bodies all over the floor. During worship one or two developed uncontrollable shaking; this recurred in their case during the time of ministry. A few roared in agony, bending over, as if they were working through some terrible grief. One or two had uncontrollable jerking, bouncing up and down for half and hour. Some fell without any special ministry at all. This was dangerous because usually there were people assigned to catch those about to fall, but nobody got hurt and those standing close by quickly caught on to be on the lookout. Some people laughed uncontrollably on the floor for twenty minutes or more.*

One of my favorite stories came from an article written by a British journalist who was sent from England to spy things out. Not a Christian, he described things through his skeptical lens. He ended his article describing his reentrance into the auditorium after going to the hotel bar for a break:

*I downed my beer and slipped back into the hall. Bodies lay everywhere. A man crawled past me on his hands and knees; another lay on his back roaring and clutching his stomach, his eyelids fluttering madly. Perhaps it was the heat, or the air of febrile intoxication coursing in the air, but I could feel myself growing giddy.*

*"Can you catch for me?" a woman asked. A body came falling toward me. I rested it on the ground, and moved on. I found myself beside John Arnott, who was moving through the crowd, blessing people, who fell like ninepins. I didn't even see his hand coming as it arced through the air and touched me gently—hardly at all—on the forehead. "And bless this one Lord..." I could feel a palpable shock running through me, then I was falling backwards, as if my legs had been kicked away from underneath me. I hit the floor—I swear this was the truth—laughing like a drain.[11]*

## MANIFESTATIONS

The center of the storm that would eventually surround the renewal had to do with the plethora of manifestations of the Holy Spirit that were present from the first night in Toronto. Most of these phenomena were not new to the Charismatic world, but their breadth and intensity were incredible.

The most obvious manifestation was people being slain in the Spirit. The British were fond of saying, "And up came the floor!" Renewal services often resembled a battlefield with bodies strewn everywhere.

Randy Clark's explanation? He thinks that when God comes on people powerfully they just can't stand up anymore. When people would fall in Vineyard meetings in the past, those praying would try to hold them up. I prayed for a girl the week before writing this who had had pesticide poisoning that was affecting her lungs. The power of God hit her and we had to have three guys to hold her up. This has been standard operating procedure in the Vineyard for years. In Toronto it was impossible because there weren't enough support people. Those who were going to fall were going to fall. The question was how to avoid injury because some of the falls were instant and powerful. To avoid injury a whole contingent of "catchers" were trained to receive people who were standing at pieces of tape put on the floor for better organization. Catchers and tape? Many debated that these things were not "Vineyard."

## HOLY LAUGHTER

One of the most criticized phenomena of the renewal was holy laughter. People would begin to laugh for no apparent reason in the middle of the meetings… and then they would laugh some more. And the laughter would often spread, first to one and then to another.

When I first saw holy laughter, I realized how much like drunkenness it looked. If this was what the day of Pentecost looked like, it is easy to see why they would have been accused of drinking. The obvious difference is that all the faculties are sharp and there is a sense of holiness over it all. Oh, and there is no hangover.

When I first saw it, I said to myself, "If that ever happens to me, it will have to be God because I don't do that." Some months later we were at a leaders' retreat, and someone began to pray for me. Suddenly, everything began to be funny. The person praying for me made me laugh, the chair I was sitting on looked funny—in fact everything I looked at was absolutely hysterical! I must have laughed for over an hour, and they had to help me to my room where my poor wife could hardly get to sleep because I was laughing so hard in bed. I can't remember in my entire life when I have had more fun than I did that night as I saw in the face of Christ "joy inexpressible and full of glory."

People have criticized the renewal, as John Wimber asked that it be called, for its holy laughter and the explanation that the Toronto leaders gave that God was throwing a party. The meetings were jokingly called "Joel's Place," in reference to the promise of the outpouring of the Spirit predicted in the Old Testament book of Joel that found its fulfillment on the day of Pentecost, where the disciples were accused of being drunk. To the critics, Toronto leaders asked, "Why couldn't, or wouldn't, God throw a party for his hurting people?" The word chosen by the Greek writers of the New Testament to connote the message of the Christ was a secular word, *euangelion,* which meant something like "holiday or celebration in honor of the emperor's birthday." The whole Christian life is the celebration of the joy of sins forgiven at the cross. Why not be so happy in the Spirit as to laugh with all our might?

Among other manifestations having some biblical and historical precedent were things like prophecy, weeping, and visions. Many of the things that were happening, however, were strange indeed and had no biblical and little historical precedent. People shook, often violently, "pogoed" up and down, twirled around, swung their arms and heads, and much, much more (we had seen these things in the Vineyard before, but not with such magnitude). Before long people in the meetings began to make sounds that sounded like animals, but we will save that for later in our discussion (these phenomena we had never seen in the Vineyard).

It all seemed so weird. I was taken beyond my comfort zone more than once. As John Arnott has said, "We are not on seeker-sensitive mode here." I am also reminded of something Paul Cain used to say during the prophetic years: "God often offends the mind to reveal the heart." While that line could be used to support an anti-intellectual approach to Christianity, I tried to use my mind while withholding judgment waiting for the fruit. It was a classic "Wimberism"—don't cut back the bush until you know what you've got.

John Arnott, in thinking about the strangeness of it all, wrote,

*Sometimes I say to my wife incredulously, 'Every night now we preach, we pray for people, and they fall down on the carpet. Every night of our lives this is what we do.' Isn't that the craziest thing you ever heard? But what is so amazing is that when people get up off the carpet, their "leprosy" is gone, and their hearts are transformed.*[12]

## THE BLESSING GOES FORTH

Randy Clark has noted that in his study of revivals, it seems that the more powerful the revival, the greater the impact it has on the countries of the world.[13] He also compares the Toronto Blessing to Azusa Street, the three-year revival in Los Angeles that birthed historic Pentecostalism (1906-9). LA is ethnically diverse, and Randy believes that it is for this same reason that the Lord sovereignly chose Toronto; United Nations statistics say that it is the most ethnically diverse city in the world.

The Airport Vineyard began to have different nationalities show up within weeks. The British were the first to fly there. Before long, there were so many coming to the meetings from England that it became difficult for businessmen to get a direct flight to Toronto because Christians had booked all of the flights.

After the English, the rest of the European community began to come. Randy wrote that as the weeks progressed, they saw Swiss, Norwegian, German, Swedish, Scottish, and Irish visitors raising their hands during the geography check-in that was included in the welcome portion of the meeting. Eventually, every continent except Antarctica would be represented. The strip mall space quickly became too small and they were forced to move to a new location.

## THE FIRE SPREADS TO BRITAIN

To date, no other country has embraced the Toronto Blessing more than England. Dr. Patrick Dixon wrote a book called *Signs of Revival* that chronicles in detail the story of what happened in Britain.[14] Many renewal movements had arisen on a smaller scale in the U.K. during the 1980s. Men like Bryn Jones, Dave Holden, Terry Virgo, Roger Mitchell, and Gerald Coates had been preaching about revival and were instrumental in planting churches and movements dedicated to renewing Britain.

Graham Kendrick became one of the principal worship leaders in Britain and started "March for Jesus" which quickly went on to become a global phenomena uniting churches of all kinds. Kendrick and missions mobilizer Steve Hawthorne collaborated on the concept of prayer-walking to cover whole cities and nations in prayer.[15]

The visits of John Wimber to the U.K. in 1984 had been pivotal for renewal there, especially within the Anglican churches. Key ministries that embraced Wimber were David Pytches' church in Chorleywood and David Watson's in York. Renewal also spread to a prominent Anglican church in London called Holy Trinity Brompton led by Sandy Miller. HTB's Alpha program, a ten-week discovery series for non-Christian seekers would explode all over the world after the release of power in 1994.

Paul Cain's prophecy about tokens of revival breaking out in England during the Vineyard conferences in October of 1990 had also caused quite a stir in the U.K. While neither Sandy Miller nor John Mumford has found any direct correlation between what broke out in England in 1990 and the events of 1994, it seems obvious that all of these factors had been preparing England for a major move of God.

Eleanor Mumford, wife of John Mumford, pastors of the South-West London Vineyard and the National Directors of the Vineyards in the U.K., brought the Toronto spark to England. At about 11:30 a.m. on May 24, 1994, during the fifth month of the renewal, "Ellie" Mumford met with a group of friends in London to share about their recent trip to Toronto. As she was sharing,

Nicky Gumbel, Curate of Holy Trinity Brompton, suddenly realized that he was late for a staff meeting. Arriving late for the meeting, he talked briefly about Mumford's experience, and then the team asked him to close in prayer. As he finished, he asked the Holy Spirit to fill everyone in the room. According to the church newspaper, *HTB in Focus*:

*The effect was instantaneous. People fell to the ground again and again. There were remarkable scenes as the Holy Spirit touched all those present in ways few had ever experienced or seen. Staff members walking past the room were also affected. Two hours later some of those present went to tell others in different offices and prayed with them where they found them. They too were powerfully affected by the Holy Spirit-many falling to the ground. Prayer was still continuing after 5 p.m.[16]*

At 4 p.m., Sandy Miller, the Vicar of HTB, was at a serious meeting of the Evangelical Alliance where he got an emergency call from the church secretary, Glenda. She said that she was sorry for the interruption but felt he needed to know that all of his staff members were on the floor and unable to work. The Evangelical Alliance looked on with anxious faces to see what this emergency might be. Sandy remembers the dialogue went something like this:

*I said to Glenda, "Is it good?"*
*"Yes, it's a very good thing, indeed," she replied.*
*So I said, "What are you doing on the telephone then?"*
*So she said, "Well I'll tell you... I have crawled to the telephone on my hands and knees."*
*So I managed to look solemn for another minute, and I said, "Thank you very much. I will get back as soon as I can."*

From that time on, the Spirit of the Lord began to break loose not only at HTB, but in fires all over Britain as plane load after plane load began the trek over to Canada. Randy Clark writes that seven thousand churches in the U.K. were affected.[17] British journalists described the significance of January 20, 1994, writing, "British Airways flight number 092 took off from Toronto airport on Thursday evening just as the Holy Spirit was landing on a small building a hundred yards from the end of the runway."[18]

## A Few Other Major Renewal Centers

### MELBOURNE, FLORIDA

In 1989, the Lord spoke to a man in our church in Indianapolis named Fred Grewe to go to Melbourne to plant a church. Fred was ready, having been Todd Hunter's assistant pastor in Wheeling, West Virginia, and now my assistant in Indy. As he and his new wife, Cindy, began to pray about Melbourne, the Lord made it clear that he was talking about Melbourne, Florida, not Australia. On the day that we sent them out, I distinctly remember prophesying that they would have trouble "three days" and then the Lord would bless them. Fred said afterward, "Gee, thanks."

They went to Florida and planted a small church where they struggled until 1995. Meanwhile, Randy Clark had had a vision of a tidal wave hitting the Florida coast. When a pastors' alliance from Florida invited him to speak at Tabernacle Church, formerly pastored by the late Jamie Buckingham, Randy knew that God was going to do a major work. In 150 days in renewal meetings, he had not been in one place that he thought had the potential to become another Toronto until Melbourne. Even though he never scheduled more than four days in one place, Randy booked "Tab" in faith for fifteen days starting January 1, 1995.

Great power broke out in Melbourne right from the beginning. Major healings took place, people from every kind of denomination worshipped together, and hundreds of people confessed faith in Christ. I had the privilege of preaching in Melbourne for three nights and can attest to the power in those meetings. So many people wanted prayer that I was exhausted by the end. I thought to myself, "How do Randy and John do this night after night?!"

Fred Grewe used his John Wimber training and became the administrator and chief trainer of the ministry teams for the meetings. He resigned his struggling pastorate to a capable man who was able to double the size of the congregation within a short time. Fred then set up an office at Tab and facilitated the meetings from there. Since that time Fred has traveled all over the world and has trained so many thousands of people to pray that he has been asked to make his training available in book and video form.

The most memorable story coming out of Melbourne was when Randy and Fred went to a local radio station to do an interview, and all the staff fell out under the power of the Spirit during the middle of the broadcast. There was no one to monitor the equipment! The station manager made it to the mic and told the listening audience that God was moving at the station and that they could come to receive prayer. Before long, the station was inundated with people, and they had to move the *ad hoc* meeting to another location.

## NEW LIFE FELLOWSHIP BAPTIST CHURCH, KELOWNA, CANADA (NOW NEW LIFE VINEYARD)[19]

As testimonies began to come in at the meetings, one of the most amazing discoveries was that God had been causing outbreaks of renewal in various parts of the world simultaneously. One example of this was in New Life Fellowship Baptist Church in Kelowna, Canada, led by Wesley Campbell, Roger Helland, and David Ruis, all men who would become leaders in the renewal. In 1985-86 the leadership was exposed to the ministry of John Wimber and began to hold conferences on the kingdom and pray for a release of power. On December 9, 1987, the eight couples who made up their elder team gathered for a Christmas party. As they entered into a time of prayer, the presence of God fell in the room and shook them like rag dolls while they spoke in tongues (these were Baptists!). Wesley's wife, Stacey, was hurled off the couch in the center of the room where she began to shake, bounce, and prophesy.

This sovereign initiation began a learning curve for the church as God taught them some years before the Toronto Blessing how to pastor in the midst of renewal. The church in Kelowna went on to become a renewal center; Wes became one of the key renewal leaders, and David Ruis became its principal worship leader. David gave us some of the most memorable songs such as "Let Your Glory Fall" with its chorus, "Let it flow forth from here to the nations," and "Break Dividing Walls" which addresses the destruction of racial barriers. Much of the electricity of the renewal has been centered in the worldwide impact of the Holy Spirit's ministry.

## MOTT AUDITORIUM[20]

I worked at the U.S. Center for World Mission for two years and remember Mott Auditorium. It had been the site of many seances when the property was occupied by the cult led by Madame Claire Prophet. Who would have thought that it would one day be the sight of a divine visitation by the Holy Spirit?

On the New Wine list on the internet, July 29, 1995, a woman from Oakland, California, wrote that she had seen a vision on April 16. In it she saw a large auditorium in a residential neighborhood in Pasadena that would become the sight of a major move of God. The Lord told her that it would become a cleansing flood.

On May 28, Che and Sue Ahn, pastors of the Vineyard of Greater Pasadena that met in Mott auditorium, were awakened in the middle of the night by their daughter and her friend. The girls were shouting, "Mott, Mott, Mott." Sue Ahn took the girls over to Mott where they saw open visions of heavenly things. An independent observer, a ministerial student returning to the church to pick up his car, said that he saw the glory of the Lord in the form of a mist hovering all over the facility and later observed enormous angels everywhere throughout the auditorium. From that point on, droves of people began to attend nightly meetings held there led by Che Ahn.

## BROWNSVILLE, FLORIDA

Brownsville, Florida, has been the greatest center of renewal outside of Toronto, and it has produced enough literature to become its own publishing industry. On Father's Day, June 18,

1995, evangelist Steve Hill spoke at Brownsville Assembly of God just outside of Pensacola. He was only planning to be there for one day, but the Holy Spirit had other plans. The power of God fell that first night, and the pastor, John Kilpatrick, fell out under the power of God and lay out for forty-eight hours. Kilpatrick asked Hill to stay on while they held meetings five nights a week. People came, just as they had in Toronto, from all over the world. The Brownsville awakening opened up major doors in the Assemblies of God to receive the new wind of the Spirit.

On July 21, Scott Weberg wrote in the New Wine list, "There are now about 4000 people attending nightly services (except Saturdays)."

The awesome part of the report was that [a total of] about 800 people got saved during the last two meetings of last week... "The meetings are going until 3:00 in the morning, and people are coming in busses."[21]

By August 1996, over 700,000 people had attended the meetings with a cumulative total of 25,000 making either first time decisions or rededications to Christ. Converts have included not only average people, but also wealthy members of the community, Satanists, drug addicts, witches, and prostitutes.[22]

## THE FIRE GOES TO MOSCOW[23]

To me, some of the most exciting stories of the renewal involved the meetings Randy Clark and his team held in Moscow in March of 1996. In 1990, Randy was present in Kansas City when Mike Bickle took a $1,200,000 offering to purchase Bibles for Russia. As Randy sat weeping, God spoke to him that he was to go to Russia and take his worship team. It seemed impossible at the time since they only had about 50 people in the church, including children. In January 1995, Randy felt impressed to ask God for $100,000 for something that God wanted to do. What it was, Randy didn't know yet, but before long he knew it was for Russia. He also knew that it would be very important for his worship team to learn the songs in Russian.

Miraculously God brought him a young couple who planned

to go to Russia as missionaries; the wife used to teach English-speaking teams in Russia how to sing phonetically in Russian! It was a setup.

The $100,000 that was eventually raised (a story in itself—they needed another $30,000 to pay all the bills) was used to finance bringing Russian leaders to the meeting in Moscow. They eventually provided sponsorships for 980 pastors and leaders attending the conference.

They held a strategic meeting of key leaders in Moscow in October 1995. The conference could not succeed without unity among the Russian denominations—a daunting task. In the end, all of the leaders who attended the strategy meeting supported the conference except for the Registered Pentecostals. Even at that, there was skepticism as to how the Russian people would respond.

What happened was beyond anyone's expectation. We got regular e-mails from Russia during this event, and we couldn't believe what we were reading. When the people heard the phonetically perfect worship (they thought the worship team was Russian), they came unglued. No other ministers in their experience had ever taken the time to learn to worship in their language. Everyone from *babushkas* to stoic Russian men wept and shouted and danced; they were filled with the joy of the Lord.

Asked how important it was to worship in Russian, one leader quoted the apostle Paul, "I would rather say five words in a language you can understand than ten thousand in one you can't."

These meetings may have had historic significance for the church in Russia.

## EVANGELICAL RENEWAL

In the revival of the mid-twentieth century, God moved simultaneously among both evangelicals and charismatics; he used the same strategy in the 1990s. As hordes of charismatically-inclined Christians streamed to places like Toronto, the evangelical world was having its own brand of Holy Spirit wind. Students at schools such as Southwestern Baptist Seminary, Wheaton College and Taylor University were extending their chapel services and openly confessing their sin. They were coming clean of things like drugs and pornography, and were bringing their paraphernalia forward for destruction.

At the North American Conference for Itinerant Evangelists in July 1994, Billy Graham noted that "America is at the center of a great revival... I am praying for a new touch of the Holy Spirit."[24]

That same month God spoke to Dr. Bill Bright, president of Campus Crusade for Christ, to go on a forty-day fast. Out of the fast Dr. Bright wrote a book called *The Coming Revival* calling the worldwide church to fast for forty days for revival. Since that time there has been a grace on the church to do just that; the phenomena of the forty-day fast has now become a worldwide movement of prayer.

PROPHECIES OF THE AWAKENING

The prophet Amos wrote, "Surely the Sovereign Lord does nothing without revealing his plan to his servants the prophets" (3:7). Renewal leaders believe that God had been speaking about this renewal through modern prophets, and that it has eschatological significance as a last-days outpouring of the Spirit. Time does not permit us to review in detail the prophetic words commonly used to support this view, but I will try to give a few highlights.[25]

At the end of a period of fasting, both Mike Bickle and Bob Jones received words independently about a worldwide move of God. God told Jones that it would be global and would crescendo in the end-time move of God. It would begin in ten years. It was then 1983, ten years from the time that the events would begin with Randy Clark.

Prophetic minister Larry Randolf received revelation in 1986 that the Lord was going to bring the rain of his Spirit on the earth. The Lord said that it would start in embryo form in the fall of 1993.

On New Year's Eve, 1993, Paul Cain was ministering at the Anaheim Vineyard and prophesied that a new wave of the Spirit was going to be released to "John and Carol" and it would bless the whole Vineyard. Later Paul went to John and Carol Wimber and told them that this didn't necessarily mean them. Within three weeks the Toronto Blessing was poured out on John and Carol Arnott, and Wes Campbell estimates that by July two-thirds of the churches in the Vineyard had been blessed by the renewal.

Prophetic minister Marc Dupont had moved to Toronto in 1992 to work with John Arnott. On his first day of work, Marc received a prophetic vision showing that God was going to cause Toronto to become a kind of Jerusalem sending base from which ministry would flow forth to the nations of the earth. In August of 1993 he told John and Carol Arnott that within seven months they would be catapulted onto the major platforms of the earth; they would speak to thousands. The word was so grandiose that John and Carol couldn't believe it.

## WHERE IS THE POWER POINTED?

John Wimber came to Canada in August of 1994 to speak at the first Canadian Vineyard pastors' conference. En route to Canada, he asked the Lord, "What should I say to the Canadians with respect to this recent visitation?" As John prayed, he had a powerful vision from the Lord. John wrote about it in the July/August issue of *Reflections* in 1994, pp. 6-7. It was a prophetic warning for all those who would embrace the renewal:

*In the vision the Lord showed me a magnificent mountain lake. Beautiful sunshine reflected off water that was fresh and inviting. The water of the lake spilled over a dam and cascaded into a river and came down the sides of a mountain into a large plain. In the plain there were thousands and thousands of acres of vineyards. I saw men working in the fields, digging irrigation ditches. Then the vision ended.*

*So I said, "Lord, what does it mean?" In my mind, He gave me, "The lake is the blessing I'm pouring out. Isn't it beautiful? Isn't it fresh?" I was so touched, I began to cry. He then said, "The cascading stream is the church.*

302

*I'm pouring it first into the church." I wept more. I just thought, "Oh thank You, Lord. Thank You for the blessing on the church."*

*Then I saw again how the water came down to the bottom of the mountain into the plain where the workers were tending the irrigation ditches. I recognized these irrigation ditches as ministry to the poor, ministry to the weak, sick, broken and lost. There were different kinds of vineyards with different kinds of fruit growing on the vines. Then He said, "That's My People. This blessing can either stay in the church, with great meetings that eventually end. Or we can pull the gates up and let the water begin flowing. If you want, you can direct the water, the blessing, into the fields."*

*I got the clear impression of co-laboring. God was pouring out His blessing. But if we didn't dig the channels, if we don't go out into the highways and by-ways, if we don't put evangelism forward, if we don't do the things God calls us to do, revival won't spread.*

Randy Clark, on the other hand, while completely agreeing with John Wimber's concerns that the renewal go outward, wrote the following in speaking of his pain over the events we will describe in the next chapter:

*This renewal which God sovereignly chose to birth in Toronto is so much bigger than any one church or any one denomination. Any attempt to box it in will fail and only harm those who try to restrain it. It is my prayer that every man on earth can experience what I have personally experienced of the grace of God. My heart is elated how God has sovereignly moved across the globe. This is no prairie fire. This is no brush fire whipped about by the wind. This is a blazing inferno that is spreading to every heart that will receive it. It is my experience that as God appears to shut some doors, He is already opening many others.[26]*

ℂℬ

303

## NOTES:

[1] As quoted by Guy Chevreau in his book *Catching the Fire* (Marshall Pickering, London, 1994, p. 2)

[2] *Vineyard Reflections*, May/June, 1994, p. 3

[3] *Lighting the Fire*, p. 101

[4] *Ibid.*

[5] Clark, p. 109

[6] Riss, in the chapter on "The Vineyard Churches"

[7] Wesley Campbell, *Welcoming a Visitation of the Holy Spirit* (Creation House, Orlando FL, 1996, p. 23-4)

[8] A whole host of literature began to come out within a short period of time, many going great lengths to demonstrate biblical and historical precedent. Some of these included, Guy Chevreau's *Catch the Fire,* Patrick Dixon's *Signs of Revival* (Kingsway, Sussex, England, 1994), Derek Morphew's *Renewal Apologetics* (an AVC position paper, 1995), Don William's *Revival: the Real Thing* (self published, 1995), Roger Helland's *Let the River Flow* (Bridge Logos, New Brunswick NJ, 1996), and Wesley Campbell's *Welcoming a Visitation of the Spirit.*

[9] While I have never been to meetings in Toronto, as I said, Randy Clark and John and Carol Arnott came to Champaign twice so we experienced "typical" renewal meetings outside the context of Toronto.

[10] Grand Rapids, Zondervan, 1995, p. 153

[11] Mick Brown, "Unzipper Heaven, Lord. Ha-ha, Ho-ho, He-he." *Telegraph Magazine*, December 3, 1994; James A. Beverly writes about this article in *Holy Laughter and the Toronto Blessing* (Grand Rapids, MI, Zondervan, 1995, pp. 96-98). He says that Brown was interviewed by the British publication *Evangelicals Now* during which Brown likened his experience in Toronto to a similar encounter he had had with an Indian religious leader named Mother Meera. He said that he had had no long-term consequences from what happened with Meera. Beverly writes that the Toronto position on Mick Brown is that the Lord had been gracious to him by granting him a touch of His power. Unfortunately Brown did not look to the Lord, but rejected a sign from heaven to him.

[12] Arnott, p. 130

[13] Clark, p. 164

[14] Kingsway Publications, 1994

[15] *Prayer-walking*, Orlando, FL, Creation House, 1993

[16] As quoted in Riss, in his chapter on Holy Trinity Brompton.

[17] Clark, p. 165

[18] Riss in his chapter on Holy Trinity Brompton

[19] This story can be found in the books by Wes Campbell and Roger Helland.

[20] Taken from Riss in his chapter on Mott Auditorium

[21] Taken from Riss in his chapter on Pensacola

[22] Helland, p. 226

[23] Clark, pp. 15-160

[24] Campbell, p. 31

[25] See the pamphlet written by Randy Clark, Prophetic Foundations for Revival (available through Vineyard Christian Fellowship, St. Louis) and Campbell, pp. 34-47.

[26] Clark, p. 163

# CHAPTER EIGHTEEN

# THE
# LIONS ROAR

# THE LIONS ROAR

### JOHN WIMBER: TRYING TO LEAD FROM A DISTANCE

As the first few months of the Toronto Blessing came to a close, John Wimber was being inundated with calls, letters, and faxes about what was going on. Most were positive at this point, but some were beginning to show great anxiety over the manifestations.

In April of 1994, a seminar was held in Randy Clark's church in St. Louis for potential church planters. I was present at these meetings and saw the Holy Spirit released in powerful ways on many of those who came. During this time, John Wimber had a private meeting with Randy where he indicated that he was essentially pleased with what was happening in Randy's life, but he also gave him lots of "fatherly" advice, warning him to not give up his church and to pace himself. He expressed genuine concern for Randy's family, telling him that it might not show up now, but his travel could greatly affect his kids in the future. John concluded by telling Randy that if he could convince him that all of the traveling was God's call on his life, then the two of them would need to sit down at a later date and discuss how to administrate his schedule.

Randy didn't immediately know how to respond to this request, so he began to reconstruct all the different ways God had prepared and called him to do what he had been doing. Randy recounts in an appendix of his book at least fifteen different prophetic words over the years, one of which was spoken by Wimber himself, that predicted the things that were happening to him.

### "VINEYARD REFLECTIONS," MAY/JUNE 1994

By late spring John felt he needed to begin to speak into the things that were happening in Toronto. He chose to use the vehicle of his *Reflections* magazine and produced a series of rapid-fire issues sharing his views.

308

In the May issue, John began to attempt to pastor the renewal from afar. He reminded us that the things that were happening in Toronto had happened in ebbs and flows in the Vineyard's history and that God was being kind to give us another measure of his grace. God himself had spoken to John that he would be bringing us into a season of "new beginnings."

Wimber asked that this stage of the Spirit's activity be called "renewal" as opposed to "revival." He then demonstrated historically what real revival looks like: mass conversions, increased holiness, societal change, and a fire to fulfill the Great Commission. His preliminary conclusions were that this very well could be the early stages of revival, but it was too early to tell.

Because of the stir about the manifestations, John looked to six principles for judging "affections" as articulated by Jonathan Edwards in the first Great Awakening ("affections" was Edwards' word for manifestations of the Spirit). Edwards exhorted the readers of his day to be patient and to judge the long-term fruit.

Wimber asked the smaller churches to avoid wearing their people out with meetings and asked the larger churches to make sure that their renewal meetings did not override the work of the church.

He asked that the renewal stay Christ-centered and not become manifestation-centered. He expressed concerns even at this stage with training catchers and putting tape on the floor. He thought that it planted the notion that people should fall, thus putting the emphasis on the manifestations and creating first and second class citizens i.e., those who experienced manifestations and those who didn't.

## "VINEYARD REFLECTIONS," JULY/AUGUST 1994

John brought the renewal to Anaheim in July with a conference called "Let the Fire Fall." About 5,000 people attended and afterward they were inundated with over a thousand phone calls, letters, faxes, and notes, the largest response they had ever gotten from a conference. Again the communications were both positive and negative.

John's *Reflections* article reiterated the need to be patient and to see the fruit. He likened the renewal to a birthing process that is messy but also mysterious. He said,

*In my opinion, it's not necessary to explain everything connected with revival any more than a young mother needs to share in detail the travail of giving birth. All she has to do is hold the baby up and everyone shares in the joy.*

John was willing to let the zeal go for the moment but had no problem speaking into the ministry model of those in the renewal. He assured renewal leaders that it was OK to pastor the meetings such as putting a stop to "holy" laughter during the preaching if it was bothersome; it would not be quenching the Spirit to do so.

He walked us through 1 Corinthians 14 where Paul asks for 1) intelligibility, 2) order, and 3) edification in a meeting. Not everyone defines order in the same way, but however it is defined, as pastors we need to make sure that our people are being edified. If they aren't, then we need to pastor our meetings to find the right balance to ensure that they are.

In this issue of *Reflections* John shared the vision of the waterfall he had seen before addressing the Vineyards in Canada. He believed it was God's word to the Vineyard as a whole: the renewal needs to lead people out into the streets with the gospel. Individual and corporate fruit would be the real test as to whether the renewal would end up where God intended it.

## "VINEYARD REFLECTIONS," SEPTEMBER/OCTOBER 1994 AND WINTER 1994-95

In the next two issues of *Reflections* John shared insights gained from counsel with noted Pentecostal leaders such as Jack Hayford, pastor of a large Four Square Gospel church in Van Nuys, California, and Vinson Synon, one of the premier Pentecostal historians.

Citing similarities to the Pentecostals who were set on fire through the Azusa Street revival from 1906-1909, Wimber again exhorted the Vineyard to take the renewal to the streets.

Pentecostalism has grown to become the largest strata of Protestant Christianity in the world in less that a century because the touch of God's Spirit drove them all over the world with the gospel. The revival was never a "bless-me" club, but was a wind that blew them outward. In this regard Wimber said,

> Our earliest commission as a group of churches was to be a church planting movement for the sake of winning the lost...For me, our historic identity provides a moral, spiritual and intellectual grid for evaluating the current renewal activity in the Vineyard. My chief concern as overseer of the Vineyard is whether the renewal activity will contribute to or hinder our ability to achieve our goals of evangelism through church planting.

John reiterated that pursuit of the renewal should not keep us from pastoring our people. He listed at least six things that must continually be going on in the local church whether it was in renewal or not: teaching the Word, administering the ordinances of baptism and communion, pastoring people's needs, equipping the saints for ministry, leading in worship, and doing the work of evangelism.

Wimber concluded, "In my opinion, any Vineyard pastor who neglects the above to pursue or gives too great a place to phenomena long-term is making a potentially fatal mistake as far as that local congregation is concerned."

Most of the Winter 94/95 issue of *Reflections* was an excerpted and adapted reprint of a lecture from Four Square scholar Guy P. Duffield at L.I.F.E. Bible College in 1956. In his lecture, Duffield made a statement which defines the essence of what the Vineyard is trying to be and do. In developing his point that preaching the Word is the heartbeat of the church, he wrote, "Our message is not the Holy Spirit and his gifts. It is Christ Jesus and his resurrection." John Wimber wanted the Vineyard to embrace the present-day ministry of the Spirit *only* as it is built off the "main and the plain" foundation of Jesus. Any other preoccupation with the Spirit's ministry is illegitimate.

## THE "LION" ROARS

The first incident of an "animal noise" was in Toronto, about five months into the renewal. Steve Long, staff member at the Airport Vineyard, wrote about the incident in an article called "What About Animal Noises?" in the October 1995 issue of *Spread the Fire*.[1]  Gideon Chui, a Vancouver-based Cantonese Chinese pastor had come to the renewal fasting. While he was there, the Lord told him to stop fasting and enjoy the feast the Lord had prepared. During one of the meetings pastor Chui began to roar like a lion. He later testified that the roaring seemed to represent God's heart over the heritage of the Chinese people and the domination of the dragon, both culturally and spiritually. He thought that it was a prophetic sign that God was going to release the Chinese people from centuries of oppression. Steve Long wrote that the people who had been most likely to roar were those from countries where the lion is a symbol.

In the same issue of *Spread the Fire*, Steve Witt, a Vineyard pastor from Canada, wrote about an incident involving the church pianist. She quickly exited the sanctuary after worship and headed down the hallway. She suddenly darted into the nursery, closed the door, and began to shake. She then acted out the sounds and bodily gestures of an angry ox, charging on all fours, snorting with flared nostrils. She went on to prophesy in first, second, and third person that the Lord was chasing the enemy back with great strength.

In his article on possible explanations for the animal sounds, Steve Long cited texts from Ezekiel 1 and Revelation 4 which talk about four creatures: a lion, an eagle, an ox, and a man. Steve wrote that it seemed that some in the renewal were acting out prophetic messages, replicating the movements of these creatures. Since that time, renewal meetings in various places have had similar incidents of these and other animal manifestations, causing no small amount of criticism. The occurrences were actually rare; we never saw any in our renewal meetings in Champaign. But in the furor caused by these bizarre behaviors, John Wimber felt that he needed to call an emergency meeting of the Vineyard board.

## EMERGENCY BOARD MEETING, SEPTEMBER 1994

Randy Clark, John Arnott, and Wes Campbell were invited to Anaheim to meet with the Vineyard's Regional Overseers and key leaders. The attendees were faxed a list of twenty possible items to be discussed, each one addressing concerns over pastoring the renewal.[2] Todd Hunter, the acting Director of the Association of Vineyard Churches, explained that the purpose of the meeting was to address the historic tension between the "bishops" and those currently "charismatically endowed."

Randy Clark, who could only stay a couple of days, expressed consternation that most of the discussion centered on the animal noises. These manifestations had not occurred in his meetings, and he had what he felt were more pertinent issues to work through. The Regional Overseers, however, had to come up with a board policy to govern the phenomena because they were devastating some of their churches.

Hardest hit was John McClure's Vineyard in Newport Beach, California. He lost 40% of his congregation, many of whom went down the street to Chuck Smith's Calvary Chapel, because they were being scared by the comments of Hank Hanegraaff, the director of the Christian Research Institute. Hanegraaff, a member of Chuck Smith's Calvary Chapel, used his radio broadcast called "The Bible Answer Man" to warn his listeners that the renewal was really a satanic deception. The loss of hundreds of people from the Newport Beach Vineyard obviously caused McClure a great deal of pastoral anguish.

John McClure would go on to take perhaps the strongest stance against the renewal on the board. This would be easy to surmise if the loss of his people were the only factor, but John's history goes deeper than this. His wife, Margie, is the daughter of Raymond Ortlund, one of the great evangelical pastors of our day and former pastor of the eminent Lake Avenue Congregational church in Pasadena, CA. John himself was a congregationalist before linking with John Wimber. Speaking in tongues had never been a part of congregationalism, let alone animal noises. John's brother, Don McClure, is one of the top pastoral leaders in

313

Calvary Chapel (it was this church that Carol Wimber had been going to after leaving the Quakers and was the link into Calvary Chapel for the Wimbers new church). Not only this, but John's father is a part of Chuck Smith's Calvary Chapel and was very close to Chuck, at one point even being the church treasurer. All this to say that John has had to pay a great price to be in the Vineyard. When Hank Hanegraaff began his tirades on the radio and the Orange County Register began writing articles on people making animal sounds, it is easy to understand at least the visceral responses and pressures on John and Margie. In a personal letter, John and Margie wrote me that despite what it may have looked, in the end their concerns were based solely in Scripture and on nothing else.

### THE BOARD REPORT

The board voted to continue to support the renewal in Toronto but issued a report outlining their concerns. Soon after the meeting, a summary of the majority consensus was published by AVC under the title, "Board Report: Summary of the Current Renewal and the Phenomena Surrounding It." The report listed nine conclusions and offered an application of 1 Corinthians 14 to the renewal. Included in the report was an excerpt from a letter written by John Wimber explaining his views on the phenomena. I will try to summarize the conclusions here in short form.

- The Vineyard has always tried to "bless what the Father is doing" and will continue to invite the Holy Spirit to come with a willingness to pastor the results.
- While we are aware that people's unique responses to the touch of God might either look bizarre or remind us of things we have seen before like lions or oxen, we should avoid a this-is-that explanation. We should definitely not try to ex plain a non-biblical manifestation with a biblical allusion or "proof-text." It is OK to make observations about the meaning of individual occurrences of phenomena, but never to catalogue them as a doctrine.
- We should never promote manifestations in any way, but

focus on the main and plain issues of Scripture such as the fruit and gifts of the Spirit, evangelism and church planting. We are after long-term fruit, not experiences. If God has truly touched a person, he or she should go home talking about Jesus, not about falling and shaking. The result of true renewal will be seen in new passion for Jesus, and the words and works of the kingdom.

- We do not want church life to revolve around renewal meetings. We want to stick to what we are about - making disciples and church planting.
- The Vineyard should refrain from equating any movement of the Spirit with any particular eschatological schema such as the beginning of a great end-time revival.

Todd Hunter concluded the report by writing:

*You may ask, "In simple terms, what does all the above mean?" It means that it is our desire to embrace all that is good about this renewal while correcting that which is excessive, long-term hurtful or contrary to biblical mandates. We also want to interact with the renewal based on our historical and firmly held vision, mission and purpose...we are committed to "power evangelism," not just "power"; we are committed to "signs and wonders and church growth," not just "signs and wonders." The Lord has clearly instructed us to direct these current blessings into practical activities that will minister to and bless those outside of our churches. It is our hope that every Vineyard pastor will do so through the grace and power of God.*

## JAMES A. BEVERLY'S HOLY LAUGHTER & THE TORONTO BLESSING[3]

Dr. James A. Beverly, professor of theology and ethics at Ontario Theological Seminary in Toronto, is a specialist in the study of modern religious movements. He had begun research on the Vineyard in 1991 when he was asked to do an article on our movement for his denominational magazine, *The Canadian Baptist*. In 1994 he was asked by *Christianity Today* to do a similar article on the Toronto Blessing (henceforth "TB") which just happened to be occurring in his own backyard. Because of the proximity, he had plenty of time to attend the meetings and try to analyze what was going on. Unlike Hank Hanegraaff, to whom we will look later, Beverly was an "open" critic in the renewal meetings, at times going forward for prayer. His conclusions on the renewal were published in book form in 1995, before the separation of the Vineyard and Toronto. I found *Holy Laughter & the Toronto Blessing* to be a fairly even-handed critique. While I never felt that he had an ax to grind and found a number of his comments astute and helpful, his analysis came through his evangelical lens, as one would expect.

Beverly wrote that there are five possible explanations for the TB:

1. The beginnings of the great end-time revival
2. A genuine outpouring of the Holy Spirit without eschatological significance
3. A mixed blessing-some wonderful, some harmful
4. Not true revival-Christians worldwide need to be warned!
5. A great satanic deception associated with the end-time delusion that is coming

Beverly clearly falls down in #3 and writes his book to speak into that which is good and call into alignment that which he thinks is bad. Before doing so, he lists ten tests for truth through which he puts the renewal and lays down the rules for fair evaluation.

As might be expected, Beverly finds positive and negative features in all the categories he considers:

- He thinks the Vineyard has made a great contribution to the church but has had an erratic track record for judging the will of God. As such, it should watch the potential of an elitist spirit, coming perhaps from all the media hype while yet so young a movement.
- He thinks that the criticism of Hank Hanegraaff and others against Rodney Howard-Browne is unfair, but has cautions about 1) Howard-Browne being a one-man-show, 2) his "anti-intellectual trends in thought," and 3) an unbiblical

emphasis on holy laughter and other manifestations.

- While the renewal leaders say that they don't emphasize manifestations, Beverly thinks they do and says that it is illegal to look at signs and wonders as proof of God's manifest presence.
- After examining three alleged cases of healing, Beverly concludes that renewal leaders haven't been as careful as they should have been in saying that someone was healed. One wonders what Beverly would have found if he had had more time to follow up on this one. Randy Clark has told me many marvelous stories about healings in his meetings, but because of the nature of the renewal, medical verification for the skeptical, however valid, is low on the priority list.

He hits the hardest on the gift of prophecy:

- He analyzes two of Marc Dupont's prophecies and concludes that of the eighteen predictions in them, fifteen of them were either general or vague, or have yet to be fulfilled. To Marc's credit, he felt so strongly that something of significance was going to happen in Toronto that he moved his family there from San Diego on the eve of the renewal!

Marc hasn't always gotten it right (no New Testament proophet does), but I know from personal experience that he can be very accurate with great benefit to the body of Christ.

BEVERLY'S CONCLUSIONS:

Some of the things Beverly thinks are *positive* about the TB:

- God's power is exalted over the devil's.
- It is bringing long-needed renewal to the church, something it continually needs.
- The renewal leaders are not satisfied with the party; they want evangelism and full-scale revival.
- The TB leaders have been exemplary in their lack of focus on money.
- The TB is non-legalistic in its approach to holiness.

Some of the things Beverly thinks *need correction*:

- He thinks that the preaching is notoriously weak.
- Renewal leaders have a limited view of the Holy Spirit; Beverly thinks that the leaders of the renewal give the impression that God is only doing one thing in Toronto. He says, "The Spirit of God landed in Toronto long before January 20, 1994. In thousands of churches and in a million ways, the Holy Spirit has been working in this great Canadian city."[4]
- The TB has an anti-intellectual spirit that gives it a theological shallowness.
- The manifestations are not in-and-of-themselves evidences of the miraculous, as they are alleged to be. They are in reality people's responses to the touch of the Spirit. Beverly urges that renewal leaders not limit the biblical definition of a miracle by equating them with manifestations.
- Finally, there is a lack of emphasis on the person of Christ, overemphasizing pneumatology (the doctrine of the Holy Spirit) to the neglect of Christology (the doctrine of Christ).

Having said all this, Beverly says that he would be disappointed if the renewal meetings shut down. He writes in his summary chapter, "If the TB is too wild, are not dead and boring services an equal, if not greater, sin?... If the Holy Spirit is over-emphasized, what shall we say against churches that ignore the Spirit?"

## HANK HANEGRAAFF'S COUNTERFEIT REVIVAL[5]

Dispensing with the more even-handed criticism of James Beverly, we now turn to "The Bible Answer Man,"Hank Hanegraaff. Early in the renewal, Hanegraaff began to criticize the TB on his radio program. He eventually shared his conclusions in a lecture entitled "Counterfeit Revival." His basis for evaluating the ministries of Rodney Howard-Browne and the TB was the premise that bad roots equal bad fruit. He sought to discredit Howard-Browne because of his link to the Word of Faith movement and then dismissed the TB because Randy Clark received his "anointing" at a Howard-Browne meeting in a Word of Faith church.

318

In the same way that the Kansas City prophets are linked to an eschatological schema, so is Hanegraaff. He believes in the pre-tribulational rapture of the church and, therefore, is looking for a great delusion as a prelude to the appearance of the Anti-Christ. He sees in the renewal the signs of a counterfeit revival paving the way for the Anti-Christ—very serious charges indeed.

Hanegraaff's lecture eventually came out as the book *Counterfeit Revival*. Tom Stipe, pastor of what was formerly the Vineyard in Denver, wrote the foreword to *Counterfeit Revival*. Tom left the Vineyard during the prophetic turmoil and now stands with Hanegraaff in an assessment that the Vineyard and the TB are seriously off the mark. Stipe likens *Counterfeit Revival* to Martin Luther's ninety-five theses nailed to the door of Wittenburg's Cathedral.

In May of 1995, J. Lee Grady, writing in *Charisma* magazine, asked the question, "Does the Church Need Heresy Hunters?" In his article, Grady cites many who think that Hanegraaff has appointed himself as the definer and defender of truth, and that he is out of bounds in doing so. In the article, Grady pointed out that at the time there was a group of thirty former employees who were asking for Hanegraaff's resignation because he has violated ethical standards and isn't accountable to anyone. Hanegraaff thought that he was being persecuted because he is standing against heresy.

Rather than try to summarize *Counterfeit Revival*, I will reference two critiques.

## DON WILLIAM'S REVIVAL: THE REAL THING[6]

Don Williams is the pastor of the Coast Vineyard in La Jolla, California, and is the author of eleven books. He holds his Ph.D. in New Testament and is one of the Vineyard's premier theologians. He did much of the work on the AVC doctrinal statement. Williams published his rebuttal in response to Hanegraaff's lecture before the book came out.

Since the premise of *Counterfeit Revival* is to discredit Howard-Browne on the root-fruit principle, Williams spends most of his book addressing the criticisms against this South African evangelist. I will give a brief overview of the charges and the defense.

## MANIFESTATIONS ARE A SATANIC DECEPTION

Hanegraaff alleges that people in renewal meetings are manipulated into a self-induced state of altered consciousness that opens them up to the world of the occult. He dismisses all emotional displays such as holy laughter as reflective of these altered states. While he thinks that most of what goes on in the Vineyard and the TB is the flesh, he asserts that there is a demonic element as well.

Williams thinks that Hanegraaff's views stem from the Platonic worldview that became the basis of Greek dualism. Plato taught that the soul and body were separate entities. Salvation sets the soul free from the prison of the body. That which affects the soul does not affect the body. Worship and Christian joy, for instance, occur in the inner life and are not to be manifest outwardly in one's emotions or physical being. Hanegraaff concludes that laughter, therefore, is a bogus expression of joy.

Williams responds by saying that the biblical worldview, Hebrew monism, sees the soul and body as separate, but integrated, impacting one another. Salvation of the soul can affect the body, and laughter or falling could be genuine expressions of redemption or empowerment. While noting that there are no clear examples of laughter in the Bible, Hebrew worship was emotional and celebrative. In the New Testament, joy and rejoicing are earmarks of salvation and these same themes are replete in church history.

In regards to the more exotic phenomena, Hanegraaff sees these as the extension of the flesh or Satan since there is no biblical precedent. William's rejoinder is that neither biblical precedent nor proof-texting is the real issue. Since the manifestations are human responses to the touch of God, the task of leadership is to discern not the manifestation, but the root cause. The real question is, "Is it the devil, the flesh, or God?" Williams says, "If we rule such phenomena out arbitrarily or *a priori* as Hanegraaff wants to do, we may quench the Spirit."[7]

## HOWARD-BROWNE IS GUILTY OF THEOLOGICAL ERRORS

Despite Hanegraaff's attempts to show that Howard-Browne and other renewal leaders have a deficient view of Scripture, Williams defends them saying that they have a very high view of the Bible. He says, "Hanegraaff does not offer one substantial example of theological error from the speaking or writing of Howard-Browne. All of it comes from inference."[8]

As to Hanegraaff's opposition to a revival at the end of the age, Williams says that the New Testament church is always under marching orders to fulfill the great commission, actively praying for and working toward a massive influx of souls. It is love, not a prophetic scenario, which propels us toward revival.

In a final word to Hanegraaff himself, Williams chides him for his negative, joyless tone and concludes, "many that are sincere are sincerely wrong."

## JAMES A. BEVERLY'S REVIVAL WARS:
### *A CRITIQUE OF COUNTERFEIT REVIVAL*[9]

When James Beverly received a pre-publication copy of *Counterfeit Revival*, he knew that despite his friendship with Hanegraaff and even his defense of Hanegraaff's sincerity to renewal leaders, he would have to write a response. He says,

*I saw immediately that much of his research was outdated and that large portions of his analysis were rooted in faulty logic, selective use of evidence and an inexplicable failure to examine data that was contrary to his own positions.*[10]

He also regrets that Tom Stipe wrote the introduction saying that he has underestimated his own involvement in the prophetic and has left out incidents that would explain Wimber's anger over Stipe's departure from the Vineyard. He hopes that *Revival Wars* will cause Stipe to re-examine his endorsement of the book.

Beverly covers much of the same ground as Williams, citing numerous errors in logic and the reduction of complex issues with sweeping statements of generalization. He is appalled at the lack of any phrase of appreciation for the renewal leaders in question. Their faults are magnified by constant repetition and absolutely no weight is given to the truth taught by these leaders or how God has used them to bring blessing and salvation to countless numbers of people. Beverly asks, "What if a similar methodology was used to target other leaders and Christian groups? What church or leader would remain standing?" In the end, it is the lack of grace that leaves one reeling.

*Revival Wars* devotes two chapters to Hanegraaff's assassination of James Ryle, then pastor of the Vineyard in Boulder, and John Wimber.

Beverly's research into the ministry and prophecies of James Ryle led him to actually take a trip to Boulder to see this "dangerous" man for himself. He found that Hanegraaff had misrepresented Ryle at a number of points and had not taken into account his overall growth or public admission of previous errors in writing and prophetic judgment. He notes that the low point of the book was the denigration of private, sensitive things in Ryle's past saying, "Hanegraaff has taken the most tragic and fragile moments in James Ryle's life, and those of his wife Belinda, and subjected them to ridicule and sarcasm."[11] He concludes that labeling Ryle as a "counterfeit revival" leader is "unfair and unworthy."

John Wimber, however, is Hanegraaff's main target, and even though Wimber has had an impact on churches all over the globe, there is not one single positive reference to him in the entire book. Beverly says that the relentless negativity amounts to bearing false witness. His view that Lonnie Frisbee's influence on the Vineyard caused structural defects because Lonnie struggled with homosexuality and died of AIDS (see Appendix 2) in 1993 is also flawed. When this position is taken to its logical conclusion, it indicts any church that Lonnie ever ministered in.

Beverly concludes that while Hanegraaff has raised some

legitimate concerns about Charismatic Christianity, he has not established any sort of reasonable case for his overall position. He has also harmed genuine renewal by causing discord where unnecessary. "So many misjudgments… have hurt his credibility as a watchman in the church."[12]

☙

NOTES:

[1] *Spread the Fire* is the renewal magazine published by what is now called Toronto Airport Christian Fellowship (pp. 17f).

[2] Randy Clark writes about these meetings in his book, pp. 125f.

[3] Zondervan, Grand Rapids, Michigan, 1995

[4] P. 155

[5] Word Publishing, Dallas, Texas, 1997

[6] Self published, La Jolla, CA, 1995

[7] P. 50

[8] P. 52

[9] Evangelical Research Ministries, Canada, 1997

[10] P. 9

[11] P. 74

[12] P. 93

THE STREAMS DIVERGE

CHAPTER NINETEEN

# THE
# STREAMS
# DIVERGE

# THE STREAMS DIVERGE

## THE HEAT IS TURNED UP

### THE MEDIA

By 1995, the Vineyard and the Toronto Blessing were getting a lot of press. In March of that year, Peter Jennings of ABC News did an hour-long special called "In the Name of God" where he looked at new trends in Christianity. He examined Bill Hybel's Willlow Creek Community Church in Barrington Hills, Illinois, which has been the primogenitor of the seeker movement, the Vineyard, and the laughing revival under Rodney Howard-Browne.

When Jennings was allowed to take footage from the services at the Anaheim Vineyard, it was in the face of a twenty-year policy to preserve the privacy and intimacy of worship and ministry. Some of the shots compromised that privacy and focused on exotic manifestations rather than on the "main and the plain."

Phil Donahue had Toronto leaders on his show, and the news show *A Current Affair* was looking into doing a piece on the renewal. The heat was on.

In 1995 John Arnott published *The Father's Blessing*.[1] It hit the bookstores just as other things began to break and only added to the tension that Wimber felt. While John Arnott's intention was to focus the renewal on Jesus and the Father, his chapter entitled "The Prophetic: Animal Sounds and Insights," solidified for many on the AVC board that Arnott was willfully not complying with the board's 1994 parameters. What was particularly hard for Wimber was that his name appeared on the back endorsing the book, but for some reason, he had not read the chapter on animal sounds before it was published.

On October 26, 1995, the *Orange County Register* (with a circulation of several million) did a front-page article in its "Accent" section on the Vineyard renewal meetings in Pasadena. In it were descriptions of:

326

- A woman "on all fours, growling and digging at the floor like a terrier after a gopher" as a ministry team member prayed, "Increase, Lord! Increase, Lord!"
- A college-aged youth doing "Jesus laps."
- A young woman "who seemed to be imitating a chicken, waddling with head jerking back and forth as if searching for grain."

In the November/December issue of *Ministries Today* magazine (pp. 15-16), John Wimber was quoted as saying in Holy Trinity Brompton's periodical, *In Focus*, that it was OK if someone "quacked like a duck for three days" if it resulted in caring for the poor and leading others to Christ. John's intent in context was to make a hyperbolic contrast to emphasize the fruit of the main and the plain over manifestations, but given the timing of the quote in the same month with the other incidents, it was easily misconstrued.

The straw that broke the camel's back was the arrival of the Toronto Airport Vineyard's magazine, *Spread the Fire,* [2] which came out right after the *Orange County Register* article. It included the articles on animal sounds and the ox in the nursery.

These occurrences finally propelled John McClure, pastor of the Newport Beach Vineyard and AVC board member, to write a series of letters to the parties involved and to key Vineyard leaders to express his concerns. In McClure's mind, these incidents were a clear violation of the 1994 board policies that manifestations would not be emphasized or explained from Scripture. At the same time, other Vineyard leaders such as Rich Nathan and Steve Nicholson were contacting Arnott in private.

### THE VINEYARD GETS COUNSEL FROM VINSON SYNAN [3]

Todd Hunter at this time contacted the Pentecostal historian, Vinson Synan, to talk about the possibility of taking a stand against Toronto. Synan told AVC that it was OK for them to govern their movement. They had laid down parameters, and the ball was now in their court to stick to their guns.

Synan pointed out that the Assemblies of God had taken a

stand against the Latter Rain movement at mid-century, and it didn't hurt them. The Latter Rain movement essentially died out while the Assemblies continued to grow.

He reminded Todd that we are ministering in the West where bizarre manifestations can destroy our credibility. He also applauded AVC's desire to stick with the main and the plain, not forbidding manifestations but putting them to the side-away from the cross, discipleship, and world evangelization.

No matter what AVC did, however, Synan wanted Hunter to know that the worldwide body of Christ was watching.

MARGARET POLOMA

On November 27, 1995, Margaret Poloma, a retired professor from Case Western Reserve University in Akron, Ohio, wrote John Wimber a letter to respond to both his latest *Reflections* and the *Ministry Today* article.[4] Poloma is considered the top specialist on the sociology of religion, and much of her work has centered on the flow from charisma to organized religion in Charismatic Christianity. As the controversy was heating up, she was engaged in active research of the Toronto Blessing and had written a preliminary study on it.

In her letter to Wimber, she sought to demonstrate that as a "participating observer" she found few examples of the cautionary concerns that Wimber raised. She said, "There are always going to be weeds mixed with the wheat, but I have been very impressed with the leadership's ability to allow the wheat to grow undisturbed without nurturing the weeds." She concluded,

> *Contrary to the suggestion that TAV has departed from Vineyard philosophy in significant ways, I believe it not only serves as a good example of the philosophy you outlined but that it is sharing this gift with the larger church.*

## THE WITHDRAWAL OF ENDORSEMENT OF THE TORONTO AIRPORT VINEYARD[5]

In early December 1995, the board made the decision to withdraw its endorsement of the Toronto Airport Vineyard.

The reasons, when distilled down, were twofold:

1. The board's perception was that TAV had a different vision and direction from AVC.

2. The board felt that TAV was not complying with the 1994 policy decisions, demonstrating that the AVC board members were not their leaders. Wimber later said that AVC could no longer endorse what it no longer had authority over.

Given these two factors, AVC was going to set Toronto free to pursue its own direction and values.

AVC informed the TAV staff that there would be a meeting on the evening of December 5. The Toronto leaders assumed that Wimber was coming to work things out, but that was not the case. AVC was coming to announce their decision and not to negotiate.

On December 4, on the way to Toronto, AVC International Director John Wimber, acting USA National Director Todd Hunter, International Coordinator Bob Fulton, and Canadian AVC Director Gary Best, met with Wes Campbell, Roger Helland, and another staff member from New Life Vineyard in Kelowna, BC, in Vancouver. AVC wanted to inform Wes and his staff of their decision due to New Life's close association with TAV. In an internet posting on the New Wine list, Roger Helland wrote on December 13 that John Wimber had made it clear to them that he and AVC believed the renewal to be a genuine move of the Holy Spirit, but that it had been poorly pastored and had redefined renewal for the Vineyard, something that Wimber was not willing to concede. This did not mean that it was bad, that John Arnott was bad, or that the fruit was bad, only that from AVC's perspective they had serious differences in direction and philosophy. The New Life Vineyard staff decided that the Lord wanted them to wait before they decided on any particular course of action.

On Tuesday evening, December 5, Wimber, Hunter, Fulton, and Best met with Arnott and ten of his staff and friends. Wimber began by announcing that the Toronto Airport Vineyard was being asked to separate from the Association of Vineyard Churches. The TAV staff was shocked.

The Toronto team did not think that they had been spoken to

clearly enough to warrant the current action. AVC disagreed.

Todd wrote in a letter to all Vineyard pastors that Wimber and others on the board had lovingly attempted to bring corrections to Arnott and his leadership team, but from AVC's perspective, their words were not being heeded.

From Toronto's perspective, AVC was not being forthright; they were whispering when TAV needed shouting.

As they closed, Wimber informed them that this decision could be "unmade" if they could show AVC where they were wrong.

Even though they had until the next day to think about it, TAV delivered a letter to Wimber's hotel within two hours complying with AVC's decision and apologizing for the heat that Wimber and the Vineyard had taken for them since the renewal began. They admitted that "some of what was happening in Toronto was outside the Vineyard model." In parting, they asked for the Vineyard's blessing.

In an open letter from Gary Best on the Toronto Airport Vineyard homepage, Best says that he met privately with Arnott and his staff the next morning and that they raised concerns over the lack of clarity in communication. Best acknowledged their concerns, having himself expressed to AVC a desire for another step in the process. On the other hand, he pointed out to them that there had been much communication that *had* been clear. He then asked them, "Do we not both recognize that ultimately we are going in different directions?"

The clear response in the room was, "Yes; a parting of the ways was probably inevitable."

In a memo to the board on December 7, Todd stated,

*For what it's worth, my reading is that this is very sad for both parties, but that the separation was inevitable. Furthermore, they are glad to be rid of the restraints that we put on them, and we are relieved not to have to answer for the excesses any more.*

While the Vineyard's Regional Overseers made the decision to refrain from teaching in Toronto and hosting Toronto-style meetings, Todd made it clear that TAV was not being "black-balled." The two movements parted on good terms. He wanted the ROs to shout to the movement that the Vineyard was *for* renewal, including the current one.

## THE AFTERMATH

As would be expected, there was quite a bit of misunderstanding about what had just transpired. By the time Todd got home, news about the separation had been posted on the internet and spread all over the world. Neither the Vineyard nor Toronto had control of the initial language that was used to explain what had happened.

One internet posting I read likened Wimber to Saul and Arnott to David. The writer predicted that the Vineyard would split right down the middle. In reality, we did lose about forty churches, but that was not half of our 700 churches at the time. In the opinion of another writer, the evangelical side of the Vineyard prevailed.

Many were appalled at what seemed to be a lack of due process. Randy Clark has expressed how hurt he was by the suddenness of it all and by the allegations that Toronto was not "Vineyard." Indeed, Don Williams had sent an eleventh hour appeal to the board, in the form of a long fax, to defend Toronto as being quintessential Vineyard. The board never saw the fax until later.

Most of us, of course, were not privy to all that had been communicated prior to AVC's decision. Having read much of this correspondence it is obvious to me that Vineyard leaders were attempting to communicate. As to why they were not able to have a meeting of the minds remains to be explained. I can see it from both sides. I hear the frustration in the Vineyard board members as I have talked with them and read their letters. I also empathize with John Arnott and his associate, Fred Wright, as they have shared with me in phone conversations how the withdrawal of endorsement seemed like an inappropriate next step.

In his notice of withdrawal of endorsement from TAV, John Wimber admitted that there had been flaws in the process and that communication had been mixed. He was not willing to concede, however, that there had not been enough clear, unambiguous communication or that the resulting course of action had not been warranted.

Within a week, TAV was preparing to appeal the decision. They believed that on the basis of Matthew 18:15-17 they were deprived of due process and that the flaws Wimber acknowledged were no light matter. The world was watching, and it behooved them to take extra care to watch their steps. The leaders in Toronto suggested that Wimber assist in forming an International Renewal Network that would set a precedent for things of this nature in the future.

## TED HAGGARD'S RECONCILIATION EFFORTS[6]

On the evening of December 2, Ted Haggard, pastor of a 5,000-member church in Colorado and leader of the AD 2000 prayer movement, felt an urgent impression from the Lord to visit TAV immediately. In obedience he arrived on December 5 at his own expense. He learned of the crucial meeting the next day and felt that the Lord had sent him there for that purpose.

Arnott had already flown to Seattle for an engagement, so Haggard flew there and met with him for eight hours. He then flew to LA to enlist the help of Jack Hayford. From there they tried to meet with Wimber, Hunter and others to discuss reconciliation efforts.

Haggard's attempts to put something together were posted on the Toronto homepage. In a letter to Todd Hunter dated December 13, Haggard said that his review of what went on exposed enough loopholes that, in his mind, AVC could be accused of injustice and lack of due process. He said, "You just can't spank your children until they thoroughly understand what they are doing wrong and what the punishment will be if they continue." Haggard, therefore, called for an improved process.

He challenged the Vineyard to create a model which would be a first step toward reversing the historical trend to break fellowship with portions of the church that are experiencing a supernatural outpouring of God's Spirit. Haggard proposed setting up a panel of five men including himself, Todd Hunter, Steve Long (from TAV), Paul Cedar (president of the Evangelical Free Church denomination), and John Holland (president of the Foursquare Gospel denomination).

After a meeting with John Wimber, Haggard reported that Wimber told him that he was "finished" and "tired" and rejected the offer on the table. Wimber and his son Chris had both been fighting cancer, and AVC had been taking heat for Toronto for two years.

VINEYARD REFLECTIONS

Wimber spent the next two issues of *Vineyard Reflections* trying to explain why AVC withdrew its endorsement from TAV. He went back to his earlier teaching on the "centered set" and pointed out that TAV was moving away from the Vineyard center. As a result, either by the sovereignty of God or by the choices Toronto was making, they had ceased to be Vineyard in the minds of many of the men on the board.

In the July 95-February 96 *Reflections*, Wimber wrote his final response to the allegations that AVC had not been clear about where TAV stood before December 5:

*They were told (they were in error), but evidently not in ways that were meaningful to them...At least five RO's attended the meetings in Toronto and discussed areas of concern with John and his leadership staff. Furthermore, I wrote several editions of* Vineyard Reflections *on this specific subject. As I reflect on all that transpired I confess that given the serious nature of our misgivings of what was transpiring at the Toronto church, I myself or perhaps Todd Hunter could have called John Arnott personally and made absolutely sure he understood those guidelines. Could he have not done the same with us? I acknowledge some degree of failure (possibly on both of our parts) and say, "Let's not allow our differences to hinder our good will or the work we do for the kingdom."*

333

On January 20, 1996, exactly two years after the renewal began, Toronto Airport Vineyard changed its name to Toronto Airport Christian Fellowship. They still had nightly meetings attended by people from all over the world and within a short time had developed their own network of churches focused on the vision for worldwide renewal and revival.

At the time of this writing, Randy Clark is still in the Vineyard, as are other renewal leaders including Wes Campbell and David Ruis. Randy and his associate, Fred Grewe, have continued to travel extensively around the world, but not in Vineyard circles. Until the withdrawal of the Vineyard's endorsement, renewal meetings were filled with evangelicals. Since the withdrawal, audiences have been almost exclusively Pentecostal and charismatic. Randy feels that he and Fred are carrying on Wimber's renewal ministry, but that the Vineyard is now unable to benefit from it. Before Wimber died, he saw at least the Toronto expression of the renewal as "changing our definition of renewal in the Vineyard."[7]

In 1996 I attended two of Randy's meetings. Steve Nicholson invited Randy, Matt Redman, (a worship leader from Chorleywood in Britain), and myself to do a conference in Evanston, Illinois. Matt led us in explosive worship, I taught the Bible, and Randy, after preaching in the evening, invited the Holy Spirit to come. Some months after this, Randy and Fred were in Florence, Kentucky, for meetings hosted in a Pentecostal church. This conference featured men from the Argentine revival that has embraced strategic level spiritual warfare. It is interesting to note that there is a Vineyard right down the street from this location, but when I stopped by their office they had, as I recall, only a vague recollection that the meetings were taking place.

As I compared the meetings in Evanston and Kentucky to the Wimber meetings I attended in 1986, I could see little difference in power or ministry models. I was personally ministered to with great affect in each environment.

Randy expressed to me that he feels the Vineyard is reverting back to its Calvary Chapel roots out of embarrassment for the

Holy Spirit's ministry. Other's would look at the lack of evangelism in the Vineyard's renewal history and see our current stance as coming back in-balance.

## METRO-VINEYARD LEAVES AVC

### RICK OLMSTEAD'S DREAM

Two years before the events I am about to describe, Rick Olmstead had a very powerful dream about Metro Vineyard.[8] Rick was, at that time, the Regional Overseer of the Rocky Mountain States for AVC, and he was the one in pastoral oversight over Bickle. Since Rick, by his own admission, does not regularly move in prophetic revelation such as dreams, it was all the more striking to him that he had one.

In the dream he found himself in the main Metro Vineyard facility in Kansas City. All through the building the signs read "Vineyard." He felt assured that Metro was really now in the movement. For some reason he saw himself in the dream go down into the basement, and there, etched in the concrete foundation of the building, were the words "Kansas City Fellowship."

Rick concluded from the dream that Mike and Metro were saying they were Vineyard but deep in their hearts they were still KCF. They had never really assimilated and had not really bought into the Vineyard values that ran upstream from theirs. Their more Arminian presuppositions never melded with Wimber's Reformed assumptions.

Rick shared the dream with Mike who felt it was from the Lord and stepped up the "Vineyardizing" program at Metro. In reality, however, the foundation of Metro Vineyard was always really KCF. John Wimber told *Christianity Today* that the Vineyard had been advising Kansas City leaders for six years to withdraw from the Vineyard but they refused on the grounds that they felt called to be in the Vineyard.[9]

### METRO VINEYARD'S ANNUAL JUNE CONFERENCE, 1996[10]

No sooner had the Toronto dust settled than the question of Mike Bickle's status in the Vineyard came to the fore. On the eve of Metro's annual June conference, Bickle says that he received, independently, the exact same prophetic word from five different people. They each told him that he needed to overcome his fear of leading out and that he must trumpet again the divinely entrusted four banner themes of the church.

Tri Robinson and Rich Nathan, both members of what used to be called the Vineyard Executive Council (i.e., the board within the board), also spoke at the conference. On Wednesday, June 19, Rich spoke on David's wife, Michal, who despised her husband out of her prideful concerns for her own reputation. God busted Bickle through this talk and, as he wept, he says God spoke to him that he, too, was concerned for his own reputation.

The next day Paul Cain met privately with Mike. With deep compassion, he delivered a prophetic word saying that the Lord wanted Mike to repent of a divided heart. Out of the fear of losing key relationships, Mike says that he had not been faithful to the message that God had given him.

Two days later Tri Robinson spoke on Gideon who blew the trumpet of God at a time of bondage and compromise in God's people. Tri had no idea that this same passage had been given to Mike as his inaugural sermon at the church.

To top it off, Mike says he received three prophetic dreams that week that confirmed all that God was trying to say. He stood up before the conference on June 23 and repented of a divided heart, pledging himself to preach the four banner themes in an uncompromising manner.

## BICKLE WRITES THE VINEYARD EXECUTIVE COUNCIL

Realizing that a new commitment to these themes threatened his status in the Vineyard, Mike wrote a fourteen-page letter to the Executive Council on July 4, 1996. In it he asked whether the Vineyard was going to begin to embrace Metro's values even as they had embraced the Vineyard's values. It had been his assumption that the goal of "Vineyard II" had been to cross-pollinate "worship and compassion" with "prophetic and intercession." As a whole, he had not seen this happening in the Vineyard.

Mike wrote, "Simply put, our immediate dilemma is this: The Lord will no longer allow me to ignore the absence of emphasis on the values and practices represented by the banner themes prophetic and intercession in our relationship to the Vineyard." Mike also reiterated the importance of "equipping the saints to seek God for an unprecedented harvest of souls and a victorious (though not perfect) end-time church" as well as the affirmation of the fivefold ministry of Ephesians 4:11.

His final request was for the Vineyard to revisit three unresolved issues:

1. The possibility that the Holy Spirit was not fully satisfied with the way AVC governed the Toronto Blessing
2. The possibility that the Holy Spirit might be grieved over the lack of due process given TAV
3. The possibility that the Holy Spirit might have objected to the lack of honor given to John and Carol Arnott

Mike ended his letter asking for a meeting to resolve these issues and the assurance of full compliance by AVC to trumpet the four banner themes. Unless all these conditions were met, they would have a hard time remaining in the Vineyard, even though they desperately wanted to stay.

In another letter, Mike and his prophetic team brought up five insights regarding AVC. They believed that the Vineyard had

1. A spirit of slumber
2. A spirit of fear of man and a spirit of jealousy regarding the renewal in Toronto
3. Been unfaithful to merge the four banner themes
4. Rewritten history regarding AVC's relationship with Metro Vineyard, especially as it relates to prophetic and intercession
5. A control spirit which results in an ever-narrowing circle of liberty within AVC

On July 11, Wimber wrote the Executive Council recommending that:

- They not call a special meeting of the Council
- They review Bickle's concerns but not assure them that AVC would comply
- They not review AVC's decision about Toronto

In late July, Rick Olmstead met with Bickle and his leadership team. After the meeting it became clear that the Vineyard was not willing to meet the conditions articulated on July 4, nor did they believe that the prophetic words about AVC were of God.

In light of AVC's decision, Mike Bickle and his church withdrew from the Association of Vineyard Churches on August 8, 1996.

ോ

NOTES:

[1] Orlando, FL, Creation House

[2] October 1995, Vol. 1, Issue 5

[3] This information comes from notes taken by Happy Leman during a board conference call and used with his permission.

[4] I was able to read this letter off the Toronto Airport Christian Fellowship (formerly the Toronto Airport Vineyard Christian Fellowship) web page.

[5] This information comes from various correspondences during this period, especially a letter from Todd Hunter to Vineyard pastors, December 13, 1995.

[6] From an article on the Toronto Airport Christian Fellowship home page entitled, "Ted Haggard's Reconciliation Efforts

[7] Given in an interview with *Christianity Today* (July 14, 1997)

[8] This dream was first reported to me by Steve Nicholson and then, later, confirmed by Rick Olmstead in a phone conversation.

[9] July 14, 1997

[10] This information was gathered from correspondance between Mike Bickle and the AVC board, perused with Happy Leman's permission.

CHAPTER TWENTY

# LOOKING
# TO THE
# FUTURE

# LOOKING TO THE FUTURE

## CHURCH PLANTING

T wo things are amazing to me as I think about all the twists and turns in the Vineyard's history. The first is that after all the side trips we've taken, the core of the Vineyard keeps coming back to its genetic moorings. While the question "What is a Vineyard?" is still hotly debated, apparently there is enough of a consensus that we consistently return to our kingdom roots as theologically defined by George Ladd and formerly applied by the late John Wimber. Irrespective of how we philosophically juggle our programs, we are a kingdom movement. The second amazing thing is related to the first. Through it all we have stayed true to our call to plant churches. Even though we have lost churches in two tumultuous periods, we have continued to expand in both national and international church planting. We now have in place functional systems for recognizing, training, and releasing church planting teams.

THE FOLLOWING GRAPH SHOWS THE CHURCH PLANTING STATISTICS THROUGH 1998.[1]

| YEAR | USA | INTERNATIONAL | # OF COUNTRIES | CHURCHES ADDED | TOTAL CHURCHES |
|------|-----|---------------|----------------|----------------|----------------|
| 1983 | 32  | 0   | 1  | 32  | 32  |
| 1984 | 49  | 0   | 1  | 17  | 49  |
| 1985 | 84  | 0   | 1  | 35  | 84  |
| 1986 | 197 | 2   | 1  | 115 | 199 |
| 1987 | 208 | 8   | 3  | 17  | 216 |
| 1988 | 221 | 15  | 3  | 20  | 236 |
| 1989 | 222 | 22  | 3  | 8   | 244 |
| 1990 | 262 | 26  | 4  | 44  | 288 |
| 1991 | 326 | 30  | 7  | 68  | 356 |
| 1992 | 336 | 41  | 8  | 21  | 377 |
| 1993 | 349 | 57  | 14 | 29  | 406 |
| 1994 | 363 | 80  | 18 | 37  | 443 |
| 1995 | 391 | 150 | 26 | 98  | 541 |
| 1996 | 411 | 192 | 30 | 62  | 603 |
| 1997 | 417 | 246 | 38 | 60  | 663 |
| 1998 | 449 | 370 | 52 | 156 | 819 |

## Vineyard International Consortium

In order to oversee the growing international expansion of Vineyard churches, John Wimber developed a collegial association made up of the key leader in every nation with a growing number of churches. This association is called the Vineyard International Consortium (VIC).[2] VIC exists for relationship and not governance. It's power is solely in its relationships and in its control over the Vineyard name. John Wimber was the international director until his death. Currently, no one person has been selected to take his place. The members will decide who will be the leader, the tenure of the appointment, and the authority of that position. In 1997, VIC had set in place the following leadership structure in countries where the Vineyard was planting churches:

| Level | Governmental Overseer | Number of Churches in Country |
|---|---|---|
| Level 4 | Bob Fulton or one of his reps | 0-5 churches - a non-national in oversight |
| Level 3 | Area Pastoral Coordinator (APC) | 5 or more churches - a national is appointed APC |
| Level 2 | Regional Overseer (RO) | 20 or more churches - a national is appointed RO |
| Level 1 | National Director (ND) | 30 or more churches - a national is appointed ND |

On the basis of this structure, the following men and women were invited to the VIC meeting in South Africa in 1997.

| Members | AVC Title | Jurisdiction |
|---|---|---|
| John & Carol Wimber | International Director | Domestic & International |
| Bob & Penny Fulton | International Coordinator | International |
| Todd & Debbie Hunter | Acting National Director | USA |
| Gary & Joy Best | National Director | Canada |
| John & Eleanor Mumford | National Director | United Kingdom |
| Costa & Lorraine Mitchell | National Director | South Africa |
| Lloyd & Vicki Rankin | National Director | New Zealand |

| GUESTS | AVC TITLE | JURISDICTION |
|---|---|---|
| Martin & Georgia Buehlmann | National Coordinator | Switzerland |
| John & Alaine McElroy | National Coordinator | Australia |
| Jan Bernard & Tineke Struik | National Coordinator | The Netherlands |
| Hans & Lotta Sundberg | National Coordinator | Sweden |

By 1998, the criterion had changed slightly and seven nations had been released, each with its own, autonomous AVC structure. These nations, their Directors and their churches are currently:

| AVC | DIRECTOR | NUMBER OF CHURCHES |
|---|---|---|
| USA | Todd Hunter | 446 |
| Canada | Gary Best | 65 |
| UK & Ireland | John Mumford | 49 |
| South Africa | Costa Mitchell | 38 |
| New Zealand | Lloyd Rankin | 17 |
| Sweden | Hans Sundberg | 12 |
| The Netherlands | Jan Bernard Struik | 6 |

There remained 46 nations yet to be released as their own AVC. The combined total saw the Vineyard in 53 different countries with 775 churches. In 1990 there were 26 VCFs outside the US in 5 nations.

## THE MATRIX MODEL OF LEADERSHIP

In addition to governmental leaders, task specialists are recognized on the basis of what has been called the "Matrix." Developed by Tri Robinson, Regional Overseer of AVC Northwest and pastor of the Vineyard in Boise, Idaho, the Matrix recognizes two types of gifting in church leadership. As Tri analyzed his church and region in 1995 he realized that some leaders are more people-oriented with relationship being the goal. He called these *generalists.* Others are more task-oriented and mobilize people to reach a goal. He called these *specialists.* He saw that only by blessing the uniqueness in these different kinds of leaders could the church become all that God had designed it to be.

Tri developed his philosophy in the following matrix (as written, the matrix reflects language before 1998).

## REPRODUCIBLE SYSTEM OF OVERSIGHT

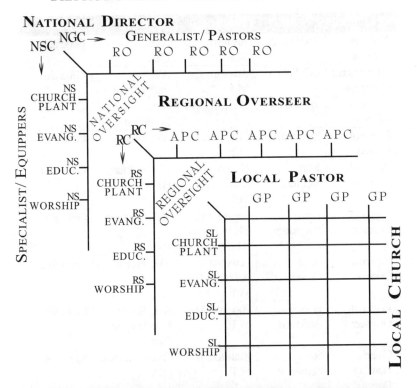

| NATIONAL LEVEL | REGIONAL LEVEL | LOCAL CHURCH |
|---|---|---|
| ND National Director | RO Regional Overseers | Local Pastor |
| NC National Coordinators | DO District Overseers | Generalist Pastors |
| RO Regional Overseers | RC Regional Coordinators | Specialist Leaders |
| NS National Specialists | RS Regional Specialists | |

Matrix thinking can be applied at any level of ministry. It can be a lens to look at the local church, as seen above, reduced to be applied to an individual ministry (e.g., youth ministry), or expanded to look at regions, countries, or denominations.

While the Matrix itself has not been officially adopted in any way, recognizing leaders with relational and task gifts has had a philosophical impact on the movement. Matrix concepts were

343

reflected in the 1997 structures in that both overseers (generalists) and task force leaders (specialists) are recognized.

THE 1997 AVC USA BOARD STRUCTURE WAS AS FOLLOWS:

| AVC Title | Name | Church | Jurisdiction | Matrix |
|---|---|---|---|---|
| National Director | Todd Hunter | Anaheim, CA VCF | AVC USA | Generalist |
| International Coordinator | Bob Fulton | Anaheim, CA VCF | AVC International | Generalist |
| Regional Overseer | Tri Robinson | Boise, ID VCF | AVC Northwest | Generalist |
| Regional Overseer | Rich Nathan | Columbus, OH VCF | AVC Great Lakes | Generalist |
| Regional Overseer | John McClure | Newport Beach, CA VCF | AVC California Hawaii | Generalist |
| Regional Overseer | Bert Waggoner | Sugar Land, TX VCF (Houston) | AVC Southern | Generalist |
| Regional Overseer | Ralph Grover | Lewiston-Auburn, MN VCF | AVC Eastern | Generalist |
| Regional Overseer | Brian Anderson | Phoenix, AZ VCF | AVC Rocky Mountains and Plains | Generalist |
| Church Planting Director | Steve Nicholson | Evanston, IL VCF | Church Planting USA | Specialist |
| Evangelism Director | Rick Olmstead | Fort Collins, CO VCF | Evangelism USA | Specialist |
| Missions Director | Bob Fulton | Anaheim, CA VCF | Missions, USA | Specialist |
| Untitled | Michael Palandro | Houston, TX VCF | Unspecified | Unspecified |

## THE THEATERS OF OPERATION

Bob Fulton, as was pointed out in an earlier chapter, believes in local church-based missions. This means that he would like to see missionaries sent out of local churches rather than out of mission agencies. To facilitate this, Bob has separated the Vineyard into what he calls theaters of operation.

Seven countries have enough Vineyards to oversee church planting movements and have been released as their own AVC. Bob divided up other countries of the world under these seven as a way to get the churches started in missions. If a local church does not have a specific direction from the Lord in regard to mission giving and sending, looking within its theater of operations would be a place to begin. The theaters are not a mandate or prison but a way of consolidating local church-based efforts. If a local church is directed toward efforts outside its theater, that is under the sovereignty of God.

THE FOLLOWING CHART REPRESENTED THE THEATERS AS THEY WERE IN 1997.[3]

| Theatre | Released AVC Nations | Unreleased AVC Nations | Missions |
|---|---|---|---|
| 1 | United States (423) | Basque People<br>Brazil<br>Chile (4)<br>Colombia (1)<br>Costa Rica (2)<br>Cuba/Caribbean<br>India (1) | Lebanon (3)<br>Mexico (8)<br>Paraguay (1)<br>Spain (2)<br>Tajikistan (1)<br>Venezuela |
| 2 | United Kingdom (39) | France (1)<br>Ireland (2)<br>Austria (4)<br>Germany (10)<br>Hungary<br>Belgium (3)<br>Estonia<br>Denmark (1)<br>Finland (1)<br>Iceland (1) | Macedonia (1)<br>Scotland<br>Romania<br>Switzerland (6)<br>Latvia<br>Netherlands (3)<br>Norway (6)<br>Russia (4)<br>Sweden (13) |
| 3 | Canada (47) | Cambodia<br>China (3)<br>Japan (3) | Korea<br>Philippines (5) |
| 4 | South Africa (22) | Kenya (1)<br>Malawi (1)<br>Nambia (2) | Zambia (5)<br>Zimbabwe (1) |
| 5 | New Zealand (17) | Australia (15) | |

◌இ

## NOTES:

[1] As is typical of new movements, accurate statistics are hard to come by. I initially worked off research done in 1990 by Steve Holt for a class for Peter Wagner at Fuller Seminary in 1991. The statistics being used here come from Marilyn Hanson at AVC and differ at numerous points from Steve's original work in the earlier years.

[2] The following information comes from the Vineyard International Consortium notes from their meeting in South Africa in April 1997 (used with the permission of AVC).

[3] At the time of this writing, three more theaters have been added, 1) Sweden, besides planting churches in its own country is taking responsibility for Russia and the Nordic countries, 2) the Netherlands facilitating work in the Benelux countries, 3) and Switzerland the Germanic states.

# CHAPTER TWENTY-ONE

# THE
# COLUMBUS
# ACCORDS

# THE COLUMBUS ACCORDS

## THE PASSING OF JOHN WIMBER

John Wimber, having suffered over the years from angina, cancer, and a stroke, incurred a massive brain hemorrhage the evening of November 16, 1997 after a fall in his house while still recovering from heart by-pass surgery. He passed away peacefully at 8:00 AM the following morning, November 17, in the presence of his family. John was sixty-three years old.

A glorious memorial service attended by 3,000 mourners was held at the Vineyard in Anaheim on Friday, November 21. Jon Panner said it well writing for *Worship Update* (1ˢᵗ Quarter, 1998):

> *Ultimately, the measure of a man is not the treasure or legacy he creates but the treasure he carries in his soul. John Wimber was a jar of clay, a vessel chipped, cracked, yet inside was a great treasure. "We have this treasure in jars of clay to show that this all-surpassing power is from God and not from us" (2 Corinthians 4:7).*
>
> *Those of us of a younger generation remember John Richard Wimber. We've considered his life's outcome. And we will imitate—however poorly—those aspects of his faith where the Treasure shone brightly.*

Even as I write this I still feel the sadness of his passing.

## THE POST-WIMBER VINEYARD[1]

We will miss John. But what did his death mean for our future? Todd Hunter had been set in place as the National Coordinator in the summer of 1994. The obvious question now was whether Todd would become the National Director in Wimber's place. We all began to ask what the post-Wimber Vineyard would look like. Would it fragment? Would its vitality decline? Was it possible to continue to grow and be vital?

Before John died he had challenged Vineyard leaders, almost in anticipation of his death, to "take the best and go." He knew that the routinization of charisma, referring back to Max Weber's term, normally sets in within a generation of the genesis of an organization. Would it be possible to build, as Wimber termed it, a "perpetually self-renewing organization?" Finke and Stark's *The Churching of America: 1776-1990* cites the example of Southern Baptists who were able to postpone debilitating institutionalization for almost two hundred years, in contrast to Methodists who began the predictable decline within the normal time frame.

Wimber thought that if we could take the best and go, the best of evangelicalism and the best of Pentecostalism, if we could continue to honor biblical tensions and stay in the radical middle, if we could continue to keep evangelism and church planting our bulls-eye, we could be perpetually self-renewed under the unction and guidance of the Holy Spirit.[2]

When the dust settled and Todd had the opportunity to think through John's vision, he felt like a man out of his league. Who was he to think that he could lead the Vineyard into this kind of vitality? As an empowered evangelical he did two things—he prayed non-stop for direction from God, and he began to read and counsel with others to discover what the questions were. It was January 1998. The next board meeting was in April. He prayed that a plan would come together fairly quickly.

Todd knew from reading Roland Allen's *The Spontaneous Expansion of the Church*[2] that the key to the perpetual vitality of the New Testament church was a continual yielding to the direction of the Holy Spirit. At a seminar held by consultants Peter Drucker and Lyle Schaller, Todd was first introduced the term "flexible architecture." He knew intuitively that self-perpetuating vitality would call for hearts that would continually yield to the direction of the Spirit, and an organization that would remain flexible enough to change at the leading of the Holy Spirit. In his assessment, the alignment and break-ups with both Kansas City and Toronto had created a kind of paralysis that fought against the risk-taking that had originally been our path to life. He realized also that we were in danger of way too much structure to adapt to any changes the Holy Spirit might want to make. The ideas of flexible architecture and minimal structure came early on in this thinking, but as the board meeting drew nearer, he wasn't sure how they applied.

Todd set about a rigorous reading schedule as he systematically explored what to do. He began by searching every New Testament reference to church polity. He then turned to systematic theology, next church history, historical theology, the sociology of religion and finally philosophy, delving into topics such as freedom, autonomy, individualism and group dynamics.

The list of those he counseled with reads like a *Who's Who?* of American Christianity. He talked to pastors (Chuck Smith, Rick Warren, Bill Hybels), theologians (Don Williams), sociologists (Margaret Paloma, Don Miller), consultants (Bob Logan, Lyle Schaller, Peter Drucker, John Maxwell), researchers (George Barna), church growth specialists (Peter Wagner, Eddie Gibbs) and denominational executives (Paul Ceder, C.J. Mahaney). He even met with therapist Henry Cloud, to determine the health of his thinking process.

Peter Wagner counseled Todd to consider breaking the Vineyard into what he called "apostolic networks."[3] This new area of research recognizes that we are entering into a postdenominational era where apostolic men are rising up in America's free market religious economy to gather around them clusters of churches, either through church planting or adoption. In response to Dr. Wagner's counsel, Todd thought through various patterns of alignment he saw in the Vineyard and recognized churches grouping around Steve Sjogren, John Arnott and Mike Bickle. Todd was willing to explore this as a possibility and called each of these men to see if they would like to have churches that were relating to them released under their care. Not one of the men was interested in such a proposal.

In a long phone conversation, Bill Hybels counseled Todd to "just lead." He said that the church in America needs the Vineyard. The seeker churches are good on "the front end," i.e. seeing people converted, but the Vineyard was good at forming people into kingdom disciples, "the back end."

Having no takers in the apostolic network direction, Todd determined after hanging up with Hybels that he would do his best to lead the movement if asked to. He "set his face like a flint" toward the board meeting that was coming up shortly in April. If they asked him to become the National Director, he began to think through those values and issues of leadership and direction he would be unwilling to compromise on. He also sought to articulate those things that were open to debate.

As he thought and prayed, the often-asked question, "What is a Vineyard?" began to trouble him. He realized that evaluating our behavior with "Is it Vineyard?" would move us toward institutionalism because in asking it we were in essence trying to become the keepers of a John Wimber museum. With all deference to John for the gift he was to us, we remember it was John himself who exhorted us to "take the best and go." To become the keepers of the "old ways" would go against all that Wimber stood for. Todd thought it more pertinent to ask "Is it true?" He ultimately narrowed his focus to four questions that became his non-negotiables:

- Is it biblical and consistent with kingdom theology?
- Is it righteous and ethical?
- Is it facilitating the Vineyard mission of church planting, evangelism and renewal?
- Is it in harmony with our values, priorities and practices?

Todd saw that we needed to fulfill the Great Commission (the evangelical tradition) in the spirit of the Great Commandments (the pietist tradition) in the power of the Holy Spirit (the Pentecostal tradition).By adding the importance of the ethical component Todd was calling for us to become a movement of *empowered evangelical pietists.*

Integrating the paradigm of the present day ministry of the Spirit to his quest to find God's will, Todd not only read and sought counsel but also listened for God to speak. One day as he was sitting in his office thinking about how to make all his research gel, he sensed the Lord say to him, "It is coming." He felt calmed in his spirit that God would put it all together.

351

The week before the April board meeting, the picture still hadn't come into focus. He had already latched onto the concept of minimal structure ("flexible architecture"). He just didn't know what that minimal structure was. Five days before the board was to arrive, Todd spent the morning with Don Greisinger, an associate of Peter Drucker's, who challenged him to provide a rationale for every layer of structure in AVC. At lunch that same day with Paul Ceder, former president of the Evangelical Free Church of America, Todd asked Dr. Ceder how many layers a denomination needed to remain viable. It was in that conversation that he says he had a "God moment" and saw that the right structure at this time was to eliminate all the District and Regional Overseers and give the pastors the freedom to choose their own Area Pastoral Coordinators (affirming relational and apostolic loyalties in addition to geography). In this way the real leaders of the regions would emerge as their gifts were recognized by those who followed them. Todd figured he could relate to about fifty Area Pastoral Overseers before AVC would need to add another layer. He would pastor and relate to those fifty guys as he would if they were his own church. Could he do it? He wanted to try.

## THE COLUMBUS ACCORDS

During the week of April 20th, 1998, the board and council met at Rich Nathan's church in Columbus, Ohio. While there Todd presented what he called *The Columbus Accords*, a multi-page document the synopsis of which can be viewed on the AVC web page. Throughout the week he lectured on all that he had discovered about avoiding the devastating effects of institutionalization. He declared that the Vineyard was at a crossroads. This week was a defining moment. He said that as we navigate the transition following the death of John Wimber, he believed that the Holy Spirit was leading the Vineyard to agree together on four priorities.

## REFRAMING THE STRUCTURE OF AVC-USA

We are called to be a force of spiritual revolution, not a stagnant institution. We need to heed John's admonition to take the best and go and not become the keepers of a museum. We are called to promote Spirit-led catalytic ministries expressed through the gift mixes of our leaders. Our atmosphere needs to be one where demonstrated purity and character are valued as highly as charisma and rhetorical skills.

Our primary focus should not be "What is Vineyard?" but:
- What is biblical and consistent with kingdom theology?
- What is righteous and ethical?
- What facilitates church planting, evangelism and renewal?
- What is in harmony with our values, priorities and practices?

## RECOGNIZING FREEDOM WITHIN AVC-USA

Our freedom comes from God, not the Vineyard, but at the same time we voluntarily submit some of that freedom to come under the AVC-USA banner. The Vineyard, on the other hand, gives those of us who are pastors the freedom to take risks and to bless what the Father is doing. We are determined to resist the routinization of charisma by maintaining our radical dependence upon the presence and power of God and the administration of the Holy Spirit. We must renew our commitment to let God be God. In so doing we bless our churches to find resources wherever they can. Our kingdom passion outweighs our desire for institutional survival.

## SHARPENING THE MISSION WITHIN AVC-USA

Clear focus on our mission is the key to maintaining our vitality. Our mission provides boundaries for directing our resources and for making decisions. Our mission must be measurable and measured. We need to ask:
- Are we developing responsible, reproducing, kingdom oriented, Spirit-empowered disciples?
- Are we developing responsible, reproducing, kingdom oriented, Spirit-empowered churches?

353

- Are we helping to renew other churches that want to do the same thing?

In light of the above, Todd conceives of AVC, to use a business analogy, as a service organization that exists in all its functions to serve 500 manufacturers whose product is more and better disciples and more and better churches.

## REDESIGNING THE STRUCTURE OF AVC-USA

Our goal for AVC structure is that it will be relational and that it will provide and promote systematic teamwork, healthy accountability, free-flowing communication and loving encouragement. We agree with Wimber that form follows function, organization supports organism. Our structure, therefore, is valuable only as it supports our mission. Our objective is to have flexible architecture and the minimum structure necessary to fulfill our goals. As we grow, we acknowledge that our structure will change under the direction of the Holy Spirit. At the current time we see the need for the governmental layers to flatten out to put the focus primarily on the Area Pastoral Coordinator's role, thus recognizing what is natural and gifted by the Holy Spirit.

## NEW WINESKINS

As Todd concluded the presentation of his four non-negotiables, it remained to be seen whether the board would tar and feather him, break up into camps, give empty lip service, or be in alignment. As I sat in Todd's office collecting the information for this chapter I could see the emotion well up in him when he described those final hours in Columbus. He said that it was his proudest moment as a leader. Rather than hold on to power, the AVC-USA board was willing to give Todd the freedom to choose a new leadership team that represented the minimal structure necessary to take the Vineyard to the next level. It was anticipated that most of the top leaders on the board would eventually retain their board appointments but in roles commensurate with their gifts and passions. The resignations of all other RO's, DO's and APC's would take effect at the November 1998 board meeting and a survey would be sent out to see who Todd's new team would be. In a first step promoting freedom and the local autonomy of Vineyard churches, the Vineyard church name policy was changed to allow any name approved by the national office.

At the conclusion of the meeting the board submitted the following affirmation:

> *Together we clearly sense the Lord's sovereign leadership and are confident and excited about the future. As the AVC-USA Board, Council and National Task Force, we unanimously affirm the appointment of Todd Hunter as the National Director of AVC-USA. We believe that his gift-mix includes a strong gift of leadership and that he is called by God to express his gifting at this time among us. As such, he is an example to us all of the ideal we are holding up to the Vineyard of Charismatic leadership that facilitates the spontaneous expansion of the church.*

We leave this section with one final thought. To those who study the relationships between organisms and organizations, it appears that structural change needs to occur with every twenty percent of growth. This means that as churches and denominations grow, structural change is a way of life. Let it not be assumed that what now happens in the Vineyard is the end of it all. Should the Lord bless us to the point that we do grow eventually to ten thousand churches, *our look has only just begun to change.* Our job is to support the life of the Vineyard with flexible architecture and minimal structure to ensure the spontaneous multiplication of the church.

Before we move on, it is fascinating to note that the same phenomenon is occurring internationally. Bob Fulton observed as he traveled around the world in 1998 that all the key leaders were talking about the need to streamline in order to keep layers of bureaucracy from blocking the spontaneous multiplication of churches through the Holy Spirit.

CB

NOTES:

[1] The material from this section came from a talk with Todd Hunter.

[2] Grand Rapids, MI, Eerdmans, 1962; cf. Allen's companion volume *Missionary Methods: St. Paul's or Ours?* Grand Rapids, MI, Eerdmans, 1962

[3] One of the first efforts to document the proliferation of "apostolic networks and congregations" was Peter Wagner's organization of the *National Symposium on the Postdenominational Church* at Fuller Seminary in May of 1996. At the symposium Dr. Wagner presented a paper entitled, "The New Apostolic Reformation: A Search for a Name." Wagner has gone on to edit *The New Apostolic Churches* (Ventura, CA, Regal Books, 1998) and has co-authored with David Cannistraci, *Apostles and the Emerging Apostolic Movement*, (Ventura, CA, Regal Books, 1998).

# CHAPTER TWENTY-TWO

# As
# I See It

# AS I SEE IT

## INTRODUCTION

### DISCLAIMERS

As we close, I will take a few pages to try and sum up what I think are the Vineyard's major contributions and opportunities for growth. I will also offer my interpretation of our history for whatever it's worth. Not everyone will see it like I do, but that's OK. History is based in perceptions of reality.

Because this is not an official Vineyard history, I have decided to use the "as I see it" approach rather than a massive polling of old-timers to offer a collective consciousness. A true history would have included sections on the amazing growth, for instance of the churches in the Northwest under the direction of Tri Robinson, the churches in the East under Lance Pitluck, the Southern churches with Bert Waggoner and the Midwestern churches under men like Rich Nathan, Steve Nicholson, Steve Sjogren, Ron Allen and Happy Leman. I would have also chronicled details of the growth of the Vineyard in many different nations of the world. After all, before the turn of the millennium there will probably be more Vineyards outside the U.S. than in it. But as I said in the introduction, this is my attempt to understand our history from the perspective of one of the rank and file guys out in the pastors' conference chair. I have tried to present accurate data, documented from either printed materials, personal communications with those involved, or my own recollections and notes. In all things I have tried to be fair, representing various sides of the issues. As I wrote I had to ask a number of questions.

### WHAT SHOULD I NAME IT?

As I wrote, I came up with two potential titles for this book: *Come, Holy Spirit!* and *The Quest for the Radical Middle.* Each one has merit.

The title *Come, Holy Spirit!* looks back to Mother's Day, 1980, at Calvary Chapel, Yorba Linda, when Lonnie Frisbee used this petition to invite the Holy Spirit into the service. It proved to be a seminal event in that it birthed the reality of power evangelism and confirmed for John Wimber his original thesis that the church can grow exponentially when accompanied by signs and wonders. Power evangelism launched the "Vineyard" that was in John's heart, and the movement was challenged by the prospect of the numinous of God.

The title, *The Quest for the Radical Middle* is reflective of John's other goal, namely the desire to develop a church and churches that would melt together the best of evangelicalism and the best of Pentecostalism. To use the term coined by Rich Nathan and Ken Wilson, John wanted to model what it means to be an "empowered evangelical." As I pointed out in the chapter on historical context, the foundation of consensus orthodoxy has been a deep commitment to the Bible as the inerrant Word of God and the priority of the evangel, the message of the gospel to the nations. Alongside consensus orthodoxy there has always existed reform, endeavoring to take the Holy Spirit out of the backroom and remind the church that we now live in the age when the Spirit energizes the ongoing ministry of Jesus to the world and the people of God. Truth is in the *radical middle*.

These titles are indicative of the two callings on John Wimber's life—*and to miss these two callings will be to miss the interpretive key to much of our history*. John is now gone, and AVC remains. While still committed to renewal around the world, in the end we are the quest for the radical middle between the Word and Spirit continuum, an empowered evangelical church planting movement—and so the name of the book.

## THE VINEYARD'S IDENTITY CRISIS

### VINEYARD MINISTRIES INTERNATIONAL (VMI)

The first call on John's life was to be a fool for Christ and address both a deficient pneumatology in the evangelical church (*pneuma* is the Greek word for *spirit*, thus pneumatology refers to the doctrine of the Holy Spirit) and a lack of intimacy in worship. John was a committed evangelical until the day he died. He was a Word man, and this is exactly why he felt he had to take a stand for the Holy Spirit's present day ministry and for the engagement of the heart in worship. He often told Pentecostals who would ask him how he got so "anointed" that it all began by reading the gospel of Luke. The Pentecostal assumption was that he had to have had a vision or impartation or something. John's position was simply that he was trying to be a true evangelical and read all of the New Testament, not only the parts that dovetailed with Enlightenment rationalism.

In regards to pneumatology, there are only two choices for an evangelical when reading the gospels: affirm the "teaching Jesus" but relegate the "power Jesus" to an anomaly of history, *or* affirm all of Jesus and take literally his commission for his disciples to heal the sick and cast out demons. The former seems to bifurcate Jesus and violate the plain meaning of the text while the latter violates our Western presuppositions. For John Wimber it was a simple choice of who he wanted to offend, God or men. He decided early on that God had called him to become a fool for Christ, and his acceptance of being a spectacle has unveiled a Trinitarian God for many.

God called John to take his willingness to be made the fool, his evangelical theology, his endearing ability to laugh at himself and set others at ease, and his naturally supernatural style to bring renewal to the church around the world. Wherever John went, he prayed, "Come, Holy Spirit!" and the Spirit came! Not only that, but John taught us, the church, how to invite the Spirit to come too. Renewal followed Wimber around the world as he left people healed, delivered, empowered, and equipped. His greatest gifts were intimate worship, faith for the kingdom coming and his simple five-step prayer model that taught us how to get off the bench and into the game to "do the stuff."

The downside of John's renewal ministry was that people often thought that the atmosphere in local Vineyard churches would or should be like that in a renewal conference. Many tried to take signs and wonders back to their congregations, but it didn't happen like at the conferences and didn't often produce exponential growth. Indeed, many Vineyard churches are effective at healing the saints, but ineffective at saving the sinners. This produced tension for John in that he knew that signs and wonders were to lead to church growth.

## ASSOCIATION OF VINEYARD CHURCHES (AVC)

The second call on John's life was to pastor, thus fathering a church and a church planting movement. Even though John remained the senior pastor of the Vineyard in Anaheim for much of his tenure there, the real work of pastoring was done by the staff to free John up to focus on renewal, take the heat, and build the infrastructure of AVC. Early on John received a vision in which he says God showed him that he was to catalyze a church planting movement that would eventually have 10,000 churches around the world, most through church planting, some through adoptions, and some "friends of the Vineyard." Those of us in AVC have owned that vision as from God and are working toward the fulfillment of that commission.

The purpose of Vineyard churches was to glorify God though contemporary worship and disciple the boomer-buster generation through evangelism, personal follow-up, healing, and care for the poor. In other words, Vineyard pastors were to be good not only at inviting the Holy Spirit but in the basic skills of reaching a new generation for Christ.

## IS THE VINEYARD VMI OR AVC?

Much of the frustration felt by the average Vineyard pastor has come from the "schizophrenia" caused by these two seemingly conflicting callings on John Wimber's life. Often, when Vineyard pastors tried to reproduce the conference model in their local congregations, the saints got better, but the church was not effective at winning the lost. Calvary Chapel criticized the Vineyard early on for going into a city to do healing seminars for ill-equipped saints and coming out with a Vineyard church. They were absolutely right. But our motive was not to steal sheep; it was to equip the saints. The problem came from our misunderstanding the tension caused by the dual call of renewal and church planting on the Vineyard.

It was the ineffectiveness of a signs-and-wonders-only paradigm that led Steve Sjogren to innovate the concept of servant evangelism to make inroads for finding Jesus' "friends" (one could put Holy Trinity Brompton's Alpha program in this category as well). Steve's breaking of the VMI model for the local church caused a healthy critique in the Vineyard that has resulted in the movement becoming better at winning the lost while trying to retain our value of equipping the saints and pursuit of renewal. Steve's innovations have forced us to look at our Sunday morning services as the main port of entry for seekers. Whether we orient our Sunday morning service around the seeker or the church is not the point. A blind spot has been pinpointed that must not be ignored. As Todd Hunter has put it, our bull's-eye on the target is evangelism and church planting. How we divvy up the program pie is not the issue. The real question is, "Are we making authentic Christian disciples and multiplying churches?"

## WILL THE REAL JOHN WIMBER PLEASE STAND UP!

Because of this schizophrenia, one of the historic problems in the Vineyard when John was alive was to pinpoint the real John Wimber. His style and posture would change depending on the setting in which you found him. His critics accused him of contradictions and inconsistencies. To address this point I switch to "as Todd sees it." In his chapter in *John Wimber*, Todd notes that while John was one man, he wore many hats; knowing that John lived on a leadership continuum, as Todd calls it, gives us insight into the many John Wimbers. In one setting he was the pastor of a large church (VCF Anaheim), in another the leader of a growing denomination (AVC), in yet another the president of a music company (VMG), and yet again a spokesman for renewal around the world (VMI). Todd says he adapted his behavior, and even his words, to fit the particular responsibility he was representing. Was John Wimber the teddy bear, the hard driving businessman, the self-deprecating healer, the crying worshipper behind the piano, the warm fuzzy pastor or the prickly target of attack? Why did John act so differently at home than when on the road doing renewal?

The following chart developed by Todd in his chapter is very insightful for those of us who are still trying to figure out where we have been.

| Placing the Hats John Wore on a Continuum | | |
|---|---|---|
| Conservative and Cautious | More Moderate and Balanced | Aggresive ("go for it") |
| Presiding Leader of a Movement | Pastor of a Local Church | Renewal Agent |
| John saw this part of his life as the place where he needed to be more responsible, to police things | | In this aspect of his ministry John saw himself as a guest. He never felt called to correct others, he felt open to experiment and adjust to the Word as he went along |
| Evangelical | | Pentecostal |
| Outreach Oriented Churches | Blended Churches | Renewal/Revival Oriented Churches |
| In the Vineyard movement, all of the facets and phases of John's ministry are extant along a similar continuum. | | |

DEFINING THE REAL VINEYARD

In 1998 I was asked by Todd Hunter to join him and two others in representing the Vineyard in a study sponsored by Hartford Seminary and funded by the Lilly Foundation. The study endeavors to examine eight denominations at the dawn of the new millennium. As we were assessing the Vineyard, it occurred to us that the debate as to what the real Vineyard is depends on when someone joined the Vineyard. If someone joined during the Calvary Chapel days then that is, for them, the true Vineyard. If they joined during the signs and wonders days, then that is the Vineyard they signed up for. If they joined during the prophetic or Toronto periods, then those days are held most precious. The following continuum shows the various Vineyard eras in relationship to John's personal journey.

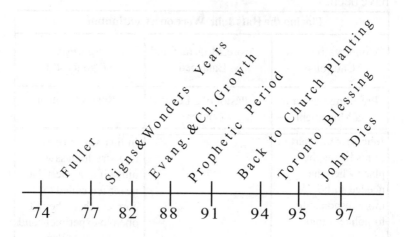

At each point it could be argued that we are either on or off track. These kinds of debates miss the John Wimber who was trying to follow an unchanging yet moving God. The real Vineyard only looks back to our evangelical moorings in the Word of God and our kingdom thesis. It looks forward propelled by our Pentecostal thesis that God is still speaking today. As Todd has said, the real question is not whether something is Vineyard but whether it is biblical. The truly biblical Vineyard is one that is moored and loosed at the same time. Looking back with fondness to the days of old as defined by our point of entry is all right as long as we don't let that nostalgia keep us from the best days that are ahead. God moves from grace to grace, faith to faith and glory to glory (John 1:16; Romans 1:17; 2 Corinthians 3:18). God is on the move and we best be moving with him. This is what John Wimber was after, not a monument to yesterday.

364

# SITUATIONAL VS. CONSTITUTIONAL GIFTING

## PUSHING BOTH PEDALS ON A BIKE

I heard a theology professor say one time that divine sovereignty and human responsibility are like pedals on a bike. It is only as the cyclist pushes one pedal after the other in repetition that the bike moves forward with stability. The moment one is not pushed, motion slows and the bike becomes unstable. In much the same way, the call on Wimber's life to focus on pneumatology was a call to focus for a season on one kingdom pedal that had been neglected, thus bringing the bike back in balance.

On the other hand, I heard a church history professor say that the definition of heresy is over-emphasizing something the church had previously under-emphasized. There is a subtle pressure to stop holding things in tension for the sake of the truth rediscovered—but this causes instability. Truth is found only in the radical middle.

## THE SITUATIONAL GIFT PEDAL

When John Wimber called attention to the concept of situational gifts, that spiritual gifts can be given to any Christian in any situation to advance the kingdom, he was swimming upstream. The standard view of spiritual gifts, even among Pentecostals by and large, was that a person could only operate in gifts they "had." Thus someone might say, "I can't pray or teach because I don't have that gift." People stood in long healing lines to get prayer from the "anointed" man of God. John pointed out exegetically from 1 Corinthians 12 that when Paul asks, "Do all prophecy, do all heal…?" he was referring to a particular gathering of the saints for worship and did not mean that one person could only operate in one gift. Once the possibility was opened up that any Christian could get words of knowledge, heal the sick, prophesy, or discern spirits, the church really did get off the bench and into the game.

The downside of Wimber pushing only the situational gifts pedal was that the bike became unstable because the constitutional gift pedal wasn't being pushed. The phenomenon of people being particularly gifted at things does exist. Of the five gift lists in the New Testament,[1] four of them clearly refer to constitutional categories of gifting and define people's place in the church as coinciding with their gifting.

Another dimension of the same problem is that not everyone operates in gifts with the same what Paul calls "measure of faith," and what charismatics would probably call "anointing." What Paul appears to be saying is that as God has graced his church, he distributes those graces according to his will. He gives to one this measure and to another that.

Knowing this explains why I've never been able to become John Wimber or Todd Hunter or Steve Sjogren or Steve Nicholson or any of my other mentors over the years. I've always been a Word man in a Spirit movement. When I finally came to terms with what God has made me to be, it took a lot of pressure off. One time Ron Allen had me come and do my through-the-Bible seminar at his church the weekend after Randy Clark had been there during the renewal. Randy's crowds, as might be expected, were huge. The next week I came to teach the Bible, and about fifteen people showed up. A few years ago, in my situational-gift-only paradigm, I would have felt like a failure. Realizing, however, that I "am what I am" (to quote the theologian Popeye), I had a great time with those fifteen people teaching the Bible. Because of what John has taught me about situational gifts, however, I paused when I was done to invite the Holy Spirit to come—and He did! I had words of knowledge, a prophetic word as I recall, and the Spirit empowered people. I operated in my own measure of faith and did not compare my results to Randy's. We were both obedient and both at peace. The Bible says, "Godliness with contentment is great gain."

Kenn Gulliksen made an absolutely fascinating comment to me in this regard. He wrote,

*I personally find it interesting that during our first nine years in West LA, we led approximately 11,000 people to Christ. When John took over and we became a movement, evangelism seemed to just stop. Several of us had the same experience. So "power evangelism" for me replaced Holy Spirit evangelism which resulted in no evangelism! I think the reason is clear. Many of us had succeeded doing what God had made us to do...the fruit came because, like Chuck Smith, I was being me and doing what God had called me to do—teach and pastor. When I found out that that wasn't enough, that I needed to...move in gifts of the Spirit that God hadn't given, evangelism ended.*

My point in saying these things is to point out, once again, that the renewal call on John's life, as exemplified by VMI, cried out for the other pedal on the church bicycle to be pushed. John was doing *his* job, and as we began to grow up, we began to do ours as well. It seems to me that Tri Robinson's "Matrix Model," even if the actual Matrix is no longer used per se in AVC literature, has had a lasting impact on our thinking. The concepts presented in it helped to bring out the differences between the giftedness of pastors. With that affirmation embedded into the movement, we now will be able to move forward with more stability.

## "APOSTOLIC" GOVERNMENT

The call on Wimber's life to found a worldwide church planting movement is apostolic by its very nature. I know this was a hot-button topic for John, and he devoted the last issue of *Vineyard Reflections* (August, 1997) to the subject of the five-fold ministry of Ephesians 4:11. The purpose in his stance was to steer the church away from holding titles without performing the functions. He must have seen a lot of out-of-touch denominational bureaucrats in his days as a church growth consultant at Fuller. I know that he also wanted to stay away from anything that hinted at restorationism (the notion that God is restoring the fivefold offices, which the devil has stolen, the last being the office of apostle). John wanted to embrace renewal without putting an eschatological spin on it.

Neither John Wimber nor anyone in church history can meet the criterion to be a member of the twelve as outlined in

367

Acts 1:21-22, but clearly Romans 16:7 and other places reference another category of apostles larger than the twelve. It is these apostles that must be referred to in Ephesians 4:11, what John called apostle with a little *a*. We could put here many in church history who have been used to found church planting movements over which they have had apostolic authority, men like Luther, Fox, Wesley, and in our day men like Chuck Smith ("pastor over many flocks") and John Wimber ("10,000 churches").[2]

We have operated until recently under the direction of an apostolic man. Historically, this form of church government, be it in denomination or church, has its strengths and weaknesses. The strength of apostolic leadership is the ability to move quickly, powerfully, to sail uncharted waters. The early adopters are pioneers attracted to the thrill of something new. God is *on* the apostolic man, and we learn new things, forgotten things, with him. We follow, at times blindly, and go on all the learning curves with the leader as he matures. There must be loyalty and grace to take a few rides because in the end, God is birthing something through imperfect people. Those who would shoot their catalyst beware. There are not many who can "make things happen." It is best to take a long view and trust that patience and lots of prayer will prevail over their quirks and dysfunction. It was Zechariah the prophet who said, "Strike the shepherd and the sheep scatter" (Zechariah 13:7). This verse was quoted by Jesus just before his arrest (Matthew 26:31 and Mark 14:27) and used to predict the scattering of the apostles (Matthew 26:56 and Mark 14:49-50).

The downside of following an apostolic man is that the path can often be erratic, first following one "word" and then the next. Our history bears this out. John confessed at the 1995 pastors' conference in Anaheim that he led us wrongly into the prophetic era. He was much more cautious with the Toronto Blessing, not wanting to lead us wrongly again. By that time the board had been more empowered, and served as a check and balance as we negotiated tricky waters.

Another downside is the failure to recognize when those who are being trained are ready to share in making decisions. During the teenage years when children want to begin to spread their wings, the wise parent has to know when to hold on and when to let go. John, at his own admission, held on too long. He had men and women around him that were trustworthy and who, if honored would have added needed council at crucial moments. Todd Hunter writes in the book *John Wimber* that during a crucial board meeting in Chicago some lively debate had erupted about whether the Vineyard should embrace a church that wanted to adopt in. As they were debating the pros and cons, Wimber at one moment got frustrated and said, "Look, you get into heaven through Jesus; you get into the Vineyard through me." The church got in, but Todd comments that "it took John many years to sort through all the fallout."

By the time the Vineyard was distancing itself from the Toronto Airport Vineyard, John had learned his lesson; the process was far more democratic and the board had legitimate input into the decision to withdraw the Vineyard's endorsement of the Toronto's administration over what was happening there.

Many of us wrongly followed John's "benevolent dictator" model of leadership into the pastorate, and found it too centered on the senior pastor. As we can see, an apostolic model of leadership is more appropriate in the early stages when the genetic code is being set. Setting a churches or movements genetic code is not subject to a democracy. God gives a leader vision and he has to "set his face like a flint" lest the vision be lost in a sea of discordant voices. But there came a point when Jesus put trust in his leaders and sent them out on their own. There was a point at which Paul delegated authority to Timothy and Titus, then to elders. Those who plant churches need to find the balance between catalytic leadership and government through elders; sensing the timing is more art than science and must be discerned by the Holy Spirit.

As we sit on the threshold of the new millennium, John's leadership has now been successfully transferred into the hands of the board. We will miss who and what John was; our history may be less catalytic, but we are in a better position to chart a straight course.

## Language for Relationship; Short at Times on Substance

Our movement has reflected the senior pastor approach to life and ministry—type A, high D, ENTJ,[3] task oriented, get to the goal line. I always appreciated the gentle, relational emphasis that Kenn Gulliksen gave us. When he left the movement, we lost something vital. I think the intent of God was for John and Kenn to bring both of their gifts into a team ministry synergism that would have created both the task and relational emphases we needed for the long haul. Our pastors' conferences have historically been go, go, go, do, do, do. I don't remember a conference where we featured how to listen, resolve conflict, deal with sexual abuse, develop a theology of counseling or build healthy teams. I think these vital things were supposed to be learned on the job, but many of us dysfunctional boomers somehow didn't get it and had to learn the hard way.

Another place this was reflected was in our pastoral oversight system. The men giving pastoral care to churches in the field were senior pastors of large, growing, reproducing churches. Two things were amiss here. *First*, these men had no time to give the proper coaching the younger ones needed. *Second*, the very gifts that made these men overseers of growing churches were the very gifts that least equipped them for the job of caring for other pastors. The system was set up for isolation and poor oversight to new churches. These problems are now being corrected by coaching systems and by setting in place overseers with the proper gifts and call.

As we settle down in the years to come—not that we pursue the Holy Spirit any less or become a boring denomination—I would like to see us develop our people skills while we keep focused on the church planting task before us.

## Can We Take the Best and Go?

It is rare in church history for a movement to sustain vitality for more than one generation. Is it possible for the Vineyard to fulfill John Wimber's vision and become vitally self-perpetuating?

Before we begin to answer that question, the Vineyard must first embrace the promise of Romans 8:28. Paul wrote, "God works all things together for good for those who love the Lord and are called according to his purpose."

Before we can look to the future we need to be sure that we hold our incredibly wonderful and at times stormy past under the sovereignty of God. Carol Wimber has written that from her and John's perspectives, it was all worth it.[4] Our journey has been God's medicine for our health. If we receive the medicine as from the hand of the Lord, it will produce in us the fragrance of Christ and we will be well on our way to taking the best and moving on.

Having said this, it should be noted that the subject of religious vitality has been attacked from many angles and various disciplines. I will highlight some of them under two main headings.

## HUNGRY FOR MEN

Sociologists Finke and Stark point out that one factor in denominational decline is the advent of denominational seminaries aimed at reproducing biblical scholars rather than church planting pastors.[5] The pursuit of truth becomes a higher priority than propagation of the truth. When this happens, the routinization process is accelerated, and dead orthodoxy is around the corner. Roland Allen wrote that in his experience as a missionary in India, the fear of false doctrine prohibits spontaneous expansion of the church by burying the zeal of new Christians under a pile of books.[6]

The father of the modern field of church growth, Donald McGavran, thought that the problem is not our desire for doctrinal correctness but the neglect of correctness in *all* doctrines. Seminaries generally neglect the great commission in pursuit of theology. In his last book before his death, *Effective Evangelism: A Theological Mandate*,[7] McGavran called for a complete curriculum reform in theological education. He wrote that evangelism and missions should be at the heart of all pastoral training. The basic problem is that we have the wrong people (those who have not proven their call to ministry in the context of the local church) being trained in the wrong place (one learns to

371

pastor and evangelize only in the context of ministry) and taught by the wrong teachers (pastors and evangelists should be trained by pastors and evangelists).

I was deeply impacted by an article I read a number of years ago called "Missionary Encounter with Culture" by Wilbert R. Shenk.[8] Shenk's comments are based on a set of lectures given by Rev. Walter Hobhouse in Oxford, England, in 1909. Hobhouse addresses the routenized church of England on the perceived to be "distasteful" subject of missionary encounter with the world. The lectures proposed that when Constantine legalized Christianity, the church lost its conscious antagonism with the world and began the long decline toward institutionalism where its goal was self-preservation rather than self-propagation. Citing Hobhouse, Shenk writes that the Bible describes the church as a dynamic missionary encounter with the world. The church is in the world but as a resident alien. It exists for mission, just as a fire exists for burning. While evangelism and nurture must be in proper balance with one another, risk-filled rescues from the kingdom of Satan must remain the initial objective. This not only applies in evangelism; it also demands church planting and world missions. Shenk writes that "the Christian faith has been saved repeatedly in nearly two thousand years of history by moving from an established heartland to a new environment."[9] If a church or denomination does not reproduce itself in multiplying churches and crossing cultures with the gospel, it will ultimately shrivel up and die.

The research of sociologist Christian Smith reveals the same phenomenon.[10] In what he calls the "subcultural identity theory of religious persistence," Smith says that religions thrive only when they provide subcultural identities (its OK to be excited about being in the Vineyard or a part of Calvary Chapel) that give members meaning and belonging and that stay in creative tension with the world. If we continue to take risks for the gospel and remain in healthy antagonism with the world, the lifeblood of the kingdom will still flow through our veins.

This is the significance of what Steve Sjogren has done with the concept of *servant evangelism*. It has given ordinary Christians the opportunity to be thrust into missionary encounter with the world. It is healthy simply because it is relatively unthreatening and gets people engaged with the unchurched. When we willfully put ourselves in a position of risk for the gospel, power is given to advance it and spiritual energy fills every fiber of our being.

Again the research of Finke and Stark is helpful. They assert that when a sect in high tension with the world seeks to lower that tension by accommodating the world's demands, vibrancy begins to abate, thus creating the climate for the emergence of new sects in the free religious market economy in America. In the process of accommodation, groups become less strict, thus making fewer demands on their constituents. Sect-like movements not only provide greater meaning by asking for greater sacrifice, but also screen out "free riders" who enjoy the benefits of the group but sap its strength because they aren't willing to contribute to its corporate life.

## HUNGRY FOR GOD

Not only must we keep the world ever before us, but our ultimate aim is to finish the work the Father gave us to do. We exist for him and to obey him. In Vineyard worship we seek his face and not his hand. In ministry John Wimber taught us to preach the words and do the works of Jesus in the same way Jesus did: he depended completely on the power of the Holy Spirit (e.g., Luke 5:17) and only did what he saw the Father doing (John 5:19). When Wimber started what is now the Anaheim Vineyard, he did so to see whether or not signs and wonders would accelerate church growth in the American context like it did in other countries of the world. While not producing the results he had hoped for, at least not in his lifetime, John was able to address a major deficiency in evangelical pneumatology and train people all around the world to "do the stuff."

It is a raging debate in the Vineyard as to how much to emphasize the Holy Spirit in our churches. Some say ministry time is our genetic DNA, and others say, "Yes, we agree, but let's create different kinds of meetings, some for evangelism and some for

Holy Spirit activity." Without getting into the middle of the "seeker" debate in the Vineyard, the greater question as we have said was framed by Todd in the Columbus Accords. The question is not "Is it Vineyard? but "Is it biblical?" It matters not how we package our programs, but whether we are reproducing disciples that look like the Jesus of the gospels. Do they know and love him? Do they know how to pray? Do they know and obey the Word of God? Do they live holy lives and know how to maintain healthy relationships? Are they released into gift-based, passion-driven ministry? Do they know how to win and disciple the lost? Can they heal the sick and cast out demons? Do they have a heart for the poor? Are they continuing to take risks for the gospel? Our DNA is *all* of Jesus, not the parts we like.

Since this is so, and Jesus did what he did, not out of his deity (although he could have), but as a man anointed with power from on high, the embracing of the power of the Holy Spirit should be a naturally supernatural part of our lives and churches. We will continue to be vibrant as long as we humble ourselves, seek the face of God and look to the power of the Spirit.

Let us not make the same mistake the Christian and Mission-ary Alliance made when, in rejecting the Pentecostalism of the Azusa Street revival, they chose to "seek not, forbid not." The Bible says to "eagerly desire spiritual gifts, especially that you might prophesy" (1 Corinthians 14:1). Despite our desire to be less weird, let us continue to eagerly desire spiritual gifts. After all, the Greek word we translate *gifts* (*charism*) is derived from the word *grace*. To desire the gifts of the Spirit is to seek the grace of God.

Religious sociologist, Donald Miller, spent two years researching what he calls "new paradigm" churches. His book *Reinventing American Protestantism: Christianity in the New Millen-nium*[11] analyzes three new church planting movements, Calvary Chapel, Hope Chapel (a renewal arm within the Foursquare Gospel denomination) and the Vineyard. He calls them a new reformation in postdenominational America. In his assessment of these new paradigm churches he says they offer what all renewal movements have throughout church history—"hope and meaning that is grounded in a transcendent experience of the sacred."[12]   What Miller means by the "sacred" is a personal encounter with God. The Word end of the Word/Spirit spectrum has historically given religious experiences a bum rap, but it was Jesus himself who said the promised Holy Spirit would bring comfort (experience) as well as truth (John 14:16-17). The apostle Paul wrote that God will continue to bestow gifts of the Spirit until we all reach unity in the faith and in the *knowledge* (the Greek word means more than just head knowledge) of the Son of God until we become mature, attaining the full measure of the stature of Christ (Ephesians 4:7-13).

We experience the sacred through the Holy Spirit, as well as through illumination of the Scriptures. But what of the renewal movements that have gone off the deep end throughout history? I like Charles Hummel's analogy: we must have the fire, but if it is to be productive rather than destructive, the fire of the Holy Spirit needs to burn in the fireplace of church leadership, philosophy and structure.[13]  It does no good to have the fire burning out in the middle of the living room out of control. Neither is the answer a dead hearth with no embers. Paul's counsel to the church in Corinth was that they should do "everything" (the fire of the Holy Spirit) "decently and in order" (the fireplace of church structure). And in doing so, let us remember that the fireplace exists to serve the fire and not the other way around. The fireplace has value only if there is fire. No matter how the fireplace is built (seeker church, classic Vineyard, or renewal), let us by all means have the fire—and let it rage. As Roland Allen has said:

*Many of our missionaries welcome spontaneous zeal, provided there is not too much of it...Such missionaries pray for the wind of the Spirit but not for a rushing mighty wind. I am writing because I believe in a rushing mighty wind, and desire its presence at all costs to our restrictions.[14]*

### So what is the end of it all?

I think that if we continue to seek God, pray for the Rushing Wind, call our people to live lives in tension with the world, risk leaving our established heartland with the gospel, create dynamic training centered on evangelism and church planting and live in the radical middle between Word and Spirit, we will stay vital.

*Come, Holy Spirit!*

ভ

### Notes:

[1] 1 Corinthians 12:7-11, 27-31; Romans 12:6-8; Ephesians 4:11; 1 Peter 4.10-11

[2] See the books by C. Peter Wagner and David Cannistraci listed in the last chapter, note 3

[3] These designations are all from various personality profile tests and describe aggressive personality patterns.

[4] "Coping with Controversy and Suffering," *John Wimber*, p. 297

[5] *The Churching of America,* pp. 145-98

[6] *The Spontaneous Expansion of the Church*, pp. 43-59

[7] Phillipsburg, New Jersey, Presbyterian and Reformed Publishing Company, 1988.

[8] *The International Bulletin of Missionary Research*, July, 1991, pp. 104-109.

[9] *Ibid.* p. 107

[10] *American Evangelicalism: Embattled and Thriving*, p. 118

[11] Berkeley, CA, University of California Press, 1997

[12] *Ibid*, p. 3

[13] *Fire in the Fireplace: Charismatic Renewal in the Nineties*, Downers Grove, IL, InterVarsity Press, 1993.

[14] *Spontaneous Expansion of the Church*, p. 12

# APPENDIX I

## TIME LINE OF KEY EVENTS:

| DATE | EVENT |
|---|---|
| February 25, 1934 | John Wimber is born in Kirksville, Missouri |
| 1949 | He plays first professional music gig at Dixie Castle in Orange, CA, at age 15 |
| 1953 | He wins Lighthouse International Jazz Festival |
| 1955 | John and Carol marry |
| 1962 | He puts together a rock group called The Righteous Brothers |
| November 1962 | Dick Heying, drummer in one of John's bands, and his wife Lynn get converted |
| 1963 | God speaks to Foursquare pastor Chuck Smith that he will be a shepherd over many flocks |
| April 1963 | John and Carol begin attending Gunner Payne's Bible study at the Heying's |
| May 1963 | John and Carol accept Christ |
| 1964 | John is filled with the Spirit in private |
| 1963-1974 | John leads hundreds to Christ in a period of intense evangelism |
| 1965 | Chuck Smith begins to pastor a little church called Calvary Chapel |
| 1968 | Lonnie Frisbee helps start the House of Miracles |
| 1968-1975 | Calvary baptizes thousands of hippie converts at a cove in Newport Beach |
| 1970 | John leads 11 Bible studies a week with over 500 people in attendance at the Yorba Linda Friends Church |
| 1971 | John joins the staff of the Yorba Linda Friends Church |
| 1974 | In West LA, Kenn and Joanie Gulliksen start an offshoot of Calvary Chapel and call it The Vineyard |
| 1974 1978 | John leaves the staff of Yorba Linda Friends Church to become the founding director of the Department of Church Growth at the Fuller Institute of Evangelism and Church Growth |
| 1977-1978 | Brent Rue and Jack Little plant the second and third Vineyards |
| May 8, 1977 | John and Carol are asked to leave Yorba Linda Friends Church; they incorporate their Bible study as Calvary Chapel of Yorba Linda |
| 1977 | John preaches on healing and spiritual gifts for 9 months |
| 1979 | Todd and Debbie Hunter plant the Wheeling, WV, Calvary Chapel out of John's church |

377

| DATE | EVENT |
|---|---|
| Mother's Day 1980 | Lonnie Frisbee says, "Come Holy Spirit" at Calvary Chapel, Yorba Linda |
| 1981 | The first two ministry trips go to England and South Africa; first two "Vineyard" albums come out under the Mercy Publishing label |
| 1982-1986 | John teaches MC510 class at Fuller Seminary |
| Spring 1982 | Calvary Chapel pastors' gathering considers tension over Wimber's approach to spiritual gifts and healing; John affiliates with Kenn Gulliksen's Vineyard churches; Kenn turns over the leadership of the Vineyards, and John calls the first meeting of Vineyard pastors at Morro Bay |
| Mother's Day 1982 | Vineyard Christian Fellowship, Anaheim, is incorporated |
| 1983 | John has a vision in which God speaks to him to start 10,000 churches |
| May 1984 | *First Fruits* magazine is published |
| 1985 | Vineyard Ministries International (VMI) and Association of Vineyard Churches (AVC) are incorporated |
| November 1985 | Wimber begins a series of medical tests; he has heart damage, is overweight, has high blood pressure and is overworked |
| 1986 | *Power Evangelism* is published |
| June 1986 | John has a severe angina attack |
| 1987 | Todd and Debbie Hunter return from Wheeling to pastor at VCF Anaheim |
| January 1987 | *Equipping the Saints* magazine replaces *First Fruits*; *Power Healing* is published |
| July 1988 | Becoming a "denomination" is stopped by consensus with the board and confirmed by Carol Wimber's dream; John receives the first word from Paul Cain |
| February 1989 | Paul Cain preaches at the Spiritual Warfare Conference |
| 1989-1991 | Vineyard experiences the prophetic years; Kansas City Fellowship becomes Metro Vineyard |
| July 1989 | Vineyard I is put on the altar as we wait for Vineyard II; the prophets are introduced to the movement |
| October 1990 | "Tokens" of revival come to the UK |
| November 1990 | At the board meeting in Snoqualmie Falls, WA, a "pioneer-homesteader" conflict develops over whether to organize for the next generation |
| January 1991 | Steve Nicholson asked to lead the Church Planting Task Force |

| Date | Event |
|------|-------|
| 1991 | VCF Anaheim moves to its new facility on La Palma |
| May 1991 | John moves away from the prophetic at the board meeting |
| July 1991 | Vineyard recommits to church planting and birthing world missions at the Denver Pastors' Conference; reorganization of the Vineyard for the next generation begins |
| 1992 | Three original Calvary pastors resign due to what they felt was a changing direction in the Vineyard: Kenn Gulliksen, Lee Bennett and Tom Stipe (Jack Little will resign in 1994); Todd Hunter catalyzes a Generation X movement in the Vineyard; Steve Nicholson begins developing a church planting system |
| 1993 | John is diagnosed with cancer |
| Fall 1993 | Randy Clark goes to hear Rodney Howard-Browne; Happy Leman gives Randy a platform to share at the Midwest Vineyard Pastors' Conference; John Arnott calls Randy and invites him to come to Toronto in January of 1994; God speaks to John Wimber that the Vineyard will enter into a season of "new beginnings" |
| January 20, 1994 | The Toronto Blessing begins |
| 1994 | John Wimber and Bob Fulton are commissioned by the board to focus on international church planting |
| 1994 | John and Carol Wimber's son, Chris, is diagnosed with cancer |
| September 1994 | Policies to govern manifestations are hammered out at an emergency board meeting with the renewal leaders present |
| January 1995 | John Wimber suffers a stroke |
| 1995 | Amidst turmoil over the renewal and bizarre manifestations, James Beverly, Hank Hanegraaff and others publish critiques |
| 1995 | Vineyard International Consortium is formed |
| July 1995 | At the International Pastors' conference in Anaheim Wimber repents for leading the Vineyard into the prophetic period; the first independent AVC is released in the nation of Canada under the direction of Gary and Joy Best |
| December 5, 1995 | Wimber, Hunter, Fulton, and Best announce to the Toronto Airport Vineyard that AVC was withdrawing its endorsement of their church while remaining positive about the renewal |
| August 8, 1996 | Metro Vineyard leaves AVC |
| 1995-1998 | Six new nations released as independent AVCs |
| November 17, 1997 | John Wimber dies of a massive brain hemorrhage due to a fall |
| 1998 | AVC has 449 USA churches, 370 International churches in 52 countries |

# APPENDIX II

I have asked David Di Sabatino, perhaps the leading historian on the Jesus People movement, to write an essay on the life of Lonnie Frisbee as a conclusion to our history of the Vineyard. David has published a bibliography on the revival, *The Jesus People Movement: An Annotated Bibliography and Resource* (Westport: CT: Greenwood Publishing, 1999). He has also been researching Lonnie's life for five years, having interviewed those who knew him closely and many others who were touched by his life. I wanted an essay on this modern day Samson (as he was eulogized at his funeral) for a couple of reasons. First, he played a crucial role in the rocketing advance of both Calvary Chapel and the Vineyard. Second, Lonnie was so controversial that legends abound; the truth needs to be discerned from myth. It is with these things in mind that I now commend David's appendix on Lonnie Frisbee.

## LONNIE FRISBEE: A MODERN DAY SAMSON

*BY DAVID DI SABATINO*

> *But peace, I must not quarrel with the will*
> *of highest dispensation, which herein*
> *Haply had ends above my reach to know:*
> *Suffices that to me strength is my bane*
> *And proves the source of all my miseries*
> *- John Milton*
> *Samson Agonistes*

There was little if anything ordinary about the life of Lonnie Frisbee. Whether talking to those that knew him well or those who met him briefly, one is left with the impression that he was larger than life, something of an Old Testament prophet having leapt out of the pages of the Bible and into the twentieth century. Much like the accounts of Elijah and Elisha, memories of Frisbee often include accounts of divine healing, miraculous occurrences, dramatic conversion experiences and other events bordering on the incredulous. Like Samson, however, whatever spiritual prowess he may have been granted was curtailed by moral failure. The stories surrounding Lonnie Frisbee are difficult to separate from myths that often fuel an inflated cult of personality that survive similar faith healers and evangelists. Not surprisingly, there is debate over how to define such a rapscallion. Some believe Frisbee was imbued with the gift of miraculous powers (1 Cor. 12:10) while others believe he was simply a gifted Christian evangelist. Others believe he was either an apostle or prophet while still others viewing him as nothing more than a hypnotist. That such a Charismatic individual exhibited such a prodigious spiritual influence despite his behavioral eccentricities make him a religious biographer's dream.

Lonnie Frisbee was countercultural hippie turned Jesus freak evangelist whose penchant for spiritual experimentation would not only shape his own life but the institutional legacies of the revival. His four years while employed at Calvary Chapel in Costa Mesa, California, serving as an evangelistic liaison between the church and the hippie counterculture from 1968 to 1971, radically transformed that church from a small two hundred member congregation to a thriving internationally renown ministry. He was also influential in the beginnings of the Vineyard church movement from 1980 to 1983, providing then leader John Wimber with a model of Pentecostal experimentalism that would influence the Vineyard's "signs and wonders" theology. His influence on these two still thriving denominations, both presently boasting several hundred affiliates worldwide[1], was integral to their periods of rapid transformation and church growth. As a zealous itinerant his various missionary endeavors throughout Sweden, Brazil, and South Africa received much fanfare.

Frisbee's influence was not solely corporate. Many individuals trace their spiritual conversions to little more than a brief encounter with the flamboyant evangelist. Evangelist Greg Laurie, pastor of Harvest Christian Fellowship and evangelist behind the southern California based Harvest Crusades, was deeply impacted by Frisbee's ministry. Both Mike MacIntosh, pastor of the Horizon

Christian Fellowship in San Diego, California, and his wife were impacted by Frisbee's ministry in the early 1970s. Kenn Gulliksen, early member of the Calvary Chapel pastoral staff and founder of the Vineyard churches, cites Frisbee as "mentoring him in the 'deeper things' of the Holy Spirit."

His death on March 12, 1993 as a result of AIDS, however, offers a puzzling end to a rather spectacular albeit brief evangelistic career. How does one reconcile the extremes that resonate throughout his biography? Lonnie Frisbee remains as enigmatic in death as he was in life.

## FROM COUNTERCULTURE TO CHRISTIANITY

Lonnie Frisbee was born on June 6, 1950 in the oceanside city of Costa Mesa, California. His early home life was marked by a number of personal and family crises that Lonnie overcame by immersing himself in his two creative passions—art and dancing. While barely a teenager Frisbee won himself a regular spot on a local dance show called *Shebang* (hosted by Kasey Kasem) while obtaining a number of awards for his paintings. In 1966 he accepted a scholarship to Academy of Art College in San Francisco which, at the age of sixteen, placed him only blocks away from the Haight-Ashbury district and the incipient hippie culture.

Though the term only came into use at the end of the 1960s, the *counterculture* was an amorphous catchall used to describe the new verve of experimentation. Following the egging of self-proclaimed gurus such as Dr. Timothy Leary, hippies were asked to propel themselves into empirical observations by turning their bodies and minds into laboratories for social study. Though he had been introduced to drugs at a young age, interaction within the Haight subculture transformed him into an aggressive LSD proselytizer coaxing others to "turn on" to the promises of mystical enlightenment. Frisbee admitted, "when I first turned on to drugs I thought that was the truth so I turned everyone on to drugs."[2] He admitted that drug use was the doorway to a self-made philosophy combining elements of metaphysical meditation, UFO worship, hypnotism, the teachings of Edgar Cayce, and the

Bible.[3] Such spiritual experimentation revealed a common quest undertaken by hippies to seek out answers to questions of ultimacy. Lonnie Frisbee's trek along this hippie "quest for truth" would eventually culminate in a direct encounter of God that would forever shape the course of his life.[4]

By 1967 a number of hippie seekers began to convert to Christianity believing that Jesus Christ was "the answer" to their search. While roaming through the California mountains near Tahquitz Falls, Frisbee claimed that God appeared to him while he was "high on acid." Of this experience of theophany he explained,

> *I was a nudist-vegetarian-hippie when the Lord called me. I was going into the desert, taking off all my clothes and I'm saying 'God, if you're really real, reveal yourself to me.' One afternoon the whole atmosphere of this canyon started to tingle and change. The Lord identified himself to me and said, 'I'm Jesus. I build nations and I tear them down. It is better for a nation to have never known me than to have known me and turned their back from me.' I thought all roads led to Rome, but he explained to me that he was the only way to know God. I accepted him and he said 'I am going to send you to the people.' Then, he gave me a vision of thousands of people and they were wandering around in a maze of darkness with no direction of purpose for their lives. He showed me that there was a light on me that he was placing on my life…and that it was Jesus Christ and I was going to bear the Word of the Lord.[5]*

Not long after this encounter, Frisbee made contact with a group of four "street Christian" couples who had begun living together in Christian community and evangelizing their hippie peers in the Haight-Ashbury.[6] The unofficial leader of the group, Ted Wise, recalled that at the time Frisbee's interpretation of his theophany experience was still nebulous. Interviewed in 1972 Wise explained that his cohort "had a Christian background… but his head was so bent out of shape from LSD that he had attached a whole lot of other junk to it,"[7] and that he was "talking incoherently about

Jesus Christ and flying saucers."[8] Noting Frisbee's sincerity, however, Wise invited him to join their community. Over a six-month period the community, dubbed the House of Acts because of the perceived affinity with first century Christianity, served as an informal seminary where Frisbee was discipled through a process of informal Christian education. The House of Acts dissolved after eighteen months with the various members each going their separate ways. Along with his young bride Connie, whom he married in early 1968, Frisbee was recruited to a small church in Costa Mesa, California called Calvary Chapel where his ministry as a Christian evangelist would flourish.

## CALVARY CHAPEL

The antecedent history to Calvary Chapel becoming a 20th century church growth phenomenon begins in 1965 when the desperate congregation staved off a vote to close the church and hired Chuck Smith as their pastor. After bringing stability to the small 200-member congregation, Smith and his wife Kay turned their attention to the large number of hippies that would flock to nearby Huntington Beach. Smith credits his wife with turning his attitude toward the hippies from disdain to an evangelistic burden. After asking their children to "bring home a real live hippie," their wish was granted in early 1968 when they were first introduced to Lonnie Frisbee who was hitchhiking through southern California. Hearing of the mission outpost in San Francisco, Chuck Smith later phoned Frisbee and recruited him to move south to begin a similar evangelistic program.[9] The decision to recruit the unorthodox couple would have immediate and long-lasting repercussions on their church.

The Frisbees moved to Costa Mesa and functioned as elders at the House of Miracles, the first of a number of similarly named communal houses established throughout the southwestern United States. Lonnie spent his days evangelizing and inviting anyone within earshot to nightly Bible studies held at the church. Within the first few weeks of the couple's arrival, Pastor Smith recalled that twenty-one young men had "accepted Christ" and more than fifty by the end of the second week.[10] Knowing they did not have the biblical knowledge to properly teach the new converts, they directed the new believers to attend nightly meetings at Calvary Chapel. The swelling church attendance soon became tangible evidence to those involved that something supernatural was happening in their midst. Such excitement was confirmed by a prophetic utterance voiced by Kay Smith: "Because of your praise and adoration before my throne tonight, I am going to bless the whole coast of California. It will move out, across the United States and then on to different parts of the world." For those in attendance, the prophecy motivated them to engage in efforts of evangelism. As the "Jesus Movement" gained international exposure the prophecy was interpreted as a divine foretelling of the revival.

Along with his daily witnessing activities at the House of Miracles (and later at a subsequent location called the Blue Top Motel), Frisbee was given the leadership of the Wednesday night Bible study at Calvary Chapel. A sociological study on Calvary Chapel conducted in 1971 captured a Wednesday night service with Frisbee at the helm:

> *A 22-year-old lay minister—a former drug user, with flowing robe, long hair and beard—leads the service...Informal songs are sung by the congregation, mostly centering on the person of Jesus and his imminent return to earth. Prayers for the sick are offered and testimonies are heard...Lonnie affirms that God desires to heal anything from 'warts to cancer.' The 'flashes' from previous LSD trips can also be cured. One woman (older than most present) testifies that she has been cured of dandruff. 'Praise the Lord!' says Lonnie. An examination of her head reveals no trace of dandruff.[11]*

Participants claimed that Wednesday became the central night in the church's weekly calendar with Frisbee playing a crucial role in attracting young hippies to the church. The report noted that attendance on other nights was "about one-third of the Wednesday night assemblage… This difference is likely due to the drawing power of the professional rock groups… plus the charisma of Lonnie."[12] Participants during this early phase of Calvary Chapel's history note Frisbee's tremendous personal magnetism and his ability to relate the Christian message in the relaxed vernacular of the times. One observer noted:

> *student leadership is emerging out of the youth culture with integrity. We are not being subjected to the embarrassing spectacle of adults who look like flower-children with pot-bellies…Lonnie Frisbee, of Calvary Chapel, wears long hair and a beard as he preaches to thousands, because Lonnie was a long-haired 'freak' before his conversion. Becoming a Christian has not meant a crew-cut because that's not Lonnie.*[13]

Adding to his appeal was his ability to identify with his generation's sense of dissatisfaction with and alienation from mainstream life. Frisbee was upfront about his past life, testifying that "God had saved him from homosexuality" and other countercultural sins.

In 1971 the Jesus People became one of the year's top stories with Frisbee receiving international exposure when his photogenic picture appeared in *Time, Society, Life*, and *Look* magazines.[14] Reporters converging on the church amplified the legendary status Frisbee had already received, writing of his reputation as an "irresistible evangelist."[15] A magazine reporter sent to southern California to cover the revival reported that it was "commonly accepted" that Frisbee was responsible for "tens of thousands of spiritual conversions." The Rev. Edward E. Plowman, editor of *Christianity Today*, documented the Frisbee's influence on Calvary Chapel by stating that the "population explosion" at the church following the couple's arrival had "skyrocketed from 150 into the thousands "within two years."[16] Chuck Smith substantiated those claims reporting that Calvary Chapel was "instrumental in 20,000 conversions to the Christian faith" while performing over "eight thousand baptisms" in a two year period.

Despite the tremendous growth surge within Calvary Chapel,

Lonnie was growing increasingly disenchanted. He began to feel as if his type of ministry was being repressed. His Wednesday night meetings began to take on an increasingly aggressive Pentecostal tack which ultimately led to a crisis point with the more staid head pastor. As his bouts of experimentation became increasingly volatile, Chuck Smith asked Frisbee to conduct post-service sessions, called "Afterglow" meetings, where spiritual gifts—speaking in tongues, prayers for healing, words of knowledge and prophecy—could be exercised. The aforementioned sociological report offered the following observations of the Frisbee-led afterglow services:

> *Lonnie invites those who want the baptism of the Spirit to come forward. A flute player provides an eerie background (he 'plays by the Spirit') while Lonnie assists those who wish to receive the Spirit, with such blandishments, as 'you may kneel, if you wish,' or 'you may extend your arms toward heaven, if you wish.' Lonnie moves in and out among those standing on the platform, touching and speaking to them. Eventually a cadence of people speaking in babble and singing in tongues, intertwines with the mystic tones of the flute...Following the afterglow, which is terminated at Lonnie's command, certain individuals remain fixed in apparent hysterical stupor. 'Counselors' help them to 'give in' to the Spirit, some of whom are unable to pull out of their babbling and hysteria.[17]*

The report concluded by stating that Frisbee was being "kept in line by the older staff members."[18] Becoming more and more convinced that a more rational teaching based theology was what was needed for their church, Smith made it clear to Frisbee that these times of Pentecostal experimentation could only take place *subsequent* to the preaching and teaching of the Bible. As the situation in the early church where the Pauline emphasis upon teaching replaced spiritual frenzy, Chuck Smith was laying the foundation for the marginalization of the ecstatic tradition that

Frisbee represented. With his marriage under increasing strain and feeling that his ministerial style was being repressed, Lonnie decided to leave Calvary Chapel in December 1971.

## FROM THE DISCIPLESHIP MOVEMENT TO THE VINEYARD

The Frisbees accepted the invitation of Bob Mumford, a Florida-based Pentecostal minister, to come to Ft. Lauderdale for the beginning of what would become the Discipleship (or Shepherding) movement. Taking note of the independent nature of the various Pentecostal and Charismatic ministries that had sprouted all over the country, Mumford and a number of other ministers began to teach about the need for personal spiritual accountability. Since Lonnie was experiencing problems in his marriage, Mumford asked him to submit to his direct spiritual supervision for a one-year sabbatical from the ministry to engender healing and restoration. After leaving the initial Ft. Lauderdale sessions, however, Lonnie struggled in his personal life. By the latter stages of 1973 the marriage was irreparably damaged and the Frisbees divorced. Lonnie moved north to Santa Cruz where he became involved with the Mission Street Fellowship. Though he was under strict guidelines to refrain from ministry until his personal issues were resolved, he craved the attention that he had received as an evangelist. Finally, after five years of fumbling through a series of odd jobs and missionary jaunts, Lonnie decided to reconcile his relationship with Chuck Smith.

By 1976 Calvary Chapel had blossomed into an internationally respected ministry overseeing the building of a new 2,300-seat auditorium, the establishment of an internationally successful music ministry (Maranatha! Music), and a host of sister church locations throughout the southwestern United States. By the late 1970s it was estimated that Calvary Chapel was selling over 50,000 books and 10,000 teaching tapes worldwide on a monthly basis.[19] Although Frisbee had been the catalyst of the church's tremendous growth, his return was a difficult one. Many of the young ministers whose lives he had spiritually nurtured had developed ministries of their own in his absence. Even more disturbing to him was the realization that Chuck Smith had replaced the aggressive Pentecostalism with an emphasis on doctrinal teaching and Bible study. Having rehired Frisbee, Smith made it clear that the spiritual experimentalism previously afforded him would no longer be tolerated.

For a short time Frisbee tried to fit into a more sedate approach to church life and briefly served as a counselor. Soon, however, he began to seek out opportunities where Pentecostal experimentalism could be implemented. His attendance at small Bible studies away from church oversight began to attract attention as reports of miracles and strange phenomena again began to circulate. His activities eventually caught the attention of John Wimber, pastor of a local Calvary Chapel affiliate in Yorba Linda, California. Although wary of Frisbee's reputation as an uncontrollable personality invited him to preach the Mother's Day evening meeting at his church in 1980.[20] At the close of the service Frisbee invited "all those under the age of 25" to come to the front altar. Wimber later recounted that upon Frisbee's prayer, "people fell to the floor. Others, who did not believe in tongues, loudly spoke in tongues. The speaker roamed among the crowd, praying for people, who then immediately fell over with the Holy Spirit resting on them."[21] Wimber notes that the event served as a powerful "watershed moment" in the life of the church and the initiation of what would eventually become a separate church denomination.

As had occurred during his first tenure at the original Calvary Chapel (in Costa Mesa), Frisbee's experimental evangelistic style had an immediate effect upon Wimber's church. Over the latter half of 1980 the church was radically transformed in similar fashion as what had happened at the original Calvary Chapel location in 1968. Lonnie Frisbee found himself once again in the center of a revival where hundreds of people were converting and experiencing dramatic healings and other spiritual manifestations. Of this period of growth Wimber stated that the church experienced "supernatural phenomena" such as manifestations of spiritual power which included "shaking," "falling over," "becoming very quiet," and "speaking in tongues" as they yielded to the Holy Spirit. Wimber cited that the church baptized over "seven hundred new converts" while increasing their attendance in upwards of two thousand members during an initial period of growth.[22] In 1982, after a Calvary Chapel pastor's retreat where Chuck Smith asked John Wimber to demarcate his church's aggressive Pentecostal doctrinal stance by placing themselves under the 'Vineyard' auspice, something resembling a church split took place between the Calvary Chapel and Vineyard churches. During the formative period of the Vineyard's rapid transition into a denomination, Lonnie Frisbee functioned as the stellar example of Wimber's "signs and wonders" theology.

In the aftermath of the "Mother's Day event," John Wimber arranged evangelistic teams to travel throughout the world to teach and visibly demonstrate what Vineyard leaders billed as a "return to New Testament Christianity." Wimber's stated desire was to fuse principles of evangelism with the experimental elements of Pentecostalism he witnessed in Frisbee's ministry. During this formative period the Vineyard's rapid transition into a denomination, Lonnie Frisbee functioned as the star example of the "signs and wonders" theology.

One Charismatic pastor involved in bringing a Vineyard evangelistic team to his church in 1982 related his experiences with them as "hugely enjoyable." The pastor mentioned that he "began to wonder whether I had made the right decision" in inviting them to his church. On Saturday morning, however, Wimber introduced Frisbee by stating it was "time to have some fun." After Frisbee took the stage and announced, "Come, Holy Spirit!" the pastor related that the events that followed were "exceedingly difficult to describe." He stated, "within seconds the Spirit of God had fallen upon a large proportion of the congregation, many of whom were trembling and shaking, speaking in tongues, calling on the Lord, prophesying, and some of whom (hard though it might seem to believe) were flapping up and down like fish upon the floor. Some of this I was able to see, but most of it passed me by since I was doing the same."[23] In his estimation Frisbee was the "trigger" for an emphasis on spiritual phenomena in those early years within the Vineyard movement.[24]

Notwithstanding his success in the Vineyard's fledgling days, during the last ten years of his life Lonnie Frisbee became embittered by the treatment he received from the leadership of the two denominations where he had once ministered. Breaking his alliance with John Wimber and the Vineyard movement in 1983, he traveled as an itinerant evangelist making missionary trips to South Africa and throughout South American countries without any church affiliation. Despite various attempts to repeat previous successes he never reestablished a center of influence for himself similar to his years at Calvary Chapel or with the early Vineyard movement. Rarely submitting himself to spiritual oversight or reprimand for his increasingly erratic behavior, he continued to alienate himself from any personal accountability. Forever seeking the validation and consuming thrill that the ministerial spotlight occasionally granted him, Lonnie vacillated between enterprising missionary jaunts and depression. At some point during this time he contracted AIDS. After a protracted illness he died on March 12, 1993 and was buried in an ostentatious ceremony at televangelist Dr. Robert Schuller's Crystal Cathedral in Garden Grove, California. In reference to his troubled life the overriding theme of the funeral speakers was to compare Frisbee to Samson, the Old Testament judge whose spiritually powerful life was cut short by moral failure.[25]

## Of Saints, Sinners and the Slur of Guilt by Association

Lonnie Frisbee's sexual confusion stemmed from an early incident that occurred when he was a youngster. At the age of eight he was homosexually molested by a male babysitter. While never using this incident as an excuse for sporadic lapses, the incident is important in placing homosexual conduct in the spectrum of his personal experience. Later on, while in the Haight-Ashbury, Frisbee was recruited by an older male figure into the gay lifestyle. After his conversion and subsequent alliance with Calvary Chapel, Frisbee openly admitted that he had been "saved out of the homosexual lifestyle." While close friends attested that he rarely (if ever) exhibited any indication that he was struggling in this area of his life, his death as a result of AIDS has been interpreted by many as an outright indictment of flagrant licentiousness unbecoming a Christian minister. It must be stated unequivocally that Frisbee never believed that homosexuality was a natural inclination. Rather, in line with most conservative evangelicals he always believed that homosexual behavior was the conscious choice of the participant.

Due to these facts about his life, however, Frisbee's legacy has been relatively neglected. Part of this unease is due to the general discomfort evangelical culture exhibits in dealing with issues related to homosexuality. Evangelicals have tended to prioritize sexual sins as deserving more attention than other actions. Tim and Beverly LaHaye evince this attitude when they state, "homosexuality seems to be the ultimate sin in the Bible that causes God to give men up."[26]

Due to this thinking, some cannot fathom that God would choose to risk His reputation by aligning Himself with someone of Frisbee's background. Evangelicals tend to prefer to view their leaders as either wholly sanctified or entirely debauched if found guilty of some evangelically incorrect actions. This despite the fact that the lives of many within the Pentecostal and Charismatic historical stream are not without blemish. While sinful behavior and personal catastrophe does point us to the fact that few leaders ever finish well, it would be a mistake to not see that God often uses broken and fragile vessels to do His bidding.

Other discomfort is evinced where Frisbee is conveniently written out of the spiritual lineage of both corporate histories and individual biographies. Not wanting their own reputations tainted, Frisbee most often shows up in recollections as "a young evangelist." Some of their concerns about their own reputations by divorcing themselves from Frisbee's memory may be well founded. The shameful tendency of American "cult" and apologetics demagogues to utilize the slur tactics of guilt by association leaves those with Frisbee in their spiritual lineage open to rancorous condemnation.

Hank Hanegraaff's *Counterfeit Revival* is the most egregious example of this perplexing style where the author impugns the Vineyard movement as having "structural defects" for even associating with Frisbee. Hanegraaff accuses Wimber of turning "his pulpit over to a... hypnotist struggling with homosexuality."[27] In his rebuttal to Hanegraaff's book, James A. Beverley writes in *Revival Wars: A Critique of Counterfeit Revival* that behind the desire to distance Christian history from someone like Frisbee "is the notion that God could not possibly use someone struggling with homosexuality."[28] Not only does Hanegraaff's logic fail to point the same accusatory finger at Calvary Chapel for having Frisbee in its spiritual lineage, but it fails to recognize the obvious biblical reality that sinless perfection is not a prerequisite for being used by God.

As embarrassing as Lonnie Frisbee's story may be to many of those who were influenced by him, the fact remains that God called him while he was an LSD-ingesting hypnotist who was experimenting with alternative sexuality just as God called Paul as he was a murderer. To miss the underlying premise of Frisbee's biography—that God would risk his reputation by aligning Himself to such a frail character—is to ignore the potential that lies resonant within each of us. That God "chose the lowly things of this world and the despised things (1 Cor. 1:28) should cause us to rejoice with humility. Ultimately, we need ask ourselves when we point to someone like Frisbee with an accusatory finger: Is the line between saint and sinner that clearly defined for any of us?

03

NOTES:

[1] Donald E. Miller, *Reinventing American Protestantism: Christianity in the New Millennium*, Berkeley, CA: University of California Press, 1997, 191-94.
[2] *The Son Worshipers*, Ventura, CA: Pyramid Films, 1971.
[3] Ibid.
[4] Robert S. Ellwood, Jr., *One Way: The Jesus Movement and Its Meaning*, Englewood Cliffs, NJ: Prentice-Hall, 1973, 53-54.
[5] Lonnie Frisbee Testimony, Anaheim: Vineyard Ministry International. Tape 003.

[6] John A. MacDonald, *The House of Acts*, Carol Stream, IL: Creation House, 1970.

[7] Brian Vachon, *A Time to Be Born*, Englewood Cliffs, NJ: Prentice-Hall Publishers, 1972, 90-96.

[8] Ronald M. Enroth, Edward E. Ericson, Jr., and C. Breckenridge Peters, *The Jesus People: Old-Time Religions in the Age of Aquarius*, Grand Rapids, MI: William B. Eerdmans Publishing Co., 1972, 13.

[9] Chuck Smith, and Hugh Steven, *The Reproducers: New Life for Thousands*, Glendale: Regal Books, 1972, 44.

[10] Smith and Steven, *The Reproducers*, p. 44.

[11] Robert Lynn Adams, and Robert Jon Fox, "Mainlining Jesus: The New Trip," *Society* February 1972, 50.

[12] Ibid., p. 50.

[13] Glenn D. Kittler, *The Jesus Kids and Their Leaders*, New York: Warner Paperback Library, 1972, 122.

[14] "The New Rebel Cry: Jesus is Coming!" *Time*, 21 June 1971, 36-47; "The Jesus Craze," *Life*, 31 December 1971, 38; Brian Vachon, "The Jesus Movement is Upon Us," *Look*, 9 February 1971, 15-21.

[15] Vachon, *A Time to Be Born*, 91.

[16] Edward E. Plowman, *The Underground Church: Accounts of Christian Revolutionaries in America*, Elgin, IL: David C. Cook Publishing Co., 1971, 44-45.

[17] Adams and Fox, "Mainlining Jesus,' p. 51.

[18] Enroth, et al, *The Jesus People*, p. 93.

[19] James T. Richardson, "Mergers, 'Marriages,' Coalitions, and Denominalization: The Growth of Calvary Chapel," *Syzygy* 2, 3-4 (1993), 206.

[20] John Wimber, "Season of New Beginnings," *Equipping the Saints*, Fall 1994, 5. Recounting his thoughts at the time, Wimber stated, "after our Sunday morning service on Mother's Day [1980], I was walking out the door behind Lonnie, and the Lord told me, 'Ask that young man to give his testimony tonight.' I hadn't even met him, though I knew who he was and how the Lord had used him in the past."

[21] John Wimber, with Kevin Springer, *Power Evangelism*, San Francisco, CA: Harper & Row Publishers, 1986, 23-24. Internal Vineyard church literature sloppily cites the Mother's Day event as occurring in 1978, 1979, and even 1981. A tape of the service from their own files is dated May 11, 1980. This date was corroborated by a number of Frisbee's own close friends

[22] Ibid., pp. 23-24.

[23] Tom Smail, Andrew Walker, and Nigel Wright. *The Love of Power or the Power of Love*, Minneapolis, MN: Bethany House Publishers, 1994, 146-47.

[24] Ibid., p. 51.
[25] Lonnie Frisbee Memorial Funeral Video, March 15, 1993.
[26] Tim and Beverly LaHaye, *The Act of Marriage*, Grand Rapids, MI: Zondervan, 1976, 261.
[27] Hank Hannegraaff, *Counterfeit Revival*, Dallas: Word Publishing, 1997, 205.
[28] James A. Beverley, *Revival Wars: A Critique of Counterfeit Revival*, Toronto: Evangelical Research Ministries, 1997, 87.

# APPENDIX 3
# THE VINEYARD STATEMENT
# OF FAITH[1]

T his document is the result of approximately ten years of work. The need for a statement of faith arose shortly after the beginning of the Vineyard movement in 1983. On one hand, we felt obliged to set forth our biblical and historically orthodox beliefs; on the other hand, we wanted to describe the values and priorities that make the Vineyard unique within the context of Evangelicalism.

While many people have worked on this project, special thanks go to John Wimber out of whose calling and vision the Vineyard, movement has emerged and matured, to John McClure, senior pastor of Vineyard Christian Fellowship Newport Beach, California, who has shepherded the process along over this decade and to Dr. Don Williams, senior pastor of Coast Vineyard in LaJolla, California, who rewrote our original statements into the cogent, biblical kingdom framework that follows.

As evangelicals, the Bible is our final authority for faith and practice. Therefore, the statements that follow reflect our best attempt to understand and live out biblical precepts. Upon further reflection, greater biblical insight, or increased wisdom through experience, these statements could be revised. Until such a time, the Association of Vineyard Churches Board of Directors formally adopts this document as our official statement of faith as of the board meeting in November 1994.

We now commend this for use by all our pastors in all our churches with the prayer that God will bless our sincere desire and humble attempt to be ambassadors of the rule and reign of His Kingdom through our lives, that His will may be done on earth as it is in heaven.

TODD HUNTER,
*National Coordinator Association of Vineyard Churches, Anaheim, California December, 1994*

## OUR STATEMENT OF FAITH
### *(REVISED NOVEMBER 1994)*

**WE BELIEVE** that God is the Eternal King. He is an infinite, unchangeable Spirit, perfect in holiness, wisdom, goodness, justice, power and love. From all eternity He exists as the One Living and True God in three persons of one substance, the Father, the Son, and the Holy Spirit equal in power and glory.

**WE BELIEVE** that God's kingdom is everlasting. From His throne, through His Son, His eternal Word, God created, upholds and governs all that exists: the heavenly places, the angelic hosts, the universe, the earth, every living thing and mankind. God created all things very good.

**WE BELIEVE** that Satan, originally a great, good angel, rebelled against God, taking a host of angels with him. He was cast out of God's presence and, as a usurper of God's rule established a counter-kingdom of darkness and evil on the earth.

**WE BELIEVE** that God created mankind in His image, male and female, for relationship with Himself and to govern the earth. Under the temptation of Satan, our original parents fell from grace, bringing sin, sickness and God's judgment of death to the earth. Through the fall, Satan and his demonic hosts gained access to God's good creation. Creation now experiences the consequences and effects of Adam's original sin. Human beings are born in sin, subject to God's judgment of death and captive to Satan's kingdom of darkness.

**WE BELIEVE** that God did not abandon His rule over the earth which He continues to uphold by His providence. In order to bring redemption, God established covenants which revealed His grace to sinful people. In the covenant with Abraham, God bound Himself to His people Israel, promising to deliver them from bondage to sin and Satan and to bless all the nations through them.

**WE BELIEVE** that as King, God later redeemed His people by His mighty acts from bondage in Egypt and established His covenant through Moses, revealing His purpose is to order our fallen race and to make us conscious of our moral responsibility. By the work of God's Spirit, it convicts us of our sin and God's righteous judgment against us and brings us to Christ along for salvation.

**WE BELIEVE** that when Israel rejected God's rule over her as King, God established the monarchy in Israel and made an unconditional covenant with David, promising that his heir would restore God's kingdom reign over His people as Messiah forever.

**WE BELIEVE** that in the fullness of time, God honored His covenants with Israel and His prophetic promises of salvation by sending His only Son, Jesus, into the world. Conceived by the Holy Spirit and born of the virgin Mary, as fully God and fully man in one person, He is humanity as God intended us to be. Jesus was anointed as God's Messiah and empowered by the Holy Spirit, inaugurating God's kingdom reign on earth, overpowering the reign of Satan by resisting temptation, preaching the good news of salvation, healing the sick, casting out demons and raising the dead. Gathering His disciples, He reconstituted God's kingdom. After dying for the sins of the world, Jesus was raised from the dead on the third day, fulfilling the covenant of blessing given to Abraham. In His sinless, perfect life Jesus met the demands of the law and in His atoning death on the cross He took God's judgment for sin which we deserve as law-breakers. By His death on the cross He also disarmed the demonic powers. The covenant with David was fulfilled in Jesus' birth from David's house, His Messianic ministry, His glorious resurrection from the dead, His ascent into heaven and His present rule at the right hand of the Father. As God's Son and David's heir, He is the eternal Messiah-King, advancing God's reign throughout every generation and throughout the whole earth today.

**WE BELIEVE** that the Holy Spirit was poured out on the Church at Pentecost in power, baptizing believers into the body of Christ and releasing the gifts of the Spirit to them. The Spirit brings the permanent indwelling presence of God to us for spiritual worship, personal sanctification, building up the Church, gifting us for ministry, and driving back the kingdom of Satan by the evangelization of the world through proclaiming the word of Jesus and doing the works of Jesus.

**WE BELIEVE** that the Holy Spirit indwells every believer in Jesus Christ and that He is our abiding Helper, Teacher, and Guide.

**WE BELIEVE** in the filling or empowering of the Holy Spirit, often a conscious experience, for ministry today.

**WE BELIEVE** in the present ministry of the Spirit and in the exercise of all of the biblical gifts of the Spirit. We practice the laying on of hands for the empowering of the Spirit, for healing, and for recognition and empowering of those whom God has ordained to lead and serve the Church.

**WE BELIEVE** that the Holy Spirit inspired the human authors of Holy Scripture so that the Bible is without error in the original manuscripts. We receive the sixty-six books of the Old and New Testaments as our final, absolute authority, the only infallible rule of faith and practice.

**WE BELIEVE** that the whole world is under the domination of Satan and that all people are sinners by nature and choice. All people therefore are under God's just judgment. Through the preaching of the good News of Jesus and Kingdom of God and the work of the Holy Spirit, God regenerates, justifies, adopts and sanctifies through Jesus by the Spirit all who repent of their sins and trust in Jesus Christ as Lord and Savior. By this they are released from Satan's domain and enter into God's kingdom reign.

**WE BELIEVE** in the one, holy, universal Church. All who repent of their sins and confess Jesus as Lord and Savior are regenerated by the Holy Spirit and form the living Body of Christ, of which He is the head and of which we are all members.

**WE BELIEVE** that Jesus Christ committed two ordinances to the Church: water baptism, and the Lord's Supper. Both are available to all believers.

**WE BELIEVE** that God's kingdom has come in the ministry of our Lord Jesus Christ, that it continues to come in the ministry of the Spirit through the Church, and that it will be consummated in the glorious, visible and triumphant appearing of Christ—His return to the earth as King. After Christ returns to reign, He will bring about the final defeat of Satan and all of his minions and works, the resurrection of the dead, the final judgment and the eternal blessing of the righteous and eternal conscious punishment of the wicked. Finally, God will be all in all and His kingdom, His rule and reign, will be fulfilled in the new heavens and the new earth, recreated by His mighty power, in which righteousness swells and in which He will forever be worshipped.

ଔଃ

NOTES:

[1] I have reproduced the AVC statement of faith just as it appears in our official publication, including Todd Hunter's introduction. I have not, however, included the voluminous footnotes to biblical texts. To obtain the AVC version, contact the national office at P.O. Box 17580, Anaheim, CA 92817 (714-777-1433).

# BIBLIOGRAPHY

BOOKS:

Allen, Roland. *Missionary Methods: St. Paul's or Ours?* Grand Rapids, MI: Eerdmans, 1962.

_____ *The Spontaneous Expansion of the Church*. Grand Rapids, MI: Eerdmans, 1962.

Armstrong, John, D. A. Carson and James M. Boice. *Power Religion: The Selling Out of the Evangelical Church?* Chicago, IL: Moody Press, 1992.

Arnott, John. *The Father's Blessing*. Orlando, FL: Creation House, 1995.

Beverly, James. *Holy Laughter and the Toronto Blessing*. Grand Rapids, MI: Zondervan, 1995.

_____ *Revival Wars: A Critique of Counterfeit Revival*. Canada: Evangelical Research Ministries, 1997.

Bickle, Mike, and Michael Sullivant. *Growing in the Prophetic*. Orlando, FL: Creation House, 1979.

Blue, Ken. *Authority to Heal*. Downers Grove, IL: InterVarsity Press, 1988.

Burgess, McGee and Alexander, eds. *Dictionary of Pentecostal and Charismatic Movements*. Grand Rapids, MI: Zondervan, 1988.

Campbell, Wesley. *Welcoming a Visitation of the Holy Spirit*. Orlando, FL: Creation House, 1996.

Chaney, Charles L. *Church Planting at the End of the Twentieth Century*, Wheaton, IL: Tyndale House, 1986

Chevreau, Guy. *Catching the Fire*. London, England: Marshall Pickering, 1994.

Coggins, James R., and Paul G. Hiebert. *Wonders and the Word, An Examination of Issues Raised by John Wilber and the Vineyard Movement*. Winnipeg, Canada: Kindred Press, 1989.

Cox, Harvey. *Fire from Heaven: The Rise of Pentecostal Spirituality and the Reshaping of Religion in the Twenty-First Century*. Reading, MA: Addison-Wesley Publishing Co., 1995.

Dawson, John. *Taking Our Cities for God*. Lake Mary, FL: Creation House, 1989.

DeArtega, William. *Quenching the Spirit: Examining Centuries of Opposition to the Moving of the Holy Spirit*. Lake Mary, FL: Creation House, 1992.

Deere, Jack. *Surprised by the Power of the Spirit*. Grand Rapids, MI: Zondervan, 1993.

Di Sabatino. *The Jesus People: An Annotated Bibliography and General Resource*. Westport, CT: Greenwood Press, 1999.

Dixon, Patrick. *Signs of Revival*. Sussex, England: Kingsway, 1994.

Engel, James. *Contemporary Christian Communications*. New York, NY: Thomas Nelson, 1979.

Fee, Gordon D. *God's Empowering Presence*. Peabody, MA: Hendrickson, 1994.

_____ *The First Epistle to the Corinthians*. Grand Rapids,MI: Eerdmans, 1987.

Finke, Roger and Rodney Stark. *The Churching of America, 1776-1990: Winners and Losers in Our Religious Economy*. New Brunswick, NJ: Rutgers University Press, 1992.

Frangipane, Francis. *The Three Battlegrounds*. Cedar Rapids, IA: Arrow Publications, 1989.

Green, Melody, and David Hazard. *No Compromise, the Life Story of Keith Green*. Eugene, OR: Harvest House, 1996.

Grudem, Wayne. *The Gift of Prophecy in the New Testament and Today*. Westchester, IL: Crossway Books, 1988.

Hanegraaff, Hank. *Counterfeit Revival*. Dallas, TX: Word, 1997.

Harrell, D.E. *All Things are Possible: The Healing and Charismatic Revivals in Modern America*. Bloomington, IN: University Press, 1975.

Hawthorne, Gerald F. *The Presence & the Power: The Significance of the Holy Spirit in the Life and Ministry of Jesus*. Dallas, TX: Word, 1991.

Helland, Roger. *Let the River Flow*. New Brunswick, NJ: Bridge-Logos, 1996.

Hollenweger, Walter. *The Pentecostals*. London, England: Student Christian Movement Press, 1992.

Hummel, Charles. *Fire in the Fireplace: Charismatic Renewal in the Nineties*. Downers Grove, IL: InterVarsity, 1993.

Hunt, Dave, and T. A. McMahon. *The Seduction of Christianity: Spiritual Discernment in the Last Days*. Eugene, OR: Harvest House, 1985.

Kallas, James. *Jesus and the Power of Satan*. Philadelphia, PA: Westminster, 1968.

_____ *The Real Satan*. Minneapolis, MN: Augsburg Publishing House, 1975.

Kendrick, Graham, and Steve Hawthorne. *Prayer-walking*. Orlando, FL: Creation House, 1993

Knox, Ronald. *Enthusiasm*. South Bend, IN: University of Notre Dame Press, 1995.

Kraft, Charles H. *Christianity in Culture*. Maryknoll, NY: Orbis Books, 1979.

_____ *Christianity with Power: Your Worldview and Your Experience of the Supernatural*. Ann Arbor, MI: Servant Books, 1989.

Lewis, David C. *Healing: Fiction, Fantasy, or Fact*. London, England:

Hodder & Stoughton, 1989.

Lindsey, Hal. *The Late Great Planet Earth*. Grand Rapids, MI: Zondervan, 1970.

Linn, Dennis and Matthew. *Healing Life's Hurts*. New York, NY: Paulist Press, 1978.

MacArthur, John F., Jr. *The Charismatics*. Grand Rapis, MI: Zondervan, 1978.

_____ *Charismatic Chaos*. Grand Rapids, MI: Zondervan, 1992.

Marsden, George. *Fundamentalism and American Culture: The Shaping of Twentieth Century Evangelicalism. 1870-1925*. New York, NY: Oxford University Press, 1980.

McGavran, Donald. *Effective Evangelism: A Theological Mandate*. Phillipsburg, PA: Presbyterian and Reformed Publishing Company, 1988.

Miller, Donald. *Reinventing American Protestantism: Christianity in the New Millennium*. Berkeley, CA: USC Press, 1997.

Murray, Ian. *The Puritan Hope*. Carlisle, PA: Banner of Truth, 1971.

Plowman, Edward. *The Jesus Movement in America*. New York, NY: Pyramid Books, 1971.

Pytches, David. *Some Said It Thundered: A Personal Encounter with the Kansas City Prophets*. Nashville, TN: Thomas Nelson, 1991.

_____. *John Wimber*. Guilford, England: Eagle Publishing House, 1998.

Riss, Richard. *A Survey of 20th Century Revival Movements in North America*. Peabody, MA: Hendrickson, 1988.

Sanford, Agnes. *The Healing Light*. Watchung, NJ: Charisma Books, 1972.

Schaeffer, Francis. *How Should We Then Live?* Old Tappan, NJ: Fleming H. Revell, 1976.

Sjogren, Steve. *Conspiracy of Kindness*. Ann Arbor, MI: Servant, 1993.

Smith, Christian. *American Evangelism: Embattled and Thriving*. Chicago, IL: The University of Chicago Press, 1998.

Smith, Chuck. *The History of Calvary Chapel*. Costa Mesa, CA: The Word for Today (undated).

_____ *Charisma vs. Charismania*. Costa Mesa, CA: The Word for Today, 1992.

Springer, Kevin, ed. *Power Encounters in the Western World*. San Francisco, CA: Harper & Row, 1988.

Synan, Vinson. *In the Latter Days: The Outpouring of the Holy Spirit in the Twentieth Century* (revised ed.). Ann Arbor, MI: Servant Publications, 1991.

Wagner, C. Peter, and David Cannistraci. *Apostles and the Emerging Apostolic Movememt*. Ventura, CA: Regal Books, 1998.

Wagner, C. Peter and F. Douglas Pennoyer, eds. *Engaging the Enemy: How to Fight and Defeat Territorial Spirits*. Ventura, CA: Regal Books,

1991.

Wagner, C. Peter, ed. *Breaking Strongholds in Your City*. Ventura, CA: Regal Books, 1993.

_____ *Confronting the Enemy*. Ventura, CA: Regal Books, 1996.

_____ *The New Apostolic Churches*. Ventura, CA: Regal Books, 1998

_____ *Wrestling with Dark Angels*. Ventura, CA: Regal Books, 1990.

Wagner, C. Peter. *How To Have a Healing Ministry Without Making Your Church Sick*. Ventura, CA: Regal Books, 1988.

_____ *The Third Wave of the Holy Spirit*. Ann Arbor, MI: Servant Books, 1988.

Watson, David. *Fear No Evil*. Wheaton, IL: Harold Shaw, 1984.

Weber, Max. *The Sociology of Religion*. Boston, MA: Beacon Press, 1993.

White, John. *When the Spirit Comes with Power*. Downers Grove, IL: InterVarsity, 1988.

William, Don. *Revival: the Real Thing*. (self-published), 1995.

Wimber, John and Kevin Springer. *Power Evangelism*. San Francisco, CA: Harper & Row, 1986.

_____ *Power Healing*. San Francisco, CA: Harper & Row, 1987.

_____ *Power Points*. San Francisco, CA: Harper & Row, 1991.

VINEYARD MAGAZINES

*WORSHIP UPDATE* (1987 – PRESENT)

Panner, Jon, "Treasure in a Clay Pot: A Tribute to the Life and Ministry of John Wimber," First Quarter 1998
Tuttle, Carl, "Effective Worship Leading," Winter 1988

*VINEYARD NEWSLETTER* (1986-1988)

Thompson, Sam, "A Vineyard Overview," Winter 1988, Vol. 3, No. 1
Wimber, Carol, "A Hunger for God—A Reflective Look at the Vineyard's Beginnings," Fall 1987, Vol. 2, No. 3
Wimber, John, "As I See It," Spring 1988, Vol. 3, No. 2
_____ "Where is God Taking Us as a Movement?" Fall 1988

*FIRST FRUITS* (1984-1986)

Dwyer, Bill, "Confessions of a Church Planter," May/June 1985
Gulliksen, Kenn, "Birthing a Vineyard," July 1985
Hunter, Todd, "Culture Shock," May 1984
_____ "Church Planting: Listen and Obey," June 1984
Little, Jack, "The Risk of Belonging to God," October 1984
Taylor, Dave, "Dear First Fruits Readers," March/April 1986

Wimber, John, "Do You Know?" May 1984
_____ "In My Opinion," July/August 1986
_____ "Risk Takers," Summer 1987

*EQUIPPING THE SAINTS* (1987 – 1996)

Hunter, Todd, "Successful Pastors: Are They Really Different?" Spring 1988, Vol. 2, No. 2
Springer, Kevin, "Paul Cain: A New Breed of Man," Fall 1989, Vol. 3, No. 4
Wimber, John, "Worship: Intimacy with God," January/February 1987, Vol. 1, No. 1
_____ "Sent into the Harvest Field," September/October 1987, Vol. 1, No. 5
_____ "Why I Don't Respond to Criticism," Summer 1988, Vol. 2, No. 3
_____ "Pure Hearts," Summer 1989, Vol. 3, No. 3
_____ "Introducing Prophetic Ministry," Fall 1989, Vol. 3, No. 4
_____ "The Way of Holiness," Fall 1989, Vol. 3, No. 4
_____ "Paul Cain," Fall 1990, Vol. 4, No. 4
_____ "A Response to Ernie Gruen's Controversy with Kansas City Fellowship," Fall 1990, Vol. 4, No. 4
_____ "The Vineyard's Call to Missions," Summer 1991, Vol. 5, No. 3
_____ "Revival Fire," Winter 1991, Vol. 5, No. 1
_____ "Season of New Beginnings," Fall 1994

*VINEYARD REFLECTIONS* (WRITTEN BY JOHN WIMBER, 1993-97)

"Who Are We and Where Are We Going?—Part 1," April/May 1993
"Who Are We and Where Are We Going?—Part 2," June/July 1993
"Season of New Beginnings," May/June 1994
"Staying Focused: The Vineyard as a Centered Set," July, 1995—February 1996
"The Five-Fold Ministry," August, 1997

*Cutting Edge* (1996-Present)

*Voice of the Vineyard* (1997-1998)

*Happy Notes* (written by Happy Leman, pastor of the Vineyard in Champaign, Illinois and reflecting the author's opinion and views)
October 31, 1990
February 8, 1991
May 7, 1991
August 26, 1991

VINEYARD BOOKLETS
Deere, Jack, *The Vineyard's Response to The Briefing—Vineyard*

*Position Paper #2*, 1992.

Grudem, Wayne, *The Vineyard's Response to The Standard—Vineyard Position Paper #3*. 1992.

_____ *Power & Truth: A Response to the Critiques of Vineyard Teaching and Practice—Vineyard Position Paper #4*, 1992.

Nathan, Rich, *A Response to Charismatic Chaos—Vineyard Position Paper #5*, 1993

Morphew, Derek, *Renewal Apologetics—Vineyard Position Paper #6*, 1995.

Wimber, John, *Why I Respond to Criticism—Vineyard Position Paper #1*, 1992.

VINEYARD TAPES AND VIDEOS

*(John Wimber's formative material—some of these sets are no longer available)*

Church Growth Leadership

Church Planning: Writing Your History in Advance

Church Planting: God's Heart for Expansion

The Cross

Healing I—IV

I'm a Fool for Christ. Whose Fool are You?

The Kingdom of God

Spiritual Gifts I & II

Signs, Wonders and Church Growth I & II

Spiritual Warfare I—III

Teach Us to Pray

Wimber on Wagner

UNPUBLISHED MANUSCRIPTS

Clark, Randy, and Wesley Campbell, *Prophetic Foundations for Revival*, 1995.

Clark, Randy, *Lighting the Fire*, 1996.

Faupel, D. William, *The Everlasting Gospel: The Significance of Eschatology in the Development of Pentecostal Thought* (Ph.D. thesis submitted to the University of Birmingham, England. 1989)

Kimla, Nikolaus, *The Historical and Empirical, Social, and Practical Theological Aspects of the Vineyard Movement* (Masters thesis for Evangelical Theological University, Wien, Vienna), February, 1994.

Riss, Richard, *A History of the Awakening of 1992-1995*. Eleventh Edition on Riss' web page, October 15, 1995

Thompson, Scott, *A Critical Analysis of the Cessationist Hermeneutic with Respect to the Issues of Miracles, Deliverance and Spiritual*

*Warfare* (a Master's thesis submitted to Talbot Graduate School of Theology), May, 1993

Wagner, C. Peter, "The New Apostolic Reformation: A Search for a Name." paper presented at the National Symposium on the Postdenominational Church at Fuller Seminary in May, 1996

MAGAZINES AND JOURNAL ARTICLES

Brown, Mick, "Unzipper Heaven, Lord. Ha-ha, Ho-ho, He-he," *Telegraph Magazine*, December 3, 1994

Grady, Lee, "Resolving the Kansas City Prophecy Controversy," *Ministries Today*,     September/October 1990

Hiebert, Paul, "The Flaw of the Excluded Middle," *Missiology: An International Review,* January 1982, Vol. 10, No. 1

Kantzer, Kenneth, "An Interview with John Wimber," *Christianity Today*, March 19, 1990

Long, Steve, "What About Animal Noises?" *Spread the Fire*, (October 1995, Vol. 1, Issue 5

Poloma, Margaret, Letter, dated November 27, 1995, on web-site of Toronto Airport Christian Fellowship

Shenk, William, "Missionary Encounter with Culture," *International Bulletin of Missionary Research,* July 1991

Shepherd, Marquis, "Gentlest of Winters Goes Out with a Blast of Snow, Cold," *Kansas City Times*, March 21, 1983

Springer, Kevin, "Applying the Gifts to Everyday Life," *Charisma*, September 1985

Stafford, Tim, "Testing the Wine from John Wimber's Vineyard," *Christianity Today*, August 8, 1986

TAV Staff, "Ted Haggard's Reconciliation Efforts" Toronto Airport Christian Fellowship Home Page, 1995

Vachon, Brian, "The Jesus Movement is Upon Us," *Look*, (February 9, 1971, Vol. 35, No. 3

Wimber, John, "Zip to 3,000 in 5 Years," *Signs & Wonders* Today (A Special Edition of *Christian Life* Magazine), 1983

_____ "An Interview," *Christianity Today*, July 14, 1997

# BOOK ORDERS

Name . . . . . . . . . . . . . . . . . . . . . . . . . . .

Address . . . . . . . . . . . . . . . . . . . . . . . . . .

. . . . . . . . . . . . . . . . . . . . . . . . . . .

Tel/Fax . . . . . . . . . . . . . . . . . . . . . . . . . .

Title . . . . . . . . . . . . . . . . . . . . . . . . . . .

Author . . . . . . . . . . . . . . Quantity . . . . . . . .

*Vineyard International Publishing*
*Books can be ordered from the following offices:*

**Australia**
Po Box 440
Sans Souci,
Sydney, NSW 2219
Fax: +61-2-95295436
Tel:  +61-2-95298811
vineyard@ssvcf.org.au

**Benelux Nations**
PO Box 1557,
3500 BN Utrecht,
The Netherlands
Fax: +31-30-2340958
Jan_Bernard_Struik@compuserve.com

**England**
Vineyard Ministries
23 Blagdon Road
New Malden
Surrey, KT3 4AH
Fax: +44-181-3366319
Tel: +44-181-3361727
vmguk@aol.com

**New Zealand**
Box 21-541
Henderson, Auckland
Tel: +64-9-8387897
Fax: +64-9-8387872
training@vineyard.co.nz

**Scandanavia**
Karrintie 2F
SF-00760 Helsinki
Fax: +358-93-881930
Web: www.vineyardsrk.fi
caj.talvio@vineyardsrk.fi

**South Africa**
PO Box 53286,
Kenilworth, 7745
Fax: +27-21-7616773
Tel: +27-21-7975332
vbi@nis.za

**Switzerland**
Association of
Vineyard Churches,
Germany, Austria
Switzerland, Liechtenstein
Postfach 108 ·
CH-3000 Bern 22
Fax: +41-31-3331519
Tel: +41-31-3330430
vineyard.bern@span.ch

**USA**
PO Box 17580
Anaheim, CA 92817
Fax: +1-714-7778841
avci@ix.netcom.com